First World War
and Army of Occupation
War Diary
France, Belgium and Germany

I0311138

48 DIVISION
143 Infantry Brigade
Royal Warwickshire Regiment
1/5th Battalion-Territorial
22 March 1915 - 9 November 1917

WO95/2755/1

The Naval & Military Press Ltd
www.nmarchive.com
Published in association with The National Archives

Published by

The Naval & Military Press Ltd

Unit 10 Ridgewood Industrial Park,
Uckfield, East Sussex,
TN22 5QE England
Tel: +44 (0) 1825 749494

www.naval-military-press.com
www.nmarchive.com

This diary has been reprinted in facsimile from the original. Any imperfections are inevitably reproduced and the quality may fall short of modern type and cartographic standards.

© Crown Copyright
Images reproduced by permission of The National Archives, London, England, 2015.

Contents

Document type	Place/Title	Date From	Date To
Heading	1/5 Bnt Royal Warwicks March 1915 Oct 1917		
Heading	48th Division 143rd Infy Bde 1-5th Bn Roy Warwicks Mar 1915 1917 Oct		
War Diary	143rd Inf Bde 48th Div. War Diary 1/5th Battn. The Royal Warwickshire Regiment March (22.3.15 To 31.3.15) 1915		
War Diary	Southampton	22/03/1915	22/03/1915
War Diary	Havre	23/03/1915	24/03/1915
War Diary	Terdeghen	25/03/1915	25/03/1915
War Diary	Bailleul	28/03/1915	31/03/1915
Heading	143rd Inf. Bde. 48th Div. War Diary 1/5th Battn. The Royal Warwickshire Regiment April 1915		
War Diary	Armentieres	01/04/1915	01/04/1915
War Diary	Bailleul	06/04/1915	06/04/1915
War Diary	Douve Trenches	12/04/1915	16/04/1915
War Diary	Hutments Near Neuve Eglise	20/04/1915	20/04/1915
War Diary	Douve Trenches	22/04/1915	24/04/1915
War Diary	Petit Pont	28/04/1915	28/04/1915
War Diary	Douve Trenches	30/04/1915	30/04/1915
Heading	143rd Inf. Bde. 48th Div. War Diary 1/5th Battn. The Royal Warwickshire Regiment May 1915		
War Diary	Douve Trenches	01/05/1915	02/05/1915
War Diary	Hutments Jonesville	05/05/1915	06/05/1915
War Diary	Trenches 61-65	07/05/1915	12/05/1915
War Diary	Point 63 Petit Pont	13/05/1915	16/05/1915
War Diary	Trenches 61-65	17/05/1915	20/05/1915
War Diary	Jonesville	21/05/1915	24/05/1915
War Diary	Trenches 61-65	25/05/1915	28/05/1915
War Diary	Point 63 Court Dreve	29/05/1915	31/05/1915
Heading	143rd Inf Bde. 48th Div War Diary 1/5th Battn The Royal Warwickshire Regiment June 1915		
War Diary	Point 63 Court Dreve	01/06/1915	01/06/1915
War Diary	Trenches 61-65	02/06/1915	05/06/1915
War Diary	Hutments Jonesville	06/06/1915	07/06/1915
War Diary	Point 63. Court Drive	08/06/1915	09/06/1915
War Diary	Douve Trenches 36-40, 61-63	10/06/1915	11/06/1915
War Diary	Romarin	12/06/1915	15/06/1915
War Diary	Trenches 1-19	16/06/1915	19/06/1915
War Diary	The Convent	20/06/1915	21/06/1915
War Diary	Ploegsteert	22/06/1915	25/06/1915
War Diary	Bailleul	26/06/1915	26/06/1915
War Diary	Vieux Berquin	27/06/1915	27/06/1915
War Diary	Hamen Artois	28/06/1915	28/06/1915
War Diary	Auchel	29/06/1915	30/06/1915
Heading	143rd Inf Bde. 48th Div. War Diary 1/5th Battn. The Royal Warwickshire Regiment July 1915		
War Diary	Auchel	01/07/1915	12/07/1915
War Diary	Houchin	16/07/1915	16/07/1915
War Diary	Auchel	18/07/1915	18/07/1915
War Diary	Beauquesne	21/07/1915	21/07/1915

War Diary	Courcelles	25/07/1915	25/07/1915
War Diary	Trenches	26/07/1915	30/07/1915
War Diary	Bayencourt	31/07/1915	31/07/1915
Operation(al) Order(s)	Operation Order No. 2 1/5th Battn Royal Warwickshire Regt	25/07/1915	25/07/1915
Heading	143rd Inf. Bde. 48th Div. War Diary 1/5th Battn. The Royal Warwickshire Regiment August 1915		
War Diary	Bayencourt	01/08/1915	03/08/1915
War Diary	Trenches Colincamps	07/08/1915	15/08/1915
War Diary	Bayencourt	16/08/1915	22/08/1915
War Diary	Trenches Colincamps	23/08/1915	25/08/1915
War Diary	Bois De Warnimont	26/08/1915	30/08/1915
War Diary	Bus	31/08/1915	31/08/1915
Operation(al) Order(s)	Operation Order No. 4 1/6th Battn Royal Warwickshire Regiment	07/08/1915	07/08/1915
Heading	143rd Inf. Bde. 48th Div. War Diary 1/5th Battn. The Royal Warwickshire Regiment September 1915		
War Diary	Bus	01/09/1915	02/09/1915
War Diary	Trenches	05/09/1915	05/09/1915
War Diary	Bayencourt	06/09/1915	07/09/1915
War Diary	Trenches	10/09/1915	10/09/1915
War Diary	Fonquevillers	14/09/1915	15/09/1915
War Diary	Trenches	18/09/1915	22/09/1915
War Diary	Bayencourt	23/09/1915	26/09/1915
War Diary	Trenches	28/09/1915	30/09/1915
Heading	Battalion Operation Order Nos. 6, 7, 8, 9, 10, 11 & 12.		
Operation(al) Order(s)	Operation Orders No. 6	01/09/1915	01/09/1915
Operation(al) Order(s)	Operation Orders No. 7 The 1/5th Battn. Royal Warwickshire Regt.	10/09/1915	10/09/1915
Operation(al) Order(s)	Operation Orders No. 8 By Lieut. Col. G.C. Sladen. Commanding 1/5th Batt. the Royal Warwickshire Regt.	14/09/1915	14/09/1915
Operation(al) Order(s)	Operation Orders No. 9 By Lieut. Col. G.C. Sladen. Commanding 1/5th Batt. The Royal Warwickshire Regt.	18/09/1915	18/09/1915
Operation(al) Order(s)	Operation Orders No. 10 by Lieut. Col. G.C. Sladen. Commanding 1/5th Batt. The Royal Warwickshire Regt.	22/09/1915	22/09/1915
Operation(al) Order(s)	Operation Orders No. 11 By Lieut. Col. G.C. Sladen. Commanding 1/5th Batt. The Royal Warwickshire Regt.	26/09/1915	26/09/1915
Operation(al) Order(s)	Operation Orders No. 12 By Lieut. Col. G.C. Sladen. Commanding 1/5th Batt. Royal Warwickshire Regt.	30/09/1915	30/09/1915
War Diary	Trenches	04/01/1916	04/01/1916
War Diary	Fonquevillers	05/01/1916	12/01/1916
War Diary	Trenches	13/01/1916	20/01/1916
War Diary	Bayencourt	24/01/1916	28/01/1916
War Diary	Trenches	30/01/1916	30/01/1916
Heading	143rd Inf. Bde. 48th Div. War Diary 1/5th Battn. The Royal Warwickshire Regiment October 1915		
Operation(al) Order(s)	Operation Order No. 24 By Lieut. Col. G.C. Sladen. Commanding 1/5th Batt. Royal Warwickshire Regt.	03/01/1916	03/01/1916
War Diary	Fonquevillers	03/10/1915	08/10/1915
War Diary	Trenches	11/10/1915	16/10/1915
War Diary	Bayencourt	17/10/1915	24/10/1915
War Diary	Trenches	27/10/1915	29/10/1915
Miscellaneous	Notice	03/01/1916	03/01/1916
Heading	Battalion Operation Order Nos 13, 14 & 15.		
Operation(al) Order(s)	Operation Orders No. 25 By Lieut. Col. G.C. Sladen. Commanding 1/5th Batt. The Royal Warwickshire Regt.	10/01/1916	10/01/1916

Operation(al) Order(s)	Operation Orders No. 26 By Major W.H. Franklin. Commanding 1/5th. Battn. The Royal Warwickshire Regt.	18/01/1916	18/01/1916
Operation(al) Order(s)	Operation Orders No. 13 By Lieut. Col. G.C. Sladen Commanding 1/5th Battn. The Royal Warwickshire Regt.	07/10/1915	07/10/1915
Operation(al) Order(s)	Operation Orders No. 14 By Lieut. Col. G.C. Sladen Commanding 1/5th Battn. The Royal Warwickshire Regt.	15/10/1915	15/10/1915
Operation(al) Order(s)	Operation Orders No. 27 By Lieut. Col. G.C. Sladen Commanding 1/5th Battn. The Royal Warwickshire Regt.	27/01/1916	27/01/1916
Operation(al) Order(s)	Operation Orders No. 15 By Lieut. Col. G.C. Sladen Commanding 1/5th Battn. R. War. R.	23/10/1915	23/10/1915
War Diary	Trenches	04/02/1916	04/02/1916
War Diary	Fonquevillers	05/02/1916	12/02/1916
War Diary	Trenches	13/02/1916	21/02/1916
War Diary	Bavencourt	28/02/1916	29/02/1916
War Diary	Trenches	29/02/1916	29/02/1916
Heading	143rd Inf. Bde. 48th Div. War Diary 1/5th Battn. The Royal Warwickshire Regiment November 1915		
Operation(al) Order(s)	Operation Orders No. 28 By Major W.H. Franklin Commanding 1/5th Battn. The Royal Warwickshire Regt.	03/02/1916	03/02/1916
War Diary	Trenches	01/11/1915	01/11/1915
War Diary	Fonquevillers	02/11/1915	09/11/1915
War Diary	Trenches	14/11/1915	17/11/1915
War Diary	Bayencourt	18/11/1915	25/11/1915
War Diary	Trenches	27/11/1915	30/11/1915
Operation(al) Order(s)	Operation Order No. 29 By Major W.H. Franklin Commanding 1/5th Battn. The Royal Warwickshire Regiment.	11/02/1916	11/02/1916
Heading	Battalion Operation Orders Nos. 16,17,18 & 19.		
Operation(al) Order(s)	Operation Order No. 30 By Lieut. Colonel G.C. Sladen Commanding 1/5th Battn. The Royal Warwickshire Regiment	20/02/1916	20/02/1916
Operation(al) Order(s)	Operation Order No. 16 By Lieut. Col. G.C. Sladen Commanding 1/5th Battn. The Royal Warwickshire Regt.	31/10/1915	31/10/1915
Operation(al) Order(s)	Operation Order No. 31 By Lieut. Colonel G.C. Sladen Commanding 1/5th Battn. The Royal Warwickshire Regt.	28/02/1916	28/02/1916
Operation(al) Order(s)	Operation Order No. 17 By Major W.H. Franklin Commanding 1/5th Battn. The Royal Warwickshire Regiment.	08/11/1915	08/11/1915
Operation(al) Order(s)	Operation Order No. 32 By Lieut. Colonel G.C. Sladen Commanding 1/5th Battn. The Royal Warwickshire Regt.	20/02/1916	20/02/1916
Operation(al) Order(s)	Operation Order No. 18 By Major W.H. Franklin Commanding 1/5th Battn. The Royal Warwickshire Regiment.	16/11/1915	16/11/1915
Heading	1/5th R Warwick Regt Vol XIII March 1916		
Operation(al) Order(s)	Operation Orders No. 19 By Lieut. Col. G.C. Sladen Commanding 1/5th Battn. The Royal Warwickshire Regt.	24/11/1915	24/11/1915
War Diary	Trenches	03/03/1916	08/03/1916

War Diary	Fonquevillers	09/03/1916	15/03/1916
War Diary	Trenches	16/03/1916	24/03/1916
War Diary	Souastre	25/03/1916	31/03/1916
Heading	143rd Inf. Bde. 48th Div. War Diary 1/5th Battn. The Royal Warwickshire Regiment December 1915		
Operation(al) Order(s)	Operation Order No. 33 By Lieut. Colonel G.C. Sladen Commanding 1/5th Battn. The Royal Warwickshire Regt.	08/03/1916	08/03/1916
War Diary	Trenches	01/12/1915	03/12/1915
War Diary	Fonquevillers	11/12/1915	11/12/1915
War Diary	Trenches	11/12/1915	19/12/1915
War Diary	Bayencourt	23/12/1915	27/12/1915
War Diary	Trenches	28/12/1915	28/12/1915
Operation(al) Order(s)	Operation Order No. 34 By Lieut. Colonel G.C. Sladen Commanding 1/5th Battn. The Royal Warwickshire Regt.	15/03/1916	15/03/1916
Heading	Battalion Operation Orders Nos. 20, 21, 22 & 23		
Miscellaneous	Report On Enterprise Carried Out By 1/5th R.War Regt	23/03/1916	23/03/1916
Operation(al) Order(s)	Operation Orders No. 20 By Lieut. Col. G.C. Sladen Commanding 1/5th Battn. The Royal Warwickshire Regt.	02/12/1915	02/12/1915
Miscellaneous	Report On Enterprise Carried Out By 1/5th R.War R.	23/03/1916	23/03/1916
Operation(al) Order(s)	Operation Orders No. 21 by Lieut. Col. G.C. Sladen Comdg 1/5th Battn. The Royal Warwickshire Regt.	10/12/1915	10/12/1915
Miscellaneous	Notice		
Operation(al) Order(s)	Operation Orders No. 36 by Lieut. Colonel G.C. Sladen D.S.O. Commanding 1/5th Battn. Royal Warwickshire Regt.	23/03/1916	23/03/1916
Operation(al) Order(s)	Operation Orders No. 22 by Lieut. Colonel G.C. Sladen D.S.O. Commanding 1/5th Battn. Royal Warwickshire Regt.	18/12/1915	18/12/1915
Operation(al) Order(s)	Operation Orders No. 37 by Major W.H. Franklin Commanding 1/5th Battn. Royal Warwickshire Regt.	30/03/1916	30/03/1916
Miscellaneous	Notice	18/12/1915	18/12/1915
Heading	1/5 R. Warwick Regt Vol XIV April 1916		
Operation(al) Order(s)	Operation Orders No. 23 by Lieut. Colonel G.C. Sladen D.S.O. Commanding 1/5th Battn. Royal Warwickshire Regt.	26/12/1915	26/12/1915
War Diary	Souastre	01/04/1916	01/04/1916
War Diary	Trenches	03/04/1916	09/04/1916
War Diary	Fonquevillers	17/04/1916	17/04/1916
War Diary	Trenches	18/04/1916	26/04/1916
War Diary	Souastre	27/04/1916	30/04/1916
Miscellaneous	Notice	26/12/1915	26/12/1915
Operation(al) Order(s)	Operation Orders No. 38 by Lieut. Colonel G.C. Sladen D.S.O. Commanding 1/5th Battn. Royal Warwickshire Regt.	07/04/1916	07/04/1916
Miscellaneous	Amendment Operation Orders No. 38	08/04/1916	08/04/1916
Operation(al) Order(s)	Operation Orders No. 39 by Lieut. Colonel G.C. Sladen D.S.O. Commanding 1/5th Battn. Royal Warwickshire Regt.	16/04/1916	16/04/1916
Operation(al) Order(s)	Operation Orders No. 40 by Lieut. Colonel G.C. Sladen D.S.O. Commanding 1/5th Battn. Royal Warwickshire Regt.	25/04/1916	25/04/1916
War Diary	Souastre	01/05/1916	06/05/1916
War Diary	J.17.c.1.7	06/05/1916	08/05/1916

War Diary	Authie	11/05/1916	11/05/1916
War Diary	Gezaincourt	12/05/1916	25/05/1916
War Diary	Couin	26/05/1916	26/05/1916
War Diary	Authie	27/05/1916	27/05/1916
War Diary	Gezaincourt	31/05/1916	31/05/1916
Operation(al) Order(s)	Operation Orders No. 41 by Lieut. Colonel G.C. Sladen D.S.O. Commanding 1/5th Battn. Royal Warwickshire Regt.	01/05/1916	01/05/1916
Operation(al) Order(s)	Operation Orders No. 42 by Lieut. Colonel G.C. Sladen D.S.O. Commanding 1/5th Battn. Royal Warwickshire Regt.	05/05/1916	05/05/1916
Operation(al) Order(s)	Operation Orders No. 43 by Lieut. Colonel G.C. Sladen D.S.O. Commanding 1/5th Battn. Royal Warwickshire Regt.	07/05/1916	07/05/1916
War Diary	Couin	01/06/1916	01/06/1916
War Diary	Trenches K17.c.30.35-K.17.a.1.8	03/06/1916	08/06/1916
War Diary	Bivouacs J.16.d	12/06/1916	12/06/1916
War Diary	Couin	22/06/1916	22/06/1916
War Diary	Trenches	24/06/1916	30/06/1916
Operation(al) Order(s)	Operation Orders No. 48 by Lieut. Colonel G.C. Sladen D.S.O. Commanding 1/5th Battn. Royal Warwickshire Regt.	07/06/1916	07/06/1916
Operation(al) Order(s)	Operation Orders No. 49 by Lieut. Colonel G.C. Sladen D.S.O. Commanding 1/5th Battn. Royal Warwickshire Regt.	21/06/1916	21/06/1916
Operation(al) Order(s)	Operation Orders No. 44 by Captain C. Retallack. Commdg. 1/5th Battn. Royal Warwickshire Regt.	10/05/1916	10/05/1916
Operation(al) Order(s)	Operation Orders No. 45 by Captain C. Retallack. Commdg. 1/5th Battn. Royal Warwickshire Regt.	24/05/1916	24/05/1916
Operation(al) Order(s)	Operation Orders No. 46 by Lieut. Col. G.C. Sladen D.S.O. Commanding 1/5th Battn. Royal Warwickshire Regt.	30/05/1916	30/05/1916
Operation(al) Order(s)	Operation Orders No. 47 by Lieut. Colonel G.C. Sladen D.S.O. Commanding 1/5th Battn. Royal Warwickshire Regt.	31/05/1916	31/05/1916
Heading	143rd Inf. Bde. 48th Div. War Diary 1/5th Battn. The Royal Warwickshire Regiment July 1916		
War Diary	Trenches K.17.c.30.35-K.17.a.1.8.	01/07/1916	04/07/1916
War Diary	Bivouacs J.1.c.8.3	05/07/1916	11/07/1916
War Diary	La Boisselle	13/07/1916	13/07/1916
War Diary	Ref Map 57d S.E. 1/20000 57d S.E. 1/10000	14/07/1916	16/07/1916
War Diary	Ref Map Orvillers 57d S.E 4 2b	17/07/1916	17/07/1916
War Diary	W.30 a	18/07/1916	18/07/1916
War Diary	Bouzincourt	19/07/1916	22/07/1916
War Diary	Trenches	23/07/1916	24/07/1916
War Diary	Unsa Redout	25/07/1916	27/07/1916
War Diary	Bouzincourt	28/07/1916	28/07/1916
War Diary	Coulonvillers	30/07/1916	30/07/1916
Heading	Appendices 1, 2, 3, 4, 5.		
Operation(al) Order(s)	143 Inf Bde Operation Order No. 69	15/07/1916	15/07/1916
Miscellaneous	O.C. 1/5 R War Regt	15/07/1916	15/07/1916
Map	Map		
Operation(al) Order(s)	144th Infantry Brigade Order No. 79		
Operation(al) Order(s)	Operation Orders No. 50 by Lieut. Colonel G.C. Sladen D.S.O. Commanding 1/5th Battn. Royal Warwickshire Regt.	22/07/1916	22/07/1916

Miscellaneous	A Form Messages And Signals		
Operation(al) Order(s)	1/5 R War R. O.O. No. 51	23/07/1916	23/07/1916
Operation(al) Order(s)	143 Inf Bde O.O. No. 75	24/07/1916	24/07/1916
Operation(al) Order(s)	143 Inf Bde Operation Order No. 76	27/07/1916	27/07/1916
Miscellaneous	Extract From Account Of The Defence Of Gommecourt	01/07/1916	01/07/1916
Heading	143rd Brigade 48th Division 1/5th Battalion Royal Warwickshire Regiment August 1916		
War Diary	Coulonvillers	01/08/1916	09/08/1916
War Diary	Longuevillette	10/08/1916	10/08/1916
War Diary	Arqueves	14/08/1916	14/08/1916
War Diary	Varennes	15/08/1916	15/08/1916
War Diary	Bouzincourt	16/08/1916	16/08/1916
War Diary	Orvillers Post	17/08/1916	17/08/1916
War Diary	Ref Map Orvillers 57d S.E. 4 1/10000 And Special Map	18/08/1916	18/08/1916
War Diary	Trenches	19/08/1916	20/08/1916
War Diary	Bivouacs W.8.c.8.4	22/08/1916	27/08/1916
War Diary	Ref 57d S.E 1/20000	28/08/1916	28/08/1916
War Diary	Varennes	29/08/1916	29/08/1916
Operation(al) Order(s)	Operation Orders No. 52 by Lieut. Colonel G.C. Sladen D.S.O. Commanding 1/5th Battn. Royal Warwickshire Regiment	08/08/1916	08/08/1916
Operation(al) Order(s)	Operation Orders No. 53 by Lieut. Col. Sladen D.S.O.	09/08/1916	09/08/1916
Miscellaneous	Notices		
Operation(al) Order(s)	Operation Orders No. 54 by Lieut. Colonel G.C. Sladen D.S.O. Commanding 1/5th Battn. Royal Warwickshire Regiment	13/08/1916	13/08/1916
Operation(al) Order(s)	Operation Orders No. 55 by Lieut. Colonel G.C. Sladen D.S.O. Comdg 1/5th Battn. Royal Warwickshire Regt.	16/08/1916	16/08/1916
Operation(al) Order(s)	Operation Orders No. 56 by Lieut. Colonel G.C. Sladen D.S.O. Commanding 1/5th Battn. Royal Warwickshire Regiment	16/08/1916	16/08/1916
Operation(al) Order(s)	143 Inf Bde Operation Order No. 81	18/08/1916	18/08/1916
Miscellaneous	48th Division Information Regarding The Enemy To Be Fought This Afternoon	18/08/1916	18/08/1916
Miscellaneous	A Form Messages And Signals		
Operation(al) Order(s)	143rd Inf Bde Operation Order No. 82-	19/08/1916	19/08/1916
Miscellaneous	B Coy Lord		
Operation(al) Order(s)	Operation Order No. 58 Relief	20/08/1916	20/08/1916
Operation(al) Order(s)	143rd Inf Bde Operation Order No. 83	20/08/1916	20/08/1916
Miscellaneous	C.O 5a War R.		
Miscellaneous	A Form Messages And Signals		
Miscellaneous	143rd Inf Bde.	19/08/1916	19/08/1916
Miscellaneous	B Form Messages And Signals		
Miscellaneous	Appendix I A		
Map	Ovillers		
Miscellaneous			
Heading	48th Division 143rd Infantry Bde. 1/5th Royal Warwickshire Regt September 1916		
War Diary	Bois De Warnimont	02/09/1916	02/09/1916
War Diary	Sarton	02/09/1916	11/09/1916
War Diary	Gezaincourt	12/09/1916	16/09/1916
War Diary	Heuzecourt	18/09/1916	30/09/1916
Operation(al) Order(s)	Operation Orders No. 59 by Lieut. Colonel C. Retallack Commdg 1/5th Battn. Royal Warwickshire Regiment	10/09/1916	10/09/1916
Operation(al) Order(s)	Operation Orders No. 60 by Lieut. Colonel C. Retallack	17/09/1916	17/09/1916

Operation(al) Order(s)	Operation Orders No. 61 by Lieut. Colonel C. Retallack Commdg 1/5th Battn. Royal Warwickshire Regt.	29/09/1916	29/09/1916
Operation(al) Order(s)	Operation Orders No. 62 by Lieut. Colonel C. Retallack	30/09/1916	30/09/1916
War Diary	Hebuterne	01/10/1916	04/10/1916
War Diary	Hebuterne & Fonquevillers	05/10/1916	05/10/1916
War Diary	St Amand	06/10/1916	18/10/1916
War Diary	Grand Rullecourt	20/10/1916	24/10/1916
War Diary	Franvillers	25/10/1916	25/10/1916
War Diary	Becourt	26/10/1916	26/10/1916
War Diary	Mametz Wood	27/10/1916	31/10/1916
Operation(al) Order(s)	Operation Orders No. 63 by Lieut. Colonel C. Retallack	01/10/1916	01/10/1916
Operation(al) Order(s)	Operation Orders No. 64 by Lieut. Colonel C. Retallack Commdg 1/5th Battn. Royal Warwickshire Regiment.	02/10/1916	02/10/1916
Operation(al) Order(s)	Operation Orders No. 65 by Lieut. Colonel C. Retallack Commdg 1/5th Battn. Royal Warwickshire Regt.	05/10/1916	05/10/1916
Operation(al) Order(s)	Operation Orders No. 66 by Captn. A.S. Alabaster, M.C. Commdg. 1/5th Battn. The Royal Warwickshire Regiment.	19/10/1916	19/10/1916
Operation(al) Order(s)	Operation Orders No. 67 by Captn. A.S. Alabaster, M.C. Commdg. 1/5th Battn. The Royal Warwickshire Regiment.	23/10/1916	23/10/1916
Operation(al) Order(s)	Operation Orders No. 68 by Captn. A.S. Alabaster, M.C. Commdg. 1/5th Battn. The Royal Warwickshire Regiment.	24/10/1916	24/10/1916
Operation(al) Order(s)	Operation Orders No. 69 by Lieut. Colonel C. Retallack Commdg. 1/5th Battn. The Royal Warwickshire Regiment.	25/10/1916	25/10/1916
Operation(al) Order(s)	Operation Orders No. 70 by Lieut. Colonel C. Retallack Commdg. 1/5th Battn. The Royal Warwickshire Regiment.	26/10/1916	26/10/1916
War Diary	Becourt	01/11/1916	01/11/1916
War Diary	Contalmaison	02/11/1916	08/11/1916
War Diary	Le Sars	09/11/1916	10/11/1916
War Diary	Martin Puich	11/11/1916	13/11/1916
War Diary	Villa Camp	14/11/1916	14/11/1916
War Diary	Contalmaison	14/11/1916	18/11/1916
War Diary	Pioneer Camp	19/11/1916	19/11/1916
War Diary	Contalmaison	19/11/1916	23/11/1916
War Diary	Le Sars	24/11/1916	27/11/1916
War Diary	Martin Puich	28/11/1916	30/11/1916
Operation(al) Order(s)	Operation Orders No. 71 by Lieut. Colonel C. Retallack Commdg. 1/5th Battn. Royal Warwickshire Regt.	08/11/1916	08/11/1916
Operation(al) Order(s)	Operation Orders No. 72 by Lieut. Colonel C. Retallack Commdg. 1/5th Battn. Royal Warwickshire Regt.	23/11/1916	23/11/1916
Operation(al) Order(s)	Operation Orders No. 73 by Lieut. Colonel C. Retallack Commdg. 1/5th Battn. Royal Warwickshire Regt.	27/11/1916	27/11/1916
War Diary	Martin Puich	01/12/1916	01/12/1916
War Diary	Scotts Redoubt	02/12/1916	02/12/1916
War Diary	Camp North X.21.b.3.5	02/12/1916	05/12/1916
War Diary	Le Sars	06/12/1916	06/12/1916
War Diary	Acid Drop Camp	06/12/1916	06/12/1916
War Diary	Martin Puich	08/12/1916	09/12/1916
War Diary	Scotts Redoubt Camp North	10/12/1916	12/12/1916
War Diary	Albert	14/12/1916	31/12/1916

Heading	War Diary Of 1/5th Bn. Royal Warwickshire Regt. From 1st December 1916 To 31st December 1916 Vol 22		
Operation(al) Order(s)	Operation Orders No. 74 by Lieut. Colonel C. Retallack Commdg. 1/5th Battn. Royal Warwickshire Regt.	01/12/1916	01/12/1916
Operation(al) Order(s)	Operation Orders No. 75 by Lieut. Colonel C. Retallack Commdg. 1/5th Battn. Royal Warwickshire Regt.	05/12/1916	05/12/1916
Miscellaneous	Orders for Working Company By Major A.S. Alabaster M.C. 5th December 1916	05/12/1916	05/12/1916
Operation(al) Order(s)	Operation Orders No. 76 By Major A.S. Alabaster, M.C. Comdg. 1/5 Battn. The Royal Warwickshire Regt.	10/12/1916	10/12/1916
Operation(al) Order(s)	Operation Orders No. 77 By Major A.S. Alabaster, M.C. Comdg. 1/5 Battn. Royal Warwickshire Regt.	13/12/1916	13/12/1916
Operation(al) Order(s)	Operation Orders No. 78 By J.H. Crosskey Comdg. 1/5 Battn. The Royal Warwickshire Regiment.	27/12/1916	27/12/1916
Heading	War Diary Of 1/5 R Warwickshire Regt Jan 1st To Jan 31st 1917 Vol 23		
War Diary	Warloy	05/01/1917	06/01/1917
War Diary	Sorel Wanel	08/01/1917	31/01/1917
Operation(al) Order(s)	Operation Orders No. 79 By Capt. J.H. Crosskey Comdg. 1/5 Battn. Royal Warwickshire Regiment.	07/01/1916	07/01/1916
Operation(al) Order(s)	Operation Orders No. 80 By Lieut. Col. C. Retallack. M.C. Commdg 1/5 Battn Royal Warwickshire Regiment.	26/01/1917	26/01/1917
Operation(al) Order(s)	Operation Orders No. 81 By Lieut. Col. C. Retallack. M.C. Commdg 1/5 Battn Royal Warwickshire Regiment.	30/01/1917	30/01/1917
Operation(al) Order(s)	1/5th R. War. R. Operation Orders	31/01/1917	31/01/1917
Operation(al) Order(s)	Operation Orders No. 81 By Lieut. Col. C. Retallack. M.C. Commdg 1/5 Battn Royal Warwickshire Regiment.	30/01/1917	30/01/1917
Operation(al) Order(s)	Operation Orders The Following Alterations Are To Be Made In Operation Order No. 81	31/01/1917	31/01/1917
Heading	War Diary Of 1/5th Bn. R. Warwickshire Regt. From 1st Feb To 28th Feb 1917 Vol 24		
War Diary	Eclusier	01/02/1917	01/02/1917
War Diary	Biaches	05/02/1917	09/02/1917
War Diary	Willkind Trench North of Herbecourt	10/02/1917	10/02/1917
War Diary	Biaches	14/02/1917	20/02/1917
War Diary	Eclusier	24/02/1918	26/02/1918
War Diary	Biache	14/02/1917	17/02/1917
Operation(al) Order(s)	Operation Orders No. 82 By Lieut. Col. C. Retallack. M.C. Commdg 1/5 Battn Royal Warwickshire Regiment.	05/02/1917	05/02/1917
Miscellaneous	Operation Orders No. 82A By Lieut Col C. Retallack M.C. Commdg 1/5th Battn Royal Warwickshire Regiment 10th February 1917	10/02/1917	10/02/1917
Miscellaneous	Appendix I.A Showing Map		
Operation(al) Order(s)	Operation Orders No. 83 By Lieut. Col. C. Retallack. M.C. Commdg 1/5 Battn Royal Warwickshire Regiment.	13/02/1917	13/02/1917
Operation(al) Order(s)	Operation Orders No. 84 By Lieut. Col. C. Retallack. M.C. Commdg 1/5 Battn Royal Warwickshire Regiment.	25/02/1917	25/02/1917

Miscellaneous	Operation Orders No. 84 By Lieut. Col. C. Retallack. M.C. Commdg 1/5 Battn Royal Warwickshire Regiment.	25/02/1917	25/02/1917
War Diary	Biaches	01/03/1917	02/03/1917
War Diary	Eclusier	03/03/1917	12/03/1917
War Diary	Biaches	13/03/1917	17/03/1917
War Diary	Front Line Trench About I 32 Central East Of Biaches	17/03/1917	17/03/1917
War Diary	Eclusier	18/03/1917	18/03/1917
War Diary	Halle	21/03/1917	24/03/1917
War Diary	Mount St Quintin	25/03/1917	25/03/1917
War Diary	St Dennis	25/03/1917	25/03/1917
War Diary	Bussu	25/03/1917	26/03/1917
War Diary	Aizecourt	25/03/1917	26/03/1917
War Diary	Driencourt	27/03/1917	27/03/1917
War Diary	Saulcourt-Villers-Faucon	28/03/1917	31/03/1917
Operation(al) Order(s)	Operation Orders No. 85 By Lieut. Col. C. Retallack. M.C. Commdg 1/5 Battn Royal Warwickshire Regiment.	02/03/1917	02/03/1917
Operation(al) Order(s)	Operation Orders No. 86 By Lieut. Col. C. Retallack. M.C. Commdg 1/5 Battn Royal Warwickshire Regiment.	06/03/1917	06/03/1917
Operation(al) Order(s)	Operation Orders No. 87 By Lieut. Col. C. Retallack. M.C. Commdg 1/5 Battn Royal Warwickshire Regiment.	12/03/1917	12/03/1917
Operation(al) Order(s)	Operation Orders No. 88 By Lieut. Col. C. Retallack. M.C. Commdg 1/5 Battn Royal Warwickshire Regiment.	18/03/1917	18/03/1917
Operation(al) Order(s)	Operation Orders No. 89 By Lieut. Col. C. Retallack. M.C. Commdg 1/5 Battn Royal Warwickshire Regiment.	24/03/1917	24/03/1917
Operation(al) Order(s)	Operation Orders No. 90 By Lieut. Col. C. Retallack. M.C. Commdg 1/5 Battn Royal Warwickshire Regiment.	25/03/1917	25/03/1917
Operation(al) Order(s)	Operation Orders No. 91 By Lieut. Col. C. Retallack. M.C. Commdg 1/5 Battn Royal Warwickshire Regiment.	27/03/1917	27/03/1917
Miscellaneous	48th Divn. No. 2924 A.X.	17/12/1915	17/12/1915
Operation(al) Order(s)	Operation Orders No. 92 By Lieut. Col. C. Retallack. M.C. Commdg 1/5 Battn Royal Warwickshire Regiment.	28/03/1917	28/03/1917
Operation(al) Order(s)	143rd Inf Bde. Operation Order No. 130	31/03/1917	31/03/1917
War Diary	Ref Map 57c S.W. 1/20000 62c N.E Chaufours Wood	01/04/1917	10/04/1917
War Diary	Cartigny	11/04/1917	14/04/1917
War Diary	Epehy	16/04/1917	17/04/1917
War Diary	Ref Map 62c 1/40000 Villers Faucon	18/04/1917	20/04/1917
War Diary	Marquaix	21/04/1917	29/04/1917
War Diary	Flamicourt	29/04/1917	30/04/1917
Operation(al) Order(s)	Operation Orders No. 93 By Lieut. Col. C. Retallack. M.C. Commdg 1/5 Battn Royal Warwickshire Regiment.	02/04/1917	02/04/1917
Operation(al) Order(s)	Operation Orders No. 94 By Lieut. Col. C. Retallack. M.C. Commdg 1/5 Battn Royal Warwickshire Regiment.	05/04/1917	05/04/1917
Operation(al) Order(s)	Operation Orders No. 95 By Lieut. Col. C. Retallack. M.C. Commdg 1/5 Battn Royal Warwickshire Regiment.	09/04/1917	09/04/1917

Operation(al) Order(s)	Operation Orders No. 96 By Lieut. Col. C. Retallack. M.C. Commdg 1/5 Battn Royal Warwickshire Regiment.	13/04/1917	13/04/1917
Miscellaneous	Dispositions Of Right Battalion Left Brigade Sector	15/04/1917	15/04/1917
Operation(al) Order(s)	Operation Orders No. 97 By Lieut. Col. C. Retallack. M.C. Commdg 1/5 Battn Royal Warwickshire Regiment.	16/04/1917	16/04/1917
Miscellaneous	Messages And Signals		
Miscellaneous	Appendix II All Units	18/04/1917	18/04/1917
Operation(al) Order(s)	Operation Orders No. 98 By Lieut. Col. C. Retallack. M.C. Commdg 1/5 Battn Royal Warwickshire Regiment.	20/04/1917	20/04/1917
Operation(al) Order(s)	Operation Orders No. 99 By Lieut. Col. C. Retallack. M.C. Commdg 1/5 Battn Royal Warwickshire Regiment.	28/04/1917	28/04/1917
Operation(al) Order(s)	Operation Orders No. 100 By Lieut. Col. C. Retallack. M.C. Commdg 1/5 Battn Royal Warwickshire Regiment.	30/04/1917	30/04/1917
Heading	War Diary Of 1/5th Bn R. War R. From 1st May 1917 To 31st May 1917 Vol 27		
War Diary	Eclusier	02/05/1917	03/05/1917
War Diary	Peronne	05/05/1917	12/05/1917
War Diary	Letransloy	13/05/1917	13/05/1917
War Diary	Fremicourt	13/05/1917	31/05/1917
Operation(al) Order(s)	Operation Orders No. 101 By Major P.H. Whitehouse, Commdg 1/5 Battn Royal Warwickshire Regiment.	02/05/1917	02/05/1917
Operation(al) Order(s)	Operation Orders No. 102 By Major W.C.C. Gell, M.C. Commdg 1/5 Battn Royal Warwickshire Regiment.	11/05/1917	11/05/1917
Operation(al) Order(s)	Operation Orders No. 103 By Major W.C.C. Gell, M.C. Commdg 1/5 Battn Royal Warwickshire Regiment.	12/05/1917	12/05/1917
Operation(al) Order(s)	Operation Orders No. 104 By Major W.C.C. Gell, M.C. Commdg 1/5 Battn Royal Warwickshire Regiment.	21/05/1917	21/05/1917
Operation(al) Order(s)	Operation Orders No. 105 By Major W.C.C. Gell, M.C. Commdg 1/5 Battn Royal Warwickshire Regiment.	30/05/1917	30/05/1917
Heading	War Diary Of 5th Royal Warwickshire Regiment From 1st June To 30th June 1917 Vol 28		
War Diary	Louverval Sector	01/06/1917	08/06/1917
War Diary	Morchies-Delsaux Farm	08/06/1917	14/06/1917
War Diary	Louverval Sector	15/06/1917	21/06/1917
War Diary	Louverval	17/06/1917	24/06/1917
War Diary	Lebucquiere	24/06/1917	30/06/1917
Operation(al) Order(s)	Operation Orders No. 106 By Lt-Col W.C.C. Gell, M.C. Commdg 1/5 Battn Royal Warwickshire Regiment.	07/06/1917	07/06/1917
Operation(al) Order(s)	Operation Orders No. 107 By Lieut. Col. W.C.C. Gell M.C. Commdg 1/5th Bn The Royal Warwickshire Regiment.	15/06/1917	15/06/1917
Operation(al) Order(s)	Operation Orders No. 108 By Lieut. Col. W.C.C. Gell M.C. Commdg 1/5th Bn Royal Warwickshire Regiment.	23/06/1917	23/06/1917
Operation(al) Order(s)	Operation Orders No. 109 By Lieut. Col. W.C.C. Gell M.C. Commdg 1/5th Bn Royal Warwickshire Regiment.	30/06/1917	30/06/1917
Miscellaneous	1/8th Royal Warwickshire Regiment Operation Orders	20/06/1917	20/06/1917
Heading	War Diary Of 1/5th Bn Royal Warwickshire Regt From 1st July To 31st July 1917 Vol 29		

War Diary	Gomiecourt	02/07/1917	04/07/1917
War Diary	Berles-Au-Bois	06/07/1917	20/07/1917
War Diary	Pommera	21/07/1917	22/07/1917
War Diary	St Janster Biezen	23/07/1917	31/07/1917
War Diary	Belgium Sheet 28 N.W. 1/20000 Woods In A30	31/07/1917	31/07/1917
Operation(al) Order(s)	Operation Orders No. 110 By Lieut. Col. W.C.C. Gell M.C. Commdg 1/5th Bn Royal Warwickshire Regiment.	02/07/1917	02/07/1917
Miscellaneous	1/5th Royal Warwickshire Regiment Entraining State	22/07/1917	22/07/1917
Operation(al) Order(s)	Operation Orders No. 111 By Lieut. Col. C. Retallack, M.C. Commdg 1/5th Bn Royal Warwickshire Regiment.	19/07/1917	19/07/1917
Operation(al) Order(s)	Operation Orders No. 112 By Lieut. Col. C. Retallack, M.C. Commdg 1/5th Bn Royal Warwickshire Regiment.	21/07/1917	21/07/1917
Miscellaneous	Administrative Instructions Issued In Conjunction With Bn. Operation O. No.112	21/07/1917	21/07/1917
Operation(al) Order(s)	Operation Orders No. 113 By Lieut. Col. C. Retallack, M.C. Commdg 1/5th Bn Royal Warwickshire Regiment.	29/07/1917	29/07/1917
Heading	War Diary Of 1/5th Royal Warwickshire Regiment From 1st August To 31st August 1917 Vol 30		
War Diary	Belgium Sheet 28 N.W. 1/20000 Wood L A 30	01/08/1917	17/08/1917
War Diary	Dambre	17/08/1917	17/08/1917
War Diary	Camp A30d 19 Ref Map Of Belgium 28 N.W. 1/20000	07/08/1917	07/08/1917
War Diary	Reigersburg Camp	08/08/1917	08/08/1917
War Diary	Vanheule Fm St Julien	10/08/1917	11/08/1917
War Diary	Canal Bank	12/08/1917	13/08/1917
War Diary	Vanheule Fm	16/08/1917	17/08/1917
War Diary	Dambre	18/08/1917	18/08/1917
War Diary	Canal Bank	19/08/1917	21/08/1917
War Diary	Dugout C.18.a.5.4	21/08/1917	24/08/1917
War Diary	Dugout C.12.c.0.2	24/08/1917	28/08/1917
War Diary	Poperinghe	29/08/1917	29/08/1917
War Diary	St Janter Biezen	30/08/1917	31/08/1917
Miscellaneous	Provisional Orders For Move	06/08/1917	06/08/1917
Operation(al) Order(s)	Operation Orders No. 114 By Lieut. Col. C. Retallack, M.C. Commdg 1/5th Bn Royal Warwickshire Regiment.	08/08/1917	08/08/1917
Operation(al) Order(s)	Operation Orders No. 115 By Lieut. Colonel C. Retallack, M.C. Commdg. 1/5th Bn. Royal Warwickshire Regiment	13/08/1917	13/08/1917
Miscellaneous	Appendix II	21/08/1917	21/08/1917
Operation(al) Order(s)	Operation Orders No. 116 by Lt. Col. C. Retallack, M.C. Commdg 1/5th Bn. Royal Warwickshire Regiment	15/08/1917	15/08/1917
Miscellaneous	Recipients Of O.O No. 116	15/08/1917	15/08/1917
Heading	War Diary Of 1/5th Royal Warwickshire Regiment From 1st September To 30th September 1917		
War Diary	St Janter Biezen	01/09/1917	17/09/1917
War Diary	Nordausques	18/09/1917	30/09/1917
Operation(al) Order(s)	Operation Orders No. 117 By Lieut. Col. C. Retallack, M.C. Commdg 1/5th Bn The Royal Warwickshire Regiment.	21/08/1917	21/08/1917

Operation(al) Order(s)	Operation Orders No. 116A By Lieut Col C. Retallack M.C. Commdg 1/5th Bn Royal Warwickshire Regiment 21st Aug 1917	21/08/1917	21/08/1917
Operation(al) Order(s)	Operation Orders No. 118 By Capt. H.S. Bloomer Comdg. 1/5th Bn. Royal Warwickshire Regiment	29/08/1917	29/08/1917
Miscellaneous	Appendix IV	26/08/1917	26/08/1917
Miscellaneous	Appendix V	23/08/1917	23/08/1917
Miscellaneous	Appendix VII	24/08/1917	24/08/1917
Heading	1/5 R Warwick Rgt Vol 32 October 1917		
Heading	D.A.G. 3rd Echelon		
Heading	War Diary Of 1/5th Royal Warwickshire Regiment From 1st October To 31st October 1917		
War Diary	Dambre Camp	01/10/1917	02/10/1917
War Diary	Reigersburg Camp	02/10/1917	03/10/1917
War Diary	Front Line	04/10/1917	07/10/1917
War Diary	Irish Farm	07/10/1917	08/10/1917
War Diary	Siege Camp	08/10/1917	08/10/1917
War Diary	Poperinghe	09/10/1917	13/10/1917
War Diary	Maroeuil	13/10/1917	13/10/1917
War Diary	Mt St Eloy	13/10/1917	16/10/1917
War Diary	Mericourt Sector	16/10/1917	16/10/1917
War Diary	Poperinghe	09/10/1917	12/10/1917
War Diary	Mt St Eloy	14/10/1917	15/10/1917
War Diary	Mericourt Sector	18/10/1917	18/10/1917
War Diary	Dambre Camp	01/10/1917	01/10/1917
War Diary	Front Line	06/10/1917	07/10/1917
War Diary	Poperinghe	09/10/1917	13/10/1917
War Diary	Fraser Camp	26/10/1917	27/10/1917
War Diary	Mericourt Sector	20/10/1917	21/10/1917
War Diary	Fraser Camp	21/10/1917	26/10/1917
War Diary	Mericourt Sector	27/10/1917	09/11/1917
Operation(al) Order(s) Miscellaneous	143rd Inf Bde Operation Order No. 169	02/10/1917	02/10/1917
Operation(al) Order(s)	Operation Orders No. 121 By Lieut. Col. W.C.C. Gell, M.C. Commdg 1/5th Bn Royal Warwickshire Regiment.	02/10/1917	02/10/1917
Operation(al) Order(s)	Operation Orders No. 123 By Lieut. Col. W.C.C. Gell, M.C. Commdg 1/5th Bn Royal Warwickshire Regiment.	03/10/1917	03/10/1917
Operation(al) Order(s)	Operation Orders No. 122 By Lieut. Col. W.C.C. Gell, M.C. Commdg 1/5th Bn Royal Warwickshire Regiment.	03/10/1917	03/10/1917
Miscellaneous	Appendix I	05/10/1917	05/10/1917
Miscellaneous	1/5th Bn Royal Warwickshire Regiment	10/10/1917	10/10/1917
Miscellaneous	48th Division F.126	11/10/1917	11/10/1917
Miscellaneous	1/5th Bn Royal Warwickshire Regiment	12/10/1917	12/10/1917
Operation(al) Order(s)	143rd Infantry Brigade Operation Orders No. 171	08/10/1917	08/10/1917
Miscellaneous	March Table To Accompany O.O. 171		
Miscellaneous	Addendum To Operation Order No. 171		
Operation(al) Order(s)	Operation Orders No. 125 By Lieut. Col. W.C.C. Gell, M.C. Commdg 1/5th Bn Royal Warwickshire Regiment.	12/10/1917	12/10/1917
Operation(al) Order(s)	Operation Orders No. 124 By Lieut. Col. W.C.C. Gell, M.C. Commdg 1/5th Bn Royal Warwickshire Regiment.	08/10/1917	08/10/1917
Miscellaneous	Entraining Table Issued With O.O. 172		

Miscellaneous	Table "B" To Accompany 48th Division Order No. 225		
Miscellaneous	Move Of 48th Division (Less Artillery)		
Miscellaneous	143rd Inf. Bde. O.O. 172		
Miscellaneous	Addendum No. 1 To 143rd Inf Bde Operation Order No. 172	12/10/1917	12/10/1917
Operation(al) Order(s)	143rd Infantry Brigade Operation Order No. 172	12/10/1917	12/10/1917
Miscellaneous	Addendum Issued With O.O. 173	14/10/1917	14/10/1917
Operation(al) Order(s)	143rd Infantry Brigade Operation Order No. 173	14/10/1917	14/10/1917
Miscellaneous	Table Of Reliefs And Moves Issued With O.O. 173		
Miscellaneous	Move Of 48th Division (Less Artillery) Table "D"		
Operation(al) Order(s)	Operation Orders No. 126 By Lieut. Col. W.C.C. Gell, M.C. Commdg 1/5th Bn Royal Warwickshire Regiment.	16/10/1917	16/10/1917
Operation(al) Order(s)	143rd Infantry Brigade Operation Order No. 174	19/10/1917	19/10/1917
Operation(al) Order(s)	Operation Orders No. 126/1 By Lieut. Col. W.C.C. Gell, M.C. Commdg 1/5th Bn Royal Warwickshire Regiment.	21/10/1917	21/10/1917
Operation(al) Order(s)	143rd Infantry Brigade Operation Order No. 175	21/10/1917	21/10/1917
Operation(al) Order(s)	143rd Infantry Brigade Operation Order No. 176	25/10/1917	25/10/1917
Miscellaneous	Relief Table Issued With 143rd Inf Bde O.O. 176		
Operation(al) Order(s)	Operation Orders No. 127 By Lieut. Col. W.C.C. Gell, M.C. Commdg 1/5th Bn Royal Warwickshire Regiment.	26/10/1917	26/10/1917
Operation(al) Order(s)	Operation Orders No. 128 By Lieut. Col. W.C.C. Gell, M.C. Commdg 1/5th Bn Royal Warwickshire Regiment.	31/10/1917	31/10/1917

1/5 BNT.
ROYAL WARWICKS

MARCH 1915 →
OCT. 1917.

48TH DIVISION
143RD INFY BDE

1-5TH BN ROY. WARWICKS.

MAR 1915-~~MAR 1919~~
1917 OCT

TO ITALY

143rd Inf.Bde.
48th Div.

Battn. disembarked
Havre from England
23.3.15.

WAR
DIARY

1/5th BATTN. THE ROYAL WARWICKSHIRE REGIMENT.

M A R C H

(22.3.15 to 31.3.15)

1 9 1 5

1

Mar '19

Instructions regarding War Diaries and Intelligence Summaries are contained in F. S. Regs., Part II. and the Staff Manual respectively. Title pages will be prepared in manuscript.

WAR DIARY
or
~~INTELLIGENCE SUMMARY~~
(Erase heading not required.)

1/5 R. WAR. R.

MARCH 1915

Army Form C. 2118.

Hour, Date, Place	Summary of Events and Information	Remarks and references to Appendices
SOUTHAMPTON 4PM 22nd	Battalion strength 30 officers 1003 other ranks 78 horses embarked for service with Expeditionary Force.	CD
HAVRE 8AM 23rd	Battalion disembarked & went into rest camp, one interpreter joined and was taken on the strength. The orderly sergeant proceeded to base & was struck off strength	CD.
" NOON 24th	Battalion entrained for CASSEL.	
TERDEGHEN 7AM 25th	Battalion detrained at CASSEL & proceeded by route march into TERDEGHEN into billets. One man admitted to hospital struck off strength.	CD
BAILLEUL 8AM 28th	Battalion marched from TERDEGHEN into billets at BAILLEUL. One horse died & one horse sick struck off strength.	CD.
" 29th	Battalion employed in digging trenches N E of NEUVE EGLISE.	
" 30th	do	CD
" 31st	do	CD.

C R Davies Capt & Adjt
1/5 R. War. R.

1247 W 3299 200,000 (E) 8/14 J.B.C. & A. Forms/C. 2118/11.

143rd Inf.Bde.
48th Div.

WAR
DIARY

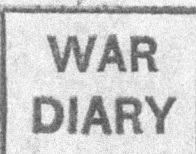

1/5th BATTN. THE ROYAL WARWICKSHIRE REGIMENT.

A P R I L

1 9 1 5

Instructions regarding War Diaries and Intelligence Summaries are contained in F. S. Regs., Part II. and the Staff Manual respectively. Title pages will be prepared in manuscript.

WAR DIARY ~~or~~ ~~INTELLIGENCE SUMMARY~~

(Erase heading not required.)

Army Form C. 2118.

1/5 R. WAR. R.

APRIL 1915.

Hour, Date, Place APRIL	Summary of Events and Information	Remarks and references to Appendices
ARMENTIERES. 1st	Battalion marched from BAILLEUL into billets at ARMENTIERES and attached to 19th Infantry Brigade for instruction in trench warfare	CD
BAILLEUL 6th	Battalion marched from ARMENTIERES back into billets at BAILLEUL.	CD
DOUVE TRENCHES 12th	Battalion marched from BAILLEUL and took over DOUVE trenches Casualties - one man wounded	CD
DOUVE TRENCHES 13th	casualties - one man killed one man died of wounds received same day	CD
— 14th	casualties - two men slightly wounded	CD
— 15th	casualties - ~~one killed~~ two men wounded.	CD
— 16th	casualties - three men killed two men wounded. On being relieved in DOUVE trenches battalion marched into hutments near NEUVE EGLISE in divisional reserve.	CD
HUTMENTS near NEUVE EGLISE 20th	Battalion marched from hutments & took over DOUVE trenches. Casualty one man wounded.	CD
DOUVE TRENCHES 22nd	casualties one man killed two men wounded.	
24th	Battalion marched into ~~hutments near~~ billets at PETIT PONT point 63	CD
PETIT PONT 28th	Battalion took over DOUVE trenches. casualty one man wounded - "at duty"	CD
DOUVE TRENCHES 30th	casualty - one man wounded.	

C. [illegible] Capt. & Adjt
1/5 R. War. R.

143rd Inf.Bde.
48th Div.

WAR DIARY

1/5th BATTN. THE ROYAL WARWICKSHIRE REGIMENT.

M A Y

1 9 1 5

Army Form C. 2118.

Instructions regarding War Diaries and Intelligence Summaries are contained in F. S. Regs., Part II. and the Staff Manual respectively. Title pages will be prepared in manuscript.

WAR DIARY or INTELLIGENCE SUMMARY

(Erase heading not required.)

1/5 R. WAR R.

MAY 1915

Hour, Date, Place	Summary of Events and Information	Remarks and references to Appendices
DOUVE TRENCHES MAY 1st	casualties 4 men killed 8 men wounded.	C.R.D.
MAY 2nd	Battalion marched to hutments at JONESVILLE	C.R.D.
HUTMENTS - JONESVILLE ... MAY 3rd C.R.	digging parties - casualty one man wounded.	C.R.D.
MAY 6th	Battalion returned to trenches - casualty one man killed	C.R.D.
TRENCHES. 61-65 MAY 7th	casualty one man killed	C.R.D.
MAY 8th	casualty ~~two~~ men wounded - Captain J.A. SEYMOUR wounded 2Lt. O.L. OWEN accidentally wounded	C.R.D.
MAY 9th	casualties 7 men killed 18 men wounded	C.R.D.
MAY 11th	casualty one man wounded	C.R.D.
MAY 12th	Battalion marched into billets at PETIT PONT - Point 63	C.R.D.
Point 63. PETIT. PONT. MAY 13th	digging parties - casualties two men killed. 2Lt. W.A.P. WATSON went to hospital as result of being thrown from his horse	C.R.D. C.R.
MAY 14th	digging party - casualty one man wounded	C.R.D.
May 15	digging parties. Lt. C.S. Riddell went to hospital for an operation - Capt and Adj C.E. DAVIES went into hospital - Capt C. RETALLACK appointed adjutant vice Capt C.E. DAVIES	Charles Retallack -
~~May 16~~	Major A.W.F. PAULI. T.D. returned to ENGLAND	
May 16.	Battalion returned to trenches - one man wounded	C.R.
TRENCHES 61-65 - MAY 17.		C.R.
MAY 18	one man accidentally wounded.	C.R.
MAY 19	one man wounded	C.R.
MAY 20	one man wounded and one accidentally wounded. Battalion marched to JONESVILLE	C.R.
JONESVILLE ..... MAY 21	digging party	C.R.
May 22	digging party	C.R.

Charles Retallack - Capt and adj 1/5 R War. R.

1247 W 3299 200,000 (E) 8/14 J.B.C. & A. Forms/C. 2118/11.

Instructions regarding War Diaries and Intelligence Summaries are contained in F. S. Regs., Part II. and the Staff Manual respectively. Title pages will be prepared in manuscript.

Army Form C. 2118.

WAR DIARY
or
~~INTELLIGENCE SUMMARY~~
(Erase heading not required.)

Place	Hour, Date, 1915	Summary of Events and Information	Remarks and references to Appendices
JONESVILLE	MAY 23	Digging Parties	CR.
	MAY 24	Battalion returns to trenches – one man wounded	CR
TRENCHES. 61 – 65	MAY 25	one man wounded	CR
	MAY 26	one man killed and one wounded	CR
	May 27	one man wounded	CR.
	May 28	Battalion march to COURT DREVE	CR
POINT. 63. COURT DREVE	MAY 29	Digging parties	CR
	MAY 30	Digging parties	CR
	MAY 31	Digging parties	CR.

The weather during May has been fine except the week beginning May 9th – the later weeks have been very hot.
Battalion Strength on May 31st – officers 22. other ranks 889.

Charles Retallack
Capt and adj.
1/5 R. Warwickshire Regt.

1247 W 3299 200,000 (E) 8/14 J.B.C. & A. Forms/C. 2118/11.

143rd Inf.Bde.
48th Div.

WAR DIARY

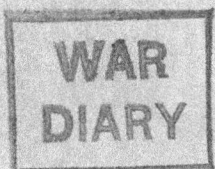

1/5th BATTN. THE ROYAL WARWICKSHIRE REGIMENT.

J U N E

1 9 1 5

Instructions regarding War Diaries and Intelligence Summaries are contained in F. S. Regs., Part II. and the Staff Manual respectively. Title pages will be prepared in manuscript.

WAR DIARY
or
~~INTELLIGENCE~~ SUMMARY
(Erase heading not required.)

Army Form C. 2118.

1st/5 Bn. R. Warwickshire. Regt
— June 1915 —

Hour, Date, Place		Summary of Events and Information	Remarks and references to Appendices
Point 63. Court DREVE June	1	Batt. returned to trenches. MAJOR GENERAL. R. FANSHAWE. D.S.O assumed command of the Division	C.R.
Trenches 61–65	2	CAPTAIN J.H. FRANCIS killed – one man wounded	C.R.
	3	2/LIEUT. R.W.L. EDGINGTON killed – one man wounded.	C.R.
	4	One man killed.	C.R.
	5	One man wounded – Battalion marched into Huts at JONESVILLE	C.R.
Hutments: JONESVILLE	6	digging parties	C.R.
	7	Battalion marched into COURT DREVE – CAPT. J.R.M. MINSULL FORD. ROYAL WELSH FUSILIERS assumed duties of Bde Major – one man accidentally wounded.	C.R.
Point 63. Court DREVE	8	digging parties	C.R.
	9	Battalion went into trenches taking up a new line – 5 new trenches being taken in on the right of the old line and 2 trenches given up on the left	C.R.
DOUVE TRENCHES 36–40, 61–63	10	The following officers have arrived from England & taken on strength of the battalion. Capt. K. JENNENS – 2 Lieut A.F. ADKIN – 2 Lieut R.W. AREND – MAJOR W.H. FRANKLIN 1st NEWFOUNDLAND REGt took Sen. Major	C.R.
	11	one man wounded – Battalion marched into Billets at ROMARIN	C.R.
ROMARIN	12		
	13		
	14	Battalion (in Divisional Reserve) turned out at 3.5 am for an alarm occasioned by the explosion of a mine but the situation dealt with by the garrison in the trenches. The Batt. was inspected in the afternoon by G.O.C. Division	C.R.
	15	Battalion took over another line of trenches Between FRELINGHIEN and PLOEGSTEERT. No. 1–19	C.R.
Trenches 1–19	16	a company of 7 Norfolks in our trenches for instruction throughout our tour	C.R.
	17	Three men wounded – one died of his wounds the following day – on night of 17/18 an effort to take a prisoner in accordance with 3rd Army Corps orders was made by a party under 2nd Lieut H.W.L. Groom who patrolled with a bomb party – No prisoner was taken, but the party threw bombs when they encountered the enemy & only retired when forced to do so by superior fire & numbers of enemy, having penetrated nearly as far as enemies trenches	C.R.
	18	Two men wounded 2/Lt Groom made another sortie on night of 18/19 but no Germans were to be found in front of their line	C.R.
	19	[illegible] men wounded – Battn went into Brigade Reserve at the [illegible] at The Convent PLOEGSTEERT	C.R.

Charles [illegible] Capt & Adjt

1247 W 3299 200,000 (E) 8/14 J.B.C. & A. Forms/C. 2118/11.

Instructions regarding War Diaries and Intelligence Summaries are contained in F. S. Regs., Part II. and the Staff Manual respectively. Title pages will be prepared in manuscript.

WAR DIARY
or
INTELLIGENCE SUMMARY
(Erase heading not required.)

Army Form C. 2118.

Hour, Date, Place		Summary of Events and Information	Remarks and references to Appendices
The Convent	June 20	} Drill and working parties	Ch
PLOEGSTEERT.	21		
	22		Ch
	23	Batn returned to Trenches 1–19 – one man wounded	
	24		
	25	Two men wounded – one died 26.6.15 of his wounds.	Ch
BAILLEUL	26	Batt left trenches 12.30 a.m and marched to BAILLEUL – inspection by Lieut General Sir W. P. Pulteney K.C.B. D.S.O. Commdg 3rd Corps – Batt marched to VIEUX BERGUIN.	Ch
VIEUX BERGUIN.	27	Batn Marched to HAM EN ARTOIS. 2nd Lieuts E. Holt and W. E. Walsh arrived from England & taken on strength of Batn	Ch
HAM EN ARTOIS	28	Batn Marched to AUCHEL and goes into CORPS reserve	Ch
AUCHEL	29	–	
	30	–	
		Weather during June has been fine and hot.	
		Batn Strength on June 30th – Officers 25 Other Ranks 886	
		Charles Retallack Capt and Adjt – 5 R War R June 30 1915	

1247 W 3299 200,000 (E) 8/14 J.B.C. & A. Forms/C. 2118/11.

143rd Inf.Bde.
48th Div.

WAR DIARY

1/5th BATTN. THE ROYAL WARWICKSHIRE REGIMENT.

J U L Y

1 9 1 5

Attached:

Battn. O.O. No. 2.

Army Form C. 2118.

Instructions regarding War Diaries and Intelligence Summaries are contained in F. S. Regs., Part II. and the Staff Manual respectively. Title pages will be prepared in manuscript.

WAR DIARY
or
~~INTELLIGENCE SUMMARY~~

(Erase heading not required.)

July 1915 1/5 R. War. R

Hour, Date, Place			Summary of Events and Information	Remarks and references to Appendices
AUCHEL	July	1.	Bath in Corps Reserve –	C.R.
	"	3	Bath inspected by General Sir Douglas Haig. Comdg First Army –	C.R.
	"	8	Bath inspected by Earl KITCHENER	C.R.
	"	11	Lieut. Col. G.C. SLADEN. (The Rifle Brigade) took over command of the Bath	C.R.
		12	Bath marched to Bivouacs. at HOUCHIN	C.R.
HOUCHIN	"	16	Bath returned to AUCHEL	C.R.
AUCHEL	"	18	Bath marched to Bivouac at BEAUQUESNE	C.R.
BEAUQUESNE	"	21	Bath marched to COURCELLES. and went into Brigade Reserve. 143rd Inf Bde take over trenches at HEBUTERNE	C.R.
COURCELLES	"	25	Bath marched to trenches and took over line as in Operation Order 2.	C.R.
TRENCHES	"	26th ~~25th~~	Three men killed and seven men wounded	G.H.C.
	"	27th	Three men wounded	G.H.C.
	"	28th	LIEUT. P.E. ROBINSON and 2/Lt W.J. BUCK arrived from HAVRE & taken on strength of Bath	C.R.
	"	29th	One man accidentally wounded.	G.H.C.
	"	30th	Battalion marched into billets at BAYENCOURT.	G.H.C.
BAYENCOURT.	"	31st	Battalion remained in billets at BAYENCOURT.	G.H.C.

Strength of Bath on July 31st 1915 –

Officers 28 – O.R. 828 –

Charles Retallack
Capt & adjt –

No. 6 COPY.

OPERATION ORDERS No.2.

July 25th. 1915.

1/5th. Battn. Royal Warwickshire Regt.

---

1. The 1/5th. Battn. will take over the right section of the Trenches at HEBUTERNE" now occupied by the 1/6th Battn., to night.

2. A.& B. Coys. will be in the front line Trenches, A. Coy. on the right, B. Coy. on the left.

3. C. Coy. will be in support in the NEW TRENCH, and D. Coy. in reserve at ROLAND & DUGUESCLIN.

4. Battalion H. Q. will be at ROLAND.

5. Dressing Station is in DUGUESCLIN near RANDON.

(signed) Charles Retallack.
CAPT. & ADJT.
1/5th. R. WAR. R.

Issued at p. m. July 25th 1915.

No.1 copy to A. Coy.

2 " B.

3 " C.

4 " D.

5 , War Diary.

6 " "

7 " Office.

143rd Inf.Bde.
48th Div.

WAR DIARY

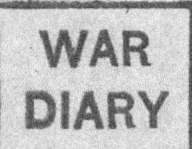

1/5th BATTN. THE ROYAL WARWICKSHIRE REGIMENT.

A U G U S T

1 9 1 5

Attached:

Battn. O.O. No. 4.

Army Form C. 2118.

Instructions regarding War Diaries and Intelligence Summaries are contained in F. S. Regs., Part II. and the Staff Manual respectively. Title pages will be prepared in manuscript.

WAR DIARY
or
~~INTELLIGENCE~~ SUMMARY
(Erase heading not required.)

5th Batt. R. War. R. —

August 1915

Hour, Date, Place		Summary of Events and Information	Remarks and references to Appendices
BAYENCOURT — AUGUST	1	Batt. in Divisional Reserve –	C.R.
" "	3	Batt. inspected by Lt. Gen. Sir T. D'O SNOW. K.C.B. Commdg VII Corps	C.R.
TRENCHES COLINCAMPS	7	Batt. relieved 4th Glosters in trenches and took over line & dispositions as in O.O. No. 4	Ch. Operation Order No. 4
	10	One man wounded (at duty) one accidental injury	Ch
	13	one O.R. wounded	Ch
	15	Batt. relieved by the 4th Glosters and marched to billets at BAYENCOURT	Ch
BAYENCOURT	16		
	17	Working parties of 375 per day & baths during stay in billets	Ch
	19	one man accidentally wounded	Ch
	20	[illegible]	Ch
TRENCHES - COLINCAMPS	23	Batt. relieved 4th Glosters in trenches taking up same dispositions as on 7th August	Ch
	24	1 O.R. killed 3 wounded (1 at duty)	Ch
	25	2. O.R. wounded. Batt. relieved by 2 Batt. Essex Regt & marched to huts in BOIS de WARNIMONT	Ch
BOIS de WARNIMONT.	26 27 28 29	[illegible] and Baths –	Ch Ch
	30	Batt. went into billets at BUS –	
BUS.	31	Working parties & Baths –	

Strength of Batt. on August 31st.
Officers 29 — O.R. 777 —

Charles [illegible]
CAPT. & ADJT.
5TH BATTN. R'L WAR. REGT.

1247 W 3299 200,000 (E) 8/14 J.B.C. & A. Forms/C. 2118/11.

War Diary

OPERATION ORDERS. No. 4.

1/8th Battn. Royal Warwickshire Regiment.

Ref. Maps August 7th. 1916.

AMIENS $\frac{1}{80,000}$ & Trench Map.

---

1. The 1/8th Battn. Royal Warwickshire Regt. will relieve the 4th. Battn Gloucester Regt. on August 7th. 1916., and will take over their dispositions.

2. The Front Trenches the Battn. will take over are as follows:-

   From 2 ARBRES ARBATUS inclusive to 303 inclusive.

   " A " Coy. in Battn. reserve Trench.
   B
   B. C. D. in the Front Trench.

3. The Battn. will relieve via COURCELLES Point 180 (at C of COLINCAMPS). COLINCAMPS and BOYEAU EMPEREUR.

4. The Transport of the Battn will be Brigaded at COIGNEUX and will take over the Transport lines at 11 am.

5. All personnel of the Grenadier Coy. will go into Trenches with their respective Units.

6. Reserve M.G. teams will rejoin their Companies.

7. The " S.O.S." signal for Artillery support is one RED followed by one GREEN rocket fired from the Trenches and repeated until support is received.

8. The Dressing Station will be ~~at~~ in Moine Trench. –

9. The Battn. H.Q. will be ~~at~~ in MOINE Trench

Issued at 11 a.m. Aug. 7th. 1916.

Charles Retallack.
CAPT.& ADJT.
1/8th. R.WAR.R.

143rd Inf.Bde.
48th Div.

WAR
DIARY

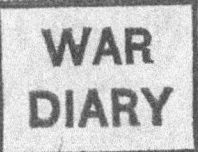

1/5th BATTN. THE ROYAL WARWICKSHIRE REGIMENT.

S E P T E M B E R

1 9 1 5

Attached:

Battn. O.Os. Nos.
6, 7, 8, 9, 10, 11
& 12.

Instructions regarding War Diaries and Intelligence Summaries are contained in F. S. Regs., Part II. and the Staff Manual respectively. Title pages will be prepared in manuscript.

WAR DIARY
or
INTELLIGENCE SUMMARY
(Erase heading not required.)

Army Form C. 2118.

September 1915

5TH BATTN. R'L WAR. REGT.

Hour, Date, Place		Summary of Events and Information	Remarks and references to Appendices
BUS —	September 1	Working parties and Baths — Capt. J.K. RABONE died at No 1 Red Cross Hospital LE TOUQUET of peritonitis after an operation for appendicitis	Ch
"	" 2	Baths — The Battn took over trenches from the French 56 Division as in O.O. No 6	Ch — O.O. No 6
TRENCHES	" 5	Reinforcements of 30 O.R. taken on strength of Battn	Ch
BAYENCOURT	" 6	Battn relieved in trenches by 6 R. War. R. and took over billets in BAYENCOURT. No casualties in trenches.	Ch.
"	" 7	½ Coy under MAJOR CARTER at work to continue defences of BAYENCOURT.	Ch
Trenches	" 10	Battn took over trenches from 6 R. War. R. as in O.O. No 7	Ch — O.O. No 7
FONQUEVILLERS.	" 14	Battn relieved by 6 R. War. R. and took over dispositions of 8 R. War. R. as in O.O. No 8	
"	" 15	one O.R. accidentally wounded. Working parties in [illegible] defences of FONQUEVILLERS	Ch — O.O. No 8.
TRENCHES	" 18	Battn relieved 6 R. War. R. in trenches as in O.O. No 9.	Ch — O.O. No 9.
	" 19	one O.R. killed.	Ch
	" 22	Battn relieved by 6 R. War. R. and took over billets of 8th R. War. R. at BAYENCOURT as in O.O. No 10	Ch.
BAYENCOURT	23	Battn Route March — Capt. E.V. JEAVONS appointed acting Q.M. vice Q.M. and hon. Major D. TAYLOR to England sick 6-9-15	Ch — O.O. No 10
	26	Battn relieved 6 R. War. R. in trenches as in O.O. No 11	Ch
TRENCHES	28	One O.R. wounded	Ch — O.O. No 11.
	30	Battn relieved by 6 R. War. R. in trenches, and took over defences of Fonquevillers and La Haie as in O.O. No 12 from 8 R. War. R.	Ch Ch — O.O. No 12

The weather in September has been generally fine & hot

Strength of Battn on Sept 30th

Officers 26 — O.R. 796

Charles Peto Yeats
Capt. & adjt.
5 R. War. R.

1247 W 3299 200,000 (E) 8/14 J.B.C. & A. Forms/C. 2118/11.

BATTALION OPERATION ORDERS NOS.
6, 7, 8, 9, 10, 11 & 12.

O P E R A T I O N O R D E R S. NO 6.

The 1/5th. Battn. Royal Warwickshire Regt.

Ref. AMIENS. 1/80,000. Sept. 1st, 1915.

---

1. 48th. Division will take over, as below, by Sept. 4th.

(a) A portion of the line now occupied by the French 56th. Divn. i.e.- the frontage of two Battalions, already designated to O.C. 5th & 7th. R.WAR.R. respectively.

(b) The Southern defences of FONQUEVILLERS, i.e., that part of the Village South of and including the road which runs S.E. below "FONQUEVILLERS" (on Plan Directeur) to CROSS ROADS in centre of Village, and thence just South of Church as far as edge of Village on CHURCH-CALVAIRE road.

(c) CHATEAU-de la HAIE.

2. 143rd Infantry Brigade will take over this portion of the line and will be permanently disposed as follows:-

1 Battn. in line on right.
1 Battn. in line on left.
1 Battn. as follows:-
  Hd. Qrs. & 2 Coys defences of FONQUEVILLERS
  2 Companies CHATEAU de la HAIE.
1 Battn. in BAYENCOURT.
Grenade Coy. (less platoons of 2 Battns in line) permanently at CHATEAU de la HAIE.
86th. Trench Mortar Battery:-
  ½ in line
  ½ in billets.in FONQUEVILLERS.

3. (a) 5th. R.WAR.R. will take over the right sub-section of the line on the night of 2/3rd September, moving via BAYENCOURT and CHATEAU de la HAIE. Guides will meet this Battn. at entrance to FONQUEVILLERS at 1.15 am. 3rd. September.

(b) The Battn after passing Chateau de la HAIE, will move in silence by platoons, and no smoking will be permitted.
The Coys will be closed up under cover of the Village by 1.15.

(c) 1 Officer per Coy. and 1 N.C.O. per platoon of French Brigade, will remain in Trenches untill mid-day 3rd Sept.

(d) The Battn. will be disposed as follows:-
A. on right)
B. in centre) in front line
C. on left)
D. in Battn. reserve.
Battn. H.Q. will be in the reserve line
The " Special Instruction" (No 17) Platoon will be attached to "D" Coy, and a platoon of " D " Coy will be attached to " B " Coy. whilst in Trenches.

O P E R A T I O N O R D E R S. NO 6.
September 1st. 1915.

---

4. The Grenade Coy. will be permanently billeted at LA HAIE,& will consist of platoons of 2 Battns out of the line, and in addition, 10 men of each of these 2 Battns for instruction.

5. M.G. Sections of all Battns, with limbers, will be at CHATEAU de la HAIE at 7 pm. on 2nd. September, and will proceed to FONQUEVILLERS at intervals of 500 yards. They will be met by Brigade Machine Gun Officer and Guides at entrance to FONQUAVILLERS.

Machine Guns will be Brigaded.

Machine Guns Sections will consist of 26 men (including Cook and Officers Servant), and 5 N.C.Os.

8 Guns will be in front line,(2 guns from each Battn),i.e. 4 guns in right sub-section and 4 guns in left sub-section. Disposal of remaining guns will be directed by Bde. M.G.O.

Each Section will bring with it necessary degchies etc.

6. Rations will be dumped at the Ration dump, about 600 yds west W of FONQUEVILLERS on CHATEAU de la HAIE - FONQUEVILLERS road at an hour after dark, which will allow of all wagons being clear of this road by 11 pm. on the night of 2nd. September.

7. Cookers will be brought into FONQUEVILLERS by 10 pm. on Sept. 2nd. No horses will be kept in the Village.

8. Orders re position of Brigade Transport will be issued later.

9. The French dispositions will be followed untill the ground is better known. (and arrangements.)

10. Great care is to be taken with regard to moving Troops and Transport. All movements for the present will be under cover of darkness, and with intervals between units and vehicles.

Single vehicles, horses, and parties of men not larger than sections, may move from LA HAIE to FONQUEVILLERS, if necessary, by day,but there is very grave risk of machine guns firing on this road.

Charles Altemach

ISSUED AT 5 pm.
Sept. 1st. 1915.

Capt. & Adjt.
1/5th. R.WAR.R.

OPERATION ORDERS. No.7.

The 1/5th.Battn. Royal Warwickshire Regt.

Ref.AMIENS. 1/80.000.

September.10th.1915.

---

1. The 1/5th R.War R. will relieve the 1/6th.R.War.R.in Trenches to-day,and will take over their dispositions.
2. A.Company will march off at 2.p.m.
   D. " " " " " 2.10.p.m.
   B. " " " " " 2.20.p.m.
   C. " " " " " 2.30.p.m.
   and will go by Platoons.

3. Route. Leave BAYENCOURT and move across country along valley N. of M in MIN 162 past Battery of dummy Guns across the SQUASTRE - FONQUEVILLERS road across valley until under cover of Village of FONQUEVILLERS - into village by road S of CHURCH.

   Guides will be placed out,and these will be picked up by Officer in rear of C.Company

4. Separate orders have been issued to Transport.

September 10th.1915.

(Signed) Charles Rettallack.
Capt & Adjt.
1/5th.R WAR R

War Diary

OPERATION ORDERS No 8.
BY
Lieut.Col.G.C.SLADEN.
Commanding 1/5th Batt.the Royal Warwickshire Regt. Sept.14th.1915

Reference Map.

Amiens 1/80.000.

(1) The 5th R War R will take over the billets and dispositions of the 6 R War R to-day at LA HAIE and FONQUEVILLERS.

(2) A and D. will take over the southern defences of FONQUEVILLERS with H.Q at the BRASSERIE. B and C. Coy's will be at CHATEAU de la HAIE.

(3) Dressing Station will be at FONQUEVILLERS

(4) B and C will go via FONQUEVILLERS and then to LA HAIE by communication Trench

ISSUED AT 11 am.
Sept.14th.1914

Charles Bell Mack
Capt & Adjt.
1/5th R WAR R.

COPY No. 7

OPERATION ORDERS No. 9
By.
Lieut.Col.G.C.SLADEN.
Commanding 1/5th Batt.The Royal Warwickshire Regt.
September.18th.1915.

Reference Map.

AMIENS. 1/80,000.

1. The 5th.R War R. will relieve the 6th.R War R. in the Trenches to-day.

2.(a) B and C Companies will relieve the centre and left Companies of the 6th.R War R. at 2-30.p.m.

(b) The centre and left Companies of the 6th R War R will then relieve A and D. Companies in the defences of FONCQUEVILLERS.

(c) A and D. Companies will then relieve the right and reserve Companies 6th.R War R. in the Trenches.

3. The Companies from CHATEAU LA HAIE will go via the communication Trench to FONCQUEVILLERS.

4. Seperate orders have been issued to Transport officer and Machine Gun Officer.

ISSUED AT 9-40.a.m.
Sept.18th.1915.

Charles [illegible]

CAPT & ADJT.
1/5th. R War R.

No.1. Copy to A.Coy.
" 2 " " B "
" 3 " " C. "
" 4 " " D. "
" 5 " " 6th. R War R.
" 6 " " Office.
" 7 " " War Diary.
" 8 " " " "

O P E R A T I O N O R D E R S (10)
by.
Lieut.Col.G.C.SLADEN.
Commanding 1/5th.Battn.The Royal Warwickshire Regt.
September, 22nd.1915.

Ref.Map
1/80000 AMIENS.

1. The 5th Battn will be relieved in the Trenches by the 6th.Battalion to-day, and will take over the billets and dispositions of the 6th.Battalion at BAYENCOURT.

2. A and C. Companies will be relieved at 2-30.p.m. and B and D Companies at 3-45.p.m.

3. A and D will leave by Thorpe Street.
B will leave by New Street and Thorpe Street.
C will leave by Inge Avenue and The Forte

Companies will then go by Platoons, and leave FONCQUEVILLERS by the road which passes just South of the Church, across the SOUASTRE- FONCQUEVILLERS road, past Battery of dummy guns, along valley North of the M in MIN 162 and into BAYENCOURT at the N.E. corner of the village.

4. The Field Cookers will remain in their positions, and be taken over by the 6th.Battalion, who will send their Cookers to BAYENCOURT, for the use of the 5th.Battalion. A receipt must be taken from an Officer of the 6th.Battalion, that the Cookers and Boilers are clean and in good order. Receipt to be sent to Orderly room

5. Separate orders have been issued to Machine Gun and Transport Officers.

ISSUED AT 10-30.a.m.
September 22nd.1915.

(Signed) Charles Retallack.
Capt & Adjt.
1/5th. R WAR R.

O P E R A T I O N ~~S~~ O R D E R S No.11
By.
Lieut.Col.G.C.SLADEN.
Commanding 1/5th The Royal Warwickshire Regt.
September.26th.1915.

Ref.Map 1/80,000

AMIENS.

No.1. The 5th R War R will take over the Trenches from the 6th R War R.to-day.

" 2. A.Coy. will go in first,followed by B.C. and D.Coys A.Coy will time its departure to arrive in Trenches at 2-15.p.m.

" 3. Companies will march in Platoons,using the Dummy Gun route.

" 4. The Quartermaster will inspect the Cookers of the 6th,Battalion,and see that they are handed over,clean and in good order,and will obtain a receipt to that effect, from a responsible Officer.
The Cookers of the 5th Battalion will be taken over by Major FRANKLIN,who will give a receipt,and report on their condition after inspection by the respective Company Cooks.

" 5. Separate orders have been issued to Transport Officer.

ISSUED AT 10 a.m.
September.26th.1915.

(Signed)

Capt & Adjt.
1/5th. R WAR R.

OPERATION ORDERS. NO.15.

By

Lieut.Col.G.C.SLADEN.

Commanding the 1/5th Battn.Royal Warwickshire Regt.

September.30th.1915.

Ref Map. AMIENS 1/40.000 - and Trench Map.

1 The 6th.R War R, will relieve the 5th.R War R, in the Trenches to-day at 2-15.p.m.

2 The 5th.R War R on relief,will take over the billets and dispositions of the 6th.R War R.

3 A and D will form part of the defences of the Southern Ilot of FONCQUEVILLERS,and will be disposed as under.-

A. Coy in and about ~~F~~. F.10.
D. " " " " F.14. 15. 16.
HEAD QUARTERS at BRASSERIE.
B and C. will be at LA HAIE,under Command of Major W.FRANKLIN,with HEAD QUARTERS at CHATEAU.

4 A and D will go out via THORPE Street.
B via NEW Street and FIFTH AVENUE.
C via INGE AVENUE and the FORTH.

5 Separate orders have been issued to Transport and Machine Gun Sections.

6. The Cookers and Limbers complete of the 5th.R War R,will be taken over,as they stand,by the 6th.R War R. The 6th R War R will send up 2 Cookers and Limbers to LA HAIE,and 2 to FONCQUEVILLERS,for the use of the 5th.R War R.

Charles [signature]

ISSUED at 10 - 30.a.m.
September.30th.1915.

Capt & Adjt.
1/5th R WAR R.

Instructions regarding War Diaries and Intelligence Summaries are contained in F. S. Regs., Part II. and the Staff Manual respectively. Title pages will be prepared in manuscript.

WAR DIARY
or
~~INTELLIGENCE~~ SUMMARY
(Erase heading not required.)

Army Form C. 2118.

January 1916 –
5th Batt. The Royal Warwickshire Regt.

Hour, Date, Place		Summary of Events and Information	Remarks and references to Appendices
Trenches –	Jan. 4th	5th R Warwk relieved by the 6 R Warwk and took over distribution of 8 R Warwk at FONQUEVILLERS as in O.O 24.	– – – O.O 24 – Ch
		Lt G.H. SKIRROW taken on strength of Battn – Jan 3rd 1915	– Ch
FONQUEVILLERS	5th	2/Lt ARENO and 2/Lt BUCK and 33 O.R's transferred to Bde M.G. Coy.	– Ch
"	12	5 R Warwk relieve 6 R Warwk in trenches as in O.O. 25	– O.O. 25 – Ch
		The following officers arrived & taken on strength of Batt Jan. 11th 1915 2/Lt C.E. Carrington – 2/Lt P.A. Grove – 2/Lt A.R. Terry – 2/Lt R.J.H. Simpkin – 2/Lt F.T. Wakeman	– Ch
Trenches	13	2 O.R's wounded	– Ch
	20	5 R Warwk relieved by the 6 R Warwk and took over billets of 8 R Warwk at BAYENCOURT – O.O. 26	– O.O 26 – – Ch
BAYENCOURT	24	2/Lt J.R. HOUGHTON taken on strength of Batt	Ch
"	25	21 O.R's arrived and taken on strength of Batt	Ch
	28th	5 R Warwk took over trenches from 6 R Warwk as in O.O 27	O.O 27 – Ch
Trenches	30	A raid on Enemy trenches was attempted in conjunction with 144th Bde on our right – but owing to the darkness & fog it had to be abandoned after reaching the enemy wire.	– Ch
		2 O.R's wounded –	– Ch
		Strength of Batt. of Jan 31st 31 Officers 775 O.R's	

Charles Retallack
CAPT. & ADJT. 5TH BATT. R. WARWICKSHIRE REGT.
for Lt Col Commdg –

1247 W 3299 200,000 (E) 8/14 J.B.C. & A. Forms/C. 2118/11.

143rd Inf.Bde.
48th Div.

WAR DIARY

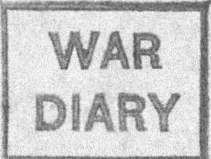

1/5th BATTN. THE ROYAL WARWICKSHIRE REGIMENT.

O C T O B E R

1 9 1 5

Attached:

Battn. O.Os. Nos.
13, 14 & 15.

OPERATION ORDERS NO. 24 Copy No. 2
BY
Lieut Col. G C SLADEN
Comdg 1/5 Batt Royal Warwickshire Regt
JANUARY 3rd 1916

Ref map 57d 1/40000
and BM 976C

1 The 5th R War R will be relieved by the 6th R War R on January 4th 1916 & will take over dispositions of the 8th R War R at FONQUEVILLERS and LA HAIE Relief will commence at 10-30 a.m. except the 6 posts which will be relieved at dark

2 Battalion Headquarters will be at Entrance Village.

Dispositions of Companies will be as under

A. LA HAIE CHATEAU

B one Platoon LA HAIE CHATEAU
one " LA HAIE F work
one " " H
one " " J

C 3 Platoons FONQUEVILLERS in Shelter F 12 13 14
1 " NORTH KEEP

D 3 Platoons FONQUEVILLERS in Shelter F 28
2 Sections at FORT DICK
2 " " JUNCTION KEEP

Major W H FRANKLIN will be in Command of the LA HAIE Detachment

3 The Route for the LA HAIE detachment will be as follows

Leave THORP STREET by the Cookers, then by VALLEY ROAD to K I D 96 on SAILLY - FONQUEVILLERS ROAD, thence by track to S.E. corner of LA HAIE

4 The Blankets of the LA HAIE Detachment will be rolled by sections & labelled & be at ARTILLERY CROSS ROADS at 9-30 A M where a wagon will be ready to take them to the CHATEAU

5 The Field Kitchens of the 5th R War R will be taken out and each Company will take their own Cookers and limbers

Horses for A & B Cookers will be at ARTILLERY CROSS ROADS at 8 a m on January 4th to take these Cookers to LA HAIE

CONTINUED

Army Form C. 2118.

Instructions regarding War Diaries and Intelligence Summaries are contained in F. S. Regs., Part II. and the Staff Manual respectively. Title pages will be prepared in manuscript.

WAR DIARY
or
~~INTELLIGENCE SUMMARY~~
(Erase heading not required.)

October 1915
5th Batt. R Warwickshire Regt

Hour, Date, Place		Summary of Events and Information	Remarks and references to Appendices
FONQUEVILLERS – October	3	Lt Col. G.C. SLADEN wounded whilst in M sector – relinquishing command	CR
"	8	5th Batt relieved 6 R Wark as in O.O. No 13	CR OO.13
TRENCHES	11	HQ's and A & B Coys of 15 Batt. R. W. Rif attached for instruction until 17th	CR
	16	5th Batt relieved by 6 R Wark. and took over billets of 8 R Wark R at BAYENCOURT as in OO. No 14	
BAYENCOURT .. "	19	Batt. Route March	CR OO. 14
	19	Working parties on BAYENCOURT defences & for R.E.	CR
	24	5 R Wark relieved 6 R Wark in trenches as in O.O. No 15	CR OO.15.
TRENCHES.	27	14th Batt R. Irish Rifles in for instruction until Nov 2nd	CR
	29	25 O.R arrived as reinforcement draft from base	CR

Strength of Batt on October 31st 1915

24 Officers 805 Other Ranks

Charles [illegible] CAPT & ADJT
5TH BATTN R'L WAR. REGT

1247 W 3299 200,000 (E) 8/14 J.B.C. & A. Forms/C. 2118/11.

6. When taking or handing over any trench or billet from another Battalion receipts must pass for all Stores, SAA, Grenades, Tools, Gumboots etc. These receipts must be made out in duplicate, and a copy forwarded to the Battalion Headquarters by 3 p.m. on January 4th. Certificate that Trenches & billets are left clean must also be handed in. No receipt or certificate is valid unless signed by an Officer.

7. Separate orders have been issued to Transport Officer.

Issued at 11 AM
January 3rd 1916

(SIGNED) Charles Ressilaeh
Capt & Adjt
1st R. War R.

NOTICE

The Transport Officer will arrange to take Officers Valises of A & B to LA HAIE and C and D to FONQUEVILLERS.

A Wagon will be at ARTILLERY CROSS ROADS at 10 a.m. to take A & B Company Officers kit and messes etc from trenches to LA HAIE.

No 1	Copy	File
2 & 3		War Diary
4		A
5		B
6		C
7		D
8		Transport

BATTALION OPERATION ORDERS NOS.
13, 14 & 15.

O P E R A T I O N O R D E R S. No.25.   Copy No....2.
B Y
Lieut.Col.G.C.SLADEN.
Commdg.1/5th.Battn.The Royal Warwickshire Regiment.
J A N U A R Y. 10th.1916.

---

1. The 5th.R.War.R, will relieve the 6th.R.War.R. on January.12nd

2. A. Company will be on the Right.

B. Company will be on the Left.

D. Company will be in Support.

C. Company will be in Reserve.

3. A and B Companies will March via SUNKEN ROAD route in half platoons, at 200 yards distance.

4. A and B Companies will relieve the Right and Left Companies of the 6th.R.War.R. at 10.a.m.

Posts 1.2.3 will be relieved at 10.a.m. 4.5.and 6.at dusk.

The Right Company 6th.R.War.R, will then relieve C.Company 5th.R.War.R.
C.Company.5th.R.War.R. will then relieve Reserve Company 6th.R.War.R.
Reserve Company 6th.R.War.R. will then relieve D.Company 5th.R.War.R.
D.Company 5th.R.War.R. will then relieve Support 6th.R.War.R.

5. Blankets of A and B Companies will be rolled and labelled by Sections. A wagon will be at LA HAIE at 8.a.m. to take them to the Trenches.

6. The Field Kitchens will be taken to the Trenches.
Horses for Kitchens of A and B will be at LA HAIE at 8.a.m.

7. When taking over or handing over any trench or billet from another Battalion, receipts must pass for all Stores, S.A.A Grenades, Tools, Gumboots, etc. These receipts must be made out in duplicate, and a copy forwarded to the Battalion Headquarters by 3.p.m. on January 12th.
Certificates that Trenches and Billets are left clean must also be handed in. No Receipts or Certificates are valid unless signed by an Officer.

8. Separate orders have been issued to Transport.

ISSUED at 8.p.m.
January.10th.1916.

Charles Rethlock
Capt & Adjt.
1/5th.Batt.The Royal Warwickshire Regt.

N O T I C E.

Officers baggage will be collected from CHATEAU LA HAIE at 9.a.m. and brought up to the Trenches, and will on return take kit back to the Transport.

No.1	Copy	File.
2&3	"	War Diary.
4	"	A
5	"	B
6	"	C
7	"	D
8	"	Transport Officer.
9	"	6th.R.War.R.

OPERATION ORDERS. No.26. Copy No....2.
BY
MAJOR.W.H.FRANKLIN.
Commanding 1/5th.Battn.The Royal Warwickshire Regt.
JANUARY. 18th.1916.

---

1. The 5th.R.War.R. will be relieved by the 6th.R.War.R.in the trenches on January 20th, and will then take over billets of 8th.R.War.R. at BAYENCOURT.
Relief will commence at 10.30.a.m. except the right and left posts, which will relieve at dusk.

2. The Reserve and Support Companies will each hand in to the Battalion Sergeant-Major by 8.a.m. 100 pairs of Gum Boots.
The right and left Companies, and all details will return their Gum boots to the Pioneers Shop before leaving.

3. Companies will move alongside the FONQUEVILLERS BOYEAU as far as LA HAIE, and then by the Trench board path to BAYENCOURT. They will move by ½ Platoons at 200 yards distance.

4. Each Company will detail 1.N.C.O. and 4 men, to be at BAYENCOURT at 8.30.a.m. The N.C.O's will take over the billets from 8th.R.War.R. and the men will report to the Garrison Q.M. at Battalion Headquarters BAYENCOURT at 8.30.a.m. This advance party will be under Major P.H.CARTER who will also take over the Defences of BAYENCOURT.

5. The Cookers and Limbers complete will be taken out to BAYENCOURT, and horses will be at ARTILLERY CROSS ROADS at 8.a.m.

6. When taking over or handing over any trench or billet from another Battalion, receipts must pass for all Stores, S.A.A. Grenades, Tools, Gumboots, etc. These receipts must be made out in duplicate, and a copy forwarded to the Battalion Headquarters by 5.p.m. on January.20th.
Certificates that Trenches and billets are left clean must also be handed in. No receipts or certificates are valid unless signed by an Officer.

7. Blankets rolled, and numbered by sections will be at ARTILLERY CROSS ROADS at 8.a.m.were a wagon will be ready to take them to BAYENCOURT.

8. On arriving in BAYENCOURT, each Company commander will take over all garrison property in his billets, from the Garrison Quarter Master at Battalion Headquarters.

9. Dinners will be on arrival at BAYENCOURT.

ISSUED at 7.30.p.m.
January.18th.1916.

Charles [illegible]
Capt & Adjt.
1/5th.Royal Warwickshire Regt.

NOTICE.

Officers baggage to be at ARTILLERY CROSS ROADS at 10.a.m. in charge of Officers servants.
Officers Chargers will be at ARTILLERY CROSS ROADS at 11.15.a.m.

No.1	Copy	File.
" 2 & 3	"	War Diary.
" 4	"	A.
" 5.	"	B.
" 6.	"	C.
" 7.	"	D.
" 8.	"	Transport Officer.
" 9.	"	6th.R. War. R.

Copy No 3

OPERATION ORDERS. Copy No.13.

By

Lieut.Col.G.C.SLADEN.

Commanding 1/5th Battn.The Royal Warwickshire Regt.

October. 7th.1915.

Ref Map.AMIENS 1/80.000

1. The 5th R War R will relieve the 6th R War R to-morrow 8.10.15 and will take over their billets and dispositions.

2. The Battalion in the line is now disposed as follows.

   Two Companies in the front line.
   One Company in support on the Pilon (FONCQUEVILLERS-HEBUTERNE) Road
   One Company in reserve in billets near the Entrance to the Village on the FONCQUEVILLERS-SOUASTRE Road.

3. D.Coy will take over the Right Company in the line
   C.Coy will take over the Left Company in the line.
   B.Coy will be in support.
   A.Coy will be in reserve.

4. B and C.Coys 5th.R War R will relieve the support and Left Coys of the 6th R War R at 2 - 30.p.m.
   These two Companies of the 6th R War R will then relieve A and D Coys 5th.R War R in FONCQUEVILLERS.
   A and D Coys 5th R War R will then relieve the reserve and right Coys of the 6th R War R.

5. D Coy will take over complete the Cooker and limber of A Coy
   A.Coy will take over complete the Cooker and limber of D Coy and manhandle it back to the village.
   Receipts must pass between the Officers concerned,stating that the Cookers are handed over and taken over clean and complete.

6. When taking over or handing over any trench or billet from another Battalion,receipts must pass for all Stores,S.A.A. Grenades etc,and also certificate that the trenches or billets are left clean.

7. Separate orders have been issued to Machine Gun and Transport Officers.

Charles [illegible]

ISSUED AT 9. p.m.
Pctober.7th.1915. (Signed)

Capt & Adjt.
1/5th R WAR R

No.	Copy.	Office.
No. 1	Copy.	Office.
" 2&3	"	War Diary
" 4	"	6th.R War R
" 5	"	A.
" 6	"	B.
" 7.	"	C.
" 8.	"	D.

O P E R A T I O N   O R D E R S   NO. 14.
BY
Lieut. Col. G. C. SLADEN.
Commanding 1/5th Battn. The Royal Warwickshire Regiment.
OCTOBER. 15th. 1915.

Ref Map AMIENS 1/80,000.

Trench Map.

1. The 5th R War R, will be relieved by the 6th R War R tomorrow (October.16th) and will take over billets and dispositions of 6th R War R at BAYENCOURT.

2. The Left and Reserve Companies will be relieved at 2.15.p.m. and the Right and Support Companies at 3.15.p.m.

3. A and C Companies will go out via THORP STREET. B.Company by INGE AVENUE and the PORTE.
All four Companies will then proceed to BAYENCOURT by the DUMMY GUN route.

4. The Field Cookers and Limbers will remain in their present position, and be taken over by the 6th R War R. The Cookers and Limbers of the 6th R War R, will be brought to BAYENCOURT for the use of the 5th R War R.
Receipts must pass between the Officers concerned, stating that the Cookers, Limbers and Boilers are handed over, and taken over clean and complete.

5. When taking over or handing over any trench or billet from another Battalion, receipts must pass for all Stores, S.A.A. Grenades etc, and also certificates that the trenches or billets are left clean.

6. Separate orders have been issued to Transport and Machine Gun Officers.

N O T I C E.

Officers baggage to be at Battalion Head Quarters at 2.30.p.m. in charge of their servants. Officers Horses will be at Artillery Cross Roads.

ISSUED AT 6.30.p.m.
October. 15th. 1915.   (Signed)

Capt & Adjt.
R WAR R

OPERATION ORDERS. No.27. Copy No...... 2

BY

Lieut.Colonel.G.C.SLADEN. D.S.O.
Commdg.1/5th.Battn.The Royal Warwickshire Regiment.
JANUARY. 27th.1916.

---

1. The 5th.R. War. R. will relieve the 6th. R. War. R. in the trenches, at 10.30.a.m. to-morrow January.28th.
The Left Posts will not be relieved until dusk.

2. The route will be as follows, and no other route will be used.
From BAYENCOURT to LA HAIE, by main road, and trench board track. Then by track from S.E. corner of LA HAIE, to SAILLY-FONQUEVILLERS road at K I D 96. The Right, Left, and Support Companies will then go via VALLEY ROAD into THORP STREET. The Reserve Company will proceed via SAILLY-FONQUEVILLERS ROAD (using the trench at side of the road) into FONQUEVILLERS. All Ranks must be warned not to take short cuts across country.
Troops will move by 2 Platoons at 200 yards distance, in the following order. - A. B. C. D.
The first party of " A " Company will pass the CROSS ROADS J11a 1.10 at 8.45.a.m.

3. Companies will be disposed as follows :-
A. Company on the right.
B. " " " left.
C. " in support.
D. " in reserve.

4. Blankets will be rolled and labelled by sections, and stacked ready to be taken to trenches by 8.a.m.

5. The travelling Kitchens will be taken to the trenches, and must be ready to move by 8.a.m.

6 When taking over, or handing over any trench or billet from another Battalion, receipts must pass for all Stores, S.A.A. Grenades, Tools, Gumboots, etc. These receipts must be made out in duplicate, and a copy forwarded to the Battalion Headquarters by 5.p.m. on January.28th.
Certificates that Trenches, and billets are left clean, must also be handed in. No receipts or certificates are valid unless signed by an Officer.

7.

ISSUED at 2.p.m.
January.27th.1916.

Charles Metcalfe [signature]

Capt & Adjt.
1/5th.Batt.Royal Warwickshire Regt.

NOTICE.

Officers baggage for trenches, will be collected, from Officers Billets at 8.30.a.m.
Another wagon will collect Officers Valises from Transport lines.

No. 1.	Copy	File.
" 2 & 3	"	War Diary.
" 4.	"	A.
" 5.	"	B.
" 6	"	C.
" 7.	"	D.
" 8.	"	Transport Officer.
" 9.	"	6th.R. War. R.

OPERATION ORDERS NO. 16.
BY
Lieut. Col. G.C.Sladen.
Commanding the 1/5th. Battn. R. War. R.
Oct. 23rd. 1915.

Ref. Map AMIENS 1/100,000.

Trench Map.

1. The 5th. R.War.R. will relieve the 6th R.War.R. in the Trenches tomorrow Oct. 24th.

2. Coys. will march by Platoons using the Dummy Gun Route.

3. A. Coy. will parade in time to relieve at 2.30pm. followed by C. D. & B.

4. Companies will be disposed as follows:-
   A. on the Right.
   C. on the Left.
   D. in Support.
   B. in Reserve in FONQUEVILLERS.

5. The Quarter Master will obtain a Certificate from an Officer of the 6th. R.War. R. that each Cooker and Limber is handed over clean and complete.

6. O/C. Coys will before taking over the Cookers and Limbers inspect and give a Certificate to the Effect, that they are clean and complete, this to include the ground around them.

7. When taking over , or handing over any Trench or Billet from another Battn., Receipts must pass for all Stores, S.A.A., Grenades etc. and also Certificates that the Trenches or Billets are left clean.

8. Separate Orders have been issued to the Transport & M/G. Officers.

2

Issued at 6.30 pm. Oct. 23rd 1915.

Charles Retallack

Capt. & Adjt.
1/5th. R. WAR. R.

NOTICE.

The Transport Officer will collect Officers baggage for the Trenches at 1.0 pm., and another waggon will collect Officers Valises for the Transport Lines.
These Carts will be sent to Officers Billets.

Instructions regarding War Diaries and Intelligence Summaries are contained in F. S. Regs., Part II. and the Staff Manual respectively. Title pages will be prepared in manuscript.

WAR DIARY
or
INTELLIGENCE SUMMARY
(Erase heading not required.)

Army Form C. 2118.

February 1916
5 Batt. The Royal Warwickshire Regt.

Hour, Date, Place		Summary of Events and Information	Remarks and references to Appendices
Trenches – February	4.	4 O.R.s wounded	C.R.
FONQUEVILLERS	5	5th R. War. R. relieved in trenches by 6 R.War.R. and took over detachment of 7 R.War.R. at Fonquevillers & La Haie as in O.O. 28.	O.O. 28 — CR
"	11	one O.R. wounded	CL
"	12	one O.R. wounded	CL
TRENCHES	13	5th R. WAR. R. relieve 6th R. WAR. R. in the trenches as in O.O. 29.	JHC
"	15 13.	~~one O.R. wounded~~; 5th R. War. R. take over trenches 13, 14 & 15 from the 7th R. War. R.	JHC
"	17	one O.R. wounded	JHC
"	20th	6 O.R's wounded.	JHC
	21st	5th R.War.R. relieved in trenches by 6th R.War.R. and take over billets of 6 R.War.R. at BAYENCOURT as in O.O. 30	JHC
BAYENCOURT	28th	2nd Lt F. C. Alabaster } 2nd Lt W. E. Curtis } taken on the strength of the Battalion.	JHC
	29th	5th R. War. R. relieve the 6th R. War. R. in the trenches as in O.O. 31 & 32.	JHC
	29th	Trenches 16, 17 & 18 are also taken over from the 8th R. War. R. on our left	JHC
TRENCHES	29th	1 O.R. accidentally wounded.	JHC

Strength of Batt. 30 officers 761 O.R.S.

J H Canning Lieut.
for Lt Col Commdg

1247 W 3299 200,000 (E) 8/14 J.B.C. & A. Forms/C. 2118/11.

143rd Inf.Bde.
48th Div.

WAR
DIARY

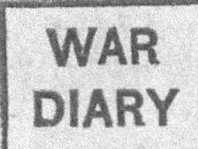

1/5th BATTN. THE ROYAL WARWICKSHIRE REGIMENT.

N O V E M B E R

1 9 1 5

Attached:

Battn. O.Os. Nos.
16, 17, 18 & 19.

OPERATION ORDERS. No. 28. Copy No. 3

BY

MAJOR W.H.FRANKLIN.

Commdg.1/8th.Battn.The Royal Warwickshire Regt.

FEBRUARY. 3rd.1916.

Ref.Map 57d 1/20,000.
and B.M.276.G.

1. The 8th.R.War.R. will be relieved by the 6th.R.War.R on February 8th.1916. and will take over dispositions of 6th.R.War.R at FONQUEVILLERS and LA HAIE.

Relief will commence at 10.30.a.m. except Nos 4,5, and 6 Posts which will be relieved at dusk.

The Garrison of FORT DICK, JUNCTION KEEP and NORTH KEEP, and Guards and Duties will be taken over from the 6th.R.War.R at 9.30.a.m.

2. Battalion Headquarters will be at Entrance Village. Dispositions of Companies will be as under.-

A. Coy. 3.Platoons FONQUEVILLERS in Shelters F.22.
2 Sections at FORT DICK.
2 Sections at JUNCTION KEEP.

B. Coy. 3.Platoons FONQUEVILLERS in Shelters F.12.13.14.
1.Platoon in NORTH KEEP.

C. Coy. LA HAIE ~~CHATEAU~~. G Work

D. Coy. ~~One Platoon LA HAIE CHATEAU.~~
2 sections ~~One Platoon~~ LA HAIE F.Work.
3 ~~One~~ Platoons LA HAIE H.Work.
2 sections ~~One Platoon~~ LA HAIE J.Work

Major P.H.CARTER will be in command of LA HAIE Detachment.

3. The route for the LA HAIE Detachment will be as follows-

Via ARTILLERY CROSS ROADS, and along CEMETERY ROAD, as far as it is metalled. Then across country by a covered route North of the SOUASTRE ROYEAU into the DUMMY GUN Valley (E.30.a.) Thence to LA HAIE, approaching LA HAIE CHATEAU from the West.

4. The Blankets of the LA HAIE Detachment, will be rolled by Sections, and labelled, and be at ARTILLERY CROSS ROADS at 9.30.a.m where a wagon will be ready to take them to the CHATEAU.

5. Horses for the Travelling Kitchens of C and D will be at ARTILLERY CROSS ROADS at 9.a.m. to take the Kitchens to LA HAIE

6. When taking over or handing over any trench or billet from another Battalion, receipts must pass for all Stores, S.A.A. Grenades, Tools, Gumboots, etc These receipts must be made out in duplicate, and a copy forwarded to the Battalion Headquarters by 4.p.m. on February 8th.

Certificates that Trenches, and Billets are left clean must also be handed in. No receipts or certificates are valid unless signed by an Officer.

Charles Reta Yaate
Capt & Adjt.
1/8th.Royal Warwickshire Regt.

ISSUED AT 2.pm.
February 3rd.1916.

NOTICE.

The Transport Officer will arrange to take Officers Valises of A. and B. to FONQUEVILLERS and C.and D. to LA HAIE.

A wagon will be at ARTILLERY CROSS ROADS at 10.a.m. to take C.and D.Coy's Officers Kit etc from Trenches to LA HAIE.

No. 1	Copy.	File	No. 6.	Copy.	C.
" 2 & 3	"	War Diary	" 7.	"	D.
" 4	"	A.	" 8.	"	Transport Officer
" 5	"	B.	" 9.	"	6th.R.War. R.
			" 10.	"	[illegible]

Instructions regarding War Diaries and Intelligence Summaries are contained in F. S. Regs., Part II. and the Staff Manual respectively. Title pages will be prepared in manuscript.

WAR DIARY
or
INTELLIGENCE SUMMARY

(Erase heading not required.)

Army Form C. 2118.

1/5 Batt. R. Warwickshire Regt

November 1915

Hour, Date, Place		Summary of Events and Information	Remarks and references to Appendices
TRENCHES	NOVEMBER 1	5th Batt. Relieved by 6th Batt. and took over the position of 6 R. Warwick R. as in O.O. 16	CR OO-16
FONQUEVILLERS	" 2	Lt Col G.C. SLADEN 1/5 R Warwick assumed temporary command of the 143 Inf Bde during absence of Brigadier General C.H.L. James on leave	CR
	" 9	5th Batt Relieved 6 R Warwick in the trenches (L sector) as in O.O. No 17. The trenches now occupied by 143rd Bde are opposite GOMMECOURT – and L sector front line is from E 27 d 76 – K 3 d 38 Ref Map France 57D 1/40000 – on the right is 144 Inf Bde and on left is 37th Division	CR — OO 17
TRENCHES	" 14	One OR wounded	CR
	" 15	A coy of 12 Bn R. Irish Rifles attached for instruction	CR
	" 17	5th R Warwick Relieved by 6 R Warwick R and marched to BAYENCOURT as in O.O. No 18	CR — OO.18
BAYENCOURT	" 18	Draft of 26 men arrived	CR
	" 22	2/Lieut E.P.G. Carter taken on strength of Batt.	CR
	" 25	5 R Warwick R Relieved 6 R Warwick in trenches as in O.O. No 19	CR — O.O.19
TRENCHES	" 27	Capt. A.S. ALABASTER and one O.R. taken on strength of Batt.	CR
	" 28	One O.R. wounded. HQrs + 2 Coys of 21st Manchester Regt in for instruction	CR
	30	Lt J.W.W. HUDSON killed	CR

The weather has been very bad indeed during the greater part of the month, and the trenches have suffered from constant rain. Strength on Nov 28th 26 officers 798 ORs.

Charles [illegible]

CAPT. & ADJT. 5TH BATT. R. WARWICKSHIRE REGT.

OPERATION ORDERS. No. 29. Copy No...... 2

BY

MAJOR W.H.FRANKLIN.

Commanding 1/5th.Battn.The Royal Warwickshire Regiment.

FEBRUARY. 11th.1916.

---

1. The 5th.R.War.R. will relieve the 6th.R.War.R. in the Trenches on February.13th.

2. D. Company will be on the Right.

C. Company will be on the Left.

B. Company will be in Support.

A. Company will be in Reserve.

3. C. and D. Companies will use the SUNKEN ROAD (J.6.b.) route, and march in half platoons, at [illegible] yards distance.

4. Relief will commence at 10.a.m. Posts 4.5. and 6. will not relieve until dusk.

5. Two platoons of the Right Company, and two platoons of the Support Company will be accommodated in the Steel roofed Huts in the Bluff.

6. The Blankets of C. and D.Companies will be rolled and labelled by sections. A Waggon will be at LA HAIE at 8.a.m. to take them to the trenches.

7. Horses for the Travelling Kitchens of C. and D.Companies will be at LA HAIE at 8.a.m.

8. When taking over or handing over any trench or billet from another Battalion, receipts must pass for all Stores, S.A.A. Grenades, Tools, Gumboots, etc. These receipts must be made out in duplicate, and a copy forwarded to the Battalion Headquarters 4.p.m. on February.13th.

Certificates that Trenches, and Billets are left clean must also be handed in. No receipts or certificates are valid unless signed by an Officer.

9. Separate orders have been issued to the Transport Officer.

Charles Rettback

ISSUED AT 7.p.m.
FEBRUARY. 11th.1916.

Capt & Adjt.
1/5th.Batt.Royal Warwickshire Regt.

NOTICE.

Officers baggage will be collected from CHATEAU LA HAIE at [illegible]a.m. and brought up to the trenches, and will on return take kits back to the Transport lines.

No. 1	Copy	File.
" 2 & 3	"	War Diary.
" 4.	"	A.
" 5.	"	B.
" 6.	"	C.
" 7.	"	D.
" 8.	"	Transport Officer.
" 9.	"	6th.R.War.R.

BATTALION OPERATION ORDERS NOS.
16, 17, 18 & 19.

O P E R A T I O N O R D E R S. No.30. Copy No..2...
B Y
Lieut.Colonel. G.C.SLADEN. D.S.O.
Commanding 1/5th.Battalion.The Royal Warwickshire Regiment.
F E B R U A R Y. 20th.1916.

---

1. The 5th.R.War.R. will be relieved by the 6th.R.War.R. in the Trenches, on February 21st, and will then take over billets of 8th.R.War.R. at BAYENCOURT.
Relief will commence at 10.a.m. except the centre Company Posts, which will relieve at Dusk.

2. The route to BAYENCOURT will be as follows :-
Via ARTILLERY CROSS ROADS, and along CEMETERY ROAD as far as it is metalled, then across country by a covered route N, of SOUASTRE BOYAU into DUMMY GUN VALLEY.

3. B. C. and D. Companies with the exception of posts, will hand over all Gum boots in their possession to Sergt THURSFIELD.J at the Pioneers Shop, THORPE STREET by 9.a.m.
A.Company will hand them over to the Pioneers Stores in the village by the same, TIME.
Posts will hand them over after being relieved.

4. Each Company will detail 1.N.C.O and 4 men to be at BAYENCOURT at 8.30.a.m. The N.C.O's will take over the billets from the 8th.R.War.R. and the men will report to the Garrison Quartermaster at Battalion Head Quarters BAYENCOURT at 8.30.a.m. This advanced party will be under Capt W.A.P.WATSON, who will also take over the defences of BAYENCOURT.

5. The Cookers and Limbers complete will be taken out to BAYENCOURT, and horses will be at ARTILLERY CROSS ROADS at 8.a.m.

6. On relief, receipts must pass for all Stores, S.A.A. Grenades, Tools, Gumboots etc. These receipts must be made out in duplicate, and a copy forwarded to Battalion Head Quarters by 5.p.m. on February.21st.
Certificates that Trenches and billets are left clean, must also be handed in. No receipts or certificates are valid unless signed by an Officer.

7. Blankets rolled and numbered by sections will be at ARTILLERY CROSS ROADS at 8.a.m. where a waggon will be ready to take them away.

8. On arriving at BAYENCOURT, each Company Commander will take over all Garrison property in his billets from the Garrison Quartermaster at Battalion Headquarters.

9. Dinners on arrival at BAYENCOURT.

10. Separate orders have been issued to Transport Officer.

ISSUED AT 5.30.p.m.
February.20th.1916.

J H Crosskey Lieut.
Acting Adjutant.
1/5th.Royal Warwickshire Regt.

N O T I C E.

Officers baggage to be at ARTILLERY CROSS ROADS at 10.a.m. in charge of Officers servants.
A Waggon will also be sent for Lewis Guns.
Officers chargers will be at ARTILLERY CROSS ROADS at 11.15.a.m.

No.	1	Copy	File.	No.	5	Copy	B.	No.8.Copy Tr
"	2 & 3	"	War Diary.	"	6.	"	C.	" 9.6.R.War
"	4	"	A.	"	7.	"	D	10 SERGT THURSFIELD

" Owing to inaccuracy of "TYPIST" these Operation Orders are substituted."

OPERATION ORDERS NO 16.
BY
Lieut.Col.G.C.SLADEN.
Commanding 1/5th Battn.The Royal Warwickshire Regt.
OCTOBER.31st.1915.

For Map reference see BM976C

1. The 5th R War R will be relieved by the 6th R War R tomorrow and will take over dispositions of the 8th R War R at FONCQUEVILLERS and LA HAIE.
Relief will commence at 1.30.p.m.

2. Battalion Headquarters will be at ENTRANCE of VILLAGE.
" A " Company ;-
3 Platoons in dug-outs behind CHATEAU.
1 Platoon in F.Work 500 yards just S.E. of CHATEAU
" B " Company ;-
3 Platoons in H Work just N.E. of CHATEAU.
1 Platoon in J Work 600 yards N of CHATEAU.
" C " Company;-
4 Platoons less 2 Sections in Shelters F14.15.16.
2 Sections in Junction Keep
" D " Company;-
3 Platoons in Shelters F28.
1 Platoon in North Keep.

3. Troops proceeding to LA HAIE will go via the communication Trench.

4. The Cookers of the 6th R War R will be brought from BAYENCOURT foh the use of the 5th R War R.

5. When taking over or handing over any Trench or Billet from another Battalion, receipts must pass for all Stores.S.A.A. Grenades etc. and also certificates that the Trenches or Billets are left clean. No receipt or certificate will be valid unless signed by an Officer.

6. Separate orders have been issued to Transport and Machine Gun Officers.

ISSUED AT 10 p.m.
October 31st.1915.

Charles Ritchie(?)

Capt & Adjt.
1/5th R WAR R.

NOTICE.

Officers baggage of A and B Companies should be at Battalion Headquarters in charge of Officers servants at 1,pm.m The Transport Officer will provide a Cart to take it to LA HAIE.
Officers of C and D Companies will make their own arrangements for baggage from Trenches to FONCQUEVILLERS.
Officers Valises of A and B Companies will be sent from Transport to CHATEAU LA HAIE, and those of C and D Companies to Battalion Headquarters.

O P E R A T I O N   O R D E R S. No.31. Copy No.2...
B Y
Lieut.Colonel.G.C.SLADEN. D.S.O.
Commanding 1/5th.Battn.The Royal Warwickshire Regt.
F E B R U A R Y. 28th.1916.

---

1. The 5th.Battn.R.War.R. will relieve the 6th.R.War.R. in the Trenches at 10.30.a.m. on February.29th.
The 3 Posts of the centre Company will not be relieved until dusk.

2. The route will be as follows, and no other route will be used.
From BAYENCOURT to LA HAIE by the main road, and trench track. Then by track from S.E. corner of LA HAIE ~~extthexmain~~ road to SAILLY-FONQUEVILLERS road at K 1 d.4.6.
The right, centre, and Support Companies will then go via VALLEY ROAD into THORPE STREET, and the DUG OUTS in the BLUFF. The left Company will proceed via SAILLY - FONQUEVILLERS ROAD(using the trench at the side of the road) into FONQUEVILLERS.
All Ranks must be warned not to take short cuts across country. Troops will move ½ Platoons at 200 yards distance in the following order - B. C. D. A.
The first party of B.Company will pass the CROSS ROADS J 11 a 1.10. at 9.45.a.m.

3. Companies will be disposed as follows :-
D. Company on the Right.
C. " in the Centre.
B. " on the Left.
A. " in Support.

4. The travelling Kitchens will be taken to the trenches and must be ready to move by 8.a.m.

5. Blankets will be rolled and labelled by sections, and stacked outside Billets ready to be taken to the trenches by 8.a.m. ^Company

6. The usual receipt for Stores.S.A.A. Grenades.Tools,and Gumboots will be given, and a copy forwarded to Battalion Head Quarters by 3.p.m. on February.29th.
Certificates that trenches and billets are in good ~~and~~ order, will also be handed in.
No receipts or certificates are valid unless signed by an Officer.

ISSUED AT 11.30.a.m.
February.28th.1916.

J.H. Crosskey Lieut.
Acting Adjutant.
1/5th.Royal Warwickshire Regt.

N O T I C E
Officers baggage for trenches will be collected from Officers billets at 8.30.a.m.
Another Waggon will collect Officers Valises for Transport lines.

No.1	Copy.	File.
" 2.& 3	"	War Diary.
" 4.	"	A.Coy.
" 5.	"	B. "
" 6.	"	C. "
" 7.	"	D. "
" 8.	"	Transport Officer.
" 9.	"	6th.R.War.R.

Copy No. 2

OPERATION ORDERS. No.17.
BY
Major W.H.FRANKLIN.
Commanding 1/5th.Battn. The Royal Warwickshire Regiment.
NOVEMBER.8th.1915.

---

1. The 5th R War R, will relieve the 6th R War R, to-morrow 9th.November.

2. A Company will be the right Company in the line.

C Company will be the left Company in the line.

B Company will be in support.

D Company will be in reserve.

The reserve Company will find the Garrison for FORT DICK.

3. The two Companies ~~will~~ from LA HAIE will use the FONQUEVILLERS BOYEAU, If this is too wet for use, the Dummy Gun route must be used.

4. A and B Companies 5th R War R will relieve the right and support Companies of 6th R War R commencing at 2.p.m.
The right Company 6th R War R will then relieve D. Company 5th R War R .
D. Company 5th R War R will then relieve the reserve Company 6th R War R.
The Reserve Company 6th R War R , will then relieve C.Company 5th R War R.
C.Company 5th R War R will then relieve left Company 6th R War R.

5. When taking over or handing over any Trench, or Billet from another Battalion, receipts must pass for all Stores, S.A.A. Grenades etc, and also certificates that the Trenches or Billets are left clean. No receipt or certificate will be valid unless signed by an Officer.

6. Thigh Gumboots are to be treated as Trench stores.
The 5th R War R will take over 81 pairs from the 6th R War R, in L sector, and will hand over 50 pairs to the 6th R War R, in LA HAIE and FONQUEVILLERS.

7. Separate orders have been issued to Transport and Machine Gun Officers.

ISSUED AT 4.p.m.
November.8th.1915.

Charles Hets Leach
Capt & Adjt.
1/5th R WAR R.

No	1.Copy	File.
"	2 & 3 Copies.	War Diary.
"	4.Copy.	A.Company.
"	5. "	B. "
"	6. "	C. "
"	7. "	D. "
"	8. "	Transport Officer.
"	9. "	6th.R War R.

NOTICE.

The Officers baggage will be collected from CHATEAU LA HAIE at 1.p.m. and brought up to Trenches. This cart will then call at Battalion Headquarters FONQUEVILLERS at 2.p.m. and take Officers Kit C and D, back to Transport, calling at LA HAIE for Officers Kit of A and B.

O P E R A T I O N   O R D E R S No.32.   Copy No.3...

B Y

Lieut Colonel G.C.SLADEN. D.S.O.

Commanding 1/5th.Battn.The Royal Warwickshire Regt.

F E B R U A R Y. 29th.1916

---

1. The 5th.R.War.R. on relieving the 6th.R.War.R in the Trenches on February 29th, will also relieve the 8th R.War R in Trenches No.16, 17, and 18.

Relief is to be complete by 6.30.p.m. except for the posts of the right centre Company, who will relieve at dusk.

2. The route will be as in Operation Order No.31. except that both the left centre, and left Company will proceed along SAILLY-FONQUEVILLERS ROAD, from point K I d 9.6.

Order of route. Troops will move by 2 Platoons at 200 yards distance in following order. A. B. D. C.

The first party of B.Company will pass the CROSS ROADS J 11 a 1.10 at 11.45.a.m.

3. Companies will be disposed as follows :-

D. Company on the Right.

C. Company in the centre right.

B. Company in the centre left.

A. Company on the left in trenches 16. 17. 18.

4. Kitchens are to be ready to move by 11.30.a.m.

5. Blankets will be taken up to FONQUEVILLERS as soon as Waggon fetches them.

6. Separate orders have been issued to Transport Officer.

ISSUED AT 9.15.a.m.
February.29th.1916.

J.H. Cooksey (signature)
Lieut.
Acting Adjutant,
1/5th.Royal Warwickshire Regt

N O T I C E.

Officers baggage for trenches will be collected from Officers billets at 11.30.a.m.

No.1	Copy.	File.
" 2 &3	"	War Diary.
" 4.	"	A. Company.
" 5.	"	B. "
" 6	"	C. "
" 7.	"	D. "
" 8.	"	Transport Officer.
" 9.	"	6th.R.War.R.

O P E R A T I O N   O R D E R S. No.16.
B Y
Major W.H.FRANKLIN.
Commanding 1/5th.Battn.The Royal Warwickshire Regiment.
NOVEMBER.16th.1916.

---

1. The 5th.R WAR R, will be relieved by the 6th.R WAR R, in the Trenches tomorrow November.17th, and will take over Billets and dispositions of 6th.R WAR R, at BAYENCOURT.

2. The relief will commence at 1.p.m.

3. Companies will march out in Platoons, and the Dummy Gun route will be used.
Attention of all ranks is directed to Battalion Order 362, dated 26.10.16.

4. The Field Cookers and Limbers will remain in their present position, and will be taken over by the 6th.R WAR R.
The Cookers and Limbers of the 6th.R WAR R, will be brought to BAYENCOURT, for the use of the 5th.R WAR R.
Receipts must pass between the Officers concerned, stating that the Cookers are taken over, and handed over clean and complete.

5. When taking over, or handing over, any trench or billet from another Battalion, receipts must pass for all Stores, S.A.A. Grenades, etc, and also certificatesh that the Trenches or Billets are left clean.
No certificate will be valid unless signed by an Officer.

6. Separate orders have been issued to Machine Gun, and Transport Officers.

Charles [illegible]

ISSUED AT 7.30.p.m.
November.16th.1916.

Capt & Adjt.
1/5th.R WAR R.

N O T I C E.

Officers baggage to be at Artillery ~~Gun~~ Cross Roads at 1.p.m. in charge of servants.
Officers horses will be at Artillery ~~Gun~~ Cross Roads at 1.30.p.m.

143
48

1/5th R. Warwick Regt

Vol XIII

March 1916.

13.T.
(8 sheets)

O P E R A T I O N   O R D E R S. No.19.
B Y
Lieut.Col.G.C.SLADEN.
Commanding 1/5th.Battn.The Royal Warwickshire Regiment.
NOVEMBER.24th.1915.

Ref Map, 57d 1/40.000.

1. The 5th.R War R,will relieve the 6th.R War R,in the Trenches to-morrow November 25th.

2. Companies will march in sections at 150 yards distance in the following order - D. B. C. A.
The first party of D. Company to pass the Cross Road J11a 1.10. at 9.a.m.

3. The following route is to be used -
To LA HAIE by the Main road, and then the sunken road from S.E. corner of La Haie to Cross roads K 1 D 96 Hence by VALLEY ROAD to Trenches.

4. The Companies will be disposed as follows :-

D. Company will be on Right.

B. Company will be on Left.

C. Company will be in support.

A. Company will be in reserve.

5. The Quarter Master will obtain a Certificate from an Officer of the 6th R War R, that each Cooker and Limber is Handed over clean and complete.

6. O.C. Companies will before taking over inspect the Cookers and Limbers, and give a certificate to the effect, that they are clean and complete, this to include the ground around them.

7. When taking over, or handing over, any Trench or Billet from another Battalion, receipts must pass for all Stores, S.A.A. Grenades etc, and also certificates that the Trenches or billets are left clean.
No certificate will be valid unless signed by an Officer.

8. Separate orders have been issued to Machine Gun, and Transport Officers.

Charles Pettbach

ISSUED AT 3.p.m.
November.24th.1915.

Capt & Adjt.
1/5th.Royal Warwickshire Regt.

N O T I C E.

The Transport Officer will collect Officers baggage for the Trenches at 8.30.a.m. Another Wagon will collect Officers valises for the Transport Lines.
These carts will be sent to Officers billets.

Instructions regarding War Diaries and Intelligence Summaries are contained in F. S. Regs., Part II. and the Staff Manual respectively. Title pages will be prepared in manuscript.

WAR DIARY
or
INTELLIGENCE SUMMARY
(Erase heading not required.)

Army Form C. 2118.

March 1916.

5th Batt. The Royal WARWICKSHIRE Regt.

Hour, Date, Place		Summary of Events and Information	Remarks and references to Appendices
TRENCHES MARCH	3rd	1 OR wounded very slightly	JHC
"	" 7th	2nd Lt J. Crawford 20th Batt. London Regt. attached to & taken on strength of the Battalion	JHC
	" 8th	5th R Warw. R. was relieved in trenches 1-12 by the 6th R Warw R & in trenches 13-18 by the 8th R Warwick R as in O.O. 33. On relief the dispositions of the 8th R Warw R were taken over at La Haie and the Southern Islet of Fonquevillers	JHC 00.33
FONQUEVILLERS March	9th	1 OR wounded	JHC
"	12	2nd Lt A. J. Farrington arrived & taken on strength of Batt.	CR
"	14	4 OR's wounded	CR
"	16	1 OR "	
Trenches	16	Relieved 6 R Warw R in trenches as in O.O. 34	CR 0034
"	19	1 O.R. wounded. 4 2nd Lt C. Buck & 80 OR's arrived & taken on strength of Batt.	CR
"	21	2/Lt G. R. Poynter arrived and taken on strength of Batt.	CR
"	23	Enterprise against Enemy trenches — Appendix A. 2nd Lt H.L.R. GROOM. 2nd Lt E. HOLT and 15 OR's wounded	CR Appx A.
"	24	Batt relieved by 6 R Warw R and took over billets of 8 R Warw R in ~~[illegible]~~ SOUASTRE as in O.O. 36	CR 0.0.36
SOUASTRE	25-31		CR

Strength of Batt.

32 Officers and 723 Other ranks

Charles [illegible]
CAPT. & ADJT. 5TH BATT. R. WARWICKSHIRE REGT.
for Lt Col Commdg.

143rd Inf.Bde.
48th Div.

WAR DIARY

1/8th BATTN. THE ROYAL WARWICKSHIRE REGIMENT.

D E C E M B E R

1 9 1 5

Attached:

Battn. O.Os. Nos.
20, 21, 22 & 23.

O P E R A T I O N   O R D E R S. No. 33.   Copy No. ..2...

B Y

Lieut Colonel G.C. SLADEN. D.S.O.
Commanding 1/8th. Battn. The Royal Warwickshire Regt.
M A R C H. 8th. 1916.

---

1. The 8th. R.War.R. will be relieved by the 6th. R.War.R. in trenches 1 - 12 and by 5th. R.War.R. in trenches 13 - 18, on March 8th. 1916. and will take over the dispositions of the 6th. R.War.R. in FONQUEVILLERS, and LA HAIE.

Relief will commence at [illegible] p.m. except for Nos 4.5.& 6 Posts which will be relieved at dusk.

The Garrison of FORT DICK and JUNCTION KEEP, Guards and Duties will be taken over at 1.p.m.

2. Battalion Head Quarters will be at "ARTILLERY HOUSE" on the ARTILLERY CROSS ROADS.

The Dispositions of the Companies will be as under :-

"A" Company.	[illegible] Platoons	in Dug-outs WEST of FORT DICK.
	[illegible] Platoon	in H.WORK.
	1 Platoon	in F.WORK.
	1 Platoon	in J.WORK.
	[illegible] Platoon	in FORT DICK.
	[illegible] Platoon	in JUNCTION KEEP.
"B" Company.	at LA HAIE in grounds WEST OF CHATEAU.	
"C" Company.	1 Platoon in NORTH KEEP	
	[illegible] Platoons in FONQUEVILLERS, in Shelters F.12.13 14.	
"D" Company	4 Platoons in FONQUEVILLERS in Shelters F 23.	

Major W.H. FRANKLIN will be in Command at LA HAIE

3. The route of the LA HAIE DETACHMENT, will be as follows:- Via ARTILLERY CROSS ROADS, along CEMETERY ROAD, as far as it is metalled. Then across country by covered route NORTH of BOUASTRE ROYAU into DUMMY GUN VALLEY. Along DUMMY GUN route to D at G [illegible], and from there to CHATEAU approaching it from the WEST

4. The " A " Company Lewis Gun will be kept at FORT DICK.
" " B " " " " " " " JUNCTION KEEP.
" " C " and " D " Companies Lewis Guns will be at Headquarters FONQUEVILLERS Garrison, and will be used for the general purposes of the Defence of the LISIERE.

5 Blankets of the LA HAIE DETACHMENT will be rolled in sections, and labelled, and be at ARTILLERY CROSS ROADS at 11.30.a.m. where a wagon will be ready to take them to the CHATEAU.

6 Horses for the travelling Kitchens of A. and B. Companies will be at ARTILLERY CROSS ROADS at 1.p.m. to take the Kitchens to LA HAIE.

7. All the usual receipts will be taken for trench stores, and certificates received that Dug-outs etc are clean, and a copy forwarded to Battalion Head Quarters by 9.p.m. on March 8th.

ISSUED AT [illegible].45.a.m.
MARCH 8th. 1916.

J.H. Cumberbatch [signature]
Lieut.
Acting Adjutant.
1/8th. Royal Warwickshire Regt.

N O T I C E.

The Transport Officer will arrange to take Valises of A and B Companies Officers, to LA HAIE and C and D Companies to FONQUEVILLERS

A Wagon will be at ARTILLERY CROSS ROADS at [illegible] p.m to take A and B Companies Mess Staff from Trenches to LA HAIE.

No. 1 Copy	File.	No. 6 Copy	C. Company.
" 2 & 3 "	War Diary.	" 7 "	D.
" 4 "	A. Company.	" 8. "	Transport Officer.
" 5. "	B.	" 9. "	6th. R.War.R.
		" 10 "	5th. R.War.R.

Instructions regarding War Diaries and Intelligence Summaries are contained in F. S. Regs., Part II. and the Staff Manual respectively. Title pages will be prepared in manuscript.

WAR DIARY
or
INTELLIGENCE SUMMARY
(Erase heading not required.)

Army Form C. 2118.

December 1915
1/5 Batt. R. Warwickshire Regt

Hour, Date, Place		Summary of Events and Information	Remarks and references to Appendices
TRENCHES — DEC. 1			
	Dec 3rd	5th Batt: relieved by 6th Batt. and took over dispositions of 8th WARWICKS at FONQUEVILLERS	JHC. O.O. No 20
FONQUEVILLERS TRENCHES	Dec 11th	5th Batt: relieved the 6th Batt in the trenches (? SECTOR).	JHC. O.O No 21
	11th	one company of the 17th Batt. Manchester Reg. attached for instruction	JHC
"	12th	a draft of 32 O.R's arrived.	JHC
"	18th	HQ and one company of the 19th Batt. Liverpool Reg. attached for instruction	JHC
"	19	5 Batt relieved by 6 R Warks and took over billets of 8 R Warks at Bayencourt	CR. O.O No. 22
BAYENCOURT	23	2/Lt. J.H. WILSON taken on strength of Batt	CR
"	25	Christmas Day	CL
"	27	5 Batt Relieved the 6 R War R in the trenches — as in O.O. No 23	CR O.O No 23
Trenches	28	—	

The weather during December has been very bad — the trenches have been discarded and held by six posts — communication trenches are all blocked except 4 —

Strength on December 31st — 28 Officers 823 Other Ranks

Charles [illegible]
CAPT. & ADJT. 5TH BATT. R. WARWICKSHIRE REGT.
Lt Col. Commdg

OPERATION ORDERS. No.34. Copy No...7....

BY

Lieut Colonel G C.SLADEN. D.S.O.

Commanding 1/5th.Battn.The Royal Warwickshire Regt.

MARCH. 15th.1916.

---

1. The 5th.R.War.R. will relieve the 6th.R.War.R. in the trenche tomorrow March 16th. Relief will commence at 10-30 a.m.
Posts 4,5 & 6 will not be relieved until dusk.

2. Companies will be disposed as under.
A. Company on the Right with 2 Platoons in the BLUFF.
B. " " " Left.
C. " in Support, with 2 Platoons in BLUFF, and 2 Platoons INLYING PICQUET in THORP STREET.
D Company in Reserve.

3. A and B Companies will use the SUNKEN ROAD route and will march in half platoons at 200 yards distance.

4. The Lewis Automatic Rifles will be placed as follows:-
1 each in Nos. 1,4 & 6 posts and
3 in THORPE STREET.

5. The blankets of A and B Companies will be rolled and labelled by sections. A wagon will be at LA HAIE at 8 a.m. to take them to the trenches.

6. Horses for the travelling kitchens of A & B companies will be at LA HAIE at 8 a.m.

7. When taking over or handing over any trench or billet from another Battalion, receipts must pass for all stores, S.A.A. Grenades, Tools, Gumboots, etc. These receipts must be made out in duplicate, and a copy forwarded to the Battalion Headquarters 3 p.m. on March 16th.
Certificates that trenches, and Billets are left clean must also be handed in. No receipts or certificates are valid unless signed by an Officer.

8. Separate orders have been issued to the Transport Officer.

Charles Retallack

ISSUED AT 11-30 a.m.
MARCH 15th, 1916.

Capt. & Adjt.
1/5th.Batt.Royal Warwickshire Regt.

NOTICE.

A wagon will collect Officers Baggage from CHATEAU LA HAIE at 9 a.m. for the trenches and will in return take kits back to transport lines.

No. 1	Copy	File.
" 2 & 3	"	War Diary.
" 4	"	A.
" 5	"	B.
" 6	"	C.
" 7	"	D.
" 8	"	Transport Officer.
" 9	"	6th. R.War.R.

BATTALION OPERATION ORDERS NOS.
20, 21, 22 & 23.

REPORT ON ENTERPRISE CARRIED OUT BY

1/5th.R.War.Regt. 23/3/16.

The whole party paraded at 10-30 p.m. and after being carefully checked moved up to the front line to take up their positions.

At 11-30 an officers patrol went out with a drum of white tape and laid a trail to within 150 yards of the German wirem having done this a messenger was sent back to bring up the advanced storming party.
This party was in position by midnignt and was followed by the main storming party which came up behind it.
All parties were in position and ready to start by 12-40 a.m., the Ready being phoned through at the same time.
The barrage started at 1-15 a.m. and after four minutes the advanced storming party moved forward laying tape followed at intervals by the other parties.
The hostile wire was reached at about 1.22 a.m. and the wire cutters got through the first belt in three minutes,the second belt was not such thick wire but very deep,this was entirely cut through by 1-45 a.m. under continually increasing rifle and machine gun fire from front trenches and salient on our left.
At this point a third belt of thick and high wire was encountered reaching as far as could be observed up to the German front trench, this was covered by a bomb screen of wire netting causing the bombs which were thrown in an attempt to silence enemy to rebound and explode outside trench.
Our casualties were increasing, and as it would have taken a considerable time to clear remaining wire the order was given to fall back.
The whole party withdrew slowly and in per f ect order, b rigin g back our wounded and equipment,the ret ir e ment throughout being covered by two parties with three Lewis guns.
The shglter trench was reached by 2-10 a.m. and all men were clear of No 3 post by 2-45 a.m.

(Signed) W.A.P.WATSON Capt.

1/5th.R.War.Regt.

O P E R A T I O N   O R D E R S. No. 20
B Y
Lieut Colonel G.C.SLADEN
Commanding 1/5th.Battn.The Royal Warwickshire Regt.
D E C E M B E R. 2nd.1915.

For Map reference see B.M.976.C.
and Map 57d. 1/40.000.

1. The 5th.R.War.R will be relieved by the 6th.R.War.R to-morrow December.3rd, and will take over dispositions of the 8th.R.War.R. at FONQUEVILLERS, and LA HAIE.
Relief will commence at 11.a.m.

2. Battalion Head Quarters will be at Entrance Village.
Dispositions of Companies will be as under :-

A. Company.	3 Platoons at F.28. 2 Sections at FORT DICK. 2 Sections at JUNCTION KEEP.
B. Company.	3 Platoons at F.14.15.16. 1 Platoon at NORTH KEEP.
C. Company	3 Platoons in H.Work just N.E. of CHATEAU 1 Platoon in F.Work,600 yds North of CHATEAU.
D. Company	3 Platoons in Dug-outs behind CHATEAU 1.Platoon in F.Work 500yds S.E. of CHATEAU.

Major CARTER will be in Command of Detachment at LA HAIE

3. Route for LA HAIE Detachment is via VALLEY ROAD to CROSS ROADS K.1 d 9 6. and SUNKEN ROAD to S.E corner of LA HAIE.

4. The Blankets of the LA HAIE Detachment, will be rolled by Sections, and be at ARTILLERY CROSS ROADS, at 10.a.m. where a Wagon will be ready to take them to the CHATEAU.

5. The Cookers of the 6th R.War.R. will be brought by that Battalion, to FONQUEVILLERS and LA HAIE, for use of the 5th.R.War.R.

6. When taking over, or handing over, any Trench or Billet from another Battalion, receipts must pass for all Stores.S.A.A Grenades etc, and also certificates that the Trenches or Billets are left clean.
No certificate will be valid unless signed by an Officer.

7. Separate orders have been issued to Machine Gun, and Transport Officers.

Charles Rethlack
Capt & Adjt.
1/5th.Royal Warwickshire Regiment.

ISSUED AT 1.p.m.
December.2nd.1915.

N O T I C E.

The Transport Officer will arrange to ~~have~~ take Officers Valises ~~taken~~ of A. and B. to FONQUEVILLERS and C. and D. to LA HAIE.
A.wagon will be at ARTILLERY CROSS ROADS at 10.a.m. to take C and D.Companies Officers kit,Messes,etc, from Trenches to LA HAIE. Officers Servants will carry Kits etc to the Wagon, and after loading up,proceed via the communication Trench to LA HAIE, meeting the wagon there.

Appendix A

REPORT ON ENTERPRISE CARRIED OUT BY 1/5th.R.WAR.R.

NIGHT OF 22nd - 23rd. MARCH 1916.

PRELIMINARY ARRANGEMENTS.

The point of exit was from No.5 strong post from which a disused and wired-in Sap ran out about 30 yards to a sunken road of 15 feet wide which is also filled with wire. Communication was made from Headquarters to the post by clearing out an old French trench and cutting a junction trench. These were boarded. The Sap was cleared of wire the night before and a strong telephone shelter was made behind No.5 post. As soon as it was dark on the night of the 22nd the entrance to the Sap was torn down the sandbags being carried to end of Sap and a traverse being built there. A passage was cut through the wired-in end of Sap and bridges laid over the wire in Sunken road A shelter trench 80 yards long and traversed, was dug about 20 yards in front of sunken road and gaps made in the forward knife rests, which this trench commanded. All this work was done with extreme care for fear of the enemy hearing.

The equipment of all ranks included 1 smoke helmet, 1 Shrapnel Helmet,- faces were blacked - officers wore thin white band on each arm.

The parties paraded at 10-30 p.m. and were carefully checked and moved to behind Battalion Headquarters. Each man was given a card with his No. name and Company marked on it, which he gave up at control stops as he returned from the enterprise.

11-0 p.m. Lieut.GROOM with patrol went out with a drum of white tape and laid a trail to within 150 yards of German wire.

11-15 p.m. Party A (wire cutters and advanced storming party) left Battalion Headquarters and moved up to post and out to their position in front of our wire; they were followed in intervals by "B" C, D, & E parties. All these men put a sandbag over each foot to deaden the noise made walking up the boarded communication trench. These bags were taken off at No.5 Post.

12-35 a.m. Messengers from Lieut.GROOM's party came back and led up the different parties and each party was in its proper position in front of our wire and ready to move by 12-35 a.m.

1-14 a.m. The Artillery barrage was delayed until 1-14 a.m. and the men suffered considerably from cold and wet during the long wait.

After 4 minutes barrage A party moved forward, the Howitzer which was playing on enemy Sap stopping, as agreed, after 3 minutes, the Field Guns continuing but lengthening a bit; during the Howitzer fire it was not practical for the party to get any closer as pieces were flying all over the men.

1-22 a.m. AS A party moved forward they continued laying the tape trail and reached the German wire at 1-22 a.m. The other parties followed, 2 telephone wires coming up with D party.

1-25 a.m. The first belt of wire 15 feet deep was cut through in 3 minutes.

1-45 a.m. The second belt of irregular wire, not as thick but about 30 yards deep, was entirely cut through by 1-45 a.m. Whilst on this belt the party was discovered by the Germans and subjected to rifle and machine gun fire, most of this hitting the wire in front of the party. B and C parties had closed up close to A party & D party to opening in first belt of wire and E party some 150 yards in rear.

Having got through the second belt a third belt was now encountered, very thick, high and reaching as far as could be observed right up to the German trench about 25 yards away. This trench was covered by a bomb screen of wire

Continued

OPERATION ORDERS No. 21

by

Lieut Col G. C. SLADEN

Comdg 1/5th Batt The Royal Warwickshire Regt

10th December 1915

1 The 5th R.WAR.R. will relieve the 6th R.WAR.R. in the trenches tomorrow 11th December. Relief is to commence at 10-30 A.M.

2 DISPOSITIONS

A	Company	2 Platoons in village
		2 Platoons in support line
B	"	in Village
C	"	2 Platoons in firing line
		2 " in support line
D	"	2 Platoons in firing line
		2 " in support line

1 Platoon of C and 1 Platoon of D will relieve platoon of 6th R.WAR.R. taking over Gum boots from them, at the top of communication trenches and then relieving the posts in the front line. These will be followed by the other 2 platoons of the same companies.

3 Companies from LA HAIE cat and VALLEY ROAD.

4. Receipts must pass for all Stores SAA Grenades etc.

5 Separate orders have been issued to Transport and Machine Gun Officers.

Issued at 7.45 PM
10th December 1915

J.H. Crosskey
for Capt & Adjt
1/5th Royal Warwickshire Regt

netting, causing the bombs thrown by our men to rebound and explode outside the trench. The fire was increasing and it was realised that the time of surprise was passed, the wire cutters were tired, and it would have taken considerable time to cut through the balance of the wire, the order was given therefore to fall back and this was done in complete order, A,B & C parties going back first through D & E parties, taking all casualties and stores with them, and took cover in the shelter trench outside our lines. Then D joined E party and remanned out till the shelter trench was partly cleared of men.

The whole retirement was made under shell and machine gun fire some 5.9's falling quite near to D & E parties. The shelter trench was cleared by a few men at a time running through the barrage and the last of E party reached the shelter trench at 2-10 a.m.

2-45 a.m. All men were clear of No.5 post at 2-45 a.m. The enemy Artillery were very slow in opening fire no barrage being put on for half an hour after ours commenced.

Lieut.Colonel.
Commanding 1/5th.Battn.Royal War.Regt.

NOTES.

PRACTICE.
I feel that only the constant practice enabled the men to be brought back in such good order.

Shelter trench in front of our lines. This saved many lives, the German barrage was mainly between this and our front line. This part of the line being also swept by machine gun fire.

Sandbagged feet. Most successful, no sound could be heard. Men should however be instructed to tie the sandbags firmly under the knee to prevent slipping.

Checking Ticket. Without some scheme of this sort it is impossible to know if all men are in.

Steel Helmets. Invaluable, many casualties being averted.

Telephones. Care should be taken to lay the wires well to a flank of the track.

Tracks. Wide R.E. tape on drums is best except after entering enemy wire when heavy paper trail should be laid.

Enemy fire. This could not be silenced by the rifles and Lewis guns of our support parties. (1) Because of narrow frontage of entering wire making the wire cutters mark the enemy and (2) the probability of giving away the position of the parti

Notice

2 G S Wagons will call at LA HAIE at 9 a.m. and as soon as possible at FONQUEVILLERS, to collect surplus blankets to BAYENCOURT

1 Limber Wagon will be at LA HAIE, at 9 a.m. to carry Officers kits back to BAYENCOURT, and one for Officers mess boxes to FONQUEVILLERS

GUM BOOTS

Only the 4 platoons that are in the firing line, will draw Gum boots, direct from 6th R WAR R. O.C. Companies will send a receipt to Headquarters, shewing the number taken over by them for these platoons.

All other Gum boots now in possession of 6th R. WAR R. will be collected at Battalion Headquarters under supervision of Sergeant Major.

J H Cross Knight
for Capt & Adj

O P E R A T I O N O R D E R S. NO.38. Copy No....2......
by
Lieut.Colonel G.C.SLADEN D.S.O.
Commanding 1/5th.Battn. Royal Warwickshire Regt.
M A R C H 23rd. 1916.

Ref. Map 57d 1/40,000.

1. The 5th.R.War.R. will be relieved by the 6th.R.War.R tomorrow March 24th, and will then take over billets of 8th.R.War.R. at SOUASTRE.
Relief will commence at 10-30 a.m. except garrisons of Nos. 4 5 & 6 posts which will be relieved at dusk.

2. All companies and details will return their gum-boots to the pioneers shop before leaving.

3. The route for Relief is as follows and no other is to be used:-
CEMETERY ROAD
DUMMY GUN ROUTE to D.30.b.3.7.
Thence along the FONCQUEVILLERS-SOUASTRE ROAD.
Companies will move by half platoons at 200 yards distance.

4. Each company will detail one N.C.O. per platoon and Headquarters one N.C.O., to report to TOWN MAJOR, SOUASTRE at 9 a.m. These N.C.O's will in conjunction with the Coy. Q.M.Sergts, take over the billets of their companies from the 8th. R.War.R..
They will be ready at the road junction D 23.C.7.6. at 11-30 a.m. to meet their platoons and lead them to their billets.

5. The Cookers and limbers complete will be taken out to SOUASTRE. Horses will be at Artillery CROSS ROADS at 9am

6. When taking over or handing over any trench or billet from another Battalion, receipts must pass for all stores S.A.A. Grenades, Tools, Gumboots, etc. These receipts must be made out in duplicate, and a copy forwarded to the Battalion Headquarters by 5 p.m. on March 24th.
Certificates that trenches and billets are left clean must also be handed in. No receipts or Certificates are valid unless signed by an Officer.

7. Blankets rolled and numbered by sections will be at ARTILLERY CROSS ROADS at 9 a.m. Two special wagons will convey them to SOUASTRE.

8. Guards and duties will take over from the 8th. R.War.R. at 8-30 a.m.

9. Dinners will be on arrival at SOUASTRE.

10. Battalion Headquarters will open at 1 p.m. at D22c6.5

11. Separate orders have been issued to Transport Officer and M.G.Officer.

Charles Reta Hack [signature]

Issued at 5 p.m.
March 23rd, 1916.

Capt. & Adjt.
1/5th.Battn.Royal Warwickshire Regt.

N O T I C E.

Officers baggage to be at ARTILLERY CROSS ROADS at 10 a.m. in charge of servants.
Officers chargers to be at ARTILLERY CROSS ROADS at 11-15 a.m.

No.1 Copy	File.		
2 & 3	War diary.	No. 7 Copy	D Coy.
" 4 "	A Coy.	" 8 "	Transport Officer.
" 5 "	B "	" 9 "	6th.R.War.R.
" 6 "	C "	" 10 "	8th.R.War.R.

Operation Orders No 22
by
Lieut Col. G.L. Sladen
Comdg 1/5th Royal Warwickshire Regt
December 18th 1915

Ref Map 1/40,000 57d

1. The 5th R. War. R will be relieved by the 6th R. War. R in the trenches tomorrow Dec 19th and will take over Billets and dispositions of 8th R. War R at BAYENCOURT
The relief will commence at 10-30 AM.

2. Two platoons of A Coy 6th R. War. R. who will relieve the right company posts will draw gum boots from 2 platoons of A Coy 5th R. War R in THORP STREET at 10-30 AM before proceeding to relieve.
Two platoons of C Coy 6th R. War R. who will relieve the left coy posts will draw gum boots from 2 platoons B Coy 5th R. War R. in THORP STREET at 10-30 AM.
The four platoons 5th R. War R in front line will hand over their Gum boots in THORP STREET to Sergt Major 6th R. War R. before leaving

3 Each Coy will detail 1 NCO and 4 men to be at BAYENCOURT at 8-30 AM tomorrow. The NCO's will take over the billets from the 8th R. War R and the men will report to the Garrison Quartermaster to obtain and place fresh straw in the billets. The advance party will be under the Command of Major CARTER who will also take over the defences of BAYENCOURT.

4. The field Cookers and Limbers will remain in their present position and will be taken over by the 6th R War R. The Cookers and Limbers of the 6th R War R will be taken to BAYENCOURT for the use of the 5th R. War. R. Receipts must pass between the Officers concerned stating that the Cookers are taken over and handed over clean and complete.
Capt JEAVONS will give receipts for the 5th R. War R after inspection of the Cookers.

5. When taking or handing over any trench or billet from another Battalion receipts must pa[ss] for all Stores, SAA Grenades, Tools Gum boots

OPERATION ORDERS. No.37. Copy No.....2...
BY
MAJOR W. H. FRANKLIN.
Commdg. 1/5th.Battn.Royal Warwickshire Regt.
MARCH 30th. 1916.

Ref.Map 57a 1/40,000

1. The 5th.R.War.R. will relieve the 6th.R.War.R. in the trenches on Saturday April 1st. Commencing at 10-30 a.m.
Nos. 4,5 & 6 Posts will not be relieved until dusk.

2. The route will be as follows and no other route will be used:-
Along SOUASTRE-FONCQUEVILLERS ROAD to point D.30.b.3.9.
Thence by DUMMY GUN ROUTE to CEMETERY ROAD.
Troops will move by half platoons at 200 yards distance in the following order:- D.C.A.B.
The first party of D Coy. will pass the road junction D.22.d.4.5. at 8-45 a.m.

3. Companies will be disposed as under:-
D on the right with 2 Platoons in the BLUFF.
C on the left.
A in support with 2 Platoons in the BLUFF and 2 Platoons Inlying Picquet in THORPE STREET.
B in Reserve.

4. The Lewis Automatic Rifles will be disposed as under:-
1 each in Nos. 1,4 & 6 Posts.
1 with Inlying Picquet.
2 in Magazine.

5. Blankets will be rolled and labelled by sections and stacked ready to be taken to trenches by 8-0 a.m.

6. Travelling Kitchens and limbers will be ready to move by 8-0 a.m.

7. When taking over or handing over any trench or billet from another Battalion, receipts must pass for all Stores, S.A.A. GRENADES, Tools, Gumboots, etc. These receipts must be made out in duplicate and a copy forwarded to the Battalion Headquarters by 3 p.m. on April 1st.
Certificates that trenches and billets are left clean must also be handed in. No receipts or Certificates are valid unless signed by an Officer.

8. Separate orders have been issued to Transport and Machine Gun Officers.

Charles Retallack
Capt. & Adjt.
1/5th.Battn.Royal Warwickshire Regt.

Issued at 5 p.m.
APRIL 30th. 1916.

NOTICE.

Officers baggage for trenches will be collected from Officers billets at 8-30 a.m.
Another wagon will collect Officers valises for Transport lines.

No. 1 Copy File.
" 2 & 3 " War Diary.
" 4 " A Coy.
" 5 " B "
" 6 " C "
No. 7 Copy D Coy.
" 8 " Transport Off.
" 9 " 6th.R.War.R.

These receipts must be made out in duplicate and a copy forwarded to the Orderly room on arrival at BAYENCOURT

Certificates that trenches and billets are left clean must also be made out.

No Receipt or certificate will be valid unless signed by an Officer.

6. The Following Route only to be used on relief

(a) By Troops in Trenches
Leave THORPE ST. by the Cookers thence by VALLEY ROAD to K.1.D.9.6 on Sailly-FONQUEVILLERS ROAD.

(b) By Troops in FONQUEVILLERS.
via FONQUEVILLERS SAILLY ROAD (keeping to the Trench by side of road) as far as K.1.D.9.6

(a) and (b) will then proceed by track to S.E corner of LA HAIE and thence to BAYENCOURT via Trench board track on Main Rd.

All Ranks are to be warned that they are not to take short cuts across country.

7. Separate Orders have been issued to Machine Gun & Transport Officers

Dinner will be on arrival at BAYENCOURT

Issued at 9 P.M
Dec. 18th 1915

Charles Bradbrook(?)
Capt & Adjt
1/6 R. War R.

NOTICE

Officer baggage will be at ARTILLERY CROSS RDS at 10 a.m. in charge of Servants.

Officers Horses will be at ARTILLERY CROSS RDS at 11 a.m.

O/C. Coys will arrange to collect and label blankets by sections and have them ready for a wagon, which will be at ARTILLERY CROSS ROADS at 10. a. m.

143/48

1/5 R. Warwick
Regt

Vol XIV

April 1916.

14 T.
(8 sheets)

OPERATION ORDERS No. 23 Copy No 2
By
Lieut Col. G C SLADEN
Comdg 1/5th Batt Royal Warwickshire Regt
DECEMBER 26th 1915

Ref Map 57D 1/40,000

1. The 5th R War R will relieve the 6th R War R in the Trenches at 10-30 AM tomorrow December 27th

2. The route will be as follows no other route will be taken. From BAYENCOURT to LA HAIE by main road and trench board track. Then Track from SE corner of LA HAIE to SAILLY-FONQUEVILLERS road at KID 96. Thence by VALLEY ROAD to Cookers by THORP STREET.
All ranks are to be warned that they must not take short cuts accross country.
Troops will move by ½ platoons at 200 yards distance in the following order D. C. A B
The first party of D Company will pass CROSS ROADS J11.a.1.10 at 8-45 am

3 Companies will be disposed as follows

D on the right
C " left
A in support
B " reserve

4 All men in isolated posts are to have 250 rounds of SAA per man within immediate access

5. The Quartermaster will obtain a certificate from an officer of the 6th R War R that each Cooker and limber is handed over clean and complete.
OC Companies will before taking over inspect the Cookers and limbers, and give a certificate to the effect that they are clean and complete. This is to include the ground around them

6. When taking or handing over any trench or billet from another Battalion receipts must pass for all stores SAA, Grenades Tools, Gumboots etc.

Continued.

Instructions regarding War Diaries and Intelligence Summaries are contained in F. S. Regs., Part II. and the Staff Manual respectively. Title pages will be prepared in manuscript.

WAR DIARY
or
INTELLIGENCE SUMMARY

(Erase heading not required.)

Army Form C. 2118.

April 1916

5TH BATT. R. WARWICKSHIRE REGT.

Hour, Date, Place			Summary of Events and Information	Remarks and references to Appendices
SOUASTRE	April	1	Relieved 6 R Warwick in trenches as per O.O. 37	O.O. 37 – CR
Trenches	April	3	2 other ranks wounded (one at duty)	CR
		5	28 O.R's arrived and taken on strength of Batt	CR
"	"	8	1 other rank wounded	CR
"	"	9	Batt relieved in trenches by 6 R Warwick and took over dispositions of 8 R Warwick at Foncquevillers & La Haie	OO 38 – CR
Foncquevillers	"	17	Batt Relieved 6 R Warwick in Trenches	OO 39 – CR
Trenches	"	18	2 ORs wounded (at duty)	CR
	"	19	4 OR's arrived & taken on strength of Batt	CR
		23	1 OR wounded	CR
	"	24	1 OR killed 2 ORs wounded	CR
	"	25	1 OR killed and 1 wounded (and at duty)	CR.
	"	26	Relieved by 8th Batt The Worcester Regt and marched into billets at SOUASTRE in Divisional Reserve – as per OO 40	CR – OO 40
SOUASTRE		28	16 ORs reinforcements arrived & taken on strength	CR
	"	30	2/Lt S.C. Squires – 2/Lt H.H. Price – 2/Lt G Cragg arrived & taken on strength.	CR

Strength of Batt on April 30th 1916

34 Officers & 733 ORs

Charles Ratcliffe Jack
CAPT. & ADJT. 5TH BATT. R. WARWICKSHIRE REGT.

for Lt Col Comdg –

1247 W 3299 200,000 (E) 8/14 J.B.C. & A. Forms/C. 2118/11.

These receipts must be made out in duplicate and a copy forwarded to the Battalion Headquarters by 2 PM on Dec 27th

Certificates that trenches and billets are left clean must also be handed in.

The receipt or certificate is valid unless signed by an Officer

7 Separate order have been issued to Transport Officer

Issued at 3-45 PM.
December 26th 1915 (SIGNED) Charles Retd Yach
Capt & Adjt
1st R. War. R

NOTICE

Officers baggage for trenches will be collected at 8-30 AM. Another wagon will collect Officers valises for Transport lines.

These carts will be sent to Officers billets.

No. 1	Copy	File
" 2 & 3	"	War Diary
" 4	"	A
" 5	"	B
" 6	"	C
" 7	"	D
" 8	"	Transport Officer
" 9	"	6th R War R

OPERATION ORDERS BY. Copy No....2.......

Lieut.Colonel G. C. SLADEN D.S.O.

Commdg.1/5th.Battn.Royal Warwickshire Regt. No.38.

APRIL 7th. 1916.

Ref.Map 57d 1/40,000

1. The 5th. R.War.R. will be relieved by the 8th.R.War.R. in the trenches on April 9th. 1916. and will then take over billets and dispositions of 8th.R.War.R. in FONCQUEVILLERS and LA HAIE.
Relief will commence at 10-30 a.m. Posts 5 and 6 will not be relieved until dusk.

2. The dispositions of the Companies and their action on alarm will be as under:-

Coy.	Where accomodated.	Alarm Post.	Note.
A	3 Platoons in FONCQUEVILLERS in ~~shelters~~ area of shelters at F.28	One platoon in F.18 on order to STAND BY.	Maintain trenches at all costs & Catch any men coming back.
		Two platoons in SOUTHERN KEEP on order to STAND BY.	Maintain KEEPS at all costs and catch any men coming back.
	1 Platoon in CENTRAL KEEP	One platoon in CENTRAL KEEP on orders to STAND BY.	
B	In FONCQUEVILLERS in ~~shelters~~ area round F.12.13.14	In breastworks behind F.15.16.17.18 in reserve of O/C FONCQUEVILLERS GARRISON on order READY TO MOVE.	At disposal of O/C. FONCQUEVILLERS GARRISON.
C	H.Q's. LA HAIE - H work.	Same.	Maintain INTERMEDIATE LINE until relieved by DIVISIONAL RESERVE.
	One Platoon in FORT DICK and shelters.	In FORT DICK on order to STAND BY.	Maintain these posts until relieved by DIVISIONAL RESERVE.
	½ Platoon in H work. ½ Platoon in JUNCTION KEEP.	In JUNCTION KEEP on order STAND BY.	
	One Platoon in F WORK. One Platoon in J WORK.	In F.G.H & J WORKS on order to STAND BY.	Maintain INTERMEDIATE LINE until relieved by DIVISIONAL RESERVE.
D	H.Q's and Coy. in grounds S.W. of LA HAIE	In G WORK on order READY TO MOVE.	In BRIGADE RESERVE.

Battalion Headquarters will open at MURRAGNE VILLAGE at 1 p.m.

The LA HAIE detachment will be commanded by Major P.H.CART[ER]

3. The Lewis Guns will be disposed as follows:-
A and B Coy. guns at H.Q's O/C. FONCQUEVILLERS GARRISON.
C Coy. 1 gun at FORT DICK.
1 gun in JUNCTION KEEP.
D " 2 guns at H.Q's O/C. LA HAIE DETACHMENT.

4. The route for the LA HAIE DETACHMENT is as follows and no other route will be used:-
Along the FONCQUEVILLERS BOYEAU to E.26.a.5.3.
Then left handed behind the SCREENS until the main road is struck again at E.25.d.5.4.
Thence across the road in rear of the guns, gaining the road again 300 yards N.E. of CHATEAU LA HAIE.
This route should be reconnoitred beforehand. Companies will march by half platoons at 200 yards distance.

5. The blankets of the LA HAIE DETACHMENT will be rolled by sectio[ns] and labelled. A wagon will be at ARTILLERY CROSS ROADS at 9-0 a.m. to take them to LA HAIE.

Continued.

6. Travelling kitchens & limbers of C & D Companies will be ready to move at 8-0 a.m.

7. When taking over or handing overany trench or billet from another Battalion, receipts must pass for all stores, S.A.A. Grenades, Tools, Gumboots, etc. These receipts must be made out in duplicate, and a copy forwarded to the Battalion Headquarters by 5 p.m. on April 9th.

Certificates that trenches and billets are left clean must also be handed in. No receipts are valid unless signed by an Officer.

8. Separate orders have been issued to Transport and Machine Gun Officers.

Charles Retallack

Issued at 12 Noon. Capt. & Adjt.

A P R I L 7th. 1916. 1/5th.Battn.Royal Warwickshire Regt.

N O T I C E.

The Transport Officers will arrange to take the Officers valises of A and B Companies to FONCQUEVILLERS and C and D Companies to LA HAIE. A wagon will be at ARTILLERY CROSS ROADS at 10 a.m. to take C and D Coys. Officers kits etc. from trenches to LA HAIE.

No. 1 Copy.	File.	No. 6 Copy	C Coy.
" 2 & 3 "	War Diary.	" 7 "	D "
" 4 "	A Coy.	" 8 "	Transport Officer.
" 5 "	B "	" 9 "	6th.R.War.R.

AMENDMENT TO OPERATION ORDERS. No 38. Copy No...2.....

B Y

Lieut.Colonel G.C.SLADEN D.S.O.

Commdg.1/5th.Battn.Royal Warwickshire Regt.

A P R I L 8th. 1916.

Refn Map. 57d 1/40,000

Para. 2. The dispositions of the companies and their action on alarm will be as under:-

Coy.	Where accomodated.	Alarm post.	Note.
A	1 Platoon in FORT DICK and shelters	In FORT DICK on order to STAND BY.	Maintain these posts until relieved by Divisional RESERVE.
	½ Platoon in JUNCTION KEEP ½ Platoon in area of shelters at F.28.	In JUNCTION KEEP on order to STAND BY	
	1 Platoon in CENTRAL KEEP.	SAME on order to STAND BY	Maintain KEEP and TRENCH F.19 at all costs and catch any men coming back.
	1 Platoon in area of shelters at F.28.	In F.19 on order to STAND BY.	
B	In FONCQUEVILLERS VILLAGE	Two platoons in breastworks behind F.15.16.17.18.in RESERVE of O/C. FONCQUEVILLERS GARRISON on order READY TO MOVE.	At disposal of O/C. FONCQUEVILLERS GARRISON.
		Two platoons in SOUTHERN KEEP on order to STAND BY.	Maintain KEEP at all costs and catch any men coming back.
C	H.Q's & 2 platoons in LA HAIE - H WORK.	In F.G.H. & J WORKS on order to STAND BY	Maintain INTERMEDIATE LINE until relieved by DIVISIONAL RESERVE.
	1 Platoon F WORK 1 Platoon J WORK		
D	H.Q's and Coy. in grounds S.W. of LA HAIE	In G WORK on order READY TO MOVE.	In BRIGADE RESERVE.

Battalion Headquarters will open at ENTRANCE VILLAGE at 1 p.m.

The LA HAIE DETACHMENT will be commanded by Capt.W.C.C.GELL.

Para 3. The Lewis Guns will be disposed as follows:-
- A Coy. Guns at FORT DICK
- B Coy. Guns at JUNCTION KEEP.
- C Coy.- 2 Guns at H.Q's O/C FONCQUEVILLERS GARRISON..
- D Coy.- 2 Guns at H.Q's O/C DETACHMENT LA HAIE.

Para 4. The screened route will be used by D Coy. only. C Coy. will use the SUNKEN ROAD route.

ISSUED AT 9 p.m.
April 8th. 1916.

Capt. & Adjt.
1/5th.Battn.Royal Warwickshire Regt.

No.1 Copy.	File.	No. 5 Copy	B Coy.
2 & 3	War Diary.	" 6 "	C "
" 4 "	A Coy.	" 7 "	D "

O P E R A T I O N O R D E R S No.39. Copy No...2......
B Y
Lieut.Colonel G.C.SLADEN D.S.O.
Commdg.1/5th.Battn.Royal Warwickshire Regt.
A P R I L 16th. 1916.

Ref.Map 57d 1/40,000

1. The 5th.R.War.R. will relieve the 6th.R.War.R. in the trenches tomorrow April 17th. Relief will commence at 10-30 a.m.
Posts 4.5 & 6 will not be relieved until dusk.

2. Companies will be disposed as under:-
A Company on the Right with 2 Platoons in the BLUFF.
B Company on the Left.
C Company in Support with 2 Platoons in BLUFF and 2 Platoons Inlying Picquet in THORPE STREET.
D Company in Reserve.

3. C and D Companies will use the SCREENED ROUTE and will march in half platoons at 200 yards distance.

4. Lewis Automatic Rifles will be placed as follows:-
1 each in Nos.1.4.6 Posts.
1 with Inlying Picquet.
2 in Magazine.

5. Blankets of C and D Companies will be rolled and labelled by sections. A wagon will be at LA HAIE at 8 a.m. to take them to the trenches.

6. Horses for the travelling Kitchens of C & D Companies will be at LA HAIE at 8 a.m.

7. When taking over or handing over any trench or billet from another Battalion, receipts must pass for all Stores, S.A.A. Grenades, Tools, Gumboots, etc. These receipts must be made out in duplicate and a copy forwarded to Battalion Headquarters by 3 p.m. April 17th.
Certificates that trenches and billets are left clean must also be handed in. No receipts or certificates are valid unless signed by an Officer.

8. Separate orders have been issued to the Transport Officer.

E R D Carter

Issued at 12 Noon.

April 16th. 1916.

Lieut.

Acting Adjutant.

1/5th.Battn.Royal Warwickshire Regt.

N O T I C E.

A wagon will collect Officers baggage far from CHATEAU LA HAIE at 9 a.m. for the trenches and will on return, take kits back to Transport Lines.

No. 1 Copy	File.		No. 6 Copy	C Company.
2 & 3 .	War Diary		" 7 "	D "
" 4 "	A Coy.		" 8 "	Transport Officer.
" 5 "	B "		" 9 "	6th.R.War.R.

O P E R A T I O N   O R D E R S   No 40   COPY No.....2.....

b y

Lieut.Colonel G.C.SLADEN D.S.O.
Commdg. 1/5th Battn. Royal Warwickshire Regt.
A P R I L 25th 1916.

Ref. Map 57d 1/40,000.

1. The 5th R.War.R. will be relieved by the 8th Worcester Regt. on April 26th and will proceed to billets at SOUASTRE.
Relief will commense at 3 p.m. except garrison of No.6 Post which will be relieved at dusk.

2. Companies and details will return all gum-boots to the Pioneers shop by 9 a.m.

3. Each company will detail one Officer per coy and one N.C.O per Platoon to remain with the incoming unit for 24 hours. They will render every possible assistance to the 8th Worcester Regt.

4. O/C Coys. will detail one guide per platoon to be at road junction D.23.C.8.8 at 1 p.m.
In addition, the two companies in the line will detail a guide for the garrisons of each post.
They will be at the Police Barrier at 2-30 p.m.

5. The route for relief is as follows and no other route is to be used:-

CEMETERY ROAD.
DUMMY GUN ROUTE TO D.30.b.3.9.
Thence along the FONCQUEVILLERS-SOUASTRE ROAD.

Companies will march by half platoons at 200 yards distance.

6. Each company will detail 1 N.C.O. per platoon and Headquarters one N.C.O. to report to Town Major, SOUASTRE at 10 a.m. These N.C.O's will, in conjunction with the company Q.M.Sergts, take over the billets of their companies.

7. The Cookers and Limbers complete will be taken out to SOUASTRE. Horses will be at Artillery CROSS ROADS at 12 Noon.

8. The stores shown on the list sent round to companies in the line today, are to be regarded as trench stores and will be handed over to the incoming unit together with an inventory, and a receipt obtained.
All stores other than those shown on the list will be taken out on relief..
A duplicate copy of the list of trench stores handed over will be sent to Battalion Headquarters by 12 Noon on April 27th.
Certificates that trenches and billets are left clean must also be handed in. No receipts or certificates are valid unless signed by an officer.

9. Blankets, rolled and numbered by sections, will be at ARTILLERY CROSS ROADS at 9 a.m. A special wagon will convey them to SOUASTRE.

10. Tea will be on arrival at SOUASTRE.

11. Separate orders have been issued to Transport & Machine Gun Officers.

Charles Retallack
Capt. & Adjt.
1/5th Battn.The Royal Warwickshire Regt.

Issued at 5-30 p.m.
A P R I L 25th, 1916.

N O T I C E.

Officers baggage to be at ARTILLERY X ROADS at 2 p.m. in charge of servants.
Officers chargers to be at ARTILLERY X ROADS at 4-30 p.m.

No. 1	Copy	File		No. 6	Copy	C Coy.
2 & 3		War Diary.		" 7	"	D "
" 4	"	A Coy.		" 8	"	Transport Officers.
" 5	"	B "		" 9	"	8th. Worcester Regt.

5TH BATT. R. WARWICKSHIRE REGT.
EW 32 B

143/48

WAR DIARY
or
INTELLIGENCE SUMMARY
(Erase heading not required.)

Army Form C. 2118.

Instructions regarding War Diaries and Intelligence Summaries are contained in F. S. Regs., Part II. and the Staff Manual respectively. Title pages will be prepared in manuscript.

May 1916

5TH BATT. R. WARWICKSHIRE REGT.
15

Hour, Date, Place		Summary of Events and Information	Remarks and references to Appendices
SOUASTRE — May	1.	Two coys relieved 2 coys 6 R Warwk at La HAIE as in O.O No 41	Ch — 00.41
" "	6	Batt marched to Bivouacs near SAILLY — as in OO No 42	Ch — 0042
J17.c.1.7	-	Batt digging cable trench at HEBUTERNE	
	7	" " " "	Ch
	8	Batt took over billets of 7 R Warwk at AUTHIE as in O.O. No 43	Ch
AUTHIE	11	Batt marched to billets at GEZAINCOURT as in O.O No 44	Ch — 00.43
GEZAINCOURT	12	Training commenced	Ch — 00.44
	22	Two men killed & 2 injured owing to premature explosion of a trench mortar shell	Ch —
	25	Batt moved to Bivouacs at COUIN for tactical exercise — 0.0 45	Ch —
COUIN	26	Batt took part in Bde scheme and billeted at AUTHIE.	Ch — 00.45
AUTHIE.	27	Batt marched back to billets at GEZAINCOURT	Ch
GEZAINCOURT	31	Batt marched to huts at COUIN as in O.O. 46	Ch
		Strength of Batt 33 Officers 862 O.R's	Ch — 00.46 —

Charles Reid Jack
Capt & adjt 5 R Warwk
for Lt Col Comdg —

15 T.
(7 sheets)

1247 W 3299 200,000 (E) 8/14 J.B.C. & A. Forms/C. 2118/11.

OPERATION ORDERS No.41. Copy No...2....

BY

Lieut.COLONEL G.C.SLADEN D.S.O.

Commdg. 1/5th Battn.Royal Warwickshire Regt.

MAY 1st, 1916.

---

1. In order to facilitat e the final handing over of the line to the 3rd. Army, the Brigade will resume charge of "L" and "M" Sections to-day.

2. A and B Companies of the 5th R.War.R. will relieve the 6th R.War.R. at LA HAIE to-day commencing at 3-30 p.m. and will occupy F.G.H. and J works and LA HAIE defences.

3. The dispositions of the Companies and their action on alarm will be as under:-

Coy.	Where accomodated.	Alarm Post.	Role.
~~A~~ B	H.Q's & 2 Platoons in LA HAIE - H Work. 1 Platoon F Work 1 Platoon J Work	In F.G.H & J Works on order to Stand By	Maintain INTERMEDIATE LINE until relieved by DIVISIONAL RESERVE.
~~B~~ A	H.Q's and Coy. in grounds S.W. of LA HAIE	In G Work on order READY TO MOVE.	In BRIGADE RESERVE.

The Lewis Guns will go with the Companies.

4. Battalion Headquarters and C and D Companies will remain at SOUASTRE.

5. Separate orders have been issued to Transport Officer.

6. The G.O.C. 143rd.Inf.Bde. will assume Command of "L" and "M" sections at 6-30 p.m. to-night.

Issued at 1-15 p.m.
~~Kxxxk~~ May 1st, 1916.

Charles [illegible]

Capt. & Adjt.

1/5th Battn.Royal Warwickshire Regt.

No. 1 Copy File.
" 2 & 3 War Diary.
" 4 " A Coy.
" 5 " B Coy.
No 6 Copy C Coy.
" 7 " D "
" 8 " Transport Office

O P E R A T I O N   O R D E R S   No.42.   Copy No......2..

b y

CAPTAIN C. RETALLACK.

Commdg. 1/5th Battn.Royal Warwickshire Regt.

M A Y   5th, 1916.

---

1. The 143rd. Infantry Brigade will be relieved by the 137th Infantry Brigade on 5th and 6th inst.

2. T he 1/5th R.War.R. will proceed to bivouacs situate about J.17.c.1.7. on May 6th.

3. A and B Companies will be relieved at 8 a.m. on May 6th by the 6th Battn.S.Staffs.Regt and, on relief being complete will march to bivouacs via BAYENCOURT and cross roads J.10.c.2.8.
Companies will march by half platoons at 200 yards interval as far as cross roads J.11.a.1.9. at which point the ordinary march formation will be adopted.

4. The battalion (less A and B coys.) will parade at road junction D.22.c.7.1. facing South ready to move off at 8-45 a.m. D Coy. leading, and will march via COIGNEUX.

5. Billets must be left absolutely clean and any billet Stores handed over to the Town Major and a receipt obtained.

6. The travelling kitchens will go with their Companies. Horses for kitchens will be at LA HAIE at 8 a.m.

7. Separate orders have been issued to the Transport Officer.

C. V. Suckling

Issued at 9-30 a.m.
May 5th, 1916.

Capt. & Acting Adjutant.
1/5th Battn.R.Warwickshire Regt.

N O T I C E S.

The Officers Mess Cart and wagon for Officers' valises will call at LA HAIE at 7-15 a.m. and at C and D Company Officers' billets at 8 a.m.

No.1 Copy	File.	No.6 Copy	C Coy.
" 2 & 3	War Diary.	" 7 "	D "
" 4 "	A Coy.	" 8 "	Transport Officer.
" 5 "	B "		

OPERATION ORDERS No.43. Copy No. 2
BY
CAPTAIN C. RETALLACK.
Commdg. 1/5th Battn. Royal Warwickshire Regt.
MAY 7th, 1916.

Ref.Map 57d 1/40,000.

1. The 5th R.War.R. will vacate their Bivouacs to-morrow May 8th at 2-30 p.m. and take over the billets of 8th R.War.R. at AUTHIE.

2. The Company Q.M.Sergts. and one N.C.O. for Headquarters will meet the Quartermaster (Lieut.E.V.JEAVONS) at Battalion H.Q's 8th R.War.R. at AUTHIE at 9-30 a.m. to-morrow to take over billets, and will be ready to meet the Battalion on their arrival at the entrance to AUTHIE VILLAGE to lead the Companies to their billets.

3. The area of the bivouac must be left absolutely clean by 2 p.m. Instructions re removal or otherwise of tents will be issued later.

4. The Companies will parade with the head of the column at the bend of the road in J.16.d.8.7. ready to march off at 2-30 p.m. in following order:-

A. B. C. D.

5. The Cookers will accompany the Battalion.

6. Blankets rolled by sections must be on the dump by the Cookers at 1 p.m.

7. Officers' valises and messes must be on the dump at 2 p.m.

Issued at 3-20 p.m.
May 7th, 1916.

Charles Retallack Capt
for Capt. & Acting Adjutant.
1/5th Battn. Royal Warwickshire Regt.

No. 1 Copy	File.	No. 6 Copy	C Coy.
2 & 3	War Diary.	" 7 "	D "
" 4 "	A Coy.	" 8 "	Transport Office
" 5 "	B "		

June 1916 – 14[3]/48 Army Form C. 2118.

1/5 Batt. The Royal Warwickshire Regiment

Vol 16

16. T (5 sheets)

Instructions regarding War Diaries and Intelligence Summaries are contained in F. S. Regs., Part II. and the Staff Manual respectively. Title pages will be prepared in manuscript.

WAR DIARY
or
INTELLIGENCE SUMMARY

(Erase heading not required.)

Hour, Date, Place	1916 June	Summary of Events and Information	Remarks and references to Appendices
Ref Map 57d S.E. 1/20,000 COUIN Trenches K17c 30.35 – K17a 1.8	1	Batt. relieved 4th Glosters in trenches as in O.O. 47	O.O. 47
	3	1 O.R. wounded	
	4	5 O.R.s "	
	5	1 O.R. "	
	6	New saps put out from front line trench – wire laid out by [illegible]. These saps to be joined up to form new front line –	
	7	2/Lt E.C. WROTH & Lt E.P.G. CARTER and 13 O.R.'s wounded.	
	8	Batt. relieved by 6th R. Warwick R. – marched to Bivouacs at J16 a	O.O. 48
Bivouac J16 a	12	Batt. went into huts at COUIN	
COUIN	22	The Batt. less A & B coy. relieved the 4th ~~Gloster~~ Batt. The Royal Berkshire Regt in H sector – A & B Coys. Bivouacs at J23 – O.O. 49	O.O. 49
Trenches U day	24	2/Lt F.C. ALABASTER and 4 O.R.'s wounded	
V day	25		
W day	26	Smoke candle demonstration from front line of H, simultaneously gas was let off from G sector – time 10.15 a.m. – A raiding party under CAPT. W.H.R. WATSON – 2/Lt H. HAMBIDGE and 2/Lt F.W. MARVIN attempted to enter enemy trenches at K17b 0.2 but was unsuccessful – Time 10.30 p.m. – Continuous bombard[ment] commenced – Casualties 2/Lt H. HAMBIDGE and 14 O.R.'s wounded –	
X day	27	A further raid under CAPT. WATSON & Lt MARVIN was attempted at same point and again unsuccessful – Time ~~12.30~~ 2 a.m. 27/26 Casualties – wounded 2/Lt F.W. MARVIN and 20 O.R.'s 3 O.R.'s missing –	

Instructions regarding War Diaries and Intelligence Summaries are contained in F. S. Regs., Part II. and the Staff Manual respectively. Title pages will be prepared in manuscript.

WAR DIARY
or
INTELLIGENCE SUMMARY
(Erase heading not required.)

Army Form C. 2118.

Hour, Date, Place 1916 June	Summary of Events and Information	Remarks and references to Appendices
Y day 28th	Smoke candle demonstration from front line at 7.15 a.m. The 7th Worcesters attempted to enter trenches opposite	
29.	The 4th GLOSTERS made a further unsuccessful raid on trenches at K17b11. Casualties 3 O.R.s	
30.	A further attempt by B Coy under Capt ALABASTER to raid enemy trenches was unsuccessful. Casualty 1 OR.	
	Strength 27 Officers 782 O.R.s	
	Strength 27 Officers 782 O.R.s	
	Charles Retallack Major 5 R War R	

1247 W 3299 200,000 (E) 8/14 J.B.C. & A. Forms/C. 2118/11.

OPERATION ORDERS No.48. Copy No. 2.
BY
Lieut.Colonel G.C. SLADEN D.S.O.
Commdg. 1/5th Battn. Royal Warwickshire Regt.
June 7th, 1916.

Map Ref. 57D N.E. 1/20,000.

1. The Battalion will be relieved by the 6th R.War.R., on the 8th, and proceed to bivouacs at J.16.D.

2. Relief will commence at about 9 a.m.

3. Route will be via VALLEY ROUTE to J.24.b.5.7., then to point 127 in J.23.A., and along road to bivouacs in J.16.D.
Companies will march by sections at 50 yards distance.

4. O.C.s A and B Coys will detail one guide per plat oon, and D Coy one per Company to parade at Battalion Headquarters at 8.15 a m., under 2nd Lieut.G.H.SKIRROW, party to meet 1/6th R.War.R., at entrance to HEBUTERNE at CROSS ROADS, K.15.a.9.9., at 8.30 a.m.

5. All baggage and Officers' kits, etc, will be stacked outside Batt n.H.Q., by 7 a m. A, B and D Coys will detail 2 men per Coy and D Coy one N C.O. in addition to load up Transport Wagons .

6. Company Quartermaster-Sergeants will meet the Battn.Quartermaster-Sergeant, at J.16 D., to take over bivouacs from 6th R.War.R., at 6.30 a.m. Company Q.M.Sergeants will then meet their Companies, at 10.30 a.m.,at J.23.A.(point 127) to guide them to their bivouacs.

7. Travelling kitchens will be ready to move at 8 a.m.

8. C Company will be relieved by a company of the 1/6th R.War.R., at about 9.30 a.m., when they will proceed to bivouacs at J.16.D.

9. When taking over or handing over any trench or billet from anot h er Battalion, receipts must pass for all Stores, S.A.A., Grenades Tools, Gumboots, etc. These receipts must be made out in duplicate and a copy forwarded to Battalion Headquarters by 5 p.m. on June 8th.
Certificates t hat trenches and billets are left clean must also be handed in. No receipts or certificates are valid unless signed by an Officer.

10. Separate Orders have been issued to the Transport and Lewis Gun Officers.

Issued at 5 p.m.
June 7th, 1916.

Signed R.S. TURNER. 2nd Lieut.
Acting Adjutant.
1/5th Bn.Royal Warwickshire Regt.

No.1 Copy.	File		No.5 Copy.	C Coy.
" 2 "	War Diary.		" 6 "	D "
" 3 "	A Coy		" 7 "	Transport Officer.
" 4 "	B "		" 8 "	6th R.War.R.

OPERATION ORDERS No.49. Copy Bo. 2.

BY

Lieut.Colonel G.C.SLADEN, D.S.O.

Commdg. 1/5th Bat tn.The Royal Warwickshire Regt.

June 21st, 1916.

Map Ref. 57D.N.E. 1/20,000.

1. The 143rd Infantry Brigade will relieve the 145th Infantry Bde. in the line to-morrow.

2. The 5th R.War.R. will relieve the 4th R.Berks Regt. in H Section Relief to commence at 11.30 a m.

3. Route will be via Road Junction J.7.b.- fork road J.17.a.- Road Junction J.23.a.- entrance to JENA J.24.b.5.7.

4. Companies will march by platoons at 200 yards distance in the following order:- D. C. A. B., the first platoonnof D Coy to pass the road junctiom J.1.b.1.3., at 9 a.m.

5. Transport will proceed by the VALLEY ROAD with an interval of 200 yards distance between vehicles.
As far as possible the Transport of the Battalion will be utilised to carry out the baggage of the 4th R.Berks Regt.
Cookers will go with the Battalion.

6. Companies will be disposed as under:-
D on the Right
C on the Left
A & B will be in Bivouacs in J.23.a., under the command of Captain C.RETALLACK.

7. When taking over or handing over any trench or billet from another Batt alion, receipts must pass for all stores, S.A.A., grenades, Tools, Gumboots, etc, These receipts must be made out in duplicate and a copy forwarded to Battalion Headquarters by 5 p.m. on June 22nd.
Certificates that trenches and billets are left clean must also be handed in. No receipts or certificates are valid unless signed by an Officer.

8. Separate orders have been issued to Transport and Lewis Rifle Officers.

Charles Retallack

CHARLES RETALLACK

Issued at 7 p.m.
June 21st, 1916.

Capt. & Adjt.
1/5th Battn.Royal Warwickshire Regt.

No.1 Copy.	File	No.5 Copy.	C Coy.
" 2 "	War Diary	" 6 "	D "
" 3 "	A Coy.	" 7 "	Transport Officer.
" 4 "	B "		

NOTICE.

As lit tle kit as possible is to be taken to HEBUTERNE. Valises and mess boxes to be at Headquarters at 9 a.m. Those of A and B Companies separated from those of C and D Companies.

Officers valises of A and B Companies will be t akan to the Bivouacs. Those of C and D to the Transport Lines.

OPERATION ORDERS No.44. Copy No. 2

BY

CAPTAIN C. RETALLACK.

Commdg. 1/5th Battn.Royal Warwickshire Regt.

MAY 10th, 1916.

Ref. Map 57d 1/40,000.

1. The 143rd Brigade will move to billets at BRETEL and GEZAINCOURT on the 11th instant.

2. The 5th Battalion will parade in Main AUTHIE ROAD facing West, with head of column at road junction at I.15.b.10.4. in the following order: A, B, C, D, ready to march off at 5-45 a.m.

3. Breakfasts will be before starting.

4. The travelling kitchens and water carts will be placed in the road leading up from the Orderly Room by 5 a.m. and will take their place in the line with the transport which is Brigaded.

5. The Officers' Mess cart will call for Officers' messes at 5 a.m.

6. Separate orders have been issued to Transport and Lewis Gun Officers.

C. V. Suckling

Issued at 1-0 p.m. on

May 10th, 1916.

Capt. & Acting Adjutant.

1/5th BattnRoyal Warwickshire Regt.

No.1 Copy	File.	No. 6 Copy	C Coy.
2 & 3	War Diary.	" 7 "	D "
" 4 "	A Coy.	" 8 "	Transport Officer.
" 5 "	B "		

O P E R A T I O N   O R D E R S   NO.45.   Copy No.......9
B Y
CAPTAIN C. RETALLACK.
Commdg. 1/5th Battn.The Royal Warwickshire Regt.
M A Y 24th 1916.

Ref. Map 57d 1/40,000.

1. The Brigade will move into bivouacs at COUIN on 25th inst.

2. The Bat talion will parade in the CANDAS - DOULLENS ROAD with the head of the column at Cross Roads G.3.c.2.9. facing N.E. ready to march off at 3.5 a.m. in following order B.C.D.A.

3. The Brigade will take part in a tactical exercise on 26th inst, under orders to be issued later.

4. On conclusion of the tactical exercise the Brigade will march to AUTHIE where it will bivouac for the night.

5. On 27th inst, the Brigade will march back to it's present billets at GEZAINCOURT.

6. On the march, all transport will be Brigaded and march in rear of the column in the same order as the units. Cookers will be at the head of their Battalion's Transport.
A halt will be made for breakfasts on 25th at about 6 a.m.

7. D Company will detail one Officer and 6 men to follow in rear of column.

8. Separate orders have been issued to Transport Officer.

Issued at 12-30 p.m. on
May 24th, 1916.

J H Cornkey. Lieutenant.
Acting Adjutant.
1/5th Bn.Royal Warwickshire Regt.

N O T I C E.

A G.S.Wagon for kits will be in H.Q. yard from 2-15 - 2-45 a.m.

MESSES. Mess wagon will be in H.Q. yard for Officer's Mess from 2-15 - 2-45 a.m.

No. 1 Copy	File.	No. 6 Copy	C Coy.
" 2 & 3	War Diary.	" 7 "	D "
" 4 "	A Coy.	" 8 "	Transport Officer.
" 5 "	B "		

2

O P E R A T I O N   O R D E R S   No.46.   Copy No.....

B Y

Lieut-Col. G.C.SLADEN D.S.O.

Commdg. 1/5th Battn.Royal Warwickshire Regt.

M A Y 30th, 1916.

Ref. Map 57d. 1/40,000.

1. The Brigade will move to billets at COUIN and COIGNEUX on the 31st instant.

2. The 5th R.War.R. will parade in the GANDAS - DOULLENS road with the head of the column at Cross Roads G.3.c.2.9. facing N.E. ready to move off at 4-5 a.m. in the following order:-
G. D. A. B.

3. All Transport will be brigaded and march in rear of the column, in the same order as units, travelling kitchens and cooks' carts leading in each unit.

4. The Company for duty (B.Coy), will detail one officer and a section to form a rear party which will march in rear of the Transport under command of the senior Officer.

5. A halt will be made for breakfasts about 6-30 a.m.

6. Separate orders have been issued to the Transport Officer.

Issued at 10-15 a.m. on May 30th, 1916.

Capt. & Adjt.
1/5th Battn Royal Warwickshire Regt.

N O T I C E.

The G.S.Wagon for kits and Officers' Mess cart will be in the Headquarters yard from 3 - 3-30 a.m.

No. 1 Copy	File.	No. 6 Copy	C Coy.
2 & 3	War Diary.	" 7 "	D "
" 4 "	A Coy.	" 8 "	Transport Officer.
" 5 "	B "		

O P E R A T I O N O R D E R S No.47. Copy No. 3
B Y
Lieut.Colonel G.C. SLADEN, D.S.O
Commdg. 1/5th Battn.Royal Warwickshire Regt.
May 31st, 1916

Map Ref. 57D 1/40,000.

1. The Brigade will take over the line held by the Div. from the 144 Inf. Bde. to-morrow, June 1st.

2. The 5th R.War.R. will relieve the 4th Gloster Regt. in H Sector.

3. The Battalion will parade in the SOUASTRE - COUIN Road, facing S.W., with the head of the column at road junction J.1.b.2.3., in following order - D. C. A. B., ready to move off at 4.15 a.m.

4. Rout e will be via road junction J.7.b.- fork road J.16.b.- point 127 in J.23.a.- entrance to JENA (J.24.b.5.7.) where guides will be found.

5. Coys will march by platoons at 200 yards distance - O.C.Coys will be responsible for keeping connection.
Breakfasts will be before starting.

6. Coys. will be disposed as under:-
D.Coy on right
C " on left
A " in support in HEBUTERNE
B " in reserve in SAILLY.

7. When taking over or handing over any trench or billet from another Battalion, receipts must pass for all stores, S.A.A., Grenades, Tools, Gumboots, etc. These receipts must be made out in duplicate, and a copy forwarded to Battalion Headquarters by 3 p.m. June 1st.
Certificates that trenches and billets are left clean must also be handed in. No receipts or certificates are valid unless signed by an Officer.

8. Separate orders have been issued to Transport and Lewis Rifle Officers.

Charles Retallack
~~CHARLES RETALLACK.~~

Issued at 9-30 p.m.
May 31st 1916.

Capt. & Adjt.

1/5th Bn. Royal Warwickshire Regt.

N O T I C E.

Valises of A and B Coys. Headquarters and mess boxes of all coys to be in field by Cookers at 6 a.m.

Valises of C and D will be sent to Transport Lines

No. 1 Copy.	File	No.6 Copy.	C Coy.
" 2 & 3 "	War Diary	" 7 "	D "
" 4 "	A Coy	" 8 "	Transport Officer.
" 5 "	B "		

143rd Inf.Bde.
48th Div.

WAR DIARY

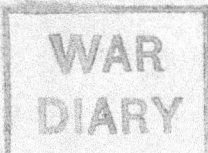

1/5th BATTN. THE ROYAL WARWICKSHIRE REGIMENT.

J U L Y

1 9 1 6

Attached:

Appendices 1 to 5.

Instructions regarding War Diaries and Intelligence Summaries are contained in F. S. Regs., Part II. and the Staff Manual respectively. Title pages will be prepared in manuscript.

WAR DIARY
or
INTELLIGENCE SUMMARY
(Erase heading not required.)

July 1916

Army Form C. 2118.

5TH BATT. R. WARWICKSHIRE REGT.

Hour, Date, Place	Summary of Events and Information	Remarks and references to Appendices
Map Ref - 57d NE 1/20,000 July		
Trenches K17c.30.35 - K17a1.8. 1	The day of attack - Z day. The front held by the 48th Division extended from JOHN COPSE K23a 3.3. to PUISIEUX ROAD. K17a1.8. the 7 R War R on the right and the 5 R War R on the left. Our rôle was to hold the trenches whilst the divisions on our right and left advanced on SERRE and GOMMECOURT respectively. our ultimate rôle depending on the line taken up by these other Divisions. The 31 Div were on our right and the 56 Div. were on our left. The time for launching the attack (Zero) was 7.30 a.m. 65 minutes before Zero the intense bombardment commenced, & 10 minutes before Zero, smoke candles and P. bombs were let off from our front line, and under cover of this screen the advance began. These attacks were successful, but by the end of the day all troops on the Corps front were driven back to their own lines again. The enemy barraged our trenches at intervals throughout the day. The night was quiet - Casualties 1 O.R. killed. 8 O.R. missing. CAPT. W.C.C. GELL (at duty) 2/Lt. P.A. GROVE. 2/Lt. H.H. PINE and 21 O.R's (5 at duty) wounded. The following officers arrived and were taken on strength of the Batt. 2/Lt. A.J.W. BROWN - W.E. WALSH - N.R. HASLUCK - W.S. TOWNSEND P.J. LAING - A.S. EIGHTEEN. J.R. BANCROFT.	CN
2.	Day quiet - Enemy lines bombarded by our Corps Artillery at 3.0 p.m and 6.30 p.m Casualties 2 O.Rs. wounded (at duty) The undermentioned officer arrived & was taken on strength 2/Lt. F.R. KYD -	OL

1247 W 3299 200,000 (E) 8/14 J.B.C. & A. Forms/C. 2118/11.

Army Form C. 2118.

Instructions regarding War Diaries and Intelligence Summaries are contained in F. S. Regs., Part II. and the Staff Manual respectively. Title pages will be prepared in manuscript.

WAR DIARY
or
INTELLIGENCE SUMMARY
(Erase heading not required.)

July 1916

5TH BATT. R. WARWICKSHIRE REGT.

Place	Hour, Date (July)	Summary of Events and Information	Remarks and references to Appendices
	3	Casualty 1 OR. wounded	C.R.
	4	Batt relieved by 5 Batt the Gloucestershire Regt - and marched to bivouacs at J1C8.3.	CL
Bivouacs J1C8.3.	5	The following officer arrived and taken on strength. 2/Lt G.B.de J. PEGLER -	CL
	9	The following officers arrived and taken on strength 2/Lt MATTS - 2/Lt HEGAN	JHC
	11	Draft of 61 OR's arrived.	CL
	11 - 13	Working parties of 500 strong found on each of these days for clearing trenches round COLINCAMPS.	JHC
LA BOISSELLE	13th - 14th	Batt. moved at 3 pm from bivouacs at J1C8.3 to BOUZINCOURT by motor lorry, moving on from BOUZINCOURT about 9 pm & marching to LA BOISSELLE. taking over at about 3 A.M. on Dugouts in trenches X13 d (Ref MAP FRANCE SHEET 57 D SE.) - being in support to 1/7th R. War. R. 3 OR wounded	JHC
Ref Map 57d SE. 1/20.000 57d SE.4 1/10 000	14 - 15	Battalion did not move - LA BOISSELLE [illegible] - 2 OR wounded.	
	15 - 16	Draft of 5 OR's arrived The Batt was ordered to attack as in Bde O.O. 69 para 3. The attack was launched at 2.3 a.m and the trenches taken without opposition and held - the Batt being disposed as shewn in map (red lines). The enemy counterattacked several times at dawn. A Coy of 6 R Warwick relieved us in trench a about midnight 16/17 Casualties - Killed - Capt D.G. LUNT - Capt C.V. SUCKLING - 2/Lt SIMPKIN and 38 ORs - wounded 2/Lt G.B. PEGLER - 2/Lt A.S. EIGHTEEN - 2/Lt R. HEGAN and 74 OR's. Missing 5.	CL CL - Appendix I

1247 W 3299 200,000 (E) 8/14 J.B.C. & A. Forms/C. 2118/11.

Instructions regarding War Diaries and Intelligence Summaries are contained in F. S. Regs., Part II. and the Staff Manual respectively. Title pages will be prepared in manuscript.

WAR DIARY
or
INTELLIGENCE SUMMARY
(Erase heading not required.)

Army Form C. 2118.

July 1916 5th Bn Warwicks

Hour, Date, Place		Summary of Events and Information	Remarks and references to Appendices
Ref/Map ORVILLERS 57D S.E.4 2B.	July 17.	Bombing attacks by enemy at intervals – The Battn was relieved by the 6 R Warwicks and bivouaced at W.30.a. Casualties (included under date 16.7.16)	CR
W 30.a.	18	400 men required for working party ~~to~~ to dig trench from X9666 to X9C55 – ~~remained~~ marched to ~~bivouac~~ billets at BOUZINCOURT	CR
BOUZINCOURT	19	wounded Lt R.S. TURNER – working party reached billets at BOUZINCOURT at 6 a.m.	CR
	22nd	The Battn moved up to ORVILLERS and CRUCIFIX as in 144 Bde OO 79 and O.O.50. The attack by 144 and 145 Bdes was carried out successfully.	CR. Appendix 2. (O.O.50)
Trenches –	23	The Battn took over from 145 Bde as in 143 Inf Bde OO. BM475 and O.O.51. Efforts to join up with ANZAC division were unsuccessful owing to enemy strong point at X3664. Several attempts aided by stokes guns were made without success. as also were attempts to bomb towards X4a46 ~~Casualties~~ –	CR. Appendix 3. (O.O.51)
	24	Further attempts made at 7.30 a.m and 4.30 p.m aided by artillery and stokes guns were unsuccessful – from subsequent aerial photographs and from information by prisoners it was proved that X3664 was a strongly fortified point held by 3 Machine Guns, & 300 men were in the vicinity ready to hold it. This point was evacuated at 10 p.m. on the 25th and taken by the 7 R Warks at 12 midnight the same date. Casualties – killed 2/Lt. F. MATTS & 4 ORs – wounded 22 ORs missing 2 ORs (continued)	CR

615

1247 W 3299 200,000 (E) 8/14 J.B.C. & A. Forms/C. 2118/11.

Instructions regarding War Diaries and Intelligence Summaries are contained in F. S. Regs., Part II. and the Staff Manual respectively. Title pages will be prepared in manuscript.

WAR DIARY
or
INTELLIGENCE SUMMARY
(Erase heading not required.)

Army Form C. 2118.

July 1916

Hour, Date, Place	July	Summary of Events and Information	Remarks and references to Appendices
Trenches.	24.	The Battn was relieved by 7 R Warwk as in 143 Inf Bde O.O. 75	Appendix 4. CL.
UNSA REDOUT	25	Battn in Brigade Reserve. 1 O.R. killed 2 O.R's wounded	CL
	26	" " Division " 1 O.R. wounded	CL
	27	Battn relieved by 8th R. FUSILIERS and marched to BOUZINCOURT as in 143 Bde O.O No 76 — 1. O.R. wounded	CL Appendix 5.
BOUZINCOURT-	28	Battn taken by Motor Bus to COULONVILLERS - 8 miles East of ABBEVILLE (Ref Map: LENS)	CL
COULONVILLERS	30	The following officers arrived & taken on strength - 2nd Lieut A.C. BRATT " " F.S. TUTE " " F. COULSON and 56 O.R's	
	31	" " " " " " " " CAPT. H.S. BLOOMER } The " E. STEELE } Manchester Regt and 14 O.R's	CL.
		Strength on July 31st 29 officers 636 O.R's	
		Total casualties in July - Killed 4 officers & 45 O.R's Wounded 8 officers & 117 O.R's Missing 5 O.R's Died of wounds . 1 officer	

[signature]
Lt Col. Comdg
1/5 R. Warw. R.

616

1247 W 3299 200,000 (E) 8/14 J.B.C. & A. Forms/C. 2118/11.

A P P E N D I C E S

1
2
3
4
5

Appendix I

Secret.

Copy No. 3

143 Inf: Bde Operation Order No. 69

15 July 1916 6/7

1. The Bde will attack OVILLERS-LA-BOISSELLE tonight in conjunction with 74 and 75 Inf: Bdes.
2. 74 Inf Bde is attacking at 1am. between the lines X8B75 (inclusive) and X8B31 (exclusive). Objective X8B56 (inclusive) – X8B24 (exclusive)
75 Inf: Bde is attacking on west of 74 Inf. Bde.
3.(a) 5th R. War. Regt will form up with their right flank on X3C51 and their left flank about X9A55 facing W by 12-55 A.M
(b) At 1 AM, at which hour the artillery barrage will lift from their first objective, they will attack between the lines X.3.C.02. and X8B75 (exclusive) to the objective X2D85.20 and X8B56 (exclusive)

618

(c) They will move to their place of assembly via X9D58 and X9B4.4

(d) M.G.C. will detail 2 MGs under an officer + 143 T.M. Batt: will detail 1 Stokes Gun under an officer with 51 rds to be at Pt. X9C82 by 1 A.M. + to there await orders from 5th R War Regt.

6th R War Regt. will provide a carrying party of 20 to report to T.M Batt: at 11 p.m. Guide from 7 R War Regt will meet this party at T.M. Batt bivouac at that hour.

4. 74 Inf: Bde is patrolling trench X3C93 – 51 – 02 after dark to ensure that none of the enemy occupy this trench. They will report to an officer. 5 R War Regt at X9D52 at 11 p.m.

5. 5th R War Regt will communicate with Bde by (a) runners through X9B66 or X9C46 to telephone office at X13D6.3 (b) visual station at X9B63

Issued and signed at 8-15 pm

Copies to Bde units
25 Div.
74 Inf: Bde

[signature] Major
BM 143 Inf: Bde

619

To O.C 1/5 R. War Reg

7th Bde have just reported Enemy MGs at X9a1.5, X9a1.4, X9a05, X3c04 and one in prolongation of the trench running from X3a5.1 to X3a02

G. I. Lee Capt
July 15. 1916 S.C 143 Inf. Bde

P.S. The first three of the above appear to be in emplacements and usually fire S.W

REF: MAP: OVILLERS 1/10000.
X CORPS. 13-7-16.

objective
ultimate disposition

049

– Appendix 2 –

SECRET.

Ref. Map
LA BOISELLE
1/5,000.

144th INFANTRY BRIGADE ORDER NO. 79.

67

1. The attack will be continued tonight 22/23rd July, 1916.

145th Bde., will attack on our right.

2. 6th Gloucesters forming up from point 47 due E. to the Railway, and advancing at zero, will capture the German trench from point 90 to point 40. Point 40 will also be attacked by 145th Bde.

Points 20, 68 and 90 will be bombarded with Stokes Mortars from – 5' to + 5'.

4th Gloucesters will hold the 1st and second lines and be prepared to hand over to 5th Royal Warwicks if require to reinforce the attack.

7th Worcesters will be in a position of readiness about RIBBLE ST., at 2 a.m. 23rd July, with a view to reinforcing or continuing the attack.

5th Royal Warwicks will send two companies to OVILLERS by 8 p.m. to-night. These Coys., will reconnoitre the 1st and 2nd lines and be ready to take over from 4th Gloucesters.

2 Coys., 5th Royal Warwicks will be at CRUCIFIX CORNER at 8 p.m. and remain there in reserve.

Brigade Machine Gun Company will cooperate according to instructions issued separately.

A Brigade Adv. Report Centre will be established at X.8.c.09. to which place all reports will be sent.

Zero time has been communicated to those concerned.

[signature]
Major.
Brigade Major.
144th Infantry Brigade.

Copies 1.2.3 – retained.
4 to 9 – Bde.Units.
10 – 5th R.War. R.
11 – 48th Divn. (for information)
12 – 145th Bde. do
13 – 143th Bde. do
~~14 – 110th Bde. R.F.A. do~~
~~15 – Right Group R.F.A. do~~
16 – 3rd Fd. Coy. R.E.
17 – Signals.

B^de^ HQ 4 [illegible] X 8 A 85
[illegible] X 8 C 15

No.50. Copy 2

OPERATION ORDERS
BY
Lieut.Colonel G.C. SLADEN, D.S.O.
Commdg. 1/5th Battn. Royal Warwickshire Regt.
22nd July. 1916.

622

Map Ref. OVILLERS.1/10,000.

1. The attack will be continued to-night 22/23rd July, 1916. The 6th Gloucesters forming up from point 47 due E. to the Railway, and advancing at zero will capture the German trench from point 90 to point 40.
   4th Gloucesters will hold the first and second lines.
   5th Royal War.R. will be attached to the 144th Brigade and will be in support to the 4th Gloucesters.

2. A and B Companies 5th R.War.R. are to be at point X8.c.2.5., at the entrance to OVILLERS by at 8 p.m. to-night. D Company is to be at the CRUCIFIX at W.11.d.8.1. by the same time.

3. O.C. Companies will arrange reconnoitring parties to reconnoitre the two front lines of trenches.

4. Lewis Gun teams and guns of C. Coy will be attached to D. Coy.

5. Brigade report centre will be at X.8.c.0.9.
   Battalion Headquarters of 4th Gloucesters will be at point X.8.a.8.5.
   Headquarters, 5thR.War.R. willbeat point W.11.d.8.1.

6. Special orders have been issued to Transport Officer.

J H Cankey
Lieut.
Acting Adjutant.
1/5th Battn. The Royal Warwickshire Regiment.

Issued at 4.45 p.m.,
22nd July,1916.

No.1.Copy. File.
" 2 " War Diary.
" 3 " A Coy.
" 4 " B "
No.5. Copy. C Coy.
" 6 " D "
" 7 " Transport Officer.

"A" Form. Army Form C. 2121.

MESSAGES AND SIGNALS.

No. of Message

Prefix ... Code ... m.	Words	Charge	This message is on a/c of:	Recd. at ... m.
Office of Origin and Service Instructions.	Sent		... Service.	Date
	At ... m.			From 6 W W
	To			
	By		(Signature of "Franking Officer.")	By

TO

Sender's Number.	Day of Month	In reply to Number	AAA
*			

7th Bn will occupy trenches between railway (which is R boundary of Div) & ALBERT road from X.9.c.8.2 to X.5.c.6.6 & LA BOISELLE (both inclusive) AAA 7th Bn will find such carrying parties as are required tonight by 5th Bn AAA Acknowledge.

From 143 I/Bde

Place

Time 5.55 pm

The above may be forwarded as now corrected.

Censor.

(Z) [illegible] Major BM

Signature of Addressor or person authorised to telegraph in his name.

* This line should be erased if not required.

(774-5) —McC. & Co. Ltd., London.— W 1789/1402. 150,000. 8/15. Forms C 2121/10.

"A" Form. Army Form C. 2121.

MESSAGES AND SIGNALS. No. of Message

Prefix Code m. | Words | Charge | This message is on a/c of: Service. (Signature of "Franking Officer.") | Recd. at m. Date. From 6 B By 6

Office of Origin and Service Instructions.

By runner

Sent At m. To By

TO: 5 Bn ~~7 Bn~~ Appendix. 3.

Sender's Number.	Day of Month	In reply to Number	AAA
* BM475	23		

The Bde is taking over from X4C42 to X3B11 (inclusive) Dividing line between Bde & 145 Inf Bde will be X3B11 X3C93 X9B66 (all inclusive to the Bde) & thence along main road to LA BOISSELLE, which will be common to both Bdes for traffic. 5th Bn will hold this front along X4C42 X3D97 X3B81 X3D22 X3B11 & will get into touch with the Anzacs on the right wherever possible & will continue working forward towards X4A43, X4A46 & R34C21. MG section attached to 5th Bn should be employed along line X9D58 to X3C93. Above relief will take place as soon after dusk as possible.

From

Place

Time

The above may be forwarded as now corrected. (Z)

Censor. Signature of Addressor or person authorised to telegraph in his name.

* This line should be erased if not required.

(774-5) —McC. & Co. Ltd., London.— W 1789/1402. 150,000. 8/15. Forms C 2121/10.

1/5 R Warwk - O.O No 51 (G?)

By Lt Col. G.C. Sladen DSO - July 23-1916

1. The 143 Bde is taking over from X4c42 to X3b1.1 (inclusive). Dividing line between Bde and 145 Bde will be X3b11. X3c93 X9b66 (all inclusive to the Bde) and thence along main road to LA BOISELLE which will be common to both Bdes for traffic.

5 Bath will hold this front along X4c42 X3d97 X3b81 X3d28 X3b11 and will get into touch with the ANZACS on the right where ever possible.

2 A coy will continue bombing towards X4a4.3 and X4c4.6 and R34C21.

B coy (2 platoons pov in reserve to A coy) will hold from X3b11 to X3b81

1 platoon from X3b81 to X3d97

1 platoon about pt X4d42

D coy will be in trench X3c92 to X9b66

HQ's to be notified

Report centre as at present until notified

56

3 Above relief will take place as soon after dark as possible.

6/7/6

4 7 Bath will occupy trenches between railway (which is right boundary of Div) and ALBERT Rd from X.9.c.8.2. to X.9.c.4.6. and LA BOISELLE (both inclusive)
They will find such carrying parties as are required by 5 Batt. Knight
— Acknowledge

Sg. J. H. Cropley
Lt
A/Adjt 5 N[illegible]

Copies to
1 File
2. Major Rotchard
3 D+B Coys
4 A Coy.

Appendix 4.

Copy No. 3.....

SECRET.

143 Inf: Bde O.O. No. 75 24 July 1916

6PM

1. 7th Bn will relieve 5th Bn today, & will continue a vigorous offensive without intermission, on the same lines.

2. 1½ Cos will relieve troops holding the front between X.3.d.9.7 & X.3.central, & bombing posts to the front, commencing at 5 p.m., using trench between X.8.b.7.8 & X.3.c.7.9, & moving by small parties.

3. Remaining dispositions will be taken over as soon after dark as possible, if daylight relief is not practicable. On relief 5th Bn will proceed to bivouacs near USNA.

4. Hdqrs of 7th Bn will be established at X.9.c.8.2.

Issued at 12-55 p.m. thro' Signals.

P R Rushall[?] Major B.M. 143 Inf: Bde.

Copies to:- Bde units
145 Inf:Bde.
48 Div.

Appendix 5.

SECRET. Copy No. 3

143 Inf: Bde Operation Order No.76.

27 July 1916

Ref: OVILLERS.1/10,000
Sheet 57D.SE.1/20,000.

1. The bde will be relieved today, by the 36 Inf:Bde & will proceed to billets at BOUZINCOURT, via railway bridge at W.23.c, new road near Brickworks at W.22.a. on to main road in W.20.d.

2. The relief will be carried out as follows:-

(a) 7th Bn, which is not being relieved will move at 2-30 p.m.

(b) 8th Bn will be relieved by 11th Middlesex Regt. and will ~~send~~ platoon guides to B.M.123.2 (X.14.a.) at 4 p.m.

(c) 6th Bn will be relieved by 7th R.Sussex Regt. & will send ~~guides~~ platoon guides to X.13.d.2.1 at 5-30 p.m.

(d) 5th Bn. will be relieved by 8th R.Fusiliers & will send Co. guides to house near W.29.b.8.6. at 5 p.m.

(e) M.G.Co relief will be completed during daylight under arrangements made between Os.C.

(f) T.M.Batt: will be relieved at 3-45 p.m. at B.M.123-2 & will provide a guide from that spot, for relief proceeding to the section in the line. Guns in the line will be handed over.

3. All 1/5,000 maps, & photographs relating to this sector, will be handed over.

4. On completion of relief referred to in 2(b), G.O.C. will hand over command of the line to G.O.C.36 Inf:Bde. After that hour, reports to BOUZINCOURT.

Major,
B.M. 143 Inf:Bde.

Issued, thro' Signals
at 12-30 p.m.

Copies to: Bde Units
48 Div.
36 Inf:Bde.

143/48

Extract from account of the Defence of Gommecourt

1st July 1916 by Major C.E.Carrington.M.C. 5/R.Warwick.

- - - - - - - - - - - - -

x x x x x

The smoke bombs had long smouldered out and the gun fire had died down, leaving the battlefield apparently empty and almost silent under a sultry clouded sky, when the observers of the 5th R.Warwick Regiment, south of Hebuterne, saw Tauscher's columns crossing the plain from Bucquoy and assembling in the dead ground near point 147. This was reported* to

---

* By the author personally by telephone.

---

the VIII.Corps artillery in vain. The target was not in their area. A message was then sent* to the London

---

* As above.

Scottish who were unfortunately unable to get the VII Corps guns to fire, for a similar reason. While the two artillery groups disputed over their boundary Tauscher's men passed on undisturbed except by desultory rifle fire at 1,500 yards range, and entered the head of the C.T's in safety. Their own artillery had no such scruples. A very severe bombardment of the English jumping off lines marked their approach. At the head of each column observers were seen controlling the fire by coloured screens showing the limits of each advance. Though the assault was made by bombers working down the trenches, the bombing parties were covered by snipers shooting over the top.

In an hour and twenty minutes (9.40 - 11 a.m.) Tauscher had assembled his men and marched two miles, from Bucquoy to point 147; in an hour and a half more (11 - 12.30) he had made his dispositions and moved 1,000 yards through battered trenches. 11th Coy. (Stolper) attacked through Roth; 12th Coy. (Winkelmann)
11.30 through Lehmann; 9th Coy. remained in 2nd Switch line in reserve. Capt.Brockmann advancing down Süd trench had already made a breach in the English defence.

x x x x x x x

143rd Brigade.

48th Division.

1/5th BATTALION

ROYAL WARWICKSHIRE REGIMENT

AUGUST 1916

Instructions regarding War Diaries and Intelligence Summaries are contained in F. S. Regs., Part II. and the Staff Manual respectively. Title pages will be prepared in manuscript.

WAR DIARY
or
~~INTELLIGENCE SUMMARY~~
(Erase heading not required.)

August 1916

Army Form C. 2118.

5TH BATT. R. WARWICKSHIRE REGT.

Hour, Date, Place		Summary of Events and Information	Remarks and references to Appendices
	August		
COULONVILLERS.	1.	Training commenced – 1 OR reinforcement	CR
	6.	Reinforcements – 30 OR:	CR
	7.	Reinforcements – 2/Lt. J.H HEYS, H.O SAGAR, D.T. PARRY, E.T. ASHTON JONES } from 5th Batt. The East Lancashire Regt	
		99 OR: from 1st Cambs (1/1 Hunts Cyclists) Batt	Ch
	9th.	Batt marched to billets at LONGUEVILLETTE – O.O. 52	Ch – OO 52
LONGUEVILLETTE	10th	" " " " " ARQUEVES – OO.53	Ch – OO 53
ARQUEVES	14	" " " " " VARENNES – O.O.54	Ch – O.O 54
VARENNES	15	" " " " " BOUZINCOURT – O.O 55	Ch – O.O.55
BOUZINCOURT	16	" relieved the 6th Glosters as in OO 56 and took over as follows. A & B coys in trenches ORVILLERS village. HQs and C & D coys " ORVILLERS post.	Ch – OO. 56
ORVILLERS POST.	19	The Batt attacked as in 143 Bde O.O. No – 81 Orders issued to O.C. coys verbally –	Appendices I and II
		The attack was successful. A coy took first objective – B coy plus two platoons of C took the second – D Coy formed the garrison of the trench 28–37 and C coy less two platoons formed a carrying party.	Map – Appendix I.a.
Ref Map ORVILLERS 57d SE. 4 1/10.000. and Special Map		The "jumping off" place was 28–88 – ladders were placed on the night of 17th/18th. and dumps formed at 28 and 88. Batt HQs were near Point 05 and advanced HQs at Pt 67.	
		At night a Coy of the York & Lanc R took over from 28–37 and	

5TH BATT. R. WARWICKSHIRE REGT.

Instructions regarding War Diaries and Intelligence Summaries are contained in F. S. Regs., Part II. and the Staff Manual respectively. Title pages will be prepared in manuscript.

WAR DIARY
or
INTELLIGENCE SUMMARY
(Erase heading not required.)

Army Form C. 2118.

1/5 R Warr R

Hour, Date, Place 1916 August	Summary of Events and Information	Remarks and references to Appendices
Ref Map OVILLERS 57D. SE-4 - 1/10.000 and Aerial Map - Trenches -	C and D Coys went forward to assist A and B Coys -	
19th	Line readjusted at daylight as shown in Appendix III	Appx III
	Patrols sent forward as in Appx IV - Pt 79 not captured	Appx IV
	Line readjusted at night as in 143 Bde O.O. 82 (Battn O.O 57)	O.O. 57 Appx V
20	The Battn was relieved at 4 pm by the 6th Glosters as in Bde O.O. No 83 and Battn O.O. 58 - and marched to Bouzincourt - W8c84	OO 58 Appx VI
	Casualties during period Aug 18 - 20th	
	Killed - 2Lt B.L. CURTIS	
	2Lt F.P. KYD and 16 OR's	
	Wounded - Capt A.L.R.J. GROOM	
	2/Lt L.S. TOWNSEND	
	2/Lt F. COULSON and 99 OR's	
	Missing - 5 OR's	
	Messages of Congratulation are shown in Appendix VII	Appendix VII
Bouzincourt W8c84 - 22	Battn relieved 8 R Warr R in trenches - On right ANZAC Corps - On left 144th Inf Bde - Front was SKYLINE Trench extending from R33a80 to X2b59.	
	Battn HQs at X8b76.	

1247 W 3299 200,000 (E) 8/14 J.B.C. & A. Forms/C. 2118/11.

Instructions regarding War Diaries and Intelligence Summaries are contained in F. S. Regs., Part II. and the Staff Manual respectively. Title pages will be prepared in manuscript.

WAR DIARY
or
INTELLIGENCE SUMMARY
(Erase heading not required.)

5TH BATT. R. WARWICKSHIRE REGT.

Army Form C. 2118.

1/5 R War R –

Hour, Date, Place		Summary of Events and Information	Remarks and references to Appendices
August 1916		On Right – C coy – on Left – A coy – Right support D coy – Left support B coy –	
	24.	Battn Relieved by 6th R War R – and disposed as follows. Battn less B and A coys at USNA Redoubt – B and D coys at OVILLERS VILLAGE in trenches from X8 c15 to X8 a 0.2	CR
		Casualties during period 22–24 killed OR's 4 wounded OR's 23	CR CR
	26	9 officers and 375 OR's employed for working party under R.E on Brigade front & support line during night 26/27 1 O.R. wounded	CR.
Ref. 57D S.E 1/20.000	27	Two coys in OVILLERS held in Reserve to Bde during an attack by 8th R-WAR-R. 2/Lt C. Buck (attach 145 Bde) wounded	CR
	28	The Battn Marched to huts at VARENNES.	CR
	29	The Battn The undermentioned officers from 3/5 Battn taken on strength – 2/Lt A. SHELDON 2/Lt H.L. WOSTENHOLM and 45 O.R's	CR
VARENNES	29	Battn Marched to huts in the BOIS DE WARNIMONT –	C.R.
		Strength of Battn on August 31st 1916 Officers – 28 O.R's 592	
		Casualties during month of August Killed – Officers 2 OR's 20 Wounded – Officers 4 OR's 123 Missing 4 OR's	

J.E. Mullin? Lt Col Comdg 5 R War R

1247 W 3299 200,000 (E) 8/14 J.B.C. & A. Forms/C. 2118/11.

OPERATION ORDERS No.52 Copy No......2

BY

Lieut-Colonel G.C.SLADEN D.S.O.
Commdg. 1/5th Battn.Royal Warwickshire Regiment.
August 8th 1916.

MAP REFERENCE
SHEET 11 (LENS)

(1) The 5th R.War.R., will move to-morrow, 9th inst., to billets at LONGUEVILLETTE.

(2) The Battalion will fall in ready to move off by 4.50 a.m., on the ST RIQUER - BERNAVILLE road, the head of the column opposite C Coy drill field.
Order of March - A. B. C. D.

(3) Breakfasts will be eaten at 3.15 a.m., and haversack rations should be taken to be eaten during the halt of about an hour's duration, which will take place about 8 a.m.

(4) The new Lewis Gun Carts will move behind their companies.
Other hand carts will go with the transport.

(5) D Coy will detail one officer and one section as Rear Party. This will march behind the Battalion, and at the Brigade rendezvous,(road junction ½ mile N.E. of MESNIL-DOMQUEUR) will fall in behind the Brigaded Transport.
Duties - to pick up and bring on stragglers of the Battn.

(6) 2nd Lieut.W.S.TOWNSHEND and the Coy. Quartermaster-Sergeants and Signalling Sergeant, will bicycle on at the hour's halt to arrange billets under the Staff Captain.
O.C.Signals will arrange bicycles for this party.

X ~~(7) Men are to wear their caps and carry the helmet slung on the handle of the bayonet.~~

(8) Special Orders have been issued to Transport Officer.

~~(Signed)~~ J.H.C. ~~J.H.C[illegible]~~.
Capt. & Adjutant.
1/5th Battn. Royal Warwickshire Regiment.

Issued at 7.30 p.m.
8th August, 1916.

No.1 Copy. File.
Nos 2 & 3. War Diary.
No. 4. A Coy.
No. 5 Copy. B Coy.
No. 6 " C "
No. 7 " D "
No. 8 " T.O. & Q.M.

NOTICE.

Officers' kits and mess boxes are to be at the cross roads by Headquarters for collection by Transport at 4.15 a.m.

No surplus kit can be taken and only one mess box per Coy.

Great care is to be taken that billets and fields are left clean and in good order.

X (7) Men are to wear their caps and carry the helmet at the back of the pack, under the supporting straps.

Aug. 9th No 52

Operation Orders

by Lieut-Col KADEN DS.O.

① The 5th R. War. R. will move from LONGUEVILLETTE to ARQUEVES tomorrow 10th inst.

② The Battalion will parade in the main street facing NE with the head of the column at the cross-roads S.E. of the E in LONGUEVILLETTE ready to move off at 4.50AM. Order of march B-C-D-A.

③ Billeting party as detailed today will report with bicycles to the Staff Captain at 6.5 AM at the fork roads ½ mile S.E. of GEZAINCOURT STN.

④ "A" Coy will detail rear party to bring in stragglers. This party will fall in in rear of the Brigaded Transport at the fork roads ½ mile SE of GEZAINCOURT STN.

⑤ No parties are to be left behind to clean up billets latrines etc, but must complete their task before the unit marches off.

9.8.16. JH Cumskey Capt & Adjt
1/5th RWar.R.

32

NOTICES.

① Breakfast will be at 3.15 AM.
Haversack rations will be carried.

② Officers Valises & offices boxes are to be dumped in the main street ~~party~~ outside HQ ready to be picked up by transport by 4.15 AM.

Officers Valises are not to exceed 35 lbs.

35

O P E R A T I O N   O R D E R S   No. ~~53~~ 54   Copy No. I......

B Y

Lieut.Colonel G.C.SLADEN D.S.O.

Commdg. 1/5th Battn.Royal Warwickshire Regiment.

August 13th 1916.

Map Reference - 11 (LENS)

1. The 5th R.War.R will move to VARENNES to-morrow August 14th.

2. The Battalion will fall in on the ARQUEVES - LEALVILLERS Road with the head of the column on the near side of the Railway crossing, ready to move off at 7 a.m.
   Order of march:- C. D. A. B.

3. A Company will detail one section under an Officer to act as Rear Party to pick up stragglers. This party will march in the rear of the Transport from the Brigade starting point at the Mill, 600 yards from ARQUEVES.

4. The company Lewis Gun carts (new pattern) will move in rear of their respective company. They are to be drawn with the guiding handle to the rear. The old pattern gun carts will all be drawn in front of the battalion Transport under the command of the O.C.Lewis Guns.
   C Coy will detail 2 Lewis Gun teams and D Coy 3 teams, to draw the carts containing their Lewis Guns and the men now attached to the Transport will draw the remainder.

5. Men are to wear their Caps and to carry the Steel Helmets under the supporting straps of the valise.

J H Cornby

Issued at 8 p.m.
August 13th 1916.

Capt. & Adjt.
1/5th Battn.Royal Warwickshire Regt.

No.1 Copy War Diary.
" 2 " do.
" 3 " A Coy.
" 4 " B "
No.5 Copy C Coy.
" 6 " D "
" 7 " Transport Officer. & Q.M.
" 8 " Signalling Officer.

N O T I C E S.

(1) Officers kits and Mess boxes will be outside Company Headquarters ready for the Transport to pick up by 6-15 a.m.

(2) O.C.Coys. will make sure that billets ~~in~~ and company areas are left clean. No men are to be left when the company parades.

OPERATION ORDERS No. 55
BY
Lieut. Col. SLADEN DSO
Comdg 1/5th Batt Royal Warwickshire Regt
AUGUST 15th/16

I The 5th R War R will move from VARENNE to BOUZINCOURT today Aug. 15th.

II The Battalion will fall in on WEST ST with the head of the column opposite the BATHS. ready to move off by 10-45 AM
Order of March D. A. B. C

III Lewis Gun Carts (old pattern) will be drawn as yesterday.

IV B Coy will detail one section under an Officer to act as rear party.

V Special Orders have been sent to Transport Officer.

J H Cronkey
Capt & Adjt
1/5th R War R

NOTICES

I Mens dinners will be cooked on the line of march & be ready on arrival

II Officers Mess boxes kits will be dumped outside Company HQ ready to be picked up by the Transport by 9-45 AM

III Steel helmets will be worn.

O P E R A T I O N   O R D E R S   No.56   Copy No.......

B Y

Lieut.Colonel G.C.SLADEN D.S.O.
Commanding 1/5th Battn.Royal Warwickshire Regiment.
A ugust 16th 1916.

---

1. The 5th R.War.R. will relieve the 6th Gloucester Regt to-day 16th inst.

2. A and B Coys will take over the OVILLERS Defences, C & D Coys at OVILLERS Post. (Old British Front line).

3. Coys. will move by platoons at 100 yards interval in the following order:- A - B - C - D.
The leading platoon of "A" Coy will move off at 1-30 p.m.
Coys. will use the new road which runs from W.~~13~~ 14.a.1.9 to W.16.b.3.8.

4. Guides from the 6th Gloucesters will be at CRUCIFIX CORNER at 3 p.m.

5. The Officers, who were detailed by Adjutant to O.C.Coys, 1 Sergt, 1 Corpl, 1 Lance Corpl and the spare Lewis Gun team per company, will proceed to the Transport lines on the SENLIS Road as soon as the Battalion has moved off.
Instructionin the Lewis Gun will be carried on by O.C.Lewis Guns for all ranks while there, the 9th Gun being used.

6. ~~O.C.Coys will have the men's packs stacked by 12 Noon to-day, in an accessible place outside coy. billets for removal to Transport lines.~~
Any Officers valises and surplus Mess kit which are not wanted in the line will be stacked outside coy. Headquarters by 1 p.m. for removal to transport lines.

7. Special orders have been issued to Transport Officer.

Issued at 10 a.m.
August 16th 1916.

J.H. Cawley [signature]
Capt. & Adjt.
1/5th Battn.Royal Warwickshire Regiment.

6 OC Coys will have the mens packs stacked by Coys in billet No 103 under arrangements of Q.M.
The Mess Cart will be available for taking Officers' ~~[illegible]~~ Mess Kit that is needed up to the Trenches

Appendix 1. Spare

SECRET. Copy No. 15

143 Inf:Bde Operation Order No. 81

18 August 1916.

Ref: OVILLERS 1/10,000

1. The bde will attack the enemy this afternoon, as follows.

   1st Objective: X.2.b.6.2 - 20 - 03, X.2.a.91-81, X.2.c.3.9.
   2nd Objective: X.2.b.5.5 - 44 - 06, X.2.a.86-76-56-43-22. x 96
   3rd Objective: (in which 145 Inf:Bde will co-operate by bombing from X.2.b.99) X.2.b.59 - 48.

2. 6th Bn will attack from the right to the line X.2.a.96, X.2.b.04 03-20 (exclusive). 5th Bn will attack the remainder of the objectives with the exception of the trench X.2.c.39 - X.2.a.22, which will be dealt with by bombing parties of the 7th Bn.

3. The Infantry advance will be by waves, the first waves capturing, consolidating, & reforming on the line of the first objective, whilst succeeding waves push on to the second objective. From the second objective, 6th Bn will secure the third objective, whilst all Bns will maintain touch with the enemy, pushing forward & establishing themselves as far (if possible) as the line R.32.D.20 X.2.a.79, X.2.a.29.

4. The sequence of artillery action will be as follows:

   (a) Corps heavy artillery & other artillery will continue their constant bombardment on the first objective, & strong points in rear until 5 p.m. when they will lift to the second objective.

   (b) At 5 p.m. a shrapnel barrage will open along the line X.2.b.62 - 20, X.2.a.80.
   At 5-5 p.m. it will lift about 100 yards, except guns on front N of X.2.b.20, through X.2.b.03 to X.2.a.91, which will not lift till 5-7 p.m.
   At 5-10 p.m. it will lift to 2nd objective.
   At 5-15 p.m. it will lift to the line ~~R.32.d.12. X.2.a.79 - 46 - 25.~~ 100 yards N of 2nd objective.
   At 5-20 p.m. it will lift to the line X2B68-59-48-X2A46-16

   After 5-20 p.m. it will work back 100 yards per 2 minutes to the bottom of the NAB - MOUQUET valley, stopping on line R33D03 R32C56-33-X2A19, & continuing at slow rate on this line

   (c) At 5-5 p.m. Heavy Artillery will lift back to outside squares X.2.a & b.

5. An R.E. officer & six sappers will report to both the 5th & 6th bns. and will follow their infantry to the 2nd objective. From there, they will send back to the R.E. Co. in OVILLERS, for such assistance & material as they require, to complete the consolidation of strong points in the line gained. They must not become involved in the infantry fighting.

6. The M.G.Co. will co-operate as follows:-

(a) A barrage will be kept up along the line R.32.d.25 - R.32.c.65 - R.32.c.33.

(b) Two guns at X.2.d.44 will watch the right flank.

(c) The THIEPVAL plateau will be searched by six guns throughout.

(d) The MOUQUET valley will be swept by two guns, if required.

7. Two guns, T.M.Batt: will be attached to the 5th, 6th & 7th Bns respectively..

8. From 5 p.m. to 5-45 p.m. there will be a discharge of smoke (if the wind is favourable) up the MOUQUET valley, from about X.2.b.33, to conceal the operations from the N. If required, this will be renewed later.

9. (a) Assaulting troops, who will move as light as possible, will carry 120 rounds S.A.A. 2 Mills bombs & 2 sandbags per man. They will also wear white distinguishing badges on the back.

(b) Yellow screens & red flares will be carried to mark the forward positions reached. S.O.S.rockets & Very lights will be sent up to the front reached, at nightfall.

(c) Officers will be dressed as like the men as possible.

(d) No maps, plans, orders or letters will be carried by anyone.

(e) Carrying parties, not taking part in the assault, need carry no arms or equipment, other than the smoke helmet.

(f) The trench X.2.d.28 - 26 - 02 will be kept clear for the evacuation of casualties.

(g) Bns will post sentries, as required, to control trench traffic & deal with stragglers.

10. Advanced Bde hdqrs will be established at X.8.a.05, by 4-30 p.m.

11·30

Issued at ~~10-40~~ a.m.

P R Nicholls. Major,
B.M. 143 Inf: Bde.

Copies to Bde units
48 Div.
145 Inf:Bde
146 Inf:Bde
Left Group, R.A.
No.2 F.Co. R.E.

Appendix II

Copy No. 4

SECRET

II Corps.
G. 362

48th Division.

18/8/16.

Information regarding the enemy to be fought this afternoon.

The following points should be brought home to all ranks taking part in the attack this afternoon. This document should then be destroyed.

1. The bombardment by our heavy guns and heavy trench mortars has now been more or less continuous on the enemy defences in X.2.a for over a week.

During the last 48 hours this bombardment has been particularly severe. No portion of our own line has ever experienced such continuous and concentrated bombardment by such heavy shells.

2. The German garrison of this area has probably been without relief for about a week: enduring this bombardment, being constantly threatened by real night attacks from the East (not mere feints) and probably short of water and food as all their communications have been kept under consistent gun and machine gun fire.

It is just possible that the garrison was relieved last night: in which case they must have had a long night march, must have suffered severely on the way and must now be very tired and short of sleep.

All recent captured letters confirm the supposition that continuous fighting and shortness of food is affecting, generally, the morale of the German troops.

3. While crossing No Man's Land our infantry may come under a certain amount of rather distant rifle or machine gun fire from the front or half-front (our flanks are quite secure): but badly aimed fire because of the smoke and dust which will be caused by our own barrage and because all likely places are being dealt with.

Those who are slow about crossing No Man's Land may come under a hostile artillery barrage: but this is unlikely to open in less than five minutes after Zero. Our counter batteries are ready to deal with this artillery and their observation posts are also being dealt with as far as possible.

4. Once across

4. Once across No Man's Land and into the 1st objectives the fight must become mostly a hand to hand one. Our barrages will continue to keep the ring but in any case neither the enemy's artillery nor his machine guns can fire into the ring without just as much chance of shooting his own men as shooting our's.

In this hand to hand fight our troops will be comparatively well fed, fit and fresh. These three advantages plus the advantage of each man meaning business and knowing what he means to do (while the enemy will be in confusion, all getting and giving different orders) and plus the acknowledged superiority of our own men in all hand to hand fighting (when they get the chance) should make the final result this afternoon a foregone conclusion.

5. Though the actual capture of the position may prove quite an easy task all ranks must remember that the German trenches will have been very badly knocked about: and that unless consolidation work is thoroughly during the night the captured positions will be uncomfortable and unhealthy tomorrow.

Maxwell

B.G.G.S.

"A" Form. Army Form C. 2121.

MESSAGES AND SIGNALS. No. of Message

Prefix........Code........m. | Words | Charge | This message is on a/c of: Offensive III Service. (Signature of "Franking Officer.") | Recd. at........m. Date........ From........ By........

Office of Origin and Service Instructions.

Sent At........m. To........ By........

TO Adjutant

Sender's Number: JC6 | Day of Month: 19th | In reply to Number | AAA

Following will be dispositions as soon as it is light AAA

B Coy — 2 Platoons & 2 Lewis guns holding 103 to 96
2 Platoons roughly about 64 & Lewis gun

A Coy — 2 Platoons about 80, 81, 91 2 Lewis guns
2 Platoons about 77, 88,

C Coy — 37 to 47 3 Lewis guns (when these get into position Company of 8Bn will go back & report at HQ 8Bn at X8C09

D Coy — To find accommodation in dug outs between 24 – 98 in German Old front line trench north of 05. (If there is room then also send two platoons of C Coy)

From
Place
Time

PTO

The above may be forwarded as now corrected. (Z)

Censor. Signature of Addressor or person authorised to telegraph in his name.

* This line should be erased if not required.

T. & W. & J. M. Ltd. London. W 14042/M44. 75,000 12/15. Forms C 2121/10.

MESSAGES AND SIGNALS. No. of Message

Prefix ______ Code ______ m. | Words | Charge

Office of Origin and Service Instructions.

Russel

Sent

At ______ m.

To ______

By ______

This message is on a/c of:

Appendix IV Service.

(Signature of "Franking Officer.")

Recd. at ______ m.

Date ______

From ______

By ______

TO { 5th Bn

Sender's Number	Day of Month	In reply to Number	AAA
* BM 33	19		

Push forward patrols to get touch with enemy as far (if possible) as X2A79 & X2A97. Report progress as soon as possible, & draw yellow screens.

* { You will hold trench X2A81 – X2C39 as far W as X2A51; 7th Bn will take beyond that.

* Col. Sladen Instructions

X { The ½ coy holding 80 81 & 91 will spread across to point X2'A51 & be in touch with 7th Bn. You will carry out the remainder of the above programme & report progress.

[illegible] [illegible]

X The starred paragraphs refer to each other

From No 3 [illegible] Bde Adv HQrs

Place

Time 7.00 am

The above may be forwarded as now corrected.

Censor.

(Z) P R [illegible] Major BM

Signature of Addresser or person authorised to telegraph in his name.

* This line should be erased if not required.

203146—W. & S. Ltd., London.—W 1780/1402—100,000—7/15 Forms C 2121/10.

"A" Form. Army Form C. 2121.

MESSAGES AND SIGNALS. No. of Message........

Prefix.........Code.........m.	Words	Charge	This message is on a/c of:	Recd. at.........m.
Office of Origin and Service Instructions.	Sent		Affidavy V Service.	Date........
	At.........m.			From........
	To........			
	By........		(Signature of "Franking Officer.")	By........

TO | OPERATION ORDER 57

Sender's Number	Day of Month	In reply to Number	AAA
*	19		

1) The 143rd Bde is moving its front to the left 1 Bay ~~[illegible]~~ of rifle.

2) The 5th Bn will move as follows to conform with this movement.

B Coy will hold from 76 exclusive, 56 – 46 – 25 – 16

A Coy from pt 64 – 22 in a single line
2 Platoons to be kept in dug-outs in old German front line 22 – 39.

C Coy 2 Platoons in trench from 81 – 39
2 Platoons in trench from 88 – 37

D Coy in reserve for carrying in dug-outs from 24 – 98.

3) All coys will wait for relief before moving out – Relief is to take place as speedily as possible.

Whenever the ~~[illegible]~~ points mentioned above are held by the 7th R[illegible]; the 7th will be relieved.

From
Place
Time

The above may be forwarded as now corrected. 6.40 pm

(Z) [illegible signature]

Censor. Signature of Addressor or person authorised to telegraph in his name.

* This line should be erased if not required.

T. & W. & J. M. Ltd., London. W 14042/M44. 75,000 12/15. Forms C 2121/10.

Return when read & clean.

SECRET.

Copy No. 3.....

143rd Inf. Bde. OPERATION ORDER NO. 82.

Ref. 1/5,000 trench maps.

19th August, 1916.

1. The Bde. will readjust its front this afternoon. On completion of this operation the Bde. front will run as follows:- X.2.b.4.8. (exclusive), X.2.b.0.6., X.2.a.9.6.-7.6.-7.9.-2.9.-1.9. thence along original British front to X.1.b.2.3.

2. In connection with the above the following movements will take place:-
(a) The 144th Inf. Bde. will relieve the 145th Inf. Bde. on our right, and at the same time will take over from the 6th Bn., up to the following line (inclusive to the 144th Inf. Bde.)
X.2.b.4.8.-4.4.-6.2., X.2.d.4.7.-4.5.-4.4., X.8.b.7.8.
The 6th Bn. will continue consolidating on this portion of their front after arrival of 144th Inf. Bde. and will not evacuate it until further instructions are received from the Div.

(b) The dividing line between 5th & 6th Bns. will be R.32.c.6.5., X.2.a.7.9.-7.6.-7.5. (all inclusive to the 6th Bn.) X.2.a.6.4.-8.1., X.2.c.8.8.-7.1., X.8.a.5.9.-4.5. (all inclusive to 5th Bn.)
The trench from X.2.a.6.4. to X.8.a.5.9. will be common to both Bns. for downward traffic only.

(c) The dividing line between 5th & 7th Bns. will be R.32.c.3.7., X.2.a.1.9. and thence along old German front line. (all inclusive to 5th Bn.) The Coy., 7th Bn., now holding right of this line is at disposal of O.C. 7th Bn. on completion of this alteration.

3. 6th Bn. will relieve garrison of two pls. 8th Bn. now in OVILLERS KEEP (X.8.b.0.2.-1.2.-0.1., X.8.a.9.1.-9.2.)
On completion of this relief Hdqrs. and 2 Cos. 8th Bn. now in OVILLERS defences will move to OVILLERS POST and this Bn. will cease to be available for carrying and working parties.

4. Times and details of all internal inter-bn reliefs will be settled by O.C.'s concerned.

B.Rickalley Major,
B.M. 143rd Inf. Bde.

Issued through Signals
at 3 p.m.
Copies to Bde units
48th Div.
7th Inf. Bde.
144th Inf. Bde.
Left Group R.A.

P.T.O

Arrange this with 6th & 7th Bns & come & see me

Bdy must be between 96–103 firstly 6 Bn

JB

P.T.O.

<u>B Coy hold</u>

~~2 Platoons~~

1st Line 76 exclusive – 56 – 46 – 25 – 16

A Coy

2nd Line 64 straight line across to 22

½ men in dugouts in old German front line between 22 – ~~[illegible]~~ 39 ~~& 91~~

C ~~D~~ Coy

3rd Line 81 – 39 2 Platoons

88 – 37 2 Platoons

dugouts at 81 & dugouts 39 – 38 & 37 – 77

D ~~2~~ Coy

Reserve for carrying.

in dugouts 24 – 98

Line to be held by strong points.

Better take the stream at 28 to 37 & not leave to 6 Bn unless 7 B are carrying a stream at 37

Operation Order 58

RELIEF.

(1) 5th R.War R will be relieved by 1/6th Gloucesters about 3.30 PM today.

(2) On completion of relief Batt will march by platoons at 100 yds distance to bivouacs at pt. W 8 C 8.4 (near BOUZINCOURT)

(3) Route via.

Along Tramway to OVILLERS POST

From OVILLERS POST → CRUCIFIX CORNER

then to W 16 b 7.2 thence by 2 forks back to BOUZINCOURT (same route as the Batt: took to come in)

(4) Lewis Guns

Lewis gun go-carts will be man-handled to OVILLERS POST ~~[illegible]~~, if the ~~carts~~ not ~~at OVILLERS~~, where pack ponies will be to help pull them to BOUZINCOURT.

Limbers for Lewis guns will be at entrance to OVILLERS on the road at pt. X 8 C 1.4.

122

(5) Mess cart will be at pt X8C 1.4 for Officers baggage etc and Officers chargers at same point.

J McCoomkey Capt Adj.
20.8.16.

2.15 pm.

S Thrape Acting OC D Coy

125

Appendix VI

SECRET. Copy No. 3

143rd Inf. Bde. OPERATION ORDER NO.83.

Ref. Trench maps 1/5,000
57D.S.E. 1/20,000.

20th August,1916

1. The Bde. (less 7th & 8th Bns. & M.G.Co.) will be relieved to-day by the 144th Inf. Bde. as soon after dinner as possible.

2. In connection with the above the following movements will take place:-

(a) 6th Bn. will be relieved by 7th Worc.Regt. & will proceed to
(b) 5th Bn. will be relieved by 6th Glouc. Regt. & will proceed to } W8C84
(c) Guns of T.M.Batt. will proceed, as relieved, to CRUCIFIX Corner, and march from there as a complete unit to bivouacs at V.12.b.70.35.

3. On completion of above reliefs, 7th & 8th Bns. & M.G.Co.(with attached guns of No. 4 M.M.G.Co. & of Hotchkiss Batt. Yorkshire Dragoons) will come under command of G.O.C. 144th Inf. Bde. who will assume command of the whole line.

4. Bde. Hdqrs. will be closed at GLOUCESTER POST, on completion of relief, and will reopen at V.12.b.70.35.

Issued through signals
at 12.30 p.m.

P R Nicholls
Major,
B.M. 143rd Inf. Bde.

Copies to Bde. units
48th Div.
7th Inf. Bde.
144th Inf. Bde.
No. 2 Co. Train.

5th Bn will provide platoon guides at X8C08 at 3 p.m.
Guns of T M Batt: will come out with your bn

X Will be notified later.

To Adj. Return this [illegible] [illegible] [illegible] [illegible] [illegible] it

Charles [illegible]
1.50 [illegible]
20.8.16

C.O. 5 abrank

Haj

"A" Form. Army Form C. 2121.

MESSAGES AND SIGNALS.

No. of Message

Prefix GM Code LE m.	Words 28 Charge	This message is on a/c of:	Recd. at m.
Office of Origin and Service Instructions. RE.	Sent At m. To By	A Hendry Service. (Signature of "Franking Officer.")	Date VII From By

TO { L G

Sender's Number	Day of Month	In reply to Number	AAA
* DM 22	18th		

Following received from GEN BIRDWOOD commanding 1st Anzac Corps aaa Well Done my hearty congratulations Ends.

From
Place LF
Time 11.25 pm

The above may be forwarded as now corrected. (Z)

Censor. Signature of Addressor or person authorised to telegraph in his name.

* This line should be erased if not required.

T. & W. & J. M. Ltd., London. W 14042/M44. 75,000 12/15. Forms C 2121/10.

48th Division.

143rd Inf. Bde.

The following wire received from Army Commander, Reserve Army is forwarded for your information:-

"Please congratulate all the troops who took part in yesterday's attack on their excellent performance. I was able to see the attack by the 143rd Inf. Bde. The way in which the infantry advanced into our barrage was beyond praise and reaped its reward. The artillery cooperation was also excellent and reflects great credit on all concerned. Please accept my best congratulations for yourself and all concerned."

19th August, 1916.

****

(1598) W. W 1539/M36 12/15. 100,000 Pads. S. B. Ltd.

"B" Form. Army Form C 2123.

MESSAGES AND SIGNALS.

No. of Message

Prefix SD Code ECSA m. Office of Origin and Service Instructions. KE — Words. 31	Received At m. From By	Sent At m. To By	Office Stamp. KE 19/8/16

TO LG

Sender's Number	Day of Month	In reply to Number	AAA
B1128	19		

The	CORPS	COMMANDER	considers	
that	the	division	have	done
very	well	and	wishes	all
ranks	to	be	informed	AAA
The	GOC	LA	cordially	endorse
this	statement			

From LF

Place

Time

...e should be erased if not required.

94/0

Appendix I.A

Map
Aug
First
Second
"Jump

Appendix I A

Map showing attack on August 18th 1916 —

First objective shown ● blue

Second ● red

"Jumping off" place 22–88 –

OVILLERS

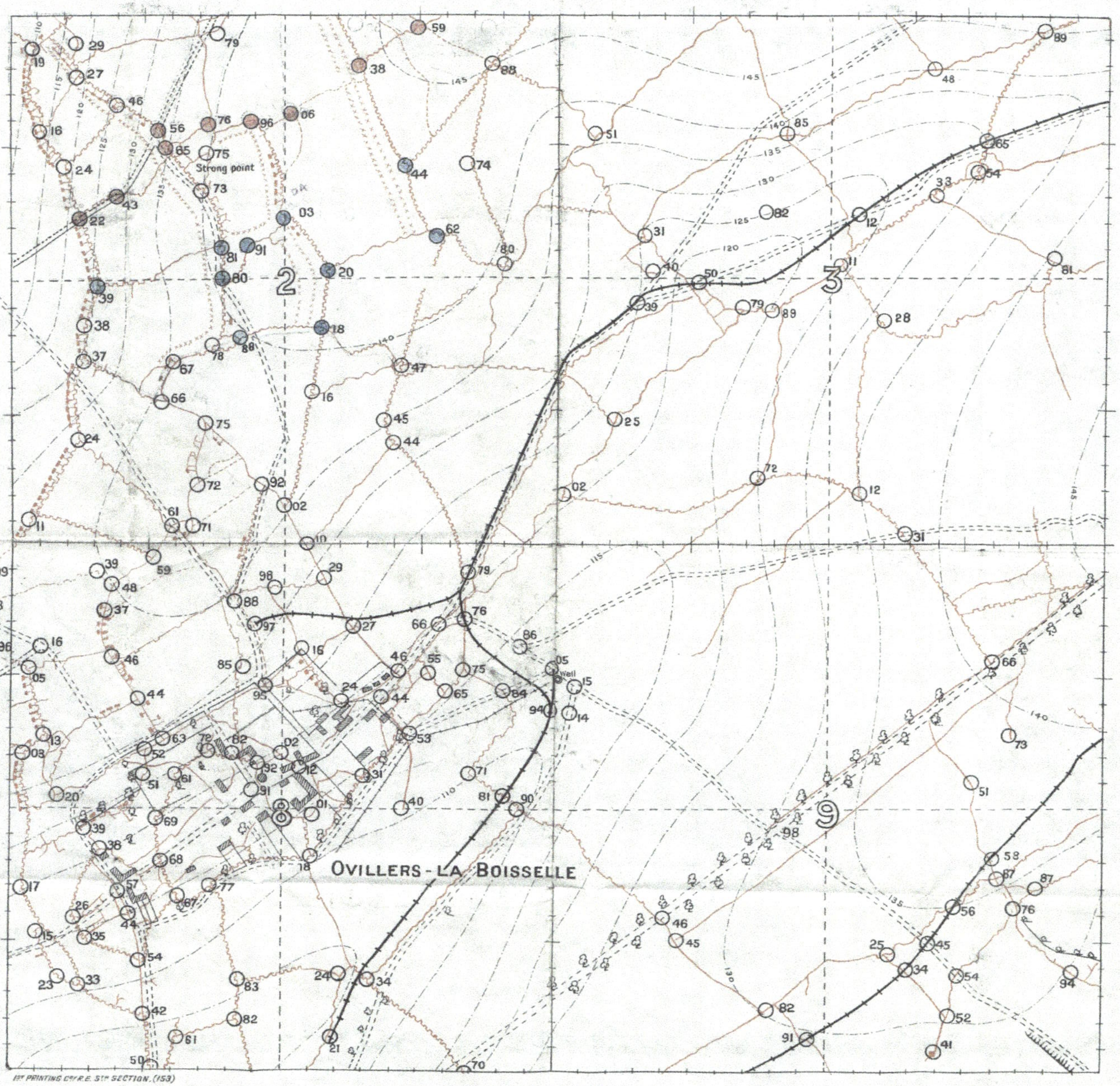

Scale-1:5,000.

Corrected on 14-8-16

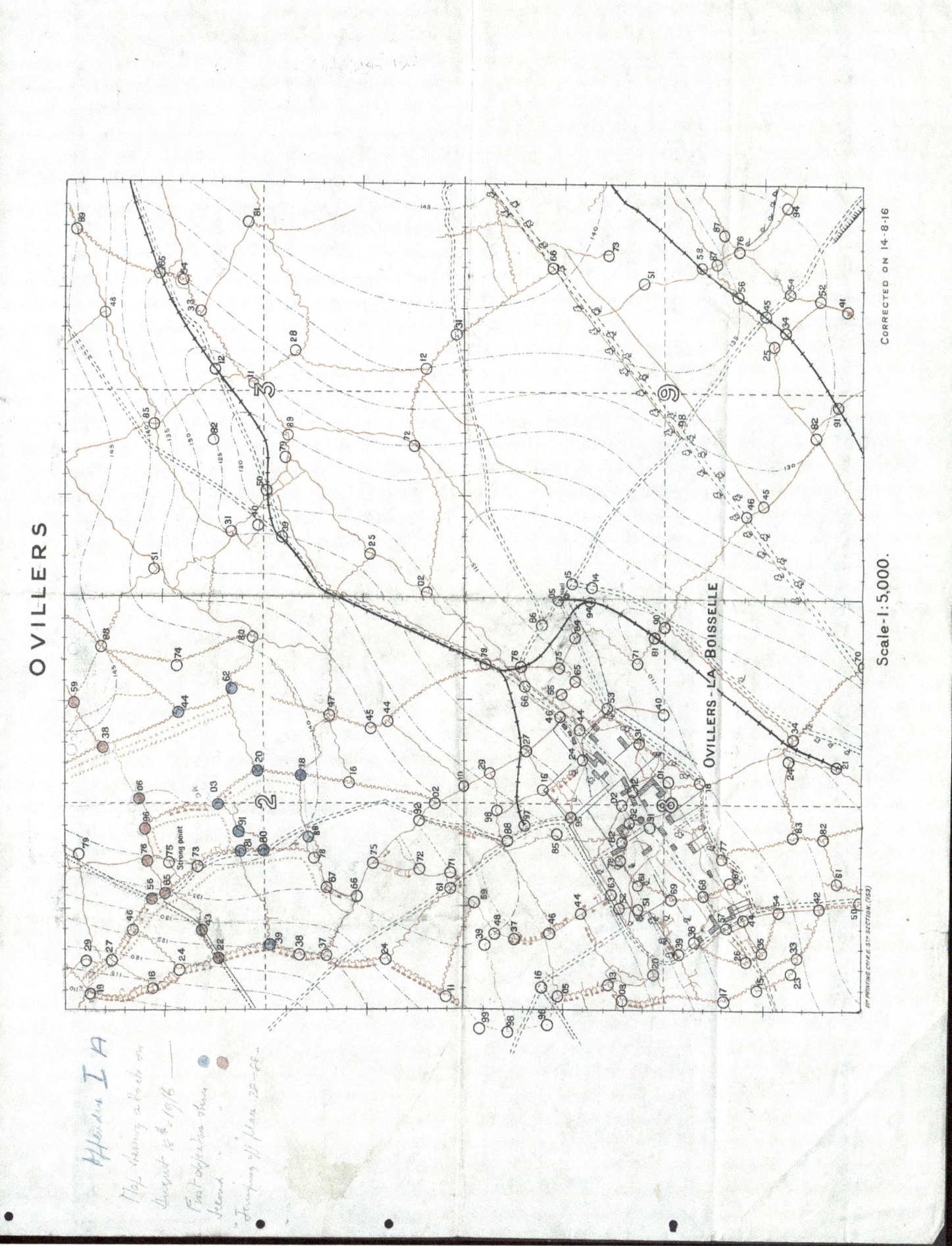

1 5 - 3 7 ~~7½~~ 1 . 16 . 9

~~4 9~~ 1 . 5 1

5 - 3 . 7

3 whs - 12 p

12 . ~~36~~ p . 1 4 9

5 - 3 . 7

1 12 3

48th. DIVISION

143rd. INFANTRY BDE.

1/5th. ROYAL WARWICKSHIRE REGT.

S E P T E M B E R   1 9 1 6.

Instructions regarding War Diaries and Intelligence Summaries are contained in F. S. Regs., Part II. and the Staff Manual respectively. Title pages will be prepared in manuscript.

WAR DIARY
or
INTELLIGENCE SUMMARY
(Erase heading not required.) September 1916

Army Form C. 2118.

1/5th BATT. R. WARWICKSHIRE REGT.

Place	Hour, Date (September)	Summary of Events and Information	Remarks and references to Appendices
Bois de WARNIMONT	2	Battn moved billets at SARTON	Ch
SARTON	4	Lt Col G.C. SLADEN. D.S.O. M.C. appointed to command of 143 Inf Bde. Major C. RETALLACK appt to command of Battn	Ch
	4	Battn inspected by G.O.C. Division (48th Div) 4 ORs arrived as reinforcements	Ch
	5	The undermentioned officers taken on strength of Battn – 2Lt A.J. FARRINGTON 2Lt W.G. LEES	Ch
	6	Battn inspected at training by the ARMY Commander (Reserve Army) 144 Ors medically or physically unfit inspected by Adjutant General The undermentioned officers taken on strength of Battn 2Lt H.L. HARCOURT. 2Lt F.S. WOOLLARD	Ch
	10	LIEUT. E. HOLT returned & taken on strength of Battn	Ch
	11	Battn moved to GEZAINCOURT as in OO. 59.	OO.59 – Ch
GEZAINCOURT	12	Reinforcements received – O.Rs. 129	A.S.G.
	14	The undermentioned officers taken on strength of batt. Maj A.W.F. PAULI 2nd Lieut L.T. O'HANLON K.O.S.B. 2nd Lt E.A. COCHRANE K.O.S.B. 2nd Lieut F.C. WATT K.O.S.B.	A.S.G.
		Reinforcements received 6 ORs	A.S.G.
	16	" " 16 ORs	A.S.G.
	17	" " 1 OR.	A.S.G.

1247 W 3299 200,000 (E) 8/14 J.B.C. & A. Forms/C. 2118/11.

Instructions regarding War Diaries and Intelligence Summaries are contained in F. S. Regs., Part II. and the Staff Manual respectively. Title pages will be prepared in manuscript.

WAR DIARY
or
INTELLIGENCE SUMMARY
(Erase heading not required.)

Army Form C. 2118.

1/5th BATT. R. WARWICKSHIRE REGT.

Hour, Date, Place	Summary of Events and Information	Remarks and references to Appendices
1916		
HEUZECOURT Sept 18.	Batt. moved to billets at HEUZECOURT & GRIMONT	O.O. 60 ASA
	The undermentioned officer taken on strength of Batt.	
	2nd Lieut Usher C.C. K.O.S.B.	A.SA.
22	Reinforcements received - 16 ORs.	A.SA.
28	Reinforcements received - 6 ORs.	ASA.
29	Batt moved to billets at HALLOY	ASA. O.O. 61
30	Batt moved to billets at SOUASTRE	OO. 62
	Strength of Batt Sept 30. 1916	
	Officers -- 35.	
	ORs -- 823.	

Charles [illegible] Lt Col
Cmdg 1/5 R Warwicks

1247 W 3299 200,000 (E) 8/14 J.B.C. & A. Forms/C. 2118/11.

OPERATION ORDERS No. 59. Copy No. 1....
BY
Lieut. Colonel C. RETALLACK,
Commdg. 1/5th Battn. Royal Warwickshire Regiment.
10th September 1916.

MAP REFERENCE.
SHEET II (LENS)

(1) The Brigade will move to GEZAINCOURT, to-morrow 11th Sept.

(2) Battns will move in artillery formation across country to the starting line mentioned in para. 3 (below). The 7th Bn. will move N of MARIEUX & the 6th Bn. S of MARIEUX.

(3) The Bde will cross the road, running from ORVILLE to BEAUQUESNE via two crossings over the tramway & the "A" of TERRAMESNIL, at 2.30 p.m., in the following order:-

5th Bn on the right. 7th Bn on the left.
8th Bn. behind the 5th. 6th Bn behind the 7th.

Bns will be formed in 2 lines of platoons at 50 yards interval & 300 yards distance. Intervals between Bns to be 100 yards & distances between Bns to be 600 yards.
The 5th & 8th Bns will direct.

(4) The 5th & 8th Bns will march with their right directed by the SARTON-DOULLENS road as far as FRESCHVILLERS whence they will move with their left directed on "Le Bon Air"

(5) The 5th R.War.R., conforming with the rest of the Brigade, will move in artillery formation across country from SARTON to the DOULLENS-LE BON AIR-BEAUVAL Road and from there along the LE BON AIR-GEZAINCOURT Road to GEZAINCOURT.

(6) The Battn. will fall in on the DOULLENS-SARTON Road, facing DOULLENS, with the head of the column opposite Hd.Qrs.Mess, ready to move off by 1 p.m.
Order of Route :- B, C, D, A.

(7) On leaving road by Church, the Battn. will deploy in Artillery formation, each coy in two lines of platoons at 50 yards interval & 300 yards distance.
Order from Right to Left:- B, C, D, A. "B" will be Coy. of direction

(8) Each Coy. will put out scouts who will march 200 yards ahead of their companies.

(9) Coys. are responsible for keeping communication from front to rear and left to right.

(10) The Lewis Gunners will march by road with the Brigaded Transport. Each Coy will send their guns, with one team per Coy. to report to T.O., at 1.30 p.m. The Lewis Gun Officer will be in charge.

(11) 2nd.Lieut.S.F.SNAPE, Coy.Q.M.Sergeants & Sergt.FLETCHER, will act as billeting party, and will meet the Staff Captain at the cross roads, by Hd.Qrs.Mess, SARTON at 10 a.m., 11th inst.
The Signalling Sergeant will arrange bicycles for this party.

(12) All Billets, Officers' quarters, etc., are to be left absolutely clean,

J H Crosskey

Issued at 8 p.m. Capt. & Adjutant.
10th Sept. 1916. 1/5th Battn. Royal Warwickshire Regiment.

No. 1	Copy.	War Diary.	No. 5	Copy.	C Coy.
" 2	"	"	" 6	"	D "
" 3	"	A Coy.	" 7	"	Signalling Officer.
" 4	"	B "	" 8	"	Transport "

NOTICES.

Officers kits & Mess Boxes will be dumped outside Coy.Hd.Qrs.by 12.30 p.m. & in charge of 1 servant per coy., and will be collected by the Transport before 12.45 p.m.

The Commanding Officer will see Coy.Commanders & Lewis Gun Officer at 9.30 a.m., to-morrow, 11th inst.

Copy No....1....

OPERATION ORDERS.
BY
Lieut.Colonel C. RETALLACK,
17th September,1916. NO. 60.

Ref: Map Sheet LENS II.

I. The 143rd Inf:Bde will march to-morrow,18th inst, to district round BERNAVILLE, the 5th Battn. moving to billets at HEUZECOURT & GRIMONT, by the route CANDAS - FIENVILLERS - BERNAVILLE.

II. The Battalion will fall in ready to move off at 8.30 a.m., on the road to LE BON AIR, facing SOUTH-WEST, with the head of the column at the cross roads 400 yards N.E., of the A in STA,(BAGNEUX) in the order C - D - A - B
The Transport will be drawn up on the BAGNEUX - BEAUVAL road, with its head on the cross road mentioned above, ready to move into the column after the Battalion.

III. New pattern Lewis Gun Hand-carts will be pulled by pack ponies behind their respective Coys. as usual; the old pattern ones will be brigaded in front of the Transport.

IV. The Coy.Q.M.Sergeants and the Signalling Sergt., under 2nd.Lieut.A.SHELDON will form the billeting party, and will meet the Staff Captain at the cross roads 400 yards N.E. of the A in STA,(BAGNEUX) at 7 a.m.
They will meet the Battalion, on arrival, at the cross roads, 400 yards South of the first E of HEUZECOURT at about 11.30 a.m.
The Signalling Sergeant will arrange bicycles for this party.

V. O.C. "D" Coy will find 8 men and a N.C.O., under an Officer, as rear party. This party will fall in in rear of the Brigade, and its duties are to collect all the Battalion's stragglers.

VI. The Sanitary squad,police & prisoners, and 1 N.C.O. and 7 men from the Coy. on duty, will stay behind as a cleaning up party, when the Battalion moves out to-morrow, and will follow as soon as their work is completed.
The Quartermaster will be in charge and will get a certificate from the Town Major that the billets are clean and in good order.

J H Cunkey
Capt. & Adjutant.
1/5th Battn.Royal Warwickshire Regiment.

Issued at 6 p.m.
17th Sept.1916.

NOTICES.

Caps will be worn,with steel helmet strapped on the back of the pack.
All mess-tins will be packed inside the valise, and no surplus luggage will be carried by the troops.
Officers' valises & Mess Boxes will be stacked on the main road outside Coy.Hd.Qrs, by 7.45 a.m.
O.C. Transport will arrange to have these collected before 8 a.m.
No one except the cleaning up party will be left off parade.
Para.VI in no way releases O.C. Coys. from the responsibility of seeing that they leave their billets and billeting areas clean and in good order.

Copy No.1	War Diary.	Copy No.5.	C Coy.
" " 2	" "	" " 6	D "
" " 3	A Coy.	" " 7	Signalling Sergt.
" " 4	B "	" " 8	Transport Officer & Quartermaster.

O P E R A T I O N   O R D E R S   No.61. Copy No..

B Y

Lieut.Colonel C.RETALLACK,

Commdg. 1/5th Battn.Royal Warwickshire Regt.

29th September 1916.

Ref: Map Sheet LENS II.

I. The 143rd Inf: Bde will march to-day to area MONDICOURT - GRENAS - HALLOY.

II. The 5th Bn. will fall in ready to move off at ~~10~~ 9.45 a.m. on the HEUZECOURT - LE MEILLARD Road, with the head of the column at the cross-roads South of the first E of HEUZECOURT, facing S.W., in the order - D, A, B, C.

III. The 1st Line Transport & baggage wagons will accompany the Battn.

IV. Packs will be dumped by 8.30 a.m., in the open space, South of the CHURCH, HEUZECOURT, by companies.
O.C. "D" Coy will detail an Officer, one N.C.O., & 6 men to remain as a loading party. The N.C.O. will meet 2/Lieut.YOUNG, attached 143rd Bde, at PROUVILLE CHURCH, at 1.45 p.m., and will wait there to conduct the lorries to the position of the packs.

V. The billeting party, consisting of 2/Lieut.A.SHELDON, the Coy.Q.M.S.s & Sergt.SHELDON., will go forward on bicycles and will meet the Staff Captain at the cross-roads by third E in L'ESPERANCE, ¾ mile N.E. of LE HALLOY at 12.20 p.m.

VI. Dinners will be cooked on route. There will be a halt at about 1 p.m., for dinners.

VII. The New pattern Lewis Gun Hand-carts will, as usual, be pulled by pack ponies in rear of their respective Coys.

VIII. O.C."C" Coy., will find one N.C.O. & 8 men, under an Officer, as rear party. This party will fall in at first behind the Battn.Transport and, at the Brigade rendezvous (the road junction W.of M in MEZEROLLES), behind the Brigade, the duties of the party being to collect any Battn.stragglers.

IX. The Sanitary Corpl, police & prisoners & one N.C.O. & 12 men from the Coy. on duty will stay behind as a cleaning up party when the Battn. moves out to-morrow, and will follow as soon as their work is completed.
The Quartermaster will be in charge and will see that all billets & the ~~xlxlx~~ vicinity of all billets are clean.

Issued at 5 a.m.
29th Sept. 1916.

J H Crosskey
Capt. & Adjt.
1/5th Battn.Royal Warwickshire Reg

N O T I C E S.

The men will march in Fighting Order, with Caps. The steel helmets will be left securely fastened to the packs.

Officers' Valises & Mess Boxes will be stacked in the village street, outside Coy.H.Q. by 8.30 a.m.

O.C.Transport will arrange to have these collected before 9.15 a.m.

Para.IX in no way releases O.C.Coys from the responsibility of seeing that they leave their billets & billeting areas clean and in good order.

No.one except the cleaning up party will be left off parade

Copy No 1.	War Diary	Copy No 5	C. Coy.
" 2	"	" 6	D "
" 3	A. Coy	" 7	Reg. Sergt. Major
" 4	B "	" 8	T.O. + Q.M.

Copy No 1.

OPERATION ORDERS.
BY
Lieut. Colonel C. RETALLACK.
30th September.1916. NO.62.

Ref. Map Sheet LENS III.

I. The 143rd Inf. Bde. will move to the area BAYENCOURT -SAILLY- SOUASTRE-ST AMAND.

II. The 5th Battn. will fall in ready to march at 10.50 a.m. on the main street HALLOY with the head of the column opposite the Church, facing South, in the order A.B.C.D. Transport.
The Transport will accompany the unit.

III. The billetting party consisting of the Coy. Q.M. Sgts. & Sgt. Sheldon under 2/Lt. E.A.COCHRANE will report to the TownMajor SOUASTRE at 12.30 p.m.

IV. Dinners will be cooked on route and will be ready for the troops immediately on arrival.

V. O.C. D. Coy will find 1 Officer, 1 N.C.O., and 8 men to act as rearparty and pick up stragglers. This party will march behind the Transport.

VI. The Sanitary Corporal, police & prisoners, & one N.C.O. & 12 men from the Coy. on duty will stay behind as a cleaning up party when the Battn. moves out and will folow as soon as their work is completed.
The Quartermaster will be in charge and will obtain a receipt from the Town Major that all billets are clean and in good order.

J.H. Crosskey

Issued at 8.15 a.m. Capt. & Adjt.
30th Sept. 1916. 1/5th Battn. Royal Warwickshire Regt.

NOTICES.

Dress Marching Order - Helmets are to be strapped on t packs.

Officers' Valises & Mess Boxes will be stacked in Main Street outside Coy Headqrs. by 9.15 a.m. and will be collected by the Transport before 10 a.m.

O.C. Coys. will see that all billets & billeting areas are clean and in good order before moving off.

No one except the cleaning up party will be left off parade.

Copies.

No 1 & 2 War Diary
No. 3-6 Companies.
No 7 Regt Sergt. Major.
No 8 Q. M. & Transport Officer.

143/48

Instructions regarding War Diaries and Intelligence Summaries are contained in F. S. Regs., Part II. and the Staff Manual respectively. Title pages will be prepared in manuscript.

WAR DIARY
or
~~INTELLIGENCE SUMMARY~~
(Erase heading not required.)

October 1916.

1/5 R Warwick Regt

Army Form C. 2118.

5TH BATT. R. WARWICKSHIRE REGT.

Vol 20

Hour, Date, Place	Summary of Events and Information	Remarks and references to Appendices
1916 Oct 1st HEBUTERNE	Batt relieved 2nd Argyle & Sutherland Highlanders in left of "W" Sector trenches	Ref O.O. 63 A.S.O.
Oct 2	Batt moved to a flank & took over trenches accordingly	Ref O.O. 64. A.S.O.
3.	1 O.R. wounded (at duty)	A.S.O.
4.	1 O.R. wounded ~~1 O.R. killed 1 O.R. missing~~ A.S.O.	A.S.O.
HEBUTERNE & FONQUEVILLERS. " 5	Batt relieved from part of line from K10 b 0.7 to K 3 d 90 05 (YUSSIF ST inclusive to 1/5 R. Berk R) by 145 Inf Brigade. On relief two companies moved to FONQUEVILLERS. Batt. HQ remained at HEBUTERNE.	A.S.O.
5	1 O.R. killed 1 O.R. missing	A.S.O.
ST AMAND 6.	Batt relieved by 1/7 R.War.R. & moved to billets at ST AMAND	Ref O.O 65 A.S.O.
7.	1 O.R. wounded. Reinforcements received - 3 O.Rs	A.S.O.
9	Undermentioned officers taken on strength of Batt. 2nd Lieut (temp Lieut) Williams, Gerald Whitfield 2nd Lt (temp Lieut) Orton Smith, Geoffrey Ewing 2nd Lieut Austin, George Elliot	A. S. Alabaster
18	Reinforcements received 5. O.Rs	A. S. Alabaster
GRAND RULLECOURT 20	Batt moved to billets at GRAND RULLECOURT	Ref O.O 66. A.S. Alabaster

20 T. (3 sheets)

1247 W 3299 200,000 (E) 8/14 J.B.C. & A. Forms/C. 2118/11.

Instructions regarding War Diaries and Intelligence Summaries are contained in F. S. Regs., Part II. and the Staff Manual respectively. Title pages will be prepared in manuscript.

WAR DIARY
or
~~INTELLIGENCE SUMMARY~~

(*Erase heading not required.*)

Army Form C. 2118.

Oct 1916

Hour, Date, Place	Summary of Events and Information	Remarks and references to Appendices
GRAND RULLECOURT Oct 24	Mounted portion 1/5 R. WAR. R moved to bivouacs in the TALMAS area	Ref O.O. 67. A.S.A.
FRANVILLERS. Oct 25.	HQs & unmounted portion 1/5 R. War R. moved by motor buses to billets at FRANVILLERS	Ref O.O. 68 A.S.A.
	Mounted portion moved by route march to FRANVILLERS	A.S.A.
BECOURT " 26	Batt. marched to tents at BECOURT Reinforcement received 1 Officer 2nd Lieut WHITE J.	A.S.A. Ref O.O. 69
MAMETZ WOOD 27	Batt. & portion of Transport marched to tents immediately S.E of MAMETZ WOOD Remainder of transport remained at BECOURT	O.O. 70 A.S.A.
28	Working parties found The following reinforcements received:— 10. O.Rs. The transport from BECOURT rejoined Batt: at MAMETZ WOOD	A.S.A.
28 – 31 both inclusive	Working parties found each day for road making	A.S.A.
	Strength Oct 31. 1916 Officers = 35 ORs = 832	

Charles Retallack
Comdg 1/5 R. Warwicks
Lt Col

1247 W 3299 200,000 (E) 8/14 J.B.C. & A. Forms/C. 2118/11.

COPY NO. 1

OPERATION ORDERS.

BY

Lieut. Colonel C.RETALLACK.

1st October, 1916. NO.63.

Ref. Map Sheet ~~LENS I.~~ 57 D NE 1:20,000.

I. The 143rd Inf. Bde. will relieve the 98th Inf. Bde in "W sector from K. 11.c.2.0 to K.10.a.7.9.

II. The 5th Battn. Royal Warwickshire Regt. will relieve the 2nd Bn. Argyll & Sutherland Highlanders on 1st October in the left Battalion Sector.

III. Companies will move from SOUASTRE with half an hours intervals and will march by platoons at 100 yards distance. The first Company will pass the road junction D. 22.c. 5.1. at 1.p.m.
Route BAYENCOURT - SAILLY - AU - BOIS.

IV. Order of March D.C.B.A. Battn. Headqrs will march with A Coy - Dress Marching Order. Men will wear their steel helmets.

V. Guides will meet the Companies at Brigade Headqrs in SAILLY- AU - BOIS ~~K.18a.5.6.~~ K18a5.6.

VI. Companies will be disposed as follows:-

Right Front	Coy.	C.
Left	"	D.
Support	"	B.
Reserve	"	A.

VII. Coy. Commanders will meet at Hqrs. Mess billet No. 72 (mounted) at 10.0. a.m. for reconnoitring the line. The Signalling Sgt. and 2 orderlies will also be there with bicycles, at the same time.

VIII. 1st Line Transport will move to COIGNEUX under O.C. Transport.

IX. On Relief signed receipts will be given by each Coy. for all stores take over. This receipt will be sent with the Adjutant by 6 pm tomorrow night.

J H Cornkey

Issued at 11.0pm. Capt & Adjutant.
30.9.16. 1/5th Battn. Royal Warwickshire Regt.

NOTICES.

Officers Mess Boxes will be dumped outside Billet No.72 before 1.45 p.m. and will be collected from there by the Mess Cart which will follow the last platoon. One Servant per Coy. may be left in charge of these boxes.
Officers valises & surplus mess boxes will be dumped outside Coy. Hqrs. by 11.15 a.m. and collected by Transport before 12 noon, for removal to Q.M.Stores.
All billets & billeting areas are to be left clean.

Nos	1 & 2.	War Diary.
"	3 - 6	Companies.
"	7.	R.Sgt. Major.
"	8.	Transport.O. & Q.M.

Copy No. 1....

OPERATION ORDERS.

BY

Lieut. Colonel C.RETALLACK. NO.64.

Commdg. 1/5th Battn. The Royal Warwickshire Regiment.

2nd October, 1916.

Ref. Map Sheet. 57 D. NE.

I. The 143rd Inf. Bde will take over from the 148th Inf. Bde. (49th Division) that part of 'Y' Sector from their present Southern boundary up to and including K. 3 d. 25.~~49~~ 40.

II. After relief the boundary between 48th & 49th Divisions will be K.3d.25.40. - JUNCTION OF SIXTH AVENUE and KELLERMAN (inclusive to 49th Division) FORT - DICK - CHATEAU de la HAIE (both inclusive) to 48th Division).

III. The relief will be carried out as follows:-
'A' Company and 1 Platoon of B under O.C. A Company will take over from 1/4th YORK & LANCS the portion of the line from their present boundary to K. 3 d.25.40. inclusive.
Arrangements for relief to be made direct between O.Cs concerned.
Relief to be completed by 6 a.m. 3rd October. O.C. 'A' Company will report relief as soon as it is completed
One Company 6th R.War.R. will take over dispositions of 'A' Company 1/5th R.War.R. in HEBUTERNE, arriving in the village about 5.30 p.m.
8th Battn R.War.R. After relief of the 4th Suffolks in right bn section of W Sector their left will be extended to YANKEE STREET inclusive. O.C. 8th Battn. will make arrangements with O.C. 5th Battn. for taking over this portion of his line.
Details will be sent to O.C. 'C' Company.

IV. The relief by the 8th R.War.R. in the portion of trench to the right of YANKEE STREET will be completed before 12 noon.
Immediately after the completion of this relief the 5th Battn. line will be readjusted as follows:-

'D' Company on the Right.
'C' " in " Centre.
'A' " on " Left.
'B' " in Support.

1 Company 1/6th R.War.R. in reserve in HEBUTERNE.

V. Company Commanders will be at Headquarters to meet the C.O. at 7.30 a.m. tomorrow to arrange the exact disposition of of their respective Companies.

Issued at
2nd October, 1916.

J H Carnkey
Capt. & Adjt.
1/5th Battn. The Royal Warwickshire Regt.

Copy No.1	War Diary.	Copy No.7.	Regtl. Sgt. Majr.
" " 2.	" "	" " 8.	Transport O. & QM
Copies 3-6.	Companies.		

COPY NO. 1.

O P E R A T I O N O R D E R S.
BY
Lieut. Colonel C. RETALLACK. No. 65
Commdg. 1/5th Battn. The Royal Warwickshire Regt.
5th October. 1916.

Ref. Map Sheet 57 D.NE. 1/20,000,

I. The 5th Battn will be relieved in the trenches from K. 3 d.9.0½. (YUSSIF STREET inclusive to K. 3d.2.5 and in FONQUVILLERS, by the 1/7th R.War.R., On relief the Battn. will march to ST. AMAND by the route - THORP STREET - FONQUVILLERS - CEMETERY ROAD- marked track (Dummy Gun Route) meeting the FONQUVILLERS - SOUASTRE -- ~~ST. AMAND~~ ROAD at D. 24 c - SOUASTRE - ST. AMAND.

II. Companies will march independently - platoons are to be at 200 yards distance, Special attention is to be paid to march discipline.

III. O.C. Companies will arrange to have 1 guide per platoon at Artillery Cross Roads, FONQUVILLERS at 1.30 p.m. to guide the Companies of the 1/7th R.War.R. The first Company will relieve "A" Company in the line, the 2nd "B" Company, and the 3rd and 4th "C" & "D" in FONQUVILLERS.

IV. O.C.Companies will send their Quartermaster Sgts. on in advance to arrange billets. They will report to the Quartermaster at ST. AMAND before 11 a.m. and take over the billets of the 1/7th R.War.R.

V. The Lewis Guns of "A" and "B" Companies will go the shortest way by road from HEBUTERNE with the Transport.

VI. The usual receipts for trench stores and certificates that the line is clean and in good order will be obtained and sent in to the Orderly Room on arrival at ST. AMAND.

Issued at
5.10.16. Capt. & Adjt.
1/5th Battn. The Royal Warwickshire Regt.

N O T I C E S.

O.C.Transport will arrange the following:-

I. Officers' chargers to be at Artillery Cross Roads FONQUVILLERS at 2.30 p.m.

II. "A" and "B" Coys. cookers)
Limber for Hqrs. Mess.)
~~Signallers for Coy. Messes A-B~~)
Limber for Coy. Messes A & B) To be at HEBUTERNE
Signallers & Pioneers Boxes) at 1 30. p.m.
Horse for Medical Cart.)
Pack ponies for Lewis Gun)
Carts of "A" & "B" Coys.)

III. Cooker horses "C" & "D" Coys.)
Pack ponies for Lewis Gun)
Carts "C" & "D") To be at FONQUVILLERS
Mess Cart for Officers' Messes) at 1.30. p.m.
"C" and "D")

Copies 1 & 2 War Diary.
" 3 to 6 Companies.
Copy 7 R.S.M.
" 8 T.O. and Q.M.

COPY NO....I........

OPERATION ORDERS. NO.66.

BY

Captn. A.S. ALABASTER, M.C.

Commdg. 1/5th Battn. The Royal Warwickshire Regiment.

19th October, 1918.

Map Ref. Sheet Lens11.

I. The 143rd Brigade Group will move tomorrow 20th inst. the 1/5th R.Warwickshire.R. moving to GRAND RULLECOURT. Route. GAUDIEMPRE - SAULTY - SOMBRIN.

II. The Battalion will fall in ready to move off by 2.25p.m. in the village street ST. AMAND facing S.W. with the head of the column opposite the Orderly Room in the order "B", "C", "D", "A".
The Transport will draw in behind the Battalion at the Transport Lines.

III. The Company Q.M. Sergts. and Sergt. SHELDON will report at 10.0.a.m. to 2/Lieut.COCHRANE and will form the billetting party. This party will report to the Staff Captain at the Church at GRAND RULLECOURT at 12 noon tomorrow (20th instant). O/C Signals will arrange bicycles for this party.

IV. All blankets will be rolled by tens and dumped in the gateway of the Headquarters Mess yard by 10.30.a.m. Each roll of blankets is to be carefully labelled. O.C. "D" Company will detail a Loading party of 1 N.C.O and 12 men which will be ready to load the lorries at 11.0.a.m. The Police Sgt. will report at Brigade Hqrs. at 11.0.a.m. and will guide the lorry to the Battalion dump.

V. O.C. "D" Company will detail 1 officer, 1 N.C.O. and 8 men to act as a rear party. This party will fall in behind the Battalion Transport and will pick up all stragglers.

VI. All billets and billetting areas will be cleaned up before the Battalion moves and a certificate to this effect sent in signed by Company Commanders before 2.p.m. to the Quartermaster.who will arrange to get a receipt from the Town Major.

J H Cronkey

Issued at 19/10/18. Capt. & Adjt.
1/5th Battalion. The Royal Warwickshire Regiment.

NOTICES.

1. Full Marching order will be worn. Men will wear their steel helmets.
2. All officers valises will be dumped outside Coy. Hqrs by 12.30.p.m. ready for removal by the Transport. O.C. Transport will arrange to collect these before 1.p.m.
3. Officers Mess boxes will be ready outside Company Hqrs. by 1.p.m. and will be collected 1.30.p.m.
4. Dinners for the troops will be at 12 noon. Cookers are to be ready for the road at 1.p.m.
Water will be boiled for tea en route.

Copy	1 & 2.	War Diary.
"	3 - 6.	Companies.
"	7.	Q.M. and T.O.
"	8.	Sig. O. & Sgt. Major.

COPY NO....../....

OPERATION ORDERS. NO.67.
BY
Captn. A.S.ALABASTER.M.C.
Commdg. 1/5th Battn. The Royal Warwickshire Regiment.
23rd October, 1916.

I. The mounted portion of the 1/8th Battalion, The Royal Warwickshire Regiment will move tomorrow under arrangements of 2/Lieut.L.ECKERSLEY at 9.30.a.m.

II. All riding horses, 1st Line Transport, Lewis Guns Carts complete with guns etc., and billeting party, will constitute the mounted portion of the Battalion. The 24 men (6 men per Company) detailed by the O.C. Lewis Guns will parade on the Transport Field with their handcarts at 8.45.a.m. tomorrow. O.C. Lewis Guns will see that the party are all in order.

III. O.C. Companies will each detail 1 Sergeant to report to 2/LieutG.de J. PEGLER at Headquarters at 9.15.a.m. tomorrow, Sergeant SHELDON will go from H.Q. and report at same time.. O.C. Signals will arrange bicycles for this party.
This party is to bivouac for the night of the 24th - 25th with the Brigaded transport, and will be at the Church in FRANVILLERS at 11.a.m. on the 25th instant where they will await the arrival of the Staff Captn.

IV. The dismounted portion of the Battalion will be moved in motor busses on 25th instant - busses are expected to arrive in the present Brigade area at about 7.30 a.m. Detailed orders will be issued later.

V. Lorries will be provided to accompany busses to carry officers' kits, rations, dixies etc.,

J.H. [signature]
Capt. & Adjutant.
1/8th Battn. The Royal Warwickshire Regt.

Issued at 8.15.p.m.
23/10/16.

Copies 1 & 2 - War Diary.
3 - 6 - Companies.
7 - T.O. & Q.M.
8 - Reg. Sgt. Major.

COPY NO..1....

OPERATION ORDERS. No. 68.
BY
Captn.A.S.ALABASTER.M.C.
Commdg 1/5th Battn. The Royal Warwickshire Regiment.
24th October, 1916.

I. The 143rd Infantry Brigade will move by motor bus tomorrow 25th instant the 1/5th Battn. The Royal Warwickshire Regiment/going to FRANVILLERS.

II. The Battalion will fall in on the road outside Headquarters ready to move off at 11.a.m. in the order "D", "C", "B", "A", with the head of the column facing S.E.

III. Each Company should be told off into parties of 20 ready for getting on the buses.

IV. Each man will carry his own blanket to use during the motor drive.

V. All Officers' Valises, mess boxes, and men's cooking degschies will be at Battalion Headquarters punctually by 8.30.a.m. for loading in the lorry.

J H Crockey
25/10/16.
Issued at 9.30.p.m. Capt. & Adjutant.
1/5th Battn. The Royal Warwickshire Regt.

NOTICE.

O.C. Companies will render a certificate by 10.15a.m. that all billets and billeting areas are clean and in good order to the Quartermaster, who will give a Certificate to this effect to the Town Major.

Blankets will be ~~folded~~ rolled and strapped on the ~~back~~ top of the packs.

Copies. 1 & 2 - War Diary
" 3 - 6 - Companies.
" 7 - Quartermaster.
" 8 - Regtl. Sgt. Major.

COPY NO..........

OPERATION ORDERS. No.69.

by

Lieut. Colonel C.RETALLACK.

Commdg. 1/5th Battn. The Royal Warwickshire Regiment.

26th October, 1916.

Ref: Sheet AMIENS.

1. The 1/5th R.War.R., will move to BECOURT to-day, 26th inst.

2. The Battn., including Transport, will fall in ready to move off at 10 a.m., on the main street, FRANVILLERS, with the head of the column at the junction of the FRANVILLERS-BEHENCOURT and the FRANVILLERS-BAZIEUX Roads, facing N, in the order: ~~D-A-B-C~~-Transport. D-A-B-C-

3. All blankets will be rolled by Sections and dumped at Orderly Room, labelled, by 8.30 a.m., where a lorry will pick them up.
   17 Platoon will find a loading party of 1 N.C.O. and 12 men, who will report at Battn. H.Q., at 8.30 a.m. 15 Regt S.M.

4. The Coy. Q.M.Sergts., and Sergt.SHELDON will report, with bicycles, at the Orderly Room to 2nd.Lieut. E.A.COCHRANE, at 9.30 a.m.
   This party will form the billetting party and will meet the Staff Captain at BECOURT at 11 a.m.

Issued at 1 a.m.
26th October 1916.

J.H.Cranley [signature]
Capt. & Adjt.
1/5th Battn.Royal Warwickshire Regiment.

Copies	1 & 2.	War Diary.
"	3 - 6.	Coys.
"	7.	T.O. & Q.M.
"	8.	Sergt.Major.

NOTICES.

O.C. Coys., will render a certificate that all billets etc., are clean by 9.30 a.m. to the Quartermaster, who will hand over to the Town Major.

Officers Valises will be dumped outside Coy. H.Q., by 8.30 am, ready for removal by transport before 9.15 a.m.

Officers Mess boxes will be at the same places by 8.45 a.m., and will be picked up before 9.30 a.m.

COPY NO....I.......

OPERATION ORDERS. NO.70.
BY
Lieut.Colonel C.RETALLACK.
Commdg. 1/5th Battn. The Royal Warwickshire Regiment.
26th October, 1916.

---

1. The 1/5th R.War.R. will move to MAMETZ WOOD tomorrow 27th instant.

II. Companies will move from the Camp as under:-
"A" COY. 5.15.a.m. "B" COY. 5.25.a.m.
"C" COY. 5.35.a.m. "D" COY. 5.45.a.m.
Companies will march to road junction at point S.13.b. 05 by the route BECOURT - LA BOISSELLE - CONTALMAISON. At point S.13.b. 05 the Battalion will form up on the NORTH Side of the CONTALMAISON - BEZENTIN LE PETIT ROAD.

III. At point S.13.b. 05 guides from the R.E. will meet Companies and show them what work is to be done on the CONTALMAISON - BEZANTIN - LE PETIT ROAD.
Companies will work from 7.a.m. - 11.a.m. and 12 noon - 2.30.p.m. After this they will move to bivouacs.

IV. Lewis Gun handcarts and guns will be left with the Transport at BECOURT with sufficient men to bring them on when required.

V. Sgt. SHELDON and the Company Q.M. Sgts. with bicycles will act as bivouac party and will meet 2/Lieut. E.A. COCHRANE at the church, CONTALMAISON at 9.a.m. They will leave the camp at 6.30.a.m. and meet their Coys. at work at 2.p.m. and guide them to bivouacs.

VI. All blankets will be rolled and left in one dump by 4.45.a.m. under a police guard at the ~~North~~ SOUTH Side of the Camp.

VII. The Transport will move as under:-
(a) The tool wagons will proceed with "A" Company at 5.15.a.m.
(b) Cookers:-
Officers Mess Cart.
Officers Valise Wagon. } will
Water Carts.
move at 8.30.a.m. to S.13.b. 05. under 2/Lieut C.C.USHER.
(c) The remainder of the Transport will await orders at BECOURT.

VIII. All Details including 17 Platoon, Signallers, Drummers etc., will parade with their Companies.

IX. Breakfast for the troops will be at 4.a.m. Dinners will be cooked en route and will be ready by 11.a.m. when Cookers will have arrived at S.13.b.05.

Issued at 10.30.p.m.
26th October, 1916.

J.H. Cankey
Capt. & Adjutant.
1/5th Battn. The Royal Warwickshire Regt.

Copies 1 & 2 - War Diary. Copy.7. - T.O. & Q.M.
" 3 - 6 - Companies. " 8.- Reg. Sgt. Major.

NOTICE.

Each Coy. will leave one servant to see that all officers valises and mess boxes are put on the Transport.

Vol II No 11

WAR DIARY
or
~~INTELLIGENCE SUMMARY~~ 1/5 R.WAR.R.
(Erase heading not required.) Nov. 1916 Vol 21

Army Form C. 2118.

143/48

Instructions regarding War Diaries and Intelligence Summaries are contained in F. S. Regs., Part II. and the Staff Manual respectively. Title pages will be prepared in manuscript.

Hour, Date, Place		Summary of Events and Information	Remarks and references to Appendices
BECOURT	Nov 1.	Batt with transport marched to huts & tents in the BECOURT area	A. S.A.
CONTALMAISON.	" 2.	Batt. less transport marched to tents in the CONTALMAISON Area; transport remained at BECOURT	A. S.A.
		Reinforcements received = 1. OR.	A. S.A.
	" 3	Working party 200 strong found for road repair	A. S.A.
	" 4.	Transport moved to ~~CHEAP~~ ~~Woods~~ CHAPES ~~WOOD~~ SPUR.	A. S.A.
	" 5	Working parties for carrying & hut building found.	A. S.A.
	" 6	" " for road repair &c found.	A. S.A.
	7.	Reinforcements received = 33 O.R.s.	A. S.A.
	8	Working parties found	A. S.A.
LE SARS	9	Batt relieved 1/4 Batt ~~[illegible]~~ GLOSTER Regt in Outpost line from M16d78. to M16a.3.9. (Ref Map ~~[illegible]~~ 57C SW.	O.O. 71. A.S.A.
		Reinforcements received = 5. O.R.s	
		Casualties 4 ORs wounded	A. S.A.
	10	" Killed = 2. ORs. Wounded = 10. ORs	A. S.A.
MARTINPUICH	11	Batt. relieved by 1/6 R.WAR.R moved back into Support in trenches N & N.E. of MARTINPUICH	A. S.A.
		Casualties Wounded = 6. ORs (1 since died) Killed = 2 ORs	A.S.A.

1247 W 3299 200,000 (E) 8/14 J.B.C. & A. Forms/C. 2118/11.

Volume II No 11

Army Form C. 2118.

WAR DIARY
or
~~INTELLIGENCE~~ SUMMARY 1/5 R. WAR. R

(Erase heading not required.)

Nov. 1916

Instructions regarding War Diaries and Intelligence Summaries are contained in F. S. Regs., Part II. and the Staff Manual respectively. Title pages will be prepared in manuscript.

Hour, Date, Place 1916		Summary of Events and Information	Remarks and references to Appendices
MARTINPUICH Nov	12	Batt found working parties strength about 350 for work in neighbourhood of LE SARS.	A.S.C.
	13	Working parties about 150 found	A.S.C.
		Casualties: Wounded = 1. OR.	A.S.C.
VILLA CAMP CONTALMAISON	14	Batt relieved by 1/4 R Berks & moved back to bivouacs between BEZANTIN LE PETIT & CONTALMAISON	A.S.C.
		Casualties = nil.	
	14	Reinforcements received :-	
		Capt J. R. WHARTON 5. R. WAR. R.	
		2nd Lieut C. L. GORDON 6(Res) SEAFORTH HIGHLANDERS	A.S.C.
	16	Working parties found ?	A.S.C.
	17	Decrease of strength	
		Capt J.R. WHARTON transferred to 2/5 R.WAR.R.	A.S.C.
		Reinforcements received 4. ORs	A.S.C.
		Casualties Killed = 3 OR. Wounded 2nd Lieut G.E. AUSTIN (at duty)	
		Wounded = 4. ORs (1 at duty).	A.S.C.
		Working parties found strength about 200	A.S.C.
	18	Reinforcements received = 9 ORs	A.S.C.
		Working parties found =	A.S.C.

1247 W 3299 200,000 (E) 8/14 J.B.C. & A. Forms/C. 2118/11.

Volume II No 11

WAR DIARY
or
~~INTELLIGENCE SUMMARY~~ 1/5 R. WAR. R.

(Erase heading not required.)

Nov 1916

Army Form C. 2118.

Instructions regarding War Diaries and Intelligence Summaries are contained in F. S. Regs., Part II. and the Staff Manual respectively. Title pages will be prepared in manuscript.

Hour, Date, Place	Summary of Events and Information	Remarks and references to Appendices
1916		
PIONEER CAMP CONTALMAISON Nov 19	Batt, less 1 Coy & transport at BECOURT, moved to huts at PIONEER CAMP CONTALMAISON. Working parties found	A. S.G.
20	Outlying company rejoined Batt at CONTALMAISON. Working parties = 400 ORs found	A.S.G.
21	Working parties found	A. S.G.
22	Reinforcements received = Capt O.W. SICHEL, Capt. F.H. HUMBY	
	Working parties found	A. S.G.
23	Working parties found	A.S.G.
LE SARS 24	Batt. Relieved the 1/4 Glosters in front line trenches from M16d7.8 to M16a.39. Casualties = 3 ORs wounded	O.O. 72 A.S.G. Ref Map 57C. S.W.
25	Reinforcements received = 4 ORs	A.S.G.
	Casualties, - Wounded = 2 ORs (1 since died of wounds)	A. S.G.
26	Reinforcements received = 4 ORs	A.S.G.
	Casualties, - Wounded = 1 OR	A. S.G.
27	Casualties Killed = 3 ORs, Wounded = 4 ORs	A. S.G.
MARTINPUICH 28	Batt relieved in the front trenches by 1/6 R. WAR R & moved back to dugouts &c in MARTINPUICH & trenches N of MARTINPUICH	Ref O.O. 73 A. S.G.
	Casualties Wounded = 2 ORs.	A. S.G.

Volume II No 11.

Instructions regarding War Diaries and Intelligence Summaries are contained in F. S. Regs., Part II. and the Staff Manual respectively. Title pages will be prepared in manuscript.

WAR DIARY
or
~~INTELLIGENCE~~ SUMMARY
(Erase heading not required.)

1/5 R. WAR. R

Nov. 1916

Army Form C. 2118.

Hour, Date, Place 1916	Summary of Events and Information	Remarks and references to Appendices
MARTINPUICH Nov 29	Carrying party 50. ORs found to LE SARS	A. S.G.
	Casualties Wounded = 1 O.R.	A. S.G.
30	Working parties found	A. S.G.
	Casualties – Wounded = 1 O.R.	A.S.G.
	Strength of Batt. Nov. 30. 1916 Officers = 28 O.Rs = 723	

Charles Pelatlack Lt Col
Comdg 1/5 R War R

1247 W 3299 200,000 (E) 8/14 J.B.C. & A. Forms/C. 2118/11.

COPY NO. 1

OPERATION ORDERS NO. 71.

by

Lieut.Colonel C.RETALLACK,
Commdg. 1/5th Battn. Royal Warwickshire Regt.
8th November 1916.

Ref: Map. 1/40,000 ALBERT COMBINED SHEET.
1/10,000 LE SARS SHEET.
1/10,000 48 Div.SECRET Map Edn.1.

1. The 143 Brigade will relieve the 144th & 145th Bdes of their front & support Battalions. After relief the 143 Bde will hold the front from M.16.d.7.8. to M.15.a.9.8.
2. Relief will take place as under:-
   On 9th November.
   5th Bn.R.Warwicks will relieve 4th Bn.Glo'ster Regt. in front line from M.16.d.7.8. to M.16.a.3.9..
   5th Bn.will march from present position, with 200 yards interval between platoons, via CONTALMAISON-Cross roads X.6.c.7.3.-MARTINPUICH. Leading platoon to be at cross roads X.6.c.7.3. at 5 p.m.
   Platoon guides & 1 guide for Bn.Hdqrs from 4th Glo'sters will meet Bn at N.E.end of MARTINPUICH M.27.c.3.1.
   Coys. will march off in the following order : B-D-A-C.
   The leading platoon of "B" Coy will pass Bn.H.Q., at 3.30 p.m.
3. Coys. will be disposed as follows:-
   B on the right.
   D on the left.
   A in Support.
   C in Reserve.
4. Packs, Blankets & Overcoats will not be taken to the trenches. Detailed orders about stacking these will be issued later.
5. Battalions taking over the front line trenches will carry on the men rations for 48 hours.
6. All trench stores, maps, photographs etc., will be taken over on relief.
7. Bns.of 143 Bde will take over from Bns they relieve, all work in hand, and this work is to be carried on until other orders are received.
8. Completion of reliefs will be reported immediately to Battn.H.Q
9. O.C.Transport will make arrangements to take Coy.Cookers back to the Transport lines, one cook per company & the Sgt.Master Cook will remain with the Cookers, the remainder will return to duty with their Coys.
10. The following inter-company relief will take place on the evening of the 10th, under arrangements made direct between Coy.Commanders:-
    A Coy. will relieve B Coy.
    C " will relieve D "
    B " will go into Support.
    D " will go into Reserve.
    One Officer for "A" & "C" Coys will reconnoitre the right & left front line respectively early on the morning of the 10th inst.
    The Battn. will be relieved by 6th R.War.R. on night of 11th, and will then go into support.

J.H. Crankey [signature] J. Herasakey [signature]
Capt.& Adjt.
1/5th Battn.Royal Warwickshire Regiment.

Issued at 8.30 a.m.
9th November 1916.

Copies 1 & 2 War Diary. Copy No.7 TBD & Q.M.
" 3 - 6 Companies. " " 8 Reg.Sergt.Major.

NOTICES.

All tents and the whole camp area must be left absolutely clean.
Arrangements for Officers' Valises, surplus mess boxes, etc., will be notified later.

Copy No....1....

O P E R A T I O N   O R D E R S   No.72.

B Y

Lieut.Colonel C.RETALLACK

Commdg. 1/5th Battn. Royal Warwickshire Regt.

23rd November 1916.

Ref:Maps 1/40,000 ALBERT COMBINED SHEET.
1/10,000 LE SARS SHEET.
1/10,000 48 Div.Secret Map.

1. The 143 Inf:Bde will relieve the 144 Inf:Bde of their front and support battalions.
2. The following relief will take place as under:-
   5th R.War.R. will relieve 4th Bn.Glo'sters in the front line fx from M.16.d.7.8. to M.16 a.3.9., on November 24th.
   The Bn. will march from present position, with 200 yards interval between platoons. Leading platoon will cross the POZIERES - BAZENTIN ridge at 4.30 p.m. Platoon guides and 1 guide for Bn. H.Q., will meet Bn where boarded track meets WILLIAM ALLEY, M.27.b.6.0., at 5.15 p.m.
   Coys will march in the following order:-
   H.Q.Details - A - C - B - D.
   H.Q. Details will pass Bn.H.Q. at 3.30 p.m.
   Route. CONTALMAISON-cross rds X.6.c.83-Trench board track to MARTINPUICH & WILLIAM ALLEY.
3. Coys will take over dispositions as under:-
   A Coy on the right.
   C Coy on the left.
   B Coy in Support.
   D Coy in Reserve.
4. Packs, Blankets & Overcoats will not be taken to the trenches. Detailed orders about stacking these will be issued later.
5. Battalions taking over the front line trenches will carry on the men rations for 48 hours.
6. All trench stores, maps, photographs, etc., will be taken over on relief.
7. Bns. of 143 Bde will take over from Bns they relieve all work in hand, and this work is to be carried on until other orders are received.
8. Completion of reliefs will be reported immediately to Battn.H.Q.
9. O.C.Transport will make arrangements to take Coy Cookers back to the Transport lines, one cook per company and the Sgt.Master Cook will remain with the Cookers; the remainder will return to duty with their Coys.
10. The following inter-company relief will take place on the evening of the 25th inst., under arrangements made direct between Coy. Commanders concerned:-
    B Coy will relieve A Coy on the right.
    D Coy " " C " " " left.
    A Coy " go into Support.
    C Coy " " " Reserve.
    The Battalion will be relieved on the night of the 26th by the 6th R.War.R., and will then go into Reserve.

Issued at 12 noon,
23rd November 1916.

Capt. & Adjutant.
1/5th Battn.Royal Warwickshire Regiment.

Copies 1 & 2	War Diary.	Copy 9	Q.M.
" 3 - 6	Coys.	" 10	T O.
Copy 7	Sig.Officer.	" 11	4th Bn.Glo'sters for
" 8	Med.Officer.	" 12	Bn.S.M.(fxinformation

N O T I C E S.

1. O.C.Coys will see that all their huts and lines are left absolutely clean.

II. O.C.Transport will arrange to have transport for the removal of officers' valises and surplus mess boxes to the Q.M.Stores at the Camp by 2.30 p.m., and to have pack ponies at the Camp by the same time for taking officers' xxxxxx messes up to the trenches, on the scale of one per coy and one for H.Q.

III. Dinner for the troops will be at 12 noon.

Copy No.....1

O P E R A T I O N O R D E R S
B Y
Lieut.Colonel C.RETALLACK,
Commdg. 1/5th Battn. Royal Warwickshire Regt.
27th November 1916.

No. 73.

I. The 1/5th R.War.R., will be relieved in the trenches tomorrow 28th inst, by the 1/6th R.War.R.and, on relief will take over the present dispositions of 1/6th R.War.R., as Left SUPPORT Battn in MARTINPUICH, and the trenches in front.

II. Relief will commence at about 6.30 p.m.

III. Coys will be relieved as under:-

B Coy, 1/5th R.War.R.	by	A Coy	1/6th R.War.R.
D " " "	"	C "	" "
A " " "	"	D "	" "
C " " "	"	B "	" "

IV. On relief Coys will take over dispositions as under:-

A Coy 1/5th R.War.R.	from	B Coy 1/6th R.War.R.	in	26th Avenue near the Mill.
B Coy " "	"	A " "	" "	MARTINPUICH.
C Coy " "	"	C " "	" "	26th Avenue near Spence Street.
D Coy " "	"	D " "	" "	MARTINPUICH.

V. O.C.Coys will send guides(1 N.C.O.per platoon & 1 Pte for Lewis Guns) for 1/6th R.War.R. These guides will report at Battn.H.Q.as under:-

C Coy at 5 p.m. A Coy at 5.20 p.m.
B " " 5.10 p.m. D " " 5.30 p.m.

O.C.Signals will arrange for a guide for Battn.H.Q.1/6th R.War.R. to be ready at 5.30 p.m.

VI. O.C.Coys will send 1 man per platoon(1 of these to be an N.C.O) to Battn.H.Q.at 6 a.m. tomorrow. These men will act as advance party for taking over dispositions of 6th R.War.R. Sergt SHELDON will take over Battn.H.Q. B & D Coys' advance party will be ready to meet their platoons at the junction of WILLIAM ALLEY and the EAUCOURT - MARTINPUICH Road (M.27.b.73) and A & C Coys parties at Battn.H.Q., at 7 p.m. They will guide their platoons from these points to new positions.

VII. O.C.Coys will hand over all trench stores on relief and will report relief complete at Battn.H.Q. in passing.

Issued thro' Signals
at 10.30 p.m.27/11/16.

Capt. & Adjt.
1/5th R.War.R.

Copies 1 & 2. War Diary.
" 3 - 6. Coys.

GUIDES NOTES.

Ours for 1/6th R.War.R.

C Coy 1/5th	meet	B Coy 1/6th	at	M.26.b.73 (where Mill Lane cuts 26th Avenue)
B " "	"	A " "	"	M.27.b.72 (junction of WILLIAM Alley and WARLINCOURT Road)
A " "	"	D " "	"	M.27.b.72
D " "	"	C " "	"	M.21.d.52 (junction of SPENCE Street and 26 AVENUE)
H.Q. "	"	H.Q. "	"	M.27.b.72.

Instructions regarding War Diaries and Intelligence Summaries are contained in F. S. Regs., Part II. and the Staff Manual respectively. Title pages will be prepared in manuscript.

WAR DIARY
or
~~INTELLIGENCE SUMMARY~~
(Erase heading not required.)

1/5 R. WAR. R.

Dec 1916

Army Form C. 2118.

Hour, Date, Place 1916	Summary of Events and Information	Remarks and references to Appendices
MARTINPUICH Dec 1	Working parties found Casualties Wounded = 1 OR.	A. S.Q.
SCOTTS REDOUBT CAMP NORTH. X21b 35 Dec 2	Batt relieved by 1/4 GLOSTERS & moved back to huts in SCOTT'S REDOUBT CAMP NORTH (X21b35) Casualties Wounded = 4 ORs	Ref O.O. 74 A. S.Q. Map ALBERT Combined sheet 1/40000
5	Working parties 262 ORs found	A. S.Q.
LE SARS. 6	Batt relieved 8th Bn WORCESTER Regt in Centre Sector	Ref O.O.75 A. S.Q.
	Reinforcements received = 1 officer 2nd LIEUT HERNE	A. S.Q.
ACID DROP CAMP	Working Coy moved to ACID DROP CAMP.	Ref OO 75 A A. S.Q.
MARTINPUICH. 8	Batt relieved by 1/6 R. WAR. R in front line trenches & moved back to shelters & dug outs in MARTINPUICH.	A. S.Q.
	Reinforcements received = 10 ORs	A. S.Q.
	Casualties 1 OR Killed 1 OR Wounded.	A. S.Q.
9.	Working parties found	A. S.Q.
SCOTTS REDOUBT CAMP NORTH 10	Batt. relieved from LEFT SUPPORT Batn by 8 Batn WORCESTER Reg & marched back to SCOTTS REDOUBT NORTH CAMP	Ref O.O.76 A. S.Q.
6	Reinforcement received = 1 OR.	A. S.Q.
12	" " = 1 OR.	A. S.Q.
ALBERT 14	Batt relieved by 11th ARGYLE & SUTHERLAND HIGHLANDERS & marched back to billets in ALBERT	Ref OO 77 A. S.Q.

1247 W 3299 200,000 (E) 8/14 J.B.C. & A. Forms/C. 2118/11.

Army Form C. 2118.

Instructions regarding War Diaries and Intelligence Summaries are contained in F. S. Regs., Part II. and the Staff Manual respectively. Title pages will be prepared in manuscript.

WAR DIARY
or
~~INTELLIGENCE SUMMARY~~ 1/5 R. WAR. R. T

(Erase heading not required.)

Hour, Date, Place	Summary of Events and Information	Remarks and references to Appendices
1916		
ALBERT Dec 15.	Working parties ORs 215 found	JHC
" 16	" " "	JHC
"	Reinforcements received = 3 O.Rs	JHC
17	Working parties 115 found	JHC
"	Reinforcements received = 8 ORs.	JHC.
" Dec 17th - 24th	Working parties found in vicinity of Albert.	JHC.
" Decr 22nd	Reinforcement received - 1.OR.	HSB
" " 23rd	Working parties found	HSB
" 24th - 27th	" " " in vicinity of ALBERT.	JHC
" 28th	Batt moved to III Corps Training area, taking over billets at WARLOY. as in OO 78.	JHC.
" 29th - 31st	Training at WARLOY	JHC.
" 29th	Reinforcements received = 9 OR.	JHC.
" 30th	Reinforcements received = 81 OR.	JHC.

Strength of Batt; Dec 31st 1916.

Officers = 33
OR's = 819.

JH Crossley Capt
Commdg 1/5th R. War R.

1247 W 3299 200,000 (E) 8/14 J.B.C. & A. Forms/C. 2118/11.

22 I.
(10 sheets)

C O N F I D E N T I A L.

War Diary of

1/5th Bn. Royal Warwickshire Regt.

From 1st December, 1916 to 31st December, 1916.

Copy No. 3

OPERATION ORDERS
BY
No.74.

Lieut.Colonel C.RETALLACK,
Commdg. 1/5th Battn.Royal Warwickshire Regt.
1st December 1916.

Ref:Maps. 1/40,000 ALBERT COMBINED SHEET.
1/10,000 LE SARS SHEET.
1/10,000 48th Div. SECRET MAP.

1. The 5th R.War.R. will be relieved by the 4th Bn.Glo'ster Reg on Dec.2nd.
2. Each Coy will provide one guide per platoon & H.Q. two guides to be at South West end of MARTINPUICH at 5.15 p.m. Each guide is to be provided with written instructions.
3. On relief the 5th R.War.R. will take over SCOTTS REDOUBT CAMP at X.21.b.35, previously occupied by 8th Worcester Reg.
4. The Quartermaster will detail the Coy Q.M.Sergts to be at SCOTTS REDOUBT Camp at 11 a.m. on December 2nd to take over the Camp from the 8th Worcesters. The H.Q.Coy,Q.M.Sergt, will also join this party.
5. The Transport Officer will deliver the packs, blankets and greatcoats, and Officers' valises, etc to the camp on the morning of the 2nd. These will be sorted out by Sections & placed by the tents or huts which the men will occupy ready for the arrival of the Battn. 2nd.Lieut.S.F.SNAPE will be at SCOTTS REDOUBT Camp at 11 a.m., and supervise arrangements.
6. Each Coy will detail one man per platoon to be at SCOTTS REDOUBT Camp at 11 a.m. Dec.2nd, to assist the Coy.Q.M.Sergts They will also act as guides and will be on the road by PEAKE WOOD STATION, X.22.a.97, by 7.30 p.m., to guide their platoons to the Camp.
7. All air photos, trench stores, log books, etc., to be handed over on relief.
8. Completion of all reliefs to be reported to H.Q.
9. Acknowledge.

Gordon
2nd.Lieut.
Acting Adjutant.
1/5th Battn.Royal Warwickshire Regiment.

Issued at 2pm.
on Decr. 1st

Copy No. 1 File.
" " 2 & 3. War Diary.
" " 4 - 7 Companies.
" " 8. Q.M. & T.O.
" " 9. 4th Glo'ster Regt.

Addendum to O.O. No 74

The Pack Ponies [illegible]
will be used as follows
A & C Coys to the Mill — M 27 c 82
B & D — [illegible] (2 miles) to the Ration Dumps at S.W. end of MARTINPUICH
Ponies to be there at 4 pm.

Copy No....1..

O P E R A T I O N   O R D E R S
B Y
Lieut,Colonel C RETALLACK,
Commdg. 1/5th Battn. Royal Warwickshire Regt.
5th December 1916.

No. 75

Ref:Map 1/40,000 ALBERT COMBINED SHEET.
1/10,000 LE SARS SHEET.
1/10,000 SECRET MAP.

1. The 143 Inf:Bde will relieve the 144 Inf.Bde.
2. The following relief will take place as under:-
   5th R.War.R. will relieve 8th Bn.Worcester Regt, in Centre Bn. Sector, on 6th December.
   The Bn. will march from present position, with 200 yards interval,between platoons. The leading platoon will cross the POZIERES - BAZENTIN ridge at 4 p.m. Five guides per Coy, and two guides for Bn.H.Q. will meet Bn on track by WILLIAM ALLEY M.27.c.60 at 4.45 p.m.
   Coys. will march in the following order:-
   H.Q.Details - A - C - B - D.
   H.Q.Details will pass Bn.H.Q., at 3.15 p.m.
3. Coys. will take over dispositions as under:-
   A Coy on the Right.
   C " " " Left.
   B " in Support.
   D " " Reserve.
4. Packs & Blankets will not be taken to the trenches. Detailed orders regarding these will be issued later.
   Overcoats will be taken to the trenches.
5. Battalions taking over the front line trenches will carry on the men rations for 48 hours, less bacon.
   Bacon, Soup, Cocoa & Fuel will be taken on pack ponies to old gun pits on West of EAUCOURT L'ABBAYE Road.(M.28.a.59)
6. All trench stores, maps, photographs, etc., will be taken over on relief.
7. Bns.of 143rd Inf:Bde will take over from Bns.they relieve all work in hand, and the work is to be carried on until other orders are received.
8. Completion of reliefs will be reported immediately to Bn.Hqrs.
9. The following inter-company relief will take place on the evening of the 7th inst., under arrangements made direct between the Coy. Commanders concerned:-
   B Coy will relieve A Coy on the right.
   D " " " C " " " left.
   A " " go into Support.
   C " " " " Reserve.
10. O.C.Transport will make arrangements to take Coy.cookers back to the Transport Lines, one cook per Coy remaining with the cookers.
   The Sgt.Master Cook & one per Coy will be in GUN PIT.(M.28.a.59
   Remainder returned to duty with their coys.

Issued at 8.30 p.m.
5th December 1916.

Gordon
2/Lt.& A/Adjt.
1/5th Battn.Royal Warwickshire Regiment

Copies 1 & 2. War Diary.
" 3 - 6 Companies.
Copy 7. Q.M. & T.O.
" 8. 8th Worcester Regt.
" 9. File.

N O T I C E S.

1. O.C.Coys will see that all their huts and lines are left absolutely clean.
2. O.C.Transport will arrange to have transport for the removal of officers' valises and surplus mess boxes to the Q.M. Stores at the Camp by 2 p.m., and to have pack ponies at the camp by the same time for taking officers' messes up to the trenches on the scale of one per coy, 2 for H.Q., and 2 for rations to GUN PITS.
3. Dinner for the troops will be at 12 noon.

Copy No. 1

ORDERS FOR WORKING COMPANY
BY
MAJOR A.S.ALABASTER, M.C.
6th December 1916.

No 75 A

Ref: Map. ALBERT COMBINED SHEET.

1. Working Coy: Strength - 2 Officers.
   10 N.C.Os & Servants.
   80 Privates,
   under 2nd.Lieut.S.F.SNAPE, will proceed to ACID DROP SOUTH CAMP, after completion of task to-morrow.

2. The company will find the following working parties - W and (X or Y) daily, commencing Decr.6th.
   Party Y will be found Decr.6th; Party X the following day, each party alternate days.

3. Tools for Party W. will be sent to VILLA STA, and should be brought back to Camp to prevent need for returning to Transport daily.

4. Battn. Quartermaster will make necessary arrangements for rationing this Coy.

5. O.C.Transport will supply transport to take packs & blankets to ACID DROP SOUTH CAMP during to-morrow morning.
   These packs, etc., will be stacked by guard tent before Coy. leaves camp in morning.

6. A guard of 1 N.C.O. and 2 men will be left in charge and will proceed with packs to new camp.

A. S. Alabaster
Major,
1/5th Battn. Royal Warwickshire Regiment.

5/12/16.

Copies 1 & 2. War Diary.
Copy 3 Coy.
" 4 Q.M. & T.O.
" 5 File.

Copy No. 1......

OPERATION ORDERS No. 76.
BY
Major A.S. ALABASTER, M.C.,
Commdg. 1/5th Battn. The Royal Warwickshire Regt.
10th December 1916.

Ref:Maps LE SARS. 1/10,000.
SHEET. 57D.S.E. 1/20,000.
ALBERT. 1/40,000.

1. The following relief will take place to-morrow.
The 1/5th R.War.R., will be relieved by 8th Worcester Reg, and will march back to SCOTS REDOUBT CAMP NORTH, X.21.b.42.
Companies will move by platoons at 200 yards distance.
2. Guides. The following guides will be found for the 1/8th Bn. Worcester Regt.

Battn.H.Q.	1 guide.	
Each Coy.	1 for Coy.H.Q.	) 5 in all.
	1 for each Platoon)	
Cooks.	1 for Cook.	

These guides will be at crossing of trench board track and light railway about M.31 d., at 5 p.m. 2/Lieut.C.L.GORDON will be in charge of guides at rendezvous.
3. All trench ~~boards~~ stores will be handed over on relief and receipt, signed by an officer, taken for them.
4. Relief to be reported to Battn. H.Q. as soon as complete.
5. Working Coy, will rejoin the Battn. at SCOTS REDOUBT CAMP to-morrow evening.
6. Sgt.SHELDON & Coy.Q.M.Sergts. will meet 2/Lieut.A.J.FARRINGTON, at Camp at 12 noon, to-morrow, to take over.
7. O.C. Transport will arrange for cookers to be taken to camp to-morrow afternoon.

A. S. Alabaster
Major,
10th December 1916. 1/5th Bn. Royal Warwickshire Regt.

Issued @ 6 pm.

Copies 1 & 2 War Diary.
" 3 - 7 Companies.
" 8. Q.M. & T.O.
" 9. File.

NOTES.

O.C. Coys. will see that lines are left perfectly clean.
T.O. will arrange for officers' valises and mess boxes to be taken to camp.
Sgt. Master Cook will see that cocoa is provided for men on return to camp, which should be about 7.30 p.m.
Pack ponies to-night in position at 4.30 p.m. as follows:-
H.Q. = 2 Pack ponies near Battn.H.Q., on brick track.
B Coy. = 1 Pack pony at railway crossing over MARTINPUICH-BAZENTIN LE PETIT Rds.
A,C & D Coys.= 3 Ponies(1 each) at the Old Mill Ruins.M.27.b.82

Copy No..1....

OPERATION ORDERS No.77.

BY

Major A S.ALABASTER, M.C.,

Commdg. 1/5th Battn. Royal Warwickshire Regt.

13th December 1916.

Ref.Map. 1/40,000. ALBERT COMBINED SHEET.

1. The 143rd Inf:Bde will be relieved in Div.Reserve by troops of the 15th Div.
2. The 5th R.War.R. will be relieved in SCOTS REDOUBT Camp by the 11th Argyle & Sutherland Highlanders, to-morrow, 14th inst and, on relief, will march to ALBERT, via FRICOURT-road junction F.8.a.50.
3. Companies will move in the order, H.Q-A-B-C-D, with 100 yards interval between coys. and platoons.
   H.Q. will march out of camp at 10 a.m.
4. Arrangements are being made for the transport of Battn's blankets and gum boots, which will be notified later.
5. A handing-over party, consisting of 2nd.Lieut.E.A.COCHRANE, and one Sergt.per coy. will remain in the camp to hand over to the incoming battalion. The N.C.Os detailed will report for orders to 2nd.Lieut.COCHRANE at 10 a.m., at C.Coy H.Q.
   When the camp has been handed over this party will march to ALBERT and rejoin the Battn.
6. 2nd.Lieut.G.de J.PEGLER, Coy.Q.M.Sergts. & Sgt.SHELDON, will proceed in advance of the Battn to ALBERT and will report to the Town Major there at 10 a.m., and take over billets.
   They will meet the Battn. on its arrival at road junction F.4.b.52, and act as guides.
7. No work will be done by the Working Coy on the day of relief This Coy.will be dissolved and the Bn will resume its normal organisation.
8. As soon as Coys, have taken over billets a report to this effect will be sent to Battn.H.Q., together with a "falling out" state.
9. The Battn.Transport will move independently under the B.T.O.
10. All Lewis Gunners, with Lewis Guns, etc., will parade under O.C.Lewis Guns at 9 a.m. at the entrance to the Camp.
11. Companies will find working parties on Dec.15th as under:-
    "A" Coy. 1 Officer 70 O.R.)
    "B" Coy. 2 Officers 70 O.R.) under O.C. "A" Coy.
    "C" Coy. 1 Officer 60 O.R.)
    Rendezvous at 9 a.m. at W.28.c.77.
    Work on ALBERT-BAPAUME Road.
    The party will report to O.C."D" Coy, 2nd Labour Bn.
    O.C."A" Coy will give all orders necessary for the parties detailed to parade under him at ALBERT in sufficient time.to reach rendezvous punctually.

J.H. Conkey

Issued at 6 p.m. Capt. & Adjt.

13th December 1916. 1/5th Battn.Royal Warwickshire Regt.

Copies 1 & 2 War Diary Copy No. 7 Q.M. & T.O.

" 3 - 6 Companies " " 8 R.Sgt.Major.

NOTICES.

1. O.C.Coys. will send in a report to the Orderly Room, by 9.45 a.m that all their coys huts, lines, etc., are clean and in good order.
2. Officers' valises and mess boxes will be packed ready for Transport by 9 a.m.
3. Officers' Charges to be at the Camp by 9.45 a.m.

Copy No. 1....

OPERATION ORDERS No.78.
BY
Capt. J. H. CROSSKEY,
Commdg. 1/5th Battn. The Royal Warwickshire Regiment
27th December 1916.

Ref: Map SHEET 11 LENS.
SHEET 17 AMIENS.

1. The 143rd Inf: Bde will mave into the III Corps Training Area, at WARLOY, to-morrow, 28th inst.
2. The 5th R.War.R., will march to WARLOY by the route ALBERT - AMIENS main road - BRESLE - BAISIEUX - WARLOY.
3. Companies will march with 100 yards between companies and platoons in the order :- H.Q. - ~~A - B~~ - C - D. - A - B,
H.Q., will pass Battn.H.Q. at 1.30 p.m.
When the Battn.has passed the Transport Lines, the remainder of Transport will fall in 100 yards in rear, with 100 yards between transport sections.
4. Lieut.G.W.WILLIAMS,Coy Q.M.Sergts & Sergt.FLETCHER will proceed in advance of the Battn to WARLOY and will meet the Acting Staff Captain at the Town Major's Officer, WARLOY, at 9.30 a.m, and take over billets. They will meet the Battn on its arrival at the entrance to the village, on the BAISIEUX-WARLOY Road, and act as guides. This party will be mounted on bicycles and will parade under Lieut.G.W.WILLIAMS at Battn.H.Q., at 8 a.m.
5. WORKING PARTIES.
Coys.will find the following working parties to-morrow, 28th inst :-

PARTY "A".

1 Sergt.)	
1 Cpl)	"D" Coy.
15 men)	

Report to O.C.,No.35 Prisoners of War,at E.3.a., at 7.30 a.m.
Work - Armed guard for prisoners of war.
Remarks - This party will be billeted at cage E.3.a., and will ~~xxxx~~ take full equipment and blankets, with rations for the 29th inst.
They will remain as guard until relieved on the afternoon of Dec.31st, when they will march to WARLOY and rejoin their company.

PARTY"C".

"A" Coy. 1 Officer, 60 O.R.)	under
"B" Coy. 1 Officer, 40 O.R.)	O.C."A" Coy.

This party will be paraded as a party, under O.C."A" Coy, before moving off.
Report to O.C."D" Coy, 2nd Labour Battn,at W.29.c.77 at 9.a.m.
Work on ALBERT - BAPAUME Road.
Remarks - Dress-Clean fatigue, with steel helmets.N.C.Os armed.

NOTE.
~~XXXXXX~~ This party and the party under the Town Major, will be dismissed at 12.30 p.m. to-morrow. O.C.Parties will see that the parties arrive punctually so as to waste as little time as possible.

PARTY UNDER TOWN MAJOR.

"B" Coy.	20 O.R.)	under
"C" Coy. 1 Officer,	44 O.R.)	O.C.
"D" Coy. 1 Officer,	36 O.R.)	"D" Coy.

Report to Town Major, ALBERT, at 8 a.m.
Work - Clearing mud in ALBERT.
Dress -Clean fatigue, with steel helmets.

6. All Blankets, rolled by sections, and all gumboots will be dumped outside Battn.H.Q., before 8.30 a.m., 28th inst, under the Battn. Guard. 3 Lorries will pick these up at 10.30 a.m. O.C."C" Coy will send 1 N.C.O. and 12 men, to H.Q. at 10.30 a.m, to act as a loading party. The Battn.Sergt.Major will supervise the loading of the lorries.

S. J. Snape

Issued at 8.30 p.m.
27th December 1916.

2nd.Lieut.& Actg.Adjt.
1/5th Battn.Royal Warwickshire Regt.

Copies 1 & 2 War Diary. Copy No. 7. Q.M. & T.O.
" 3 - 6 Companies. " " 8. Reg. Sergt. Major.

NOTICES.

1. All billets, Officers' quarters, etc., to be left absolutely clean. O.C. Coys will arrange that their "light" duty men clean up company areas during the morning.
2. Special attention will be paid to march discipline during the move.
3. Transport. Officers' Chargers will report by 1 p.m.
Officers' Mess Cart will pick up Officers' Mess boxes by 1 p.m.
Officers' Valise Wagon will pick up Officers' Valises by 12.30 p.m.
Cooker Horses and Medical Cart horse will be ready will be ready by 12.30 p.m.
This Transport will fall in 100 yards behind the Battn.
4. Officers' Valises and mess boxes are to be ready punctually for the Transport to pick up at Coy.H.Q.
5. O.C.Coys will send 14 men per coy. to report to O.C.Lewis Guns at 12 noon, to help with the loading up of the Lewis Guns. Light duty men, etc., are to be used for this work.
6. Dinner for the troops will be at 1 p.m.

23 T
(6 sheets)

Vol 23

Confidential

War Diary

of

1/5 R Warwickshire Regt.

Jan 1st to Jan 31st 1917

Instructions regarding War Diaries and Intelligence Summaries are contained in F. S. Regs., Part II. and the Staff Manual respectively. Title pages will be prepared in manuscript.

WAR DIARY
or
~~INTELLIGENCE SUMMARY~~
(Erase heading not required.)

1/5th R. WAR R.

JANUARY 1917

Army Form C. 2118.

Hour, Date, Place 1917 ~~1916~~	Summary of Events and Information	Remarks and references to Appendices
WARLOY Jan 5	Reinforcements received = 4 ORs	A. S.A.
6	" " = 10 ORs	A. S.A.
SOREL & WANEL 8	Batt moved by train & route marches to billets in SOREL & WANEL. Transport moved by road to the same place starting from WARLOY on Jan 7 & arriving SOREL & WANEL on Jan 8. 1917.	Ref O.O. 79 A. S.A.
9	Reinforcements received LIEUT E. C. WROTH.	A. S.A.
10	Reinforcements received = 14 ORs.	A. S.A.
19	" " = 1 OR.	A. S.A.
23	" " = 4 ORs	A. S.A.
25	Transport moved by Road from SOREL to MERICOURT-SUR-SOMME rejoining battalion on Jan 27. 1917	A. S.A.
27	Batt. less Transport moved by Rail & Route marches to MERICOURT-SUR-SOMME where transport rejoined it	Ref O.O. 80. A.S.A.
29	Reinforcements received = 8 ORs	A. S.A.
31	Batt moved to G 30 b & d & took over trenches from the French	Ref O.O. 81. A. S.A. Ref 62 C NW 1/20,000
	Strength of Batt Jan 31. 1917 Officers = 32 ORs = 764	

Charles Retallack - Lt Col

W 3299 200,000 (E) 8/14 J.B.C. & A. Forms/C. 2118/11.

Copy No. 1.

OPERATION ORDERS NO.79.
BY
Capt. J. H. CROSSKEY,
Commdg. 1/5th Battn. Royal Warwickshire Regiment.
7th January, 1916.

Ref: Maps, LENS & AMIENS.

1. The 5th R.War.R., will move into billets at SOREL - WANEL, in the No.5 Training Area, to-morrow, 8th inst.
2. The Battn. will march, with 100 yards intervals between companies and platoons, in the order:- H.Q.- C - B - D - A. H.Q. will pass the junction of the Rue BISTALLA and the BAIZIEUX road at 12 noon.

   Route:- BAIZIEUX.
   Road junction 800 yds South of the second I of BAIZIEUX.
   RIBEMONT.
   MERICOURT.

   At MERICOURT the Battn. will entrain for AIRAINES, and will march from there to SOREL.
   Lewis Gun Handcarts will be taken with their companies.
3. 2/Lieut. L.T.O'HANLON and the Coy.Q.M.Sergeants will act as billetting party.
   They will proceed with the Battalion by train, and will proceed from AIRAINES to SOREL by bicycles, which will be ready at AIRAINES.
4. Each man will carry one blanket. Surplus blankets and other stores - including officers' valises and mess boxes - will be dumped at Battn.H.Q., for loading on lorries.
   O.C. "A" Coy, will detail a loading party of 1 N.C.O. & 12 men - 4 of these men are to be ready to proceed with the lorry. The Regtl.Sergt.Major will be in charge of the dump.
   Times will be notified later to-night.

S. J. Snape

Issued at 5.15 p.m.,
7th January, 1917.

2/Lieut.
Acting Adjutant.
1/5th Battn.Royal Warwickshire Regiment.

Copies 1 & 2	War Diary.	Copy No. 7	Regtl.Q.M.S.
" 3 - 6	Companies.	" " 8	Regtl.Sergt.Major.

NOTICES.

All details - Pioneers, Police, H.Q. servants, Signallers, Stretcher Bearers - will parade under the Signalling Officer.

All billets & billetting areas are to be left clean & in good order, and O.C.Coys will render a certificate to the Orderly Room, by 11.30 a.m., to this effect.

The Battn. will probably detrain at AIRAINES about 2 a.m., on the 9th inst.

All men are to be warned that nobody is to get out of the train at any time until the "fall out" has been sounded on the bugle.

Every man will carry rations for the train journey.

There will be tea for the troops at AIRAINES and breakfast as soon as possible on arrival at billets.

Copy No. 1

OPERATION ORDERS No.80.
BY
Lieut.Col.C.RETALLACK.M.C.
Commdg 1/5th Battn Royal Warwickshire Regiment.
26th January.1917.

Ref: Maps,

Sheet 14.	ABBEVILLE.	1/100,000
" 17.	AMIENS.	1/100,000
" 62.	D.	1/40,000.

1. The 143rd Inf.Bde. will move tomorrow 27th inst. to the Area round MERICOURT - SUR - SOMME.
2. The 1/5th R.War.R. will fall in ready to move at 7a.m. on the main AIRAINES -PONT REMY ROAD with the head of the column at the road junction of the SOREL-HALLENCOURT and AIRAINES-PONT REMY roads facing N.W., in the order:- H.Q.-A-B-C-D Coys. The Battn will entrain at PONT REMY and detrain at CERISY, and thence move by road to MERICOURT-SUR-SOMME.
3. Lewis Gun handcarts will be man-handled behind their respective Coys.
4. All blankets, rolled by sections, Officers kits, mess boxes and all other stores will be taken to the railhead by motor lorries and will be dumped by 6.15.a.m. as under:-

   H.Q.)
   A.Coy) at Battn H.Q. SOREL.
   B. ")
   C.Coy.) at H.Q. C.Coy.
   D. ") WANEL.

   O.C."B"Coy will detail one N.C.O. and 12 men as loading party at SOREL.No.928. C.S.M.TOWNLEY.F.M.C. will be in charge of the dump.
   O.C."C"Coy will detail one N.C.O. and 12 men as loading party at WANEL.No.72.C.S.M.HEMMING.E. will be in charge.
5. "D"Coy will be ready to act as a loading party at the entraining station and "B"Coy as an unloading party at the detraining station.

J M Cronkey

Issued at 7.30.p.m.
26/ January.1917.

Capt & Adjutant
1/5th Battn Royal Warwickshire Reg

Copies 1 & 2 War Diary. Copy No. 7.Regtl.Q.M.S.
" 3 - 6 Companies. " " 8. A/ R.S.M.

NOTICES.

All billets and billetting areas must be left clean and a certificate rendered by O.C.Coys that their billets have been inspected and are in good order.

No one is to leave the train until the "fall out" has been sounded on the Bugle. In the case of the "fall out" being sounded all ranks must re-entrain when the "fall in" sounds.

Every man will carry rations for the train journey.

All men will wear their great-coats on parade tomorrow morning.

Copy No. 1

OPERATION ORDERS
BY
No.81.
Lieut.Col.C.RETALLACK.M.C.
Commdg. 1/5th Battn Royal Warwickshire Regiment.
30th January.1917.

Ref Maps :-
Sheet AMIENS 17.
Trench Map 62c N.W.

1. The 5th R.War.R. will relieve the Reserve Battalion of the 152nd French Division in the SOPHIE Trench(about G 30 central) tomorrow 31st.inst.

2. The Battalion will fall in on the road outside the camp ready to move by 8.30.a.m. in the order H.Q.-A-B-C-D coys,facing E. with the head of the column opposite the East end of the camp.

ROUTE.
FROISSY.- CAPPY - ECLUSIER - road to HERBICOURT.
If the weather is clear there will be 100yds interval between platoons after ECLUSIER.

DRESS. Great coats will be worn with fighting order.

3. Company Commanders,(mounted) 1 Sergt per Coy(on bicycles) and the Interpreter will preceed the Battalion,leaving the camp at 8.30.a.m. and take over their Company dispositions.

4. Lewis Guns will be taken up to the trenches in the handcarts as before.

5. One blanket per man- rolled in bundles of ten - with Officers mess boxes and kits for the trenches,will be dumped by the road at the East end of the camp by 7.30.a.m. ready for the Transport.

O.C."D"Coy will detail 1 N.C.O. and 12 men as loading party.

The remaining blankets (rooled in bundles of ten), mens valises and surplus mess boxes will be dumped in the "Chapel" hut by 7.30.a.m.

O.C."A"Coy will detail 1 N.C.O. and 4 men to remain as guard until they are removed by the transport.

6. O.C.Transport will arrange transport as under:-
Wagons to carry one blanket per man to the trenches,& remaining stores (second blankets, Officers and mens valises,Officers surplus mess boxes) to Camp 50. near ECLUSIER.

The Company Cookers to accompany their companies.

Pack ponies to assist Lewis Gunners with the Lewis Gun handcarts.

One limber wagon to be at the camp by 8.15.a.m. for the transport of Officers mess stuff and kits which are required for the trenches.

7. WORKING PARTY.
"D"Coy will find working parties as under tomorrow 31st.inst

1. Officer.
5. N.C.O's
70. Men.

To report to Div Bombing Officer at 10.30.a.m. at G.29.a.o.3.
Haversack rations will be taken.
DRESS Fighting Order and Great Coats.
O.C."C"Coy will send a good N.C.O. to act as guide for this party. After the work is finished this party will rejoin the Battalion in the trenches.

8. The Battalion will be relieved on the afternoon of Feb.1st. by a Battalion of the 144th.Inf.Bde.and on relief will march to Camp No.50.

Issued at 8.15.p.m.
30th.January.1917.

J H Carter [signature]

Capt & Adjutant.
1/5th Bn Royal Warwickshire Regiment.

Copies. 1 & 2	War Diary	Copy No.7.	R.Q.M.S. + TO.
" 3 - 6	Companies	" No.8	A/ R.S.M.

NOTICE

Great care is to be taken in the rolling of blankets as badly rolled blankets greatly hinder transport.

The Camp is to be left absolutely clean. O.C.Coys will render to the Adjutant by 3.p.m. that their huts and areas were left absolutely clean.

Breakfast for the troops at ~~X.XX.a.m.~~ 6.30.a.m.
Dinners will be cooked on the march and will be ready as soon as possible on arrival.

1/5th R.War.R.

OPERATION ORDERS

The following alterations are to be made in Operation Orders No.81.

Para. 2.

The Battalion will move tomorrow 31st.inst. as under:-

By platoons at 100yds interval in the order H.Q.-A-B-C-D Coy. H.Q. will pass the starting point(the road at the West end of the camp) at 10.45.a.m. Companies will be ready to follow in the above order.

ROUTE. - ETINEHE - BRAY - SUZANNE - ECLUSIER.

Para 5.

Blankets etc. will be stacked by 10.a.m.

Para.7.

"D"Coy Cooker will accompany the working party which leaves camp at 8.a.m. and have the mens dinners ready at the Div. Dump by midday.

NOTICES.

Breakfast for the troops 7.30.a.m.

J.H. Comley

Capt & Adjutant.

1/5th.Bn Royal Warwickshire Regt

31/1/17.

Copy No. /

OPERATION ORDERS No.81.
BY
Lieut.Colonel C.RETALLACK,M.C.,
Commdg. 1/5th Battn.Royal Warwickshire Regiment
30th January 1917.

Ref:Maps Sheet AMIENS 17.
Trench Map 62c N.W.

1. The 5th R.War.R., will relieve the Reserve Battalion of the 152nd French Division in the SOPHIE Trench(about G.30 Central), to-morrow, 31st inst.
2. The Battn will fall in on the road outside the camp ready to move by 8.30 a.m., in the order:- H.Q.-A-B-C-D Coys, facing E., with the head of the column opposite the East end of the camp.
   ROUTE:- FROISSY-CAPPY-ECLUSIER-road to HERBECOURT.
   If the weather is clear there will be 100 yards interval between platoons, after ECLUSIER.
   DRESS:-Great coats will be worn with fighting order.
3. Coy.Commanders(mounted), 1 Sergt per Coy(on bicycles) and the Interpreter will preceed the Battn. leaving the camp at 8.30 a.m., and take over their Company dispositions.
4. Lewis Guns will be taken up to the trenches in the handcarts, as before.
5. One blanket per man - rolled in bundles of ten - with Officers' mess boxes and kits for the trenches, will be dumped by the road at the East end of the camp by 7.30 a.m., ready for the Transport.
   O.C."D" Coy will detail 1 N.C.O. & 12 men as loading party.
   The remaining blankets (rolled in bundles of ten), mens valises and surplus mess boxes, will be dumped in the "Chapel" hut by 7.30
   O.C."A" Coy will detail 1 N.C.O. & 4 men to remain as guard until they are removed by the transport.
6. O.C.Transport will arrange transport as under:-
   Wagons to carry one blanket per man to the trenches & remaining stores (second blankets, Officers' & mens' valises, Officers' surplus mess boxes) to Camp 50, near ECLUSIER.
   The Company Cookers to accompany their companies.
   Pack ponies to assist Lewis Gunners with the Lewis Gun Handcarts.
   One limber wagon to be at the camp by 8.15 a.m., for the transport of Officers mess stuff and kits which are required for the trenches.
7. WORKING PARTY.
   "D" Coy will find working parties as under tomorrow,31st inst:-
   1 Officer.
   5 N.C.Os.
   70 Men.
   to report to Div.Bombing Officer at 10.30 a.m., at G.29.a.8.3.
   Haversack rations will be taken.
   Dress:- Fighting Order, with Greatcoats.
   O.C. "C" Coy will send a good N.C.O., to act as guide for this party. After the work is finished this party will rejoin the Battalion in the trenches.
8. The Battalion will be relieved on the afternoon of Feb:1st., by a Battalion of the 144th Inf:Bde and, on relief, will march to Camp No.50.

Issued at 8.15 p.m. — Capt. & Adjt.
30th January, 1917. — 1/5th Battn.Royal Warwickshire Regt.

Copies 1 & 2. War Diary. Copy No.7. R.Q.M.S. & T.O.
" 3 - 6 Companies. " " 8. A/R.S.M.

NOTICES.

Great care is to be taken in the rolling of blankets, as badly rolled blankets greatly hinder transport.

The Camp is to be left absolutely clean. O.C.Coys will render to the Adjutant by 3 p.m., that their huts & areas were left absolutely clean.

Breakfast for the troops at 6.30 a.m.

Dinners will be cooked on the march and will be ready as soon as possible on arrival.

1/5th R.War.R.

O P E R A T I O N   O R D E R S.

The following alterations are to be made in Operation Orders No. 81.

Para. 2.

The Battalion will move tomorrow, 31st inst, as under:-
By Platoons, at 100 yds interval, in the order:-
H.Q.-A-B-C-D Coys. H.Q. will pass the starting point (the road at the West end of the Camp) at 10.45 a.m. Companies will be ready to follow in the above order.
ROUTE:- ETINEHEM - BRAY - SUZANNE - ECLUSIER.

Para.5.

Blankets, etc., will be stacked by 10 a.m.

Para.7.

"D" Coy Cooker will accompany the working party which leaves Camp at 8 a.m., and have the mens' dinners ready at the Div.Dump by mid-day.

NOTICE.

Breakfast for the troops at 7.30 a.m.

Capt. & Adjt.

31/1/17. 1/5th Battn.Royal Warwickshire Regiment.

Vol 24

24 .T.
(12 sheets)

CONFIDENTIAL.

WAR DIARY of

1/5th Bn. R. WARWICKSHIRE REGT.

From 1st FEB. To 28th FEB. 1917.

****

Instructions regarding War Diaries and Intelligence Summaries are contained in F. S. Regs., Part II. and the Staff Manual respectively. Title pages will be prepared in manuscript.

WAR DIARY
or
~~INTELLIGENCE SUMMARY~~
(Erase heading not required.)

Army Form C. 2118.

1/5 R. WAR. R.
Feb. 1917

Hour, Date, Place 1917		Summary of Events and Information	Remarks and references to Appendices
ECLUSIER	Feb. 1.	Batt relieved by 1/8 WORCESTERS & marched back to Camp at ECLUSIER	A. S[?]
BIACHES	5.	Batt relieved 1/6 R. War. R. in the front line trenches between I. 31d 25.30 & I 31 b. 25.35	Ref. Map 62 C. N.W. 1/20,000 Edition 4a. & O.O. 82. A. S[?]
		Reinforcements received 16 ORs	A. S[?]
	6	Casualties Killed = 3 ORs Wounded = 4 wounded (1 since died)	A. S[?]
	7.	Casualties Wounded. 1 O.R.	
	9.	Dispositions changed, 3 companies going into the line & frontage extended northwards as far as I 31 b 2.7 taking over from 1/8 R. War. R.	Ref Sheet 62 C. N.W. Edition 4a. A. S[?]
WILKIND trench north of HERBECOURT	10.	Batt. relieved in front line trenches by 1/8 R. War. R. & moved back into Brigade Reserve in WILKIND	Ref OO. 82 A. A. S[?]
BIACHES	14	Batt. relieved the 1/6 R. WAR. R. in front line trenches between I 31 d ~~[illegible]~~ 35.50 & I 31 b 27	Ref OO. 83 & sheet 62 C N.W. Ed 4A 1/20,000 A. S[?]
	17	Reinforcements received = 4 ORs. " received 1 Off: 2nd Lieut D. COWLES The weather changed today & the severe frost of the last 6 weeks gave way to thaw & rain. The trenches started giving way, & by Feb 20 were in a deplorable condition.	A. S[?]

1247 W 3299 200,000 (E) 8/14 J.B.C. & A. Forms/C. 2118/11.

Instructions regarding War Diaries and Intelligence Summaries are contained in F. S. Regs., Part II. and the Staff Manual respectively. Title pages will be prepared in manuscript.

WAR DIARY
or
~~INTELLIGENCE~~ SUMMARY 1/5 R. War R.

(Erase heading not required.)

Feb. 1917

Army Form C. 2118.

Hour, Date, Place 1917	Summary of Events and Information	Remarks and references to Appendices
BIACHES Feb. 20	Batt was relieved in front line trenches by 1/6 R. War R. The relief was extremely slow & difficult owing to darkness & state of ground & trenches. Relieving troops did not reach front line until 4 a.m. on Feb. 21. It took several hours to get men dug out of the mud into which they had floundered; the mud in places being nearly 4 ft deep. After relief the battalion moved back to rest billets at ECLUSIER where it became part of Divisional Reserve	A. S. A.
ECLUSIER Feb 24	~~Batt~~ Reinforcements received = 60 O.R.s.	
26	Batt relieved the 1/6 R. War R. in Right sector of front line on the night of Feb 26/27. 1917 between I 31 d 4.5. & I 31 b 3.3.	Ref O.O. 84 A. S. A.
BIACHE 14	The following officer reinforcement received; 2Lt ~~H. C. Davies~~ H. C. DAVIES.	A. S. A.
17	~~2 Lieut D. Cowles~~ A. S. A.	
	Total strength Feb 28. 1917 Officers = 35 O.R.s = 760 (ration strength = 650)	A. S. A.

Charles Retallack Lt Col
Cmdg 1/5 R. War R.

1247 W 3299 200,000 (E) 8/14 J.B.C. & A. Forms/C. 2118/11.

O P E R A T I O N   O R D E R S
B Y
Lieut.Col. C. RETALLACK.M.C. No.82.
Commdg 1/5th Battn Royal Warwickshire Regiment.
5th February 1917.

Copy.No. 1

Ref.Maps:Trench Map.Sheet 62c N.W.
French Trench Map of PERONNE.

1. The 5th R.War.R. will relieve the 1/6th.R.War.R. in the right Battalion trenches of the left Brigade today 5thinst.

2. Companies will march to the trenches in the order:- H.Q. - C - B - A by the route HERBECOURT - ROMAIN DESFOSSES Trench.
H.Q. will leave camp at 4.p.m.
There will be an interval of 200 yards between platoons.
DRESS:- Fighting Order wearing Great-coats and carrying one blanket per man.
The 1/6th R.War.R. are arranging to have one guide for H.Q., one per Coy.H.Q., and one per platoon at the junction of the SUNKEN ROAD and the ROMAIN DESFOSSES Trench(immediately south of BOIS DESIRE) ~~to meet each platoon~~.

3. "A" Coy 1/5th.R.War.R. will relieve "D" Coy 1/6th.R.War.R.
"B" Coy. " " " "B" " "
"C" Coy. " " " "C" " "

4. The Lewis Guns of A - B & C Coys (3 per Coy with one box of magazines per gun) will be taken by limbers wagon to trench head following the last platoon of the leading Coy and will be manhandled from there.
Two boxes of magazines per gun will be taken over from 1/6th R.War.R.

5. O.C. Coys will report relief completed to Battalion H.Q. as soon as possible by runner.

6. Orders for "D" Coy will be issued when recieved.

J H Cumbley
Capt & Adjutant.
1/5th Battn Royal Warwickshire Regiment.

Issued at 1.45.p.m.
5th.February.1917.

Copies 1 & 2 War Diary. Copy.No.7. R.Q.M.S. & T.O.
Copies 3 - 6 Companies. " " 8. A/R.S.M.

N O T I C E S

TRANSPORT. The limbers for Lewis Guns will be at the water point by H.Q. at 3.15.p.m.
Officers mess cart to carry light mess boxes to the trenches will be at the same point at the same time.
30 full petrol tins of water will be carried by Transport. The Officers mess cart and the wagon containing the water will follow the Battalion,leaving camp at 5.p.m. and will carry to the ration dump.
4 Officers servants per Coy and 2 platoons of "D"Coy under an Officer will proceed with these wagons and will carry from the dump to the Coy.H.Q. in the line on the scale of :-
8 tins of water per Coy.
6 " " " for H.Q.

BLANKETS The second blankets ~~per man~~ will be rolled by tens and dumped with packs at the Quarter Master's Stores in ECLUSIER.

BILLETS. The Camp is to be left absolutely clean and a certificate to this effect rendered to the Orderly Room before leaving Camp.
During relief the greatest quietness is to be exercised.

Men in the front line are not to be in their dug-outs by night and all movement by day limited as far as possible.

Water bottles are all to be full before leaving camp and men will carry rations for tomorrow. Hot dinners will be brought up at dusk tomorrow night.

Copy No. - 1

OPERATION ORDERS NO.82A.

by

Lieut.Col. C. RETALLACK,M.C.,
Commdg. 1/5th Battn.Royal Warwickshire Regiment.
10th February, 1917.

Ref:Map Sheet 62C.N.W. 1/20,000.
PERONNE 1/20,000.

I. The Battn. will be relieved in the trenches to-night by the 1/6th Battn.R.War.R., and, on relief, will take over the dispositions of the 1/8th R.War.R., about TRENCH WILLKIND, thereby becoming Brigade Reserve.

2. Guides for the 1/6th R.War.R., on the scale of one per Battn.H.Q one for each coy H.Q., and one per platoon, will be found as under
From "A" & "D" Coys. - At Ration Dump at 6.30 p.m.
& Stettin at 7.30 p.m.

3. Coys will be relieved by the incoming coys in the following order:-
"C" Coy,1/5th R.War.R., by "C" Coy, 1/6th R.War.R.
"B" " " " " " "D" " " " "
"A" " " " " " "B" " " " "
"D" " " " " " "A" " " " "

All boxes of Lewis Gun Drums (on the scale 3 boxes per gun) will be handed over on relief with all trench stores, bombs, S.A.A. etc, and a receipt obtained.

Periscopes & other coy stores will be brought.

4. After relief the Battn. less "D" Coy, & 2 platoons of "B" Coy, will proceed to WILLKIND TRENCH, via AUBERT & GUERRIERS.

"A" Coy will occupy that part of WILLKIND, south of GUERRIERS, as far as DOLFUS.

"C" Coy & 2 platoons "B" Coy will be in WILLKIND, North of GUERRIERS.

"D" Coy will be at Camp 50 Bis.

"B" Coy, less 2 platoons, will take up a position south of BAZINCOURT FARM, on the South bank of the SOMME.

"A" & "C" Coys, & 2 platoons "B" Coy, will be met by guides at the junction of GUERRIERS & WILLKIND, who will show them their dug-outs.

3 guides from 1/8th R.War R. (1 for Coy.H.Q. & 1 per platoon) will be at Ration Dump at 9 p.m., for "B" Coy (less 2 platoons)

They will take with them their 3 Lewis Guns & teams, and one Lewis Gun & team of "A" Coy will be taken over ar Ration Dump by "B" Coy. 2 guns will then be allotted to each platoon.

Issued at 6.30 p.m.
10th February.1917.

Capt & Adjt.
1/5th R.War.R.

5th R. War. Regt

Appendix I A

Appendix 1. A.

Appendix 1. A
- Showing Map -

Copy No. 1

OPERATION ORDERS NO.83.
BY
Lieut.Col. C.RETALLACK, M.C.,
Commdg. 1/5th Battn.Royal Warwickshire Regiment.
13th February, 1917.

Ref:Maps 62 C. N.W. 1/20,000.
PERONNE. 1/10,000.

I. The 1/5th R.War.R., will relieve the 1/6th R.War.R., in the trenches to-morrow, 14th inst.

2. Coys.will leave their present positions & pass the junction of Trenches WILLKIND & GUERRIERS, as under:-

"C" Coy	-	4.30 p.m.
"A" "	-	4.50 p.m.
"B" "(2 Platoons)		5.10 p.m.
"D" "	-	5.30 p.m.

These coys. will proceed via GUERRIERS-AUBERT to the front, support & reserve lines.

"B" Coy, less 2 platoons-(now in the trenches on the SOMME) will move as soon as relieved by the 1/6th R.War.R.

Guides from the 1/6th R.War.R., will meet "A" & "C" Coys at the junction of STETTIN & AUBERT, at 7.30 p.m., 2 platoons of "B" Coy and "D" Coy at 6.30 p.m., at the ration dump (H.30.d.27) and "B" Coy (less 2 platoons) at the same place at 8 p.m.

3. Coys will take over the following dispositions:-
"A" Coy on the right,relieving "D" Coy,1/6th R.War.R.
"C" " " " left " "C" " " "
"B" " in support in IGLAU Trench,relieving "B" Coy.1/6th R.War.R.
"D" " " reserve in DESIRE " " "A" " " "

4. O/C Coys will arrange the following guides to take the 1/6th R.War.R., to the positions now held by coys:-
"D" Coy, for "A" Coy,1/6th R.War.R., 1 guide pr Coy.H.Q., and 1 pr platoon at the ration dump at 10 p.m.
"B" Coy, for "B" Coy.1/6th R.War.R.(less 2 platoons) proceeding to the trenches by the SOMME., 1 guide pr Coy.H.Q., & 1 pr platoon at the ration dump at 6.30 p.m.

5. All Lewis Gun boxes of ammunition, complete with magazines & S.A.A on the scale of 3 per gun, will be left dumped at Battn.H.Q., for the 1/6th R.War.R., to take over, and a similar number will be taken over from the 1/6th R.War.R., in the front line system.
The Lewis Gun ammunition in the SOMME trenches will be handed over there by O/C "B" Coy, and a receipt obtained.

6. The water and rations will be brought up by the Transport to the Ration Dump (H.30.d.27)
These will be carried to the coys in the front & support by the Reserve Coy("D"), as soon after relief as possible.
All empty petrol tins which will be handed over by the 1/6th R.War.R., in the trenches, will be taken back the same night by D Coy to the wagons, for removal to Transport.

7. All mens' packs will be dumped in the sunken road near Battn.H.Q by 3 p.m., for removal by Transport. These are to be brought along by men in small parties.
The 2nd blanket per man will be packed inside the pack.
The Battn.will proceed to the front line in fighting order, wearing the great coat & carrying one blanket per man.
Officers' valises & mess boxes will be taken to the same place before the Battn.moves off.
~~All~~ All mess - stuff for the trenches will be man-handled.

Issued at 10 p.m.
13th February.1917.

J H Carnby
Capt. & Adjt.
1/5th Battn.Royal Warwickshire Regiment.

Copies 1 & 2. War Diary. Copy No.7. T.O. & Q.M.
" 3 - 6. Companies. " " 8. R.S.M.

NOTICE.

All dug-outs are to be left clean and a certificate rendered to the Orderly Room to this effect by 4 p.m.

O P E R A T I O N   O R D E R S. No. 84.   Copy No 1

B Y

Lieut. Col. C. RETALLACK, M.C.,

Commdg. 1/5th Battn. Royal Warwickshire Regiment.

25th February, 1917.

Ref: Maps 62 C N.W. 1/20,000.
PERONNE. 1/10,000.

1. The 5th R.War.R., will relieve the 6th R.War.R., in the Right Sector to-morrow, 26th inst.
2. Coys will pass the junction of the ECLUSIER-FRISE & ECLUSIER-HERBECOURT road, in the order:- H.Q.-B-C-A., the leading platoon of "B" Coy passing at 4.45 p.m.
   ROUTE :- HERBECOURT,
   Ration Dump, &
   Trench Board Track to the front line & IGLAU Trench.
   "D" Coy will proceed to WILLKIND Trench by the route:-
   ECLUSIER-FRISE-Road junction, H.15.a.12.,
   leaving camp at 5 p.m.
   Companies & platoons will march at 100 yards interval.
   DRESS:- Fighting Order, with great coats rolled,
   Box Respirators at the alert position.
   Blankets will not be taken.
3. Companies will take over the following dispositions:-
   "B" Coy. - 2 platoons in front line.
   2 platoons in STETTIN.
   "C" Coy. - 1 platoon in GRAND WOOD.
   3 platoons in IGLAU.
   The platoon in Grand Wood & one of the IGLAU platoons will form the inlying piquets.
   "A" Coy. - in HERBECOURT.
   "D" Coy. - in WILLKIND TRENCH.
4. Lewis Guns will be loaded on their limbers, which will be at the Camp by 3.45 p.m., and will preceed the Battn. by ten minutes. Lewis Gun teams will go with the guns under O/C Lewis Guns; guns will be unlimbered at the Ration Dump and there await their companies.
   No Lewis Gun ammunition will be taken up to the trenches, but will be taken over from the 6th Battn, on arrival.
   O/C Lewis Guns will make arrangements to hand over to the Q.M., 1/6th R.War.R., the same ~~number~~ as will be handed over by the 6th Battn. The Lewis Guns will be disposed as follows:-
   3. "B" Coy guns in front line.
   1. "B" Coy gun in reserve in STETTIN, under O/C "B" Coy.
   1. "C" Coy gun in Grand Wood.
   2. "C" Coy guns in position in IGLAU.
   1. "D" Coy gun in position in IGLAU, under O/C "C" Coy.
   12. "D" Coy guns in Battn. Reserve in IGLAU.
   32. "A" Coy guns in " " " "
5. One guide per platoon, and 1 for Coy. H.Q., from the 6th Battn, will meet Battn. H.Q., B & C Coys at the East end of the new trench board track from the Ration Dump to DESIRE at 6.45 p.m., and "A" Coy at the west end of the village of HERBECOURT.
6. Blankets will be rolled by Sections and dumped at Q.M. Stores, as under:-
   H.Q. - 1.30 p.m.
   "B" Coy - 1.40 p.m.
   "C" Coy - 2.- p.m.
   "D" Coy - 2.20 p.m.
   "A" Coy - 2.40 p.m.
   The Regt. Sergt. Major will supervise the dump.
   Officers' kits & spare mess boxes will be dumped at the same place before leaving Camp.
7. O/C Transport will arrange the following transport:-
   (a) Limbers for Lewis Guns at the Camp at 3.45 p.m.
   (b) 1 Limber for Officers' messes & baggage for the trenches at the Camp at 4.30 p.m. This limber will leave in rear of the Battn. 1 servant per coy will go with the cart. The load will be dumped at the Ration Dump for B & C Coys, at HERBECOURT for "A" Coy.
   (c) The light mess-cart for "D" Coy mess. to proceed to WILLKIND.
   The A, B & C Coy cookers will be parked in a sheltered spot in HERBECOURT, and the "D" Coy cooker will be taken to WILLKIND Trench.
8. Relief complete will be notified to Battn. H.Q., as soon as possible over the telephone, by code.

Issued at 10.50 pm
25th Feb 1917.

[signature]
CAPT. & ADJT. 5TH BATT. R. WARWICKSHIRE REGT.

Copies 1 & 2 War Diary.
" 3 - 6 Companies.

Copy No.7 T.O. & Q.M.
" " 8. Reg.Sergt.Major.

NOTICES.

I. The Camp will be left absolutely clean & O/C Coys will render a certificate to the Orderly Room that their huts and lines are clean before leaving camp.

II. Two orderlies per coy will report to Signals at Battn.H.Q., as soon after relief as possible.

Copy No 1

ADDENDUM TO OPERATION ORDERS NO.84.
B Y
Lieut.Col. C.RETALLACK, M.C.,
Commdg. 1/5th Battn.Royal Warwickshire Regiment.
25th February,1917.

---

1. The following reliefs will take place on the night 28/29th inst:-
"A" Coy will relieve "B" Coy in the front line,
"B" Coy will proceed to HERBECOURT.
On the night March 2/3, "D" Coy will relieve "A" Coy in the front line; "A" Coy will proceed to WILLKIND Trench.
2. Relief of Lewis Gunx teams on the night of Feby 28th:-
3 "A" Coy guns) from Reserve in IGLAU, will go to
1 "D" Coy gun) front line,
and relieve 3 guns of "B" Coy & one of "D",
the 3 "B" Coy guns going to position in IGLAU & the 1 "B" Coy gun to position in Grand Wood
The 3 "C" Coy & 1 "D" Coy guns thereby relieved will go into reserve in IGLAU by Battn.H.Q.
On the night March 2nd, the 3 "C" Coy & 1 "D" Coy guns from reserve, relieve the 3 "A" & 1 "D" Coy guns in the front line.
On relief the 1 "D" Coy gun goes to position in Grand Wood, and the 3 "A" guns to position in IGLAU.
The 3 "B" Coy & 1 "D" Coy guns thereby relieved go to reserve in IGLAU.
3. The undermentioned will draw gum boots, thigh, on the scale of one pair per man, from the Q.M.Stores, to-morrow morning:-
"B" Coy
"A" Coy.
All Lewis Gunners.
2 Working platoons of "C" Coy,
Any surplus to this number will be drawn by "D" Coy, except for 10 pairs which will be reserved for the signallers.
O/C A,B & C Coys will notify the Q.M., by/9 a.m., to-morrow, of the number they will require.
The Q.M., will notify O/C "D" Coy the number available for his Coy.
On relief on the night of March 2nd, O/C "D" Coy will draw from O/C "B" Coy, the number of gum boots he requires to make his establishment up to one pair per man, before proceeding to the front line.
The ankle boots of all men wearing gum boots will be dumped at HERBECOURT, or WILLKIND, under Coy.arrangements.

J H Cranbury

25th February,1917.

Capt. & Adjt.
1/5th Battn.Royal Warwickshire Regiment.

N O T I C E.

The greatest care will be taken by O/C Coys, Platoon Commanders and sergeants to see that men mark their ankle-boots, and do not lose either gum-boots or ankle-boots.
All men are to be warned of the penalties they will incur by such negligence.

48

Instructions regarding War Diaries and Intelligence Summaries are contained in F. S. Regs., Part II. and the Staff Manual respectively. Title pages will be prepared in manuscript.

WAR DIARY
or
~~INTELLIGENCE SUMMARY~~
(Erase heading not required.)

1/5 R Warwick Regt

March 1917

Vol 25

Army Form C. 2118.

Hour, Date, Place	Summary of Events and Information	Remarks and references to Appendices
1917		
BIACHES Mar 1.	Casualties –	
	Lieut G. E. ORTON-SMITH missing believed killed	
	Wounded = 6. ORs.	
	Died = 1. OR.	A. S. G.
2	Casualties	
	Killed = 1. OR. Wounded = 2. ORs	A. S. G.
ECLUSIER 3	Casualties – Wounded = 8 ORs	A. S. G.
	Batt was relieved in the front line trenches by the 1/8 Worcestershire Reg. & moved back to No 56 Camp between CAPPY & ECLUSIER.	Ref O.O. 85 A. S. G.
7.	Working parties up to 350 formed for work on QUERRIER.	A. S. G.
	Batt moved from Camp 56 to Camp 50 bis	Ref OO 86 A. S. G.
	Reinforcements received = 7. ORs	
12	Reinforcements received.	A. S. G.
	Lieut E. P. Q. CARTER	
	2nd Lieut (temp) F. G. HALL	A. S. G.
BIACHES 13	Batt relieved the 1/6 R. Wark in the Right Sector	Ref O.O 87 A. S. G.
15	Casualties Wounded = 2. ORs	A. S. G.
16	Reinforcements received = 1 OR	A. S. G.
	Casualties Killed = 1 OR. Wounded = 2. ORs	A. S. G.

25 T.
(150 sheets)

1247 W 3299 200,000 (E) 8/14 J.B.C. & A. Forms/C. 2118/11.

Instructions regarding War Diaries and Intelligence Summaries are contained in F. S. Regs., Part II. and the Staff Manual respectively. Title pages will be prepared in manuscript.

WAR DIARY
or
~~INTELLIGENCE SUMMARY~~
(Erase heading not required.)

Army Form C. 2118.

March 1917

Hour, Date, Place	Summary of Events and Information	Remarks and references to Appendices
1917 BIACHES Mar 17.	An attack was made by two Batts of the 145 Bde @ 2.30 a.m. on MAISONETTE farm & the neighbouring trenches. Should this attack prove successful the 1/4 R. Berks R. in conjunction with the 1/7 R. Warks on their left were to seize & occupy the enemy trenches from I 31 d 6.7. to I 31 b 7.5. The batt. was ordered to be in position for a zero hour of 4.50 am & was forming up in English front line when operation orders was cancelled; the right battalion of 145 Bde had attained its objective though the left had not yet done so. About 6 a.m. a report was received that the left battalion 145 Bde ~~on the left~~ had taken its objective. About 8 a.m. men of 145 Bde being observed on the top, patrols were pushed over to the German line which was then found to be deserted. 1 Front line Coy & 1 Support Coy (A & D respectively) were thereupon moved over & German front & support lines occupied. Patrols from A Coy were pushed forward during this move & occupied old German trench from I 32 c 8.6. to I 32 b 15.15. Patrols were again pushed on as far as I 33 c 6.5. & I 32 d 8.2 as soon as 'D' Coy had taken over trench I 32 c 8.6. to I 32 b 15.15. Patrols came in contact with enemy patrols about I 32 d 8.2.	Ref. Map 62 c NW. also Peronne Map 62 c NW. 4. A.S.Q.

1247 W 3299 200,000 (E) 8/14 J.B.C. & A. Forms/C. 2118/11.

Instructions regarding War Diaries and Intelligence Summaries are contained in F. S. Regs., Part II. and the Staff Manual respectively. Title pages will be prepared in manuscript.

WAR DIARY
or
~~INTELLIGENCE SUMMARY~~
(Erase heading not required.)

March. 1917

Army Form C. 2118.

Hour, Date, Place 1917	Summary of Events and Information	Remarks and references to Appendices
Front line trenches about I 32 central East of BIACHES Mar 17.	Casualties – Wounded – 2nd Lieut D.T. PARRY 2nd " H.L. HARCOURT (since died of wounds) also wounded = 2.ORs	A. S.H.
ECLUSIER Mar 18.	A battalion of the 144 Bde moved through the battalion area & took up an outpost line in front of the line we had occupied during the night, along the line of the river SOMME. The 1/5 R WAR R. then marched back to billets at Camp 50 bis ECLUSIER Casualties = 1 OR.	Ref O.O. 88 & Map 62 C. N.W. 1/20,000 A. S.H.
HALLE Mar. 21	Batt found working parties for road making & bridge repair 2 Coys BIACHES & 2 Coys DOIGNT. On completion they moved to billets at HALLE. Transport & HQrs also moved to HALLE.	Ref Map 62C N.W. 1/20,000
22	Working parties 4 Coys found for road making & bridging PERONNE (FAUBOURG DE PARIS) (Casualties = 1 OR. wounded)	A. S.H.
23 & 24	Working parties again found as above.	A.S.H. A. S.H.
MOUNT ST QUENTIN & ST DENNIS 25	Batt moved to billets at MOUNT ST. QUENTIN & ST DENNIS about 9.30 a.m.	Ref O.O 89 & Map 62 C N.W 1/20,000 & Peronne 62 C N.W 4 1/10,000 A. S.H.

1247 W 3299 200,000 (E) 8/14 J.B.C. & A. Forms/C. 2118/11.

Instructions regarding War Diaries and Intelligence Summaries are contained in F. S. Regs., Part II. and the Staff Manual respectively. Title pages will be prepared in manuscript.

WAR DIARY
or
~~INTELLIGENCE SUMMARY~~
(Erase heading not required.)

Mar 1917

Army Form C.

Hour, Date, Place 1917	Summary of Events and Information	Remarks and references to Appendices
Mar 25 (cont) 6 p.m. BUSSU & AIZECOURT.	Batt ~~[illegible]~~ less transport moved again. HQ & 2 Coys to BUSSU & 2 Coys to AIZECOURT. Transport remained between MOUNT ST QUENTIN & QUINCONCE.	O.O. 90 Ref Map 62 C 1/40,000. A. S.G.
	Reinforcements received:- 2nd Lieut F. COULSON 2nd Lieut A. J. LILLY	A. S.G.
	Summer time (advanced 1 hr) adopted midnight 24/25.	A. S.G.
Mar 26.	Work on RED line BUSSU, DRIENCOURT, CI. DERRIERE Wood done by companies	A. S.G.
DRIENCOURT Mar 27.	Batt (less transport) moved to billets & dug outs at DRIENCOURT by 10 a.m.	Ref O.O. 91. Map 62 C NE. 1/20,000.
	Reinforcements received:- 15 OR.	A. S.G.
	2nd Lieut R. HEGAN	A. S.G.
	Work continued by companies on RED line.	A. S.G.
SAULCOURT - VILLERS-FAUCON Mar 28	Batt. relieved the 7/8 R. War. R. in the outpost line between E 17. a. 25. & E 23 a. 25 with an advance post at CAPRON Copse	Ref O.O. 92 A. S.G. Map 62 C NE 2A 1/20,000
Mar 29	Picquet & Support line companies (two) relieved by 1/6 GLOUCESTERS. These two companies then moved back to bivouacs near TINCOURT WOOD. H.Q.s & 2 Coys remained	Ref Map 62 C NE 2A 1/20,000 A. S.G.

Instructions regarding War Diaries and Intelligence Summaries are contained in F. S. Regs., Part II. and the Staff Manual respectively. Title pages will be prepared in manuscript.

WAR DIARY
or
~~INTELLIGENCE SUMMARY~~
(Erase heading not required.)

Mar 19. 1917

Army Form C. 2118.

Hour, Date, Place	Summary of Events and Information	Remarks and references to Appendices
1917		
Mar 28. 1917	Casualties Killed = 3 O.Rs Killed (accidently) = 1 O.R. Wounded = 8 O.R. (1 since died of wounds)	A. S. A.
~~29~~/30	Working parties (strength two companies) dug 3 cruciform posts on Army line between E 26 a. 8.3. & K 3 a 7.0.	A. SA.
31	Working parties strength 4 companies for work on Army line between E 26 a 8.3 & K 3 a 7.0	A. SA.
	Strength Officers = 35 O.Rs. = 693.	

Charles Retallack Lt Col

G. W. Mirale

1247 W 3299 200,000 (E) 8/14 J.B.C. & A. Forms/C. 2118/11.

Copy No. 1

OPERATION ORDERS. NO.85.

by

Lieut.Col. C.RETALLACK, M.C.,
Commdg. 1/5th Battn.Royal Warwickshire Regiment.
2nd March, 1917.

Ref:Map. 62C.N.W. 1/20,000.

I. The 5th R.War.R., will be relieved by 2 coys.1/8th Worcester Reg, to-morrow night, March 3rd/4th.
On relief the Battalion will move to Camp 56 (G.20.b.66) on the ECLUSIER - CARPY Road.
"B", "C" & "D" Coys will move by the route, HERBECOURT-ECLUSIER. "A" Coy, via cross roads H.15.a.12-FRISE-ECLUSIER-CAMP 56.
In the case of "C" & "D" Coys, each platoon will move off independently, when relieved; "A" & "B" Coys, who will not be relieved, will move off as coys, with 100 yards between platoons at 6 p.m., unless required for working parties.

2. "D" Coy, 1/5th R.War.R., will be relieved in the front line by "B" Coy, 1/8th Worcester Reg., & "C" Coy, by "A" Coy.
O/C "C" & "D" Coys will each send 1 guide for Coy H.Q., 1 per platoon & 1 per Lewis Gun to the point where the trench board track from the front meets the HERBECOURT-BIACHE Road, by 7 p.m.
O/C "C" Coy will send an officer to supervise & see that each coy gets its proper guides.

3. All trench stores, including S.O.S. signals will be handed over on relief. All Lewis Gun ammunition, periscopes, digschies, hot-food containers and water tins will be brought out.
Hot-food containers & water tins will be handed over to transport of 1/8th Worcesters on the ration dump, on the HERBECOURT-BIACHE road.
Lewis Guns & their ammunition & digschies will be loaded on the 5th Bn Transport at the same place.
O/C Transport will arrange to have transport for the above at the dump by 8 p.m., as well as a wagon for H.Q., C & D Coy Officers' messes, signallers & pioneers equipment.

4. O/C Transport will also arrange to have the Officers' chargers for H.Q., C & D Coys, at HERBECOURT, by 10 p.m.; for O/C B Coy by 6 p.m.
Horses will be sent to pick up the cookers at HERBECOURT & WILLKIND, and transport to WILLKIND for "A" Coy Officers' mess. "B" Coy Officers' mess will be picked up at HERBECOURT by the wagons returning from the Ration dump. It will be dumped on the road ready, under a servant.

5. The Quartermaster will instruct Coy.Q.M.Sergeants to act as billetting party & to report to the B.T.O., at 10 a.m., to-morrow to take over the centre line of huts at Camp 56.
He will also arrange with O/C Transport for the conveyance of blankets, packs, Officers' valises, etc , to the camp, and see that arrangements are made for the men to bathe their feet in hot water on arrival at the camp.

Issued at 9 p.m.
2nd March 1917.

J.M.Cowley [signature]
Capt. & Adjt.
1/5th Battn.Royal Warwickshire Regiment.

Copies	1 & 2.	War Diary.	Copy No.8	T.O.
"	3 - 6	Companies.	" " 9.	M.O.
"	7.	Q.M.	" "10.	R.S.M.

Copy No 1.

OPERATION ORDERS NO.86.
BY
Lieut.Col. J.RETALLACK,M.C.,
Commdg.1/5th Battn.Royal Warwickshire Regiment.
6th March, 1917.

Ref:Map. 62C.N.W. 1/20,000.

1. The 1/5th R.War.R., will move to Camp 50 Bis, on the evening of the 7th/8th March.
2. Coys will leave Camp 56 as under:-

   H.Q. - 5.55 p.m.
   A Coy. - 6 p.m.
   B " - 6.10 p.m.
   C " - 6.20 p.m.
   D " - 6.30 p.m.

   Men will carry full equipment, with blankets.
3. H.Q.Coy.Q.M.S. & Coy Q.M.Sergts will proceed to Camp 50 Bis, reporting there at 10 a.m., and will take over the huts of the 1/8th R.War.R. They will then return and act as guides to their respective companies.
4. O/C Transport will arrange to have transport for the Lewis Guns and ammunition at Camp 56 by ~~4~~ 6 p.m.
   O/C Lewis Guns will supervise the loading and unloading of the guns.
   Transport for Officers' valises & mess boxes will be at Camp 56 by ~~4~~ 5.30 p.m.
   Coy Cookers will move at ~~4~~ 6 p.m.
5. O/C Coys will inspect their men's huts & the officers' mess kitchens to see that everything is clean.
   The Orderly Officer for the day will report to the Camp Commandant Camp 56 at 5 p.m., and obtain a certificate from him that the Battn. area is clean and in good order. This certificate will be forwarded to the Orderly Room by the same evening.

Issued at 5.15 p.m.
6th March,1917.

Capt. & Adjutant.
1/5th Battn.Royal Warwickshire Regiment.

Copies 1 & 2 War Diary.
" 3 - 6 Companies.
Copy No.7 T.O & Q.M.
" " 8. R.S.M.

NOTICE.

Troops will have tea ~~after arrival at~~ before departure to Camp 50 Bis.

Copy No 1.

OPERATION ORDERS NO.87.

by

Lieut.Colonel C.RETALLACK,M.C,
Commdg.1/5th Battn.Royal Warwickshire Regiment.
12th March,1917.

Ref: Maps 62C.NW. 1/20,000.
PERONNE 1/10,000.

1. The 5th R.War.R., will relieve the 6th R.War.R., in the Right Sector to-morrow, 13th inst.
2. Companies will take over the following dispositions:-
   "B" Coy in the front line, with 4 Lewis Guns.
   "D" " " support in IGLAU trench with 4 Lewis Guns.
   "C" " " reserve in XXXXXXX HERBECOURT with 3 Lewis Guns
   "A" " " " " WILLKIND with 3 Lewis Guns.
3. The Battn. will move off in the following order:-
   H.Q.-B-D-C-A Coys, with 100 yards interval between coys and platoons. H.Q., will pass the entrance to the Camp at 5.30 p.m.
   H.Q-B-D & C Coys will proceed by the route:-
   HERBECOURT,
   Ration Dump,
   Trench Board Track.
   "A" Coy by the route:-
   ECLUSIER,
   FRISE,
   Rd junction H.15.a.12.
   Dress - Fighting Order, greatcoats rolled & Box Respirators in the Alert position. Blankets will not be taken.
4. H.Q., will meet 1 guide, B & D Coys 1 guide per platoon & 1 for coy H.Q., at the Warwick Dump, at 7 p.m., & C Coy 1 guide per platoon & 1 for coy H.Q., at the West end of HERBECOURT.
5. Limbers for Lewis Guns will be at the Camp by 4.45 p.m. These limbers will preceed the Battn, under O/C Lewis Guns, Lewis Gunners and guns of the front & support coys will rejoin their coys at the Warwick Dump, and those of "C" Coy at HERBECOURT.
   A separate limber will be sent for the "A" Coy guns, which will go with "A" Coy. I Box containing 4 Lewis Gun Magazines will be taken up for each of the eight guns in the front and support lines, and 3 full boxes of Lewis Gun magazines for each of the six guns in reserve.
6. Blankets will be rolled, by sections, and be dumped at the Q.M. Stores, under the supervision of the Reg.Sergt.Major at the following times:-
   H.Q. - 1.30 p.m.
   "B" Coy- 1.40 p.m.
   "D" " - 2. p.m.
   "C" " - 2.20 p.m.
   "A" " - 2.40 p.m.
   Officers' kits & mess boxes will also be dumped with the Quartermaster before the Battn. moves off.
7. Limber wagons for Lewis Guns and a limber wagon for the trench mess boxes and baggage of H.Q-B-C & D Coys, will be at the Camp by 4.45 p.m.
   A limber for the Orderly Room boxes, "A" Coy trench mess box & baggage will be at the Camp by 5 p.m.
   The "C" Coy cooker will proceed to HERBECOURT. The "A" Coy digschies will be taken to WILLKIND, where a field kitchen will be made.
   All mess stuff,etc., is to be left in charge of 1 servant per coy who will march with the wagon.
8. The following reliefs will take place on the night of the 15/16th inst:- "A" Coy will relieve "B" Coy in the front line.
   "B" Coy on relief will move to WILLKIND.
   On the night of 17th/18th inst., "C" Coy will relieve "A" Coy in the front XXXXXXX line. "A" Coy will then move to HERBECOURT.
   When "B" & "A" Coys are relieved in the front line they will hand over the fourth Lewis Gun and ammunition then in their possession to the incoming company who will finda team to man it.

Issued at 6.45 p.m.
12th March,1917.

J H Cranbury (signature)
Capt. & Adjt.
1/5th Battn.Royal Warwickshire Regt.

Copy 1 & 2 War Diary.　　　Copy No. 7. T.O. & Q.M.
" 3 - 6 Companies.　　　" " 8. Reg. S.M.

NOTICES.

I. The Camp will be inspected before moving out and a certificate that it is clean and in good order will be rendered by O/C Coys to the Orderly Room by 5 p.m.

II. Reports, foot rubbing certificates,etc., are required as usual in the trenches.

III. All Gum boots will be taken up to the trenches and worn in the front line.

IV. On days when no relief takes place, the coy situated in HEREBCOURT will be responsible for detailing two platoons as Ration & Water-carrying parties to the front line.
O/C Support coy will be responsible for detailing his own Ration party.. On relief nights the relieving coy will take up with them their rations, and any extra water they require

Copy No 1

O P E R A T I O N   O R D E R S   NO.88.

BY

Lieut.Colonel C.RETALLACK,M.C,
Commdg. 1/5th Battn.Royal Warwickshire Regiment.
18th March, 1917.

Ref: Map PERONNE. 1/40,000.

I. When the enemy has been completely cleared from the ground west of the SOMME, the 144 Inf: Bde will cover the whole of the Divisional Front, with outposts.

2. Ref: para.1., when the 144 Inf: Bde have taken up outposts, the 143rd Inf: Bde will withdraw.

3. In accordance with para.2, the 5th R.War.R., will move out to Camp 50 bis, at ECLUSIER in the order :-

The front line garrison will withdraw first, via MENARIx ~~T~~RENCH-BIACHE-BIACHE-HERBECOURT Road.

The garrison of O.G.1 & 2 will move next via SUNKEN ROAD-BIACHE-FLAUCOURTROAD-~~543-[illegible]~~TRENCH BOARD TRACK-BIACHE HERBECOURT ROAD.

The garrison of the old British front line will move by the Trench Board Track and HERBECOURT-BIACHE Road.

The IGLAU garrison will go by the same route at the time ordered by Batt.H.Q.

4. Time for the commencement of the move will be notified later. If the withdrawal is in daylight, platoons will move back under cover as much as possible, with 500 yards interval

5 All trench stores, bombs, surplus S.A.A., etc., must be dumped in dumps central for the outposts of the 144th Inf: Bde, handed over and receipts obtained.
All Battn.& coy. stores, digschies, hot food containers, water tins, very pistoals, gum boots, wire cutters, bomb bags & bomb cups, platoon flags, must be brought out, All Heavy stores will be dumped by the men at the junction of the trench board track and the BIACHE-HERBECOURT road, under the provost Corporal, The last orders also apply to Lewis Guns and their drums.

6. Separate orders have been issued to the Transport Officer and Quartermaster.

J.H. Canby (signature)
Capt. & Adjt.
1/5th Battn.Royal Warwickshire Regiment.

Issued at 9 a.m.
18th March 1917.

Copies 1 & 2. War Diary.
" 3 - 6. Coys.
7. O/C Detachment.

Copy No. 1

OPERATION ORDERS NO.89.
BY
Lieut.Col. C.RETALLACK, M.C.,
Commdg. 1/5th Battn.Royal Warwickshire Regiment.
24th March,1917.

Ref:Map. PERONNE.62C.NW.4.1/10,000.

1. The Battn.will move to MOUNT ST.QUENTIN & ST.DENIS, to-morrow, 25th inst.
2. Coys will pass the road junction at I.19.b.90,85, as under:-

H.Q.	9 a.m.
A Coy.	9.5 a.m.
B "	9.15 a.m.
C "	9.25 a.m.
D "	9.35 a.m.

Route - via cross roads I.14.d.89.

3. Men will carry one blanket, placed under the oil sheet - rolled on top of valise.- Steel helmets will be carried outside the pack, under the supporting straps.
4. Blankets, rolled by tens, will be dumped opposite the Medical Inspection room by 7.30 a.m.
5. Officers' valises and mess boxes will be at transport lines by ~~8.30 a.m.~~ 9 am
6. O.C. Coys are responsible that their billets and the area around them are left clean.
7. Separate orders have been issued to the Transport Officer.

Issued at 8.30 p.m.
24th March,1917.

E P 2 Carter
Lieut.
Actg.Adjt.
1/5th Battn.Royal Warwickshire Regiment.

Copies 1 & 2. War Diary.
" 3 - 6. Companies.
Copy No.7. T.O. & Q.M.
" " 8. Reg.Sergt.Major.

Copy No. 1

OPERATION ORDERS NO.90.
BY
Lieut.Col. C.RETALLACK, M.C.,
Commdg.1/5th Battn.Royal Warwickshire Regiment.
25th March, 1917.

Ref: Map 62 C. 1/40,000.

1. The 5th R.War.R., will move to BUSSU and AIZECOURT and take over billets vacated by the 7th R.War.T.
2. H.Q., and A & D Coys will move to BUSSU, B & C Coys will move to AIZECOURT.
3. Men will carry one blanket, placed in the oil sheet, rolled on top of the valise. Steel helmets will be carried outside the pack, under the supporting straps.
4. The remaining blankets, rolled by tens, will be dumped outside Coy.H.Q. These will be collected by the Quartermaster, and returned to Ordnance.
5. Officers' valises and mess boxes will be stacked outside Coy.H.Q., and picked up by the Transport.
6. Coys will move off independently, by platoons, and must be clear of the present area by 6 p.m. to-night.
7. Battn.H.Q., will open at I.18.b.5.2., at 7 p.m.
8. Separate orders have been issued to the Transport Officer.
9. One N.C.O., per Coy., will proceed at once to find billets for their companies.

Issued at 5 p.m.
25th March.1917.

Lieut.
Actg.Adjutant.
1/5th Battn.Royal Warwickshire Regiment.

Copies 1 & 2. War Diary.
" 3 - 6. Companies.
Copy No.7. Q.M. & T.O.
" " 8. Reg.S.M.

Copy No. 1

OPERATION ORDDERS NO.91.
by
Lieut.Col. C.RETALLACK, M.C.,
Commdg. 1/5th Battn. Royal Warwickshire Regiment.
27th March,1917.

Ref:Map 62C.N.E. 1/20,000.

1. The 5th R.War.R., will move to DRIENCOURT to-day.
2. Coys. will march out independently, and on arrival will be disposed as under:-
   H.Q., "B" & "C" Coys = DRIENCOURT.
   "A" Coy. = In dug-outs at J.9.c.62.
   "D" Coy. = In dug-outs at J.9.c.65.
   Coys. are to be clear of BUSSU and AIZECOURT by 9.15 a.m.
3. Officers' valises and mess boxes will be stacked outside Coy.H.Q., in the charge of a sick man, and will be picked up by transport.
4. Steel helmets will be worn. Blankets will be carried, rolled on top of the valise.
5. Battn.H.Q., will open at DRIENCOURT at 10 a.m.
6. 1 N.C.O., per coy., will proceed to DRIENCOURT in advance to find billets.
7. Separate orders have been issued to the Transport Officer.

Issueed at 4 a.m.
27th March,1917.

E P L Carter Lieut.
Actg.Adjutant.
1/5th Battn.Royal Warwickshire Regiment.

Copies 1 & 2. War Diary. Copy No. 7. T.O. & Q.M.
" 3 - 6. Companies. " " 8. Reg.S.M.

HEADQUARTERS
No. P.B.R.W.5.F.
Date 17.12.15
143rd INFANTRY BRIGADE

A.G's Office at the Base.
140/592.

48th DIVN. No. 2924 A.X.

48th Division.

The following are the ~~6~~ chief points to be observed in rendering War Diaries, and are sent to you in order to avoid considerable correspondence which is inevitable if Units in the field fail to comply with the Regulations.

1. Make up Diaries by complete months and render the "Original" on the last day of each month to this office, marked "Confidential" or "Secret" & addressed to the Officer i/c A.G's Office at the Base, vide Field Service Regulations, Part 11, Section 140.

2. Write clearly on the War Diary the name of the unit to which it refers.

3. "Duplicate" copies to Home Records. In the case of Formations, e.g., Infantry Brigade H. Qrs., the "Duplicate" copies should be sent here, & clearly marked "Duplicate".

4. Volumes will be rendered by months.

5. O. C. Unit will sign the Diary.

Attached is also an extract from a War Office letter, (marked X) which it is requested may be circulated to units.

G.H.Q., 3rd Echelon,
12th Decr., 1915.

(sd) J. Scott, Major
for Major General, D. A. G.

EXTRACT FROM WAR OFFICE LETTER No. M.O.1. dated 27th OCTOBER, 1915.

X X X

The Diaries of several other units also failed in this respect but not to so marked a degree. "For historical purposes it is very necessary that the position of the trenches occupied should be capable of being identified on the map".
"It would be advantageous if the units whenever possible, make a practice of stating what units were on their flanks, or elsewhere in touch with them".

I am, etc. (sd) M.G.TALBOT, Colonel,
for Director of Military Operations.

-2-

O.C. 5th Bn, R. War. R.

For information.

[signature] Capt,
Acting Bde Major,
143rd Infantry Brigade.

17th December, 1915.

Copy No. 1

OPERATION ORDERS NO.92.
BY
Lieut.Col.C.RETALLACK.,M.C.,
Commdg.1/5th Battn.Royal Warwickshire Regiment.
28th March,1917.

Ref:Map 62C,N.E. 1/20,000.

1, The Outpost Line of Resistance for the Brigade to-night,XXXX 28/29th inst.,will be along road from E,23,a,25 to E,17,a,95, thence to East edge of SAULCOURT.
2. The dividing line between Battalions will be GREDAUSSART WOOD-JEAN COPSE-E,17;a,95.,all inclusive to the Left Battn,
3, The 5th R,War.R.,will relieve the 8th R.War.R.,in the Right Sector this afternoon. The 145 Inf:Bde will be on their right, and the 6th R,War.R.,will be on their left.
4. Coys will be disposed as under:-
   - B Coy - The outpost line of resistance from E.23.a.25 to E.17.a.95.
   - C Coy.- The dug-outs in the sunken road leading from E.22.d.78 to E.22.b.15.
   - A Coy. The line from road junction K.3.a.70-GROS WOOD-GUILLEMET COPSE.
   - D Coy. In LONGAVESNES and trenches East & South of LONGAVESNES.
   - Battn.H.Q. In Balloon Shed E.27.a.
5. Guides from 8thRWar.R. will be at LONGAVESNES E.26.d.38 at 4.30 p,m.
6. Coys will march by platoons at 100 yards interval in the following order:-
   - H.Q.
   - B Coy.
   - C Coy.
   - A Coy.
   - D Coy.
7. Route - Road junction J.4.d-J.5b-E.25.d.36. The first platoon of B Coy to pass road junction J.4.d.,at 3.45 p,m,
8. Dress - Fighting Order, with greatcoats & blanket.
9. Pack mules & Lewis Gun limbers will go with their coys.
10. Reports to Battn.H.Q. as soon as relief is complete.
11. Officers valises & surplus mess boxes will be collected by the Transport Officer and returned to Q.M.Stores.
12. Separate orders have been issued to the Transport Officer,

Issued at 2.45 p.m.
28th March,1917.

Lieut. & A/Adjt.,
1/5th Battn,Royal Warwickshire Regiment.

Copies 1 & 2. War Diary.
" 3 - 6. Companies.
Copy No.7. T.O. & Q.M.
" " 8. 143th Inf:Bde,

Appendix I 3

SECRET.

Copy No. . . . .

143rd Inf. Bde. OPERATION ORDERS NO, 130.

Ref. maps.
Sheet 62C N.E. 1/20,000
,, 57C S.E. ,,

31st March, 1917.

1. The 143rd and 144th Inf. Bdes. will attack and capture EPEHY and PEIZIERE to-morrow 1st April.

2. The boundaries of the 143rd Inf. Bde. are :-
Right CAPRON COPSE - EPEHY Railway Station F.1.a.9095 (both exclusive)
Left. Line from E.9.b.03 - X.19.c.00

3. The attack of the 143rd Inf. Bde. will be carried out by the 6th Bn. with the 5th Bn. in support

4. The final objective of the 6th Bn. will be the railway line N.E. of PEIZIERE from the railway station F.1.a.9095 (exclusive) to X.19.c.20, ~~which~~ but positions will be taken up in accordance with the nature of the ground.

5. The 6th Bn. will deploy for the attack on a line running through Eastern edge of CAPRON COPSE and CHAUFOURS WOOD.
The 5th Bn. will assemble just west of SAULCOURT
O.C. 6th Bn. may call direct on O.C. 5th Bn. for 2 Coys. if required but the remaining 2 Coys. of the 5th Bn. will be in Bde. reserve.
The 5th and 6th Bns. will be in the above positions by 4-30 a.m. to-morrow.

6. The 6th Bn. will advance to the attack from their position of deployment at 5 a.m. to-morrow 1st April.
1 Coy. of the 6th Bn. will advance on the left flank of the Bde. boundary and should be advanced to about W.29.c. by 5 a.m. in order to reach the high ground at F.25.a.26 at the same time as the remainder of the Bn. reaches the Western edge of PEIZIERE so as to ~~reach~~ cut off the enemy's retreat.

7. 2 Coys. of the 5th Bn. will advance in support of the 6th Bn. at 5 a.m. but will halt in about E.5.c. unless the 6th Bn. require support.
The remaining 2 Coys. to remain in Bde. Reserve West of SAULCOURT.

8. 143 M.G.Coy. will place 4 guns at the disposal of O.C. 6th Bn. 1 of the guns will advance with the detached Coy. round the left flank and 3 will advance in rear of the Bn. to help in consolidation of objective when gained. 4 guns will be in GREBAUSSART WOOD in Bde. Reserve.

9. The 241 Bde. R.F.A. will be prepared to assist in the attack of the 6th Bn. but will not fire unless a signal (S.O.S.) is fired from the left flank of the Bn. when the Western edge of PEIZIERE will be bombarded for 5 minutes..
A slow barrage will be placed 200 yds. E. of the final objective at 6-30 a.m. and, after 6-30 a.m. if the S.O.S. signal is fired from troops holding the objective, a heavy barrage will be formed.

10. A contact aeroplane will fly over PEIZIERE at 7 a.m. or 1 hour after the mist clears, when ~~the~~ aeroplane flares will be lighted by the troops holding the most forward positions.

11. The 144th Inf. Bde. will be advancing on our right from on the line through Eastern edge of CHAUFOURS WOOD and CAPRON COPSE at 5 a.m.

/12

12. The 7th and 8th Bns. will be ready to move from their present positions at short notice.

13. Advanced Dressing Station will be formed at LONGAVESNES and ambulances will run to SAULCOURT for stretcher cases.

14. Advanced Bde. Hdqrs. will open at GREBAUSSART WOOD at 4-30 a.m.

15. ACKNOWLEDGE.

Captain,

Issued through Signals
at 10 p.m.

B.M. 143rd Inf. Bde.

Copy No. 1 and 2 retained
3 to 9 Bde. units.
10 144th Inf. Bde.
11 145th Inf. Bde.
12 24rd Inf. Bde.
13 48th Division.
14 241 Bde. R.F.A.
15 & 16 War Diary.

Vol 26

Army Form C. 2118.

WAR DIARY
or
~~INTELLIGENCE SUMMARY~~
(Erase heading not required.) - April 1917 -

1/5 Battn The Royal Warwickshire Regt

Instructions regarding War Diaries and Intelligence Summaries are contained in F. S. Regs., Part II. and the Staff Manual respectively. Title pages will be prepared in manuscript.

Ref Maps 57c S.W. 1/20,000 62c N.W.

Hour, Date, Place	April	Summary of Events and Information	Remarks and references to Appendices
4.30 a.m. CHAUFOURS WOOD	1.	The 5th Battn were in support to 143 Bde Attack on PEIZIERE EPÈHY as in 143 Inf Bde O.O. No 130. The 6th R Warwick reached their objective by 10.30 a.m. & 5th R Warwick were disposed as follows: HQrs, B, C } GRESSAUSSART WOOD; A SAULCOURT WOOD; D E 5 c under orders of C.O. 6 R Warwick.	~~Appendix I~~
		Casualties { Killed 3 OR's - accidentally Killed 1 OR; under date 29/3/17 { Wounded 4 OR's. On strength 2nd Lt. D.H. BARR from 3/8 R War. R & 40 R's	Appendix 1. Ch.
10 p.m.	2.	5 Battn relieved 6 R Warwick in outpost line as in O.O. No 93 - The 144 Bde were on right and 8th Division on left	O.O. 93
		Casualties ~~Nil~~ 1. O.R.	Ch
	3	Casualties. Nil	
	4	Casualties. 2/Lt A.J. LILLY Killed - 3. O.R. wounded	
10.15 p.m.	5th	5 R Warwick relieved by 8th Battn as in O.O. 94 - ~~2 O.R.s wounded~~ Casualties - Wounded 2 OR's	O.O. 94 - Ch
5.30 p.m.	8th	5 R Warwick relieved by 5th Bn Lancs Fusiliers and marched to billets at TEMPLEUX LA FOSSE	Ch
	9th	2/Lt F.S. TOTE taken on strength of Battn	Ch
	10th	5th R Warw. R. Move to CARTIGNY as in O.O. 95	O.O. 95 JRC
	10th	Reinforcements received - 20 R.	JRC
	~~12th~~	~~Reinforcements received - 7 OR.~~	JRC

1247 W 3299 200,000 (E) 8/14 J.B.C. & A. Forms/C. 2118/11.

26 I. (17 sheets)

Instructions regarding War Diaries and Intelligence Summaries are contained in F. S. Regs., Part II. and the Staff Manual respectively. Title pages will be prepared in manuscript.

WAR DIARY
or
~~INTELLIGENCE SUMMARY~~
(Erase heading not required.)

Army Form C. 2118.

5 R Warwk
April 1917

Hour, Date, Place	Summary of Events and Information	Remarks and references to Appendices
CARTIGNY April 11–12	Working parties found about 800 strong per day Reinforcements · 6 OR:	Ch
" 14.	Battn Relieved 6 Battn LANCS. FUS. in Right Sector EPEHY Line – OO96 ~~Reinforcements: 14 ORs~~	Ch. – OO96 –
EPEHY 16	The Battn attacked enemy outpost line as in OO. 97. The night was exceedingly dark and with continuous rain & snow operations were very much hampered. CATALET COPSE was found to be strongly wired & fortified and the attack was held up owing to difficulty in getting in & turning out the Enemy. At dawn 17th April we had dug a line from about X28 a 73 and joined with 6th Battn at X22 C53. When light came Catalet Copse & LITTLE PRIEL FARM were found to be evacuated by enemy & the line F4 d 99 – LITTLE PRIEL FARM – CATALET COPSE X28 a 99 was taken up & held Casualties. Killed · 18 ORs Wounded. Lt. J. H. HEYS – 2/Lt. G. W. WILLIAMS & ~~38~~ 40 ORs	Ch O.O. 97 & Appendix 2
17.	Battn relieved by 7th R Warwk & and disposed as under Battn less C & D coys · VILLERS FALCON C & D coys – cellars in EPEHY Reinforcements 2/Lt. F. W. HALE (4 Res Battn The Buffs) 14 OR's	

Instructions regarding War Diaries and Intelligence Summaries are contained in F. S. Regs., Part II. and the Staff Manual respectively. Title pages will be prepared in manuscript.

WAR DIARY
or
~~INTELLIGENCE SUMMARY~~
(Erase heading not required.)

April 1917

1/5 R Warwick

Army Form C. 2118.

Hour, Date, Place		Summary of Events and Information	Remarks and references to Appendices
Ref Map 62c 1/40000	April 18	Major A.H. WHITEHOUSE 1/5 R Warwick temp attached as 2nd in Command vice Major A.S. ALABASTER to Senior Infantry Officers Course England	CR
VILLERS FAUCON	20.	The Bn. relieved by the 9th Manchesters & marched to MARQUAIX – 4 ORs reinforcements –	O.O. 98 CR
MARQUAIX	21st	Capt. J.H. CROSSKEY to act as Ty Major on HQ 1/6 Glosters –	CR
		2/Lt R.E. COOKE and 1 OR reinforcement –	CR
	25		CR O.O. 99
10 a.m.	29	Bn marched to FLAMICOURT – O.O. 99 –	
FLAMICOURT	29	2/Lt S.F. SHARPE – rejoined from leave	
		2/Lt H.C. DAVIES " hospital	CR
		18 ORs reinforcements	
10 a.m.	30	Bn marched to ECLUSIER – O.O. 100	CR – O.O. 100
		Total Strength 33 officers 663 ORs	
		Casualties in month. Killed: 1 officer 10 ORs Wounded: 2 " 44 ORs Died of wounds: 2 ORs	CR

Charles [illegible] Lt Col
Cg 1/5 R Warwick

Copy No 1

O P E R A T I O N   O R D E R S   NO.93.
B Y
Lieut.Col. C.RETALLACK,M.C.,
Commdg. 1-5th Battn.Royal Warwickshire Regiment.
2nd April:1917.

Ref:Maps 62C.N.E. 1/20:000.
57C.S.E. 1/20:000.

1. The 5th R.War.R., will relieve the 6th R.War.R., in the Outpost Line to-night, from X.25.c.90.,to W.24.d,44.
2. Coys will be disposed as under:-
   "D" on the Right, from X.25.c.90 to Bridge at X.25.a.17, with 3 platoons out in front of the railway line: and 1 platoon on railwaynline.
   "A" on the Left,X.25.a.17 to W.24.A.44:-
   By day 3 platoons in railway cutting
   1 platoon in support in road from W.30.b.74-W.30.b25
   By night 3 platoons in trenches in front of cutting
   1 platoon in cutting.
   Coy.H.Q. at W.30.b.54.
   "B" in Support, with 2 platoons in road from W.30.a.92-W.30.a22
   and 2 platoons in trenches about W.30.C & D.
   Coy.H.Q. in road about W.20.a.52.
   "C" in Reserve in trenches at E.6.B.
   Coy.H.Q. at E.6.b.29.

   Battn.H.Q.: in CHAUFOURS WOOD,E.10.B.
   Adv.H.Q. and Report Centre at Cellar on road at X.30.D.52., to which all reports and messages are sent.
3. Vicars machine guns are distributed:-
   2 to Right Coy.
   1 to Left Coy.
   1 at W.30 Central.
4. Coys.will go by platoons at 200 yards distance.
   Dress - Fighting Order & wearing greatcoats.
5. Guides will be at North side of Western entrance tonPEIZIERE, W.30.d.40.
   Coys. will go in following order:-
   D - A - B - C: the first platoon of "D"; to be at W.30.d.40, at 8 p.m.
6. One coy of 6th R.War.R., will be in position at E.5.c., and will be under orders of the C.O.,5th R.War.R., for tactical purposes.
7. The pack mules will be at stables in SAULCOURT.
8. Regtl Aid Post at E.9.d.38.
9. The packs,with blankets inside, of A,B & C Coys & H.Q.,will be dumped by cookers and collected by Transport at 6 p.M,
   D Coy will dump theirs at road junction,E.10.c.16.,by 6.15 p.m.
   Officers' mess boxes will be collected at Coy H.Q.;at 6.30 p.m., and dumped at W.30.d.40.

E R Cartwright [signature]

Issued at 4.30 p.m.,
2nd April,1917.

Lieut. & A/Adjt.,
1/5th Battn.Royal Warwickshire Regiment.

Copies 1 & 2. War Diary.
" 3 - 6. Companies.
Copy NO.7 T.O. & Q.M.
" " 8. Retained.

Copy No 1

OPERATION ORDERS NO.94.
BY
Lieut.Col. C.RETALLACK,M.C.,
Commdg. 1/5th Battn. Royal Warwickshire Regiment.
5th April,1917.

Ref:Map 62C.N.E., 1/20,000.

1. The 5th Battn. will be relieved by the 8th R.War.R.,to-night, April 5th.
2. One guide per coy.H.Q., and one guide per platoon will be at entrance to village at 7.45 p.m.
   O/C A Coy will also find a guide for Battn.H.Q., of the 8th Battn., which will be situated at W.30.d.15.
3. The Right Coy will be taken over by A Coy of 8th Battn.
   " Left " " " " " " B " " " "
   " Support" " " " " " D " " " "
   " Reserve" " " " " " C " " " "
4. Picks and shovels will be stacked at entrance to village and will be taken over by the 8th Battn.
   S.A.A.,S.O.S.signals,bivouac sheets will also be handed over.
   A duplicate receipt for all these stores xk must be taken, and a copy sent to Battn.H.Q., by 10 a.m.,to-morrow morning.
5. Limbers for Lewis Guns & ammunition & for officers' messes will be at entrance to village by 8 p.m. Also limbers for cooking utensils.
6. After relief:
   A & D Coys will proceed to SAULCOURT.
   B & C " " " " GREBAUSSART WOOD.
   Battn.H.Q. will remain at CHAUFOURS WOOD.
7. Each coy will detail an advance party of 1 N.C.O. per platoon, and 1 for coy H.Q., to report to Battn.H.Q., CHAUFOURS WOOD,at 5 p.M.to-day, to arrange billets for their companies.
   They will then act as guides to their platoons and will meet them on the SAULCOURT-PEZIERES road, just South of CHAUFOURS WOOD at 9 p.m.
8. Officers' valises, messes and mens packs will be dumped ready for the arrival of companies.
9. One officer per coy of the 8th R.War.R., will be at Report Centre at 6 p.m.,to-night, and will be taken by the orderlies to coys.H. Q. O-C Coys will show them their dispositions and hand over the work in hand.
10. Separate orders have been issued to the Transport Officer.
11. Completion of relief to be reported to Battn.H.Q.

Issued at 4 p.m.,
5th April,1917.

Lieut. & A/Adjt.,
1/5th Battn.Royal Warwickshire Regiment.

Copies 1 & 2. War Diary.
" 3 - 6. Companies.
Copy No. 7. Transport Officer.
" " 8. Quartermaster.

NOTICE.

The M.O. has provided a soup kitchen at his Dressing Station at SAULCOURT at E.9.d.38. Soup will be available from 9.30 p.m., onwards.

Copy No 1

OPERATION ORDERS NO.95.

BY

Lieut.Col. C.RETALLACK,M.C,
Commdg.1/5th Battn.Royal Warwickshire Regiment.
9th April,1917.

Ref:Maps 62C.N.E. 1/20,000.
62C.S.E. 1/20,000.

1. The 5th R.War.R., will move to CARTIGNY to-morrow, April 10th. The Battn. will also bathe and receive clean clothes at TINCOURT J.24.a.84. Rate of bathing: 40 men per hour.
2. Battn. will move in accordance with following march table:-

A COY. 40 men to be at the baths at 8.30 a.m.
After bathing proceed to CARTIGNY via BUIRE and road junction J.33.a.09.

B COY. 40 men to be at the baths at 9.30 a.m.
40 " " " " " " " 10.30 a.m.
40 " " " " " " " 11.30 a.m.
After bathing proceed to CARTIGNY.

C COY. The coy, marching by half-coys at 100 yards distance, will rendezvous at J.24.c.89 at 11.a.m., where coy will halt and have dinner. The cooker will accompany the coy.
The coy, will then bathe as under:-
40 men to be at the baths at 12.30 p.m.
40 " " " " " " " 1.30 p.m.
40 " " " " " " " 2.30 p.m.
After bathing each party will march to CARTIGNY.

D COY. The coy will march by half-coys at 100 yards distance to CARTIGNY, via TINCOURT,BUIRE and road junction J.33.a.09. To be clear of TEMPLEUX-LA-FOSSE by 9 a.m.
After dinner in CARTIGNY, the coy will march in clean fatigue to bathe as under:-
40 men to be at baths at 3.30 p.m.
40 " " " " " " 4.30 p.m.
40 " " " " " " 5.30 p.m.

TRANSPORT. The Transport (less C Coy cooker) will march as a complete unit and be clear of cross roads, J.10.b, by 10 a.m.

3. ALL details, except H.Q.servants,and Transport, will go with their own coys, and O/C Coys are responsible that their details are warned as to place and hour of parade.
4. The Advance Party, as under, will rendezvous at Battn.H.Q., at 7.30 a.m:-
Lieut. C.E.CARRINGTON.
No.7171 Sgt.Dmr.ROWLES P.C.
4 Coy. Q.M. Sergeants.
On arrival at CARTIGNY they will report to the Town Major, arrange billets and act as guides for their respective coys.
5. Officers' valises and mess boxes will be ready for collection by 8.30 a.m. - outside Coy.H.Qs.
Blankets; rolled in tens, will be dumped outside Coy.H.Qs, ready for collection by 7 a.m. One man per coy left in charge.
6. Separate orders have been issued to the Transport Officer.

E R L Carter

Lieut. & A/Adjutant.
1/5th Battn.Royal Warwickshire Regiment.

Issued at 7 p.m.
9th April, 1917.

Copies 1 & 2, War Diary. Copy No. 7, T.O. & Q.M.
" 3 - 6, Companies. " " 8, Reg. Sergt,M.

Copy No. 1

OPERATION ORDERS NO.96.

BY

Lieut.Col. C.RETALLACK,M.C.,
Commdg.1/5th Battn.Royal Warwickshire Regiment.
13th April,1917.
4

Ref:Map

62C. 1/40,000.
57C. 1/40,000.

1. The 143 Inf:Bde will relieve the 125th Inf:Bde in the EPEHY Sector on the 14th/15th April.
2. The 5th R.War.R., will move from CARTIGNY and relieve the 6th Battn.Lancashire Fusiliers in the Right Battn.Sector.
3. The Battn.will fall in on the main CARTIGNY road, facing S.E, with the head of the column at cross roads P.4.c.36, ready to march off at 2 p.m., in the following order:- A-B-C-D.

XX Route:- CARTIGNY.
BRUSLE.
~~BOUCHY.~~
TINCOURT.
MARQUAIX.
ROISEL.
St.EMILIE.
EPEHY.

Dress - Fighting Order,with greatcoats rolled.

A halt of one hour will take place East of ROISEL for teas, after which the Battn.will proceed by half-coys at 100 yards distance.

4. After the first ten minutes halt one officer per coy (mounted) will ride on to EPEHY to reconnoitre.
5. All billets and area round billets & cookers,etc., must be left clean.
6. Officers' valises for transport lines and officers' mess boxes etc., for trenches must be stacked outside Coy.H.Q. ~~by 12 P.M.~~ at Transport. Men's packs, with blankets inside will be stacked outside ~~Coy H.Q.~~, by 12 noon. One L.D.man per coy to be left in charge.
7. Further details re disposition of coys will be notified as soon as possible.
8. Box Respirators will be carried in the Alert position from commencement of march.
9. Guides from 6th Battn.Lancashire Fusiliers will be at entrance to EPEHY at 7.45 p.m.
10. Separate orders have been issued to the Transport Officer.

Charles Retallack Lt Col

Issued at 11 a.m.,
14th April,1917.

for
Lieut. & A/Adjt.,
1/5th Battn.Royal Warwickshire Regiment.

Copies 1 & 2. War Diary. Copy No. 7. T.O. & Q.M.
" 3 - 6. Companies. " " 8. R.S.M.

1/5th Battn. The Royal Warwickshire Regiment.

Ref Map 62c NE 1/20.000 57c SE 1/20.000

DISPOSITIONS OF RIGHT BATTALION - LEFT BRIGADE SECTOR.

A **OUTPOST COY.**

1 Platoon in MALASSLEE FARM.
1 Platoon in No.12 Copse.
1 Platoon in No.13 Copse, F.4.a.09.
2 Sections in No.14 Copse, X.27.c.67.
2 Sections in RED RUIN, X.27.a.41.
Coy.H.Q., in Railway Cutting, F.2.c.24.

B **COY. HOLDING BROWN LINE.**

From F.8.a.34 to F.1.a.99., with
1 Platoon in East Edge of TETARD WOOD.
Coy.H.Q., F.1.d.60.

C **SUPPORT COY.**

2 Platoons in Cutting from F.1.d.60-F.1.b.62.
2 Platoons in cellars about F.1.b.04.
Coy.H.Q., F.1.b.11.

D **RESERVE COY.**

In cellars round Battn.H.Q.
Coy.H.Q., F.1.c.69.

BATTN.H.Q.

F.1.c.55.

Carter Retaliation -

15th April, 1917.

Lieut.COL., Commdg.,
1/5th Battn. R. War. R.

1/5th Battn.

Copy No. 1

OPERATION ORDERS NO.97.
BY
Lieut.Col. C.RETALLACK,M.C.,
Commdg. 1/5th Battn.Royal Warwickshire Regiment.
16th April,1917.

---

1. The 48th Division will attack and hold the following line on the night of April 16th:-
   TOM BOIS FARM.
   LITTLE PRIEL FARM.
   CATELET COPSE.
   LINE OF ROAD THROUGH X.22.c.90-cross roads X.28.c.66-X.22.a.24-X.15.d.94.
2. The 145 Inf:Bde will attack on the Right, and the 143 Inf:Bde on the Left.
3. The 143 Inf:Bde will attack on a two-Battn front:- the 5th R.War.R. on the Right & the 6th R.War.R. on the Left.
4. The Boundary between the 5th R.War.R. & the 145 Inf:Bde on Right is a line from Level Crossing,F.2.a.43 to a point 500 yards South of LITTLE PRIEL FARM,inclusive to 5th R.War.R.
   That between 5th R.War.R. & the 6th R.War.R.on Left is EPEHY STATION,F.1.a.99 (inclusive to 6th R.War.R.)thence along the Southern line of 140 Contour through X.25.c & b.- X.27.a & b and X.25.a.99.
5. At ZERO, C Coy, with 2 platoons of D Coy, will capture line Cross roads,F.4.b.18 - CATELET COPSE (both inclusive) aling line of road to Northern boundary at X.28.a.99.
   After line in taken 2 platoons of C Coy will be reorganised to support attack on LITTLE PRIEL FARM.
   The 2 platoons of D Coy, less a small garrison left at F.4.b.18 will then reorganise and come under orders of O/C D Coy, for attack on LITTLE PRIEL FARM.
   As soon as this line is held, the attack on LITTLE PRIEL FARM will be launched.
   D COY, with 1 platoon of A Coy in support, will attack from South, having its Left on road from F.4.b.18 to LITTLE PRIEL FARM.
   B COY, with 2 platoons of C Coy in support, will attack on North, having its Right on road from F.28.d.15 to F.28.d.51.
   A coy of the 7th R.War.R., will be in Reserve.
   The 143 Bde M.G.Coy will establish gun positions as follows:-
   2 guns in LITTLE PRIEL FARM.
   1 gun in CATELET COPSE.
   1 gun in No.13 COPSE.
6. Report Centre will be at No.13 COPSE, where all messages will be sent.
7. Coys will use the road MALASSLEE FARM-CATELET COPSE.
   C Coy, plus 2 platoons of D Coy, will pass MALASSLEE FARM as soon as they can move unobserved, and will form up ready to deploy from road junction, F.4.a.08 at 9.40 p.m.
   The remainder will pass MALASSLEE FARM 10 minutes after C Coy, and will then proceed as follows:-
   (D Coy,(less 2 platoons)) to
   (a coy, 7th R.War.R.) valley between
   (1 platoon of A Coy.) Nos 12 & 13 Copse.
   B Coy. about F.3.b.67.
   where they will await orders to move to position of deployment for attack.
8. A dump of tools will be at No.13 COPSE.
9. Aeroplane flares will be carried. A contact aeroplane will pass over at 6.30 a.m. on April 17th.
10. Regtl. Aid Post will be at MALASSLEE FARM.
11. Hour of ZERO will be at 10 p.m.

Issued at 3.30 p.m.,
16th April,1917.

Lieut. & A/Adjt.,
1/5th Battn.Royal Warwickshire Regiment.

(continued)

Copies 1 & 2. War Diary. Copy 7. 143 inf?Bde for informn.
" 3 - 6. Companies. " 8. 6th R.War.R. " "
" 9. 7th R.War.R. " "
" 10. Retained.

ADDENDUM TO O.O. NO.97.

I. A COY, less 1 platoon, will hold the present Outpost Line as follows:-
1 Platoon in No.12 COPSE.
1 Platoon in No.13 COPSE.
1 Platoon in No.14 COPSE.

2 coys, 8th R.War.R., will be in Bde Reserve and take over dispositions of B & C Coys, and platoon of A Coy in MALASSLEE FARM.

II. ARTILLERY ARRANGEMENTS. There will be no previous bombardment or barrage fire on the enemy's position.

Should our infantry require artillery support during the attack, they will fire an S.O.S. signal and artillery fire will be brought to bear on the enemy's position for 5 minutes in the direction of the signal.

Artillery will also be prepared to fire on any other hostile positions East of our objectives, if required.

Form

MESSAGES AND SIGNALS.

Army Form C. 2128.
(In books of 100.)

No. of Message

Prefix SM Code BGS Words 55	Received From S1 By	Sent, or sent out At m. To By	Office Stamp. IB 17/4/17
£ s. d. Charges to collect			
Service Instructions. 1 of 3 adds			

Handed in at S1 Office m. Received 3.15 pm.

TO IB

*Sender's Number	Day of Month	In reply to Number	AAA
GB 409	17		

The corps commander congratulates the Division on its success last night aaa He considers that the ~~lead~~ leading of the different parties up to their objective under the weather conditions of last night shows the result of very good reconnaissance and careful arrangements aaa addressed all units of Division

Orders

FROM S1

PLACE & TIME 1 pm

* This line should be erased if not required.

(B 8188) Wt. w. 7496–M857 250,000 Pads. 1/17 H & S (E489.) Forms/C.2123/3.

Appendix II

All Units.
****

Following message from Army Commander begins. Please convey to 48th Div. my admiration of their success last night. To have carried out a successful night attack on a wide front in the midst of such a storm reflects the highest credit on all ranks and especially on the leadership of subordinate commanders. My best congratulations and thanks to all troops engaged including the artillery. Genl. RAWLINSON.

Orders

HEADQUARTERS 143rd INFANTRY BRIGADE

Copy No. 1

OPERATION ORDERS NO.98.
BY
Lieut.Col. C.RETALLACK,M.C.,
Commdg. 1/5th Battn.Royal Warwickshire Regiment.
20th April, 1917.

---

1. The 143rd Inf:Bde will be relieved by the 126 Inf:Bde on April 20th.
2. The 5th Battn.R.War.R., will be relieved by the 9th Bn.The Manchester Regt.(less 1 coy) and will march to MARQUAIX.
Relief by the Manchester Regt., to be complete by 1 p.m.
ROUTE for C & D Coys: EPEHY.
ST.EMILIE.
ROISEL.
MARQUAIX.
ROUTE for A & B Coys: VILLERS FAUCON.
ROISEL.
MARQUAIX.
Coys to march by half-coys at 100 yards distance as soon as relieved.
DRESS - Marching Order.The blanket to be rolled on top of the valise.
3. Coys will send an Advance Party of 1 N.C.O. per platoon & 1 per coy H.Q., to rendezvous at the Church,VILLERS FAUCON, at 11 a.m. This party will be under the command of 2/Lieut. L.T.O'HANLON.
This party will then act as guides, and await their platoons at the Eastern entrance to MARQUAIX.
4. ALL billets, etc., must be left clean.
5. Officers' valises, etc., of EPEHY coys will be stacked outside 7th R.War.R., H.Q., by 1 p.m. One servant per coy will be left in charge until picked up by the Transport Officer. Transport for Lewis Guns and cookers will be sent to EPEHY by 1 p.m. Officers' charges at EPEHY at 1 p.m.
Officers' valises, etc., of VILLERS FAUCON coys will be collected by Transport Officer at 2 p.m.
Transport for Lewis Guns and cookers will be sent at 1 p.m.
6. On April 21st, B Coy,complete, will march to CARTIGNY and will arrive there at 6.30 a.m., and take over the billets of one coy of the 9th Manchester Regt.
The coy will then report to Corps Camp, LE CATELET at 8 a.m., to work under 428 Field Coy, R.E.
This work will continue daily till further orders, the coy remaining at CARTIGNY.
7. Completion of all reliefs and moves to be reported to Battn. H.Q.
8. Separate orders have been issued to the Transport Officer.
9. ACKNOWLEDGE.

E P J Carter

Lieut. & A/Adjt.,
1/5th Battn.Royal Warwickshire Regiment.

Issued at 10 a.m.
20th April, 1917.

Copies 1 & 2. War Diary. Copy 7. T.O. & Q.M.
" 3 - 6. Companies. " 8. R.S.M.

Copy No. 1

OPERATION ORDERS NO.99.

BY

Lieut.Col. C.RETALLACK,M.C.,

Commdg.1/5th Battn.Royal Warwickshire Regiment.

28th April,1917.

Ref:Map 62C N.E. & 62C.N.W.

1. The 143 Inf:Bde will move to-morrow, the 29th inst.
2. The 5th Battn,will march to FLAMICOURT via TINCOURT,BUIRE, DOINGT - Distance ~~XXX~~ 6 1/2 miles.
3. The Battn.will parade on the main street facing West with the head of the column opposite Bde H.Q., in the following order:-
   Battn.H.Q.- A - B - C - D - Transport, ready to move off at 10 a.m.
   Dress - Marching Order. The oilsheet will be rolled inside flap of valise. Steel hats will be carried under the cross straps of valise.
4. "D" Coy will detail 1 N.C.O. & 4 men to collect stragglers. The party will march in rear of transport and will proceed at pace of slowest.
5. An Advance Party of 1 N.C.O. per platoon & 1 per coy.H.Q., and 1 for Battn.H.Q., under 2/Lieut.L.T.O'HANLON, will rendezvous at Battn.H.Q., at 8 a.m., and report to Town Major,FLAMICOURT.
6. All billets and spaces round cookers,etc., must be left clean. Tents and bivouacx sheets will be taken over by the Town Major.
7. Blankets, rolled by tens, will be dumped outside Battn.H.Q.by 8 a.m
8. Officers' valises and mess boxes will be dumped opposite B Coy H.Q. at 8.30 a.m.
   Horses for cookers will be sent at 9.15 a.m.
9. Dinners will be on arrival at FLAMICOURT.
10. The march will be resumed on the 30th inst.
11. Separate orders have been issued to the Transport Officer.
12. ACKNOWLEDGE.

E P L Carter

Lieut.& A/Adjt.,
1/5th Battn.Royal Warwickshire Regiment,

Issued at 11.50 p.m.,
28th April,1917.

Copies 1 & 2. War Diary. Copy 7. Q.M. & T.O.
" 3 - 6. Companies. " 8. R.S.M.

Copy No 2

OPERATION ORDERS. NO.100.

BY

Lieut.Col. C.RETALLACK, M.C.,
Commdg. 1/8th Battn.Royal Warwickshire Regiment.
30th April, 1917.

Ref:Map Sheet 62C.NW.1/20,000.

1. The 143 Inf:Bde (less 7th & 6th Bns) will move to-day,30th inst.
2. The 8th R.War.R. will march to ECLUSIER, via BIACHES-HERBECOURT. Distance - [illegible] miles.
3. The Bn will parade in the street, with the head of the column opposite Bn H.Q., facing WEST, in the following order:-
   Bn.H.Q.-B-C-D-A-Transport,
   ready to move off at 10 a.m.
   Dress - Marching Order,The oilsheet will be rolled underneath the flap of valise. Steel hats will be carried under the cross straps of valise.
4. "A" Coy will detail 1 N.C.O. & 4 men to collect stragglers. The party will march in rear of transport and will proceed at the pace of the slowest.
5. An advance party of 1 N.C.O. per platoon and 1 per Coy.H.Q., & 1 for Battn.H.Q., under 2/Lieut.L.T.O'HANLON, will rendezvous outside Bn.H.Q., at 8 a.m., and will meet the Staff Captain at the Church,ECLUSIER at 10.30 a.m.
6. Blankets, rolled by tens, will be dumped outside PERONNE-FLAMICOURT Station by 8.30 a.m.
   Leather jerkins will be rolled in bundles of tens and dumped outside transport lines at 7 a.m. They will then be returned to Ordnance.
7. Officers' valises & mess boxes will be dumped outside coy.H.Q., by 8 a.m.
   Horses for cookers will be sent at 9.15 a.m.
8. A halt will be made for dinners.
9. Separate orders have been issued to the Transport Officer.
10. ACKNOWLEDGE.

E.B. Carter

Issued at 9.10 p.m., 30th April,1917.

Lieut. & A/Adjt., 1/8th Battn.Royal Warwickshire Regiment.

Distribution - normal.

27.T
(8 sheets)

143/148

Confidential

War Diary of

1/5th Bn. R. War. R.

From. 1st. May 1917
to. 31st. May 1917.

WO 95/2756

Instructions regarding War Diaries and Intelligence Summaries are contained in F. S. Regs., Part II. and the Staff Manual respectively. Title pages will be prepared in manuscript.

WAR DIARY
or
~~INTELLIGENCE SUMMARY~~

(*Erase heading not required.*)

Army Form C. 2118.

1/5 Bn The Royal Warwickshire Regt

May 1917

Hour, Date, Place		Summary of Events and Information	Remarks and references to Appendices
ECLUSIER	May 2	Reinforcements – Capt E.A.M. Bindloss (from 3/5th Bn R War R) 2nd Lt R Crighton " T.L. Goode " " A.G. Foster Sutton (from 4th Bn The Buffs) 3. O.Rs Rejoined from Base – 2nd Lt C.L. Gordon	H.S.B.
	3	From C.C.S. – 2. O.Rs.	H.S.B.
"	9.0 am 3	The Battn moved to PERONNE (O.O. 101) – in billets –	O.O. 101. H.S.B.
	3	Major W.C.C. GELL MC rejoined the Bn as 2nd in Command	
PERONNE	5	Rejoined from base – 2nd Lt F. Coulson Reinforcements – 26 O.Rs 4 O.Rs	H.S.B.
"	7	Major J.H. Crosskey posted to 1/7th R. War R	H.S.B.
"	9	Reinforcements – 27 O.Rs.	H.S.B.
	10	860 O.Rs inoculated	H.S.B.
"	5.15 am 12.	The Battn (less 86 O.Rs inoculated) moved to LE TRANSLOY O.O. 102.	O.O. 102 H.S.B.
LE TRANSLOY	7.0 am 13	The Battn marched to a point just south of FREMICOURT and bivouaced for the day	O.O. 103 H.S.B.

W C C Gell Major 1/5 R War R

1247 W 3299 200,000 (E) 8/14 J.B.C. & A. Forms/C. 2118/11.

Instructions regarding War Diaries and Intelligence Summaries are contained in F. S. Regs., Part II. and the Staff Manual respectively. Title pages will be prepared in manuscript.

WAR DIARY
or
~~INTELLIGENCE SUMMARY~~
(Erase heading not required.)

Army Form C. 2118.

1/5th Battn The Royal Warwickshire Regt

May 1917

Hour, Date, Place	Summary of Events and Information	Remarks and references to Appendices
May		
FREMICOURT 9.0 pm 13	The Battn relieved the 5th Bn Dorset Regt in Bde Reserve in the line of the LAGNICOURT - BEAUMETZ Road	O.O. ~~104~~ 103 HSB
14	The 86 ORs inoculated rejoined	HSB
15	2nd Lt F. Coulson took over the duties of Town Major MORCHIES.	
15	Casualties - 1 OR (accidentally) wounded	HSB
17	2nd Lt R E Coombe transferred to 2/5th Bn R War R	HSB
17	Major J H CROSSKEY awarded the MC	
16	Reinforcements 2nd Lt ?? Farmer (from 3/5th Bn R War R.) 6 ORs from Base Depot 1 O.R.	HSB
21	Casualties 1 OR wounded (accidental)	HSB
night of 22-23	The Battn was relieved by the 6th Bn Glouc Regt and marched into Divisional reserve at Fremicourt	O.O. 104 HSB
FREMICOURT 23	Reinforcements. Rejoined from III Corps L Rly 6 O.Rs.	HSB
24	Reinforcements Lt F.J. Breeden (from 3/5 Bn R War R) 2nd Lt A.F. Foreman " " " J.H. ~~Lade~~ Lade (from 2/1 Warw Yeomy) " T.C. Magness (from 3/5 Bn R War R) 5 ORs	HSB HSB
27	Casualties - wounded 1 O.R. (accidental)	HSB
"	Increase - 1 O.R. from III Corps Light Rly.	
29	Casualty - 1 O.R. (accidentally injured)	HSB
night - 30/31	The Bn relieved the 6th Bn Glouc Regt in Bde Reserve	O.O. 105 HSB

W.G. Bell Major
Cmdg 1/5 R War R

Copy No 1

OPERATION ORDERS NO.101.
BY
Major P.H.WHITEHOUSE,
Commdg. 1/5th Battn. Royal Warwickshire Regiment.
2nd May, 1917.

Ref:Map 62C, 1/40,000.

1. The 143 Inf:Bde (less 7th & 8th Bns) will move to PERONNE to-morrow.
2. The 5th R.War.R., will parade on the FRISE-ECLUSIER road, with the head of the column at the cross roads, facing WEST, ready tommove off at 9 a.m.
3. Coys will form up in the following order:-
   Bn.H.Q.-C-D-A-B.
   Dress - Full marching-order. Steel helmets will be worn, sefvice caps slung over the bayonet. Oilsheets folded under the cross straps of the valise.
4. O/C "B" Coy will detail 1 N.C.O. and 4 men to march in rear of the Bn, and collect stragglers; the party to move at the pace of the slowest man.
5. Coys will detail 1 N.C.O. per platoon and 1 per coy H.Q., and 1 for Bn,H.Q., as an advance party. This party will parade under 2/Lieut.L.T.O'HANLON, outside Bn,H.Q., at 6.30 a.m., and will report to Staff Captain at Town Major's Office,PERONNE at 9 a.m.
6. Blankets will be rolled in tens and stacked outside Transport Billet (No.25) by 7.30 a.m.
7. Officers' valises will be stacked outside Transport Billet (No.25) by 7.30 a.m.; Mess Boxes by 8 a.m.
8. Horses will be sent for cookers at 8.30 a.m.
9. Dinners will be had on arrival at PERONNE.
10. Separate orders have been issued for the Transport Officer.
11. ACKNOWLEDGE.

E P I Carter

Issued at 10.30 p.m., 2nd May, 1917.

Lieut. & Actg.Adjt., 1/5th Battn.Royal Warwickshire Regiment.

Copies 1 & 2. War Diary.
" 3 - 6. Companies.
Copy No.7. T.O. & Q.M.
" " 8. R.S.M.

Copy No 1

OPERATION ORDERS NO.102.

BY

Major W.C.C.GELL,M.C.,

Commdg. 1/5th Battn.Royal Warwickshire Regiment.

11th May,1917.

Ref:Map 63C. 1/40,000.
" 57C. "

1. The 143rd Inf:Bde will move into the area LE TRANSLOY-ROCQUIGNY-MESNIL, to-morrow, the 12th inst.
2. The 5th R.War.R.,(Less the men inoculated on 10th inst.) will parade on the PERONNE-DOINGT road, with the head of the column outside the Quartermaster's stores, in the FAUBOURG de BRETAGNE facing East, ready to move off, at 5.15 a.m., in the following order:- H.Q.-D - A - B - C.
   Destination to be notified later or on the march.
   Dress - Full marching order. Steel helmets will be worn, service caps slung over the bayonet. Oilsheets folded under the cross straps of the valise.
3. An interval of 400 yards will be maintained between Battns, and 200 yards between other units, on the march.
4. The men inoculated will remain in their present billets under O/C "B" Coy, ~~HXXXXXXX~~ who will report to H.Q.,144 Inf:Bde at 3 p.m. to-morrow, for details as to march, to the new area.
5. O/C "A" Coy will detail 1 N.C.O. & 4 men to march in rear of the Battn., and collect ~~IXXXX~~stragglers.
6. All C.Q.M.Ss, and Cpl PARSONS will act as billeting party. This party will parade, with bicycles, under 2/Lieut.R.CRICHTON, outside Bn.H.Q., at 5.30 a.m., and will join the Bde party at the cross roads, I.15.d.99, at 6 a.m.
7. Blankets will be rolled and carried by each man on the top of his valise.
   Officers' valises & coy mess boxes will be stacked outside Bn.H.Q., at 4.45 a.m.
8. Particular attention will be paid to leaving the present billets scrupulously clean.
9. Separate orders have been issued for the Transport Officer.
10. ACKNOWLEDGE.

S. F. Knape

Issued at 8.15 p.m.,
11th May, 1917.

2/Lieut. & Asst.Adjt.,
1/5th Battn.Royal Warwickshire Regiment.

Copies 1 & 2. War Diary.
" 3 - 6. Companies.
Copy No. 7. TO & QM.
" " 8. R.S.M.

Copy No. 1

O P E R A T I O N   O R D E R S   NO.103.

BY

Major W.C.C.GELL, M.C.,
Commdg. 1/5th Battn.Royal Warwickshire Regiment.
12th May, 1917.

Ref:Map 57C. 1/40,000.

1. The 143 Inf:Bde will move to-morrow, 13th inst., & will relieve the 34 Inf:Bde on the night 13/14th inst.
2. The 5th R.War.R., will march to a point just SOUTH of FREMICOURT.
   Route: Cross roads N.18.a.00-VILLERS AU FLOS-Cross roads O.2.a.96.
   Distance: 5 miles.
3. Coys will fall in ready to move at 7 a.m., in the following order:
   H.Q.- C - D - A - B.
   Head of the column at cross roads,O.25.a.32,facing EAST.
   Coys will march at 100 yards distance.
   Dress: Full marching order, oilsheet folded under the cross straps of the valise.
4. O.C."B" Coy will detail 1 N.C.O. & 4 men to march in rear of the Bn to collect stragglers; the pace of the party to conform to that of the slowest man.
5. Blankets will be rolled in tens and stacked outside Q.M.Stores by 6 a.m.
   Officers' valises will be stacked outside Bn.H.Q., by 6.15 a.m.; mess boxes by 6.30 a.m.
6. The Bn. will relieve the 5th Dorset Regt., in Bde Reserve on the night of 13/14th inst.
7. Coys will fall in in the following order:H.Q.-D-C-A-B., ready to move at 9 p.m. Place will be notified later.
   A guide will meet the Bn. at Main Dressing Station,BEUGNY.
   Coy guides will meet the Bn.at I.11.c.
8. Relief will be carried out as follows:-
   B Coy will relieve A Coy, 5th Dorset Regt.
   A " " " B " " " "
   C " " " C " " " "
   D " " " D " " " "
9. Lewis Gun Limbers will go with their coys.
10. All maps, photographs,etc, will be handed over by Units of 34 Inf: Bde, to relieving units of the 143 Inf:Bde.
11. Completion of reliefs will be reported to Bn.H.Q.
12. Separate orders have been issued to the Transport Officer.
13. ACKNOWLEDGE.

E P J Carter

Issued at 10.40 p.m., 12th May, 1917.

Lieut. & Actg.Adjt.,
1/5th Bn.Royal Warwickshire Regiment.

Copies 1 & 2. War Diary. Copy 7. Q.M. & T.O.
" 3 - 6. Companies. " 8. R.S.M.

Copy No 1

OPERATION ORDERS NO.104.

BY

Major W.C.C.GELL,M.C.,
Commdg. 1/5th Bn.Royal Warwickshire Regiment.
21st May, 1917.

Ref:Map 57C.N.E. 1/20,000.

1. The 143 Inf:Bde will be relieved by the 144 Inf:Bde on the night 21/22 and 22/23 May.
2. The 5th R.War.R. will be relieved by the 6th Gloucesters, on the night, 22/23 May and, after relief, will be in Divisional Reserve.
3. One guide per platoon & 2 for Bn.H.Q., will be detailed to report to 2/Lieut.S.F.SNAPE, at "C" Coy H.Q., at 8.15 p.m.,on 22nd May. O/C "B" Coy will also detail one guide to direct the relieving Bde working party to I.12.a.95.
4. Coys will be relieved by corresponding coys of the 6th Gloucesters and, on relief, will march to FREMICOURT.
   Coys will march as far as BEUGNY by sections, at 300 yards distance: West of BEUGNY by platoons at 200 yards distance.
5. Lewis Gun Limbers will report to their Company Headquarters as soon as possible after dusk and will take back Lewis Guns and Officers Mess boxes. On completion of move Lewis Guns will remain on the Transport.
6. Dinners, or tea, will be served on arrival at FREMICOURT under coy arrangements
7. C.Q.M.S's will be responsible for taking over billets from the 6th Gloucesters.
8. All work in progress will be carefully handed over to the relieving battalion.
9. All sketches (<u>not</u> official maps) aeroplane photos and trench stores will be handed over on relief and a receipt forwarded to this Office by 11 a.m.,23rd May.
10. Completion of moves to be reported to Bn.H.Q.
11. Separate orders have been issued to Transport Officer.
12. ACKNOWLEDGE.

E P L Carter

Lieut. & Actg.Adjt.,
1/5th Bn. Royal Warwickshire Regiment.

Issued at midnight,
21/22 May,1917.

Copies 1 & 2. War Diary.
" 3 - 6. Companies.
Copy 7. T.O. & Q.M.
" 8. 6th Glosters,for information.

Copy No. 1

OPERATION ORDERS NO.105.
BY
Major.W.C.C.GELL.M.C.
Commdg 1/5th.Bn,Royal Warwickshire Regiment.
30.th.May.1917.

Ref:Map.57c.N.E. 1/20000.

1. The 5th.R.War.R. will relieve the 6th Gloucester.R. in reserve on the night 30-31st.May.
2. Coys will march by platoons at 200 yards distance & will move off as under:-

"D"Coy	8.30.p.m.
H.Q.	8.40.p.m.
"C"Coy.	8.50.p.m.
"B" "	9.p.m.
"A" "	9.10.p.m.

East of BEUGNY, Coys will march by sections at 300 yards distance.
Dress:- Fighting Order. Great-coats rolled round haversacks.

3. On completion of reliefs, Coys will be disposed of as under:-

"D"Coy.	Front.
"A" "	Left.
"C" "	Centre.
"B" "	Right.

Guides will not be provided by the 6th.Gloucester.R.

4. Lewis Guns will be packed under the direction of Sergt.MILLER.
5. Officers valises will be stacked outside Coy H.Q. by 7.30.p.m.
6. Officers Mess boxes will be stacked outside each Coy H.Q. 15 minutes before the Coy moves off.
7. Receipts for Stores taken over will be forwarded to Orderly Room by 6.p.m. 31st.
8. Completion of all reliefs to be reported in code to H.Q.
9. Seperate orders have been issued to the Transport Officer.
10. ACKNOWLEDGE.

E R L Carter

Lieut & Actg Adjt.,
1/5th.Bn.Royal Warwickshire Regiment.

Issued at 3.15.p.m.
30th.May.1917.

Copies 1 & 2.War Diary. Copy 7. T.O. & Q.M.
" 3 - 6.Companies. " 8.R.S.M.

28 A.
(15 sheets)

C O N F I D E N T I A L.

W A R D I A R Y

of

5th ROYAL WARWICKSHIRE REGIMENT.

==*=*=*=*=*=*=*

From 1st June to 30th June, 1917.

* * * * * * * * * *

9028

Instructions regarding War Diaries and Intelligence Summaries are contained in F. S. Regs., Part II. and the Staff Manual respectively. Title pages will be prepared in manuscript.

WAR DIARY
or
~~INTELLIGENCE SUMMARY~~
(Erase heading not required.)

Army Form C. 2118.

1/5th Bn The Royal Warwickshire Regt

June 1917

Hour, Date, Place		Summary of Events and Information	Remarks and references to Appendices
LOUVERVAL SECTOR	June 1	Casualties. 2 O.Rs. wounded	
		Major W.C.C. GELL M.C. granted acting rank of Lt Col.	
		Lt Col C. RETALLACK M.C. and Major A.S. ALABASTER M.C. off strength	HSB.
	1.2&3	Work carried on with wire in front of reserve line. Generally improving accomodation. working on mined dug-outs. building incinerators & latrines.	
		Movement by day being forbidden. all work is done by night	HSB.
	4	125 O.Rs employed on digging new posts at J4C 6.4. J4A 64. J4A 45 and D19C 53. respectively.	HSB
	night 5/6	The work on the new posts carried on. all available men employed	
	5th	Reinforcements – 2nd Lt F.H.D. ALLENBY 10. O.Rs.	
		Major J.H. CROSSKEY ~~proceeds~~ takes temporary command of 1/4 Glosters	HSB.
	night 6/7	New posts continued. all available men employed.	HSB.
	" 7-8	The Battalion was relieved by the 7th WORCESTERS and then relieved the 8th WARWICKS in the MORCHIES – BEUGNY area. Dispositions as follows. Bn HQ A+B Coys in left section of the BEAUMETZ – MORCHIES line. C+D Coys at DELSAUX FARM.	O.O. 106 HSB

1247 W 3299 200,000 (E) 8/14 J.B.C. & A. Forms/C. 2118/11.

Instructions regarding War Diaries and Intelligence Summaries are contained in F. S. Regs., Part II. and the Staff Manual respectively. Title pages will be prepared in manuscript.

WAR DIARY
or
~~INTELLIGENCE SUMMARY~~
(Erase heading not required.)

Army Form C. 2118.

1/5th Bn The Royal Warwickshire Regt

June 1917

Hour, Date, Place June		Summary of Events and Information	Remarks and references to Appendices
MORCHIES – DELSAUX FARM	8	The Battalion being in bivouacs the day was spent in improving these – building ovens latrines incinerators etc	HSB
	9	A+B being in the forward area + movement restricted by day no training was done the time being spent in work on the respective billets. C+D Companies carried out training during morning + evening – Rifle range built	HSB
	10-11-12	C+D Companies carried on training	HSB
	11	Reinforcements – 2 ORs	HSB
	12	88 ORs inoculated	
	13	1 ORs "	
		The 143rd Bde carried out a tactical exercise all battalions taking part	HSB
	14	1 ORs transferred from 1/6th RWarR.	
	14	C+D Coys carried out training	HSB
LOUVERVAL SECTOR	night 15/16	The Battalion relieved the 1/7 Bn The Worcestershire Regt in Bde Reserve in the BEAUMETZ – LAGNICOURT line	OO 197 HSB
	16	Reinforcements – 2nd Lieut J.B. FLORANCE (from Reserve Bn) 2 ORs	HSB
	16-21	The usual large working parties found each night for work on the reserve posts and on a new line along the BEAUMETZ – LAGNICOURT Road.	HSB

1247 W 3299 200,000 (E) 8/14 J.B.C. & A. Forms/C. 2118/11.

Instructions regarding War Diaries and Intelligence Summaries are contained in F. S. Regs., Part II. and the Staff Manual respectively. Title pages will be prepared in manuscript.

WAR DIARY
or
~~INTELLIGENCE~~ SUMMARY
(Erase heading not required.)

Army Form C. 2118.

1/5 Bn The Royal Warwickshire Regt

June 1917

Place	Hour, Date	Summary of Events and Information	Remarks and references to Appendices
	June		
LOUVERVAL	17	Decrease - Captain A. SHELDON ordered a medical board in England & struck off strength	KSB.
"	night 18/19	The 16th Bn carried out a raid on enemy post at K1B97. The 5th Bn provided one Company (B) to act in support. The company was not called up & there were no casualties	HSB
"	19 20 21	Usual working parties supplied	KSB.
	night 21/22	The 8th Bn RWarR carried out a raid on enemy posts. Two Companies of the 5th Bn were in support. We had no casualties. Two prisoners were captured.	Appendix I KSB
"	21	Reinforcements - 3 O.Rs.	KSB
"	22 & 23	Usual working parties	KSB
		During this tour in the trenches a certain amount of hay was cut & carried at night down to the transport where it was made & stacked. Two men with scythes were engaged during the day out on a patch situate at about J7a. For two or three nights 2 scythes & 8 sickles were worked at about J2a.	KSB.
	night 23/24	The Bn was relieved by the 6th Gloucester Regt and moved to billets in LEBUCQUIERE. 1 Coy in huts - 3 Coys in huts O.O. 108	O.O. 108 KSB

1247 W 3299 200,000 (E) 8/14 J.B.C. & A. Forms/C. 2118/11.

Instructions regarding War Diaries and Intelligence Summaries are contained in F. S. Regs., Part II. and the Staff Manual respectively. Title pages will be prepared in manuscript.

WAR DIARY
or
~~INTELLIGENCE SUMMARY~~
(Erase heading not required.)

Army Form C. 2118.

1/5th Bn The Royal Warwickshire Regt

June 1917

Hour, Date, Place	Summary of Events and Information	Remarks and references to Appendices
LEBUCQIERE June 24	Major WCC GELL MC to be acting Lt Col whilst in command of the Battalion (Div Orders 18.5.17)	
	Captn RETALLACK relinquishes acting rank of Lt Col on ceasing to command the Battalion (3.5.17)	HJB
" 24 – 30	Training carried out in the LEBUCQIERE district special attention being paid to musketry route marching and Company tactical schemes.	HJB
	During this period the Bn found several working parties varying in strength from 40 OR to 2 Coys. This greatly interfered with training.	
30	The Bn was relieved by the 8th Bn East Yorks and marched to GOMIECOURT	OO 109 HJB
28	Reinforcements – 3 ORs.	
30	Reinforcements – 69 ORs.	HJB

W. C. C. Gell Lt Col
Cmdg 1/5 R War R

1247 W 3299 200,000 (E) 8/14 J.B.C. & A. Forms/C. 2118/11.

Copy No. 1

OPERATION ORDERS. No.106.

BY

Lt-Col. W.C.C.GELL M.C.

Commdg 1/5th Bn.Royal Warwickshire Regiment.

7th.June,1917.

Ref.Map:- 57c N.W.1/20,000.

1. The 5th.R.War.R. will be relieved by the 7th Worcesters on the night 7th-8th June and will then relieve the 8th.R.War.R. in the MORCHIES - BEUGNY area.
2. On completion of reliefs Coys will be disposed as under:-
   Bn.H.Q., A & B in the left section of the [illegible]-MORCHIES line. H.Q. at old Bde.H.Q.
   "A" on the left.
   "B" on the right.
   "C" & "D" at [illegible].
3. One guide per platoon & 2 for Bn.H.Q. will report to 2/Lieut. S.F.SHARPE at "C" Coy at 8.[illegible]p.m. 7th.June.
4. Coys will march by sections at 300 yds distance.
5. Lewis Gun limbers will report to their Company H.Q. as soon as possible after dark & will take back Lewis Guns & Officers Mess boxes. On Completion of move Lewis Guns will be in the charge of their platoons.
6. Dinners will be served under Coy arrangements.
7. All work in progress will be carefully handed over to the relieving Bn.
8. All sketches(not Official maps), aeroplane photos, and trench stores will be handed over to the relieving Bn and a reciept forwarded to Orderly Room by 11.a.m. 8th.June.
   Copies of reciepts given for trench stores,etc., taken over from the 8th.R.War.R. will be forwarded to Orderly Room by 11.a.m. 8th.June.
9. Completion of all reliefs will be reported to Bn.H.Q.
10. Separate orders have been issued to the Transport Officer.
11. ACKNOWLEDGE.

E P L Carter

Lieut & Actg Adjt,
1/5th.Bn.Royal Warwickshire Regiment.

Issued at 12.a.m.
7th.June.1917.

Copies 1 & 2. War Diary.
" 3 - 6. Companies.

Copy No.7. [illegible]
" No.8. 7th.Worcesters.
for information.

Copy No. 1

OPERATION ORDERS No. 107.
BY
Lieut.Col. [illegible]
Comm'g 1/6th. Bn. The Royal Warwickshire Regiment,
June 15th, 1917.

Ref:Map:57c. 1/40,000.

(1). The 6th. R.War.R. will relieve the 7th. Worcesters on the night 15th-16th June & after relief will be in [illegible] reserve.

(2). Coys will move off independently, "[illegible]" Coy leading.
The garrison of the posts held by "A" Coy will not move until relieved by the 8th. Sussex.

(3). Coys will march by sections at [illegible] yds distance.
DRESS. Fighting Order.

(4). Lewis Gun limbers will report to [illegible] "C" "D" Coy H.Q. at 8.45 p.m. to take up Lewis Guns & mess boxes.
Limbers will report to "A" "B" Coy H.Q. at [illegible].50 p.m. to take up mess boxes.

(5). Officers valises and mens packs of C & D Coys will be stored outside Coy H.Q. by [illegible] p.m. and will be sent down by returning ration limbers. O.C. "D" Coy will detail a guard to take charge of C & D Coy [illegible] until they are taken over by the 7th. Worcesters.
Officers valises and mens packs of A & B Coys will be stored outside A Coy H.Q. by [illegible].10 p.m. O.C. A Coy will detail a guard to take charge of them until they are removed by the transport.

(6). Officers chargers of C & D Coys will be [illegible] at Coy H.Q. at [illegible] pm

(7). Meals will be served under Coy arrangements.

(8). All work in progress will be taken over and continued.

(9). Completion of reliefs will be reported to Bn. H.Q. The Code word for this will be [illegible].

(10). Copies of receipts for stores etc taken over [illegible] will be sent in to Bn. H.Q. by [illegible] 16th. inst.

(11). Separate Orders have been issued to the Transport Officer.

(12). ACKNOWLEDGE.

E P L Carter

Issued at [illegible]
15th. June. 1917.

[illegible]
1/6th. Bn. Royal Warwickshire Regiment.

Copies 1 [illegible]. [illegible] [illegible]
" [illegible] - [illegible] Companies. " [illegible] [illegible]

Copy.No. 1

OPERATION ORDERS No.108.
BY
Lieut.Col.W.C.C.GELL.M.C.
Commdg 1/5th.Bn.Royal Warwickshire Regiment.
June 23rd.1917.

Ref:Map:57c. 1/40,000.

1. The 5th.R.War.R. will be relieved by the 6th.Gloucester.R. on the night 23-24th.June. and on relief will move to [redacted]. LE BUCQUIERE.

2. Coys will march via cross roads I17d58 by sections at 300yds distance and on completion of move will be disposed as under:-
Bn.H.Q., "A" "B" "C" in tents at I.30.d.03.
"D" in huts at J.17.c.15.

3. On completion of moves Lewis Guns will be with their Coys.

4. O.C."D"Coy will detail 6 guides under an officer to meet "C"Coy of the relieving Bn at cross roads J.8.c.22. at 9.45.p.m.

5. O.C.Coys will detail an advance party of 3 men per Coy to report to "C"Coy.H.Q. at 4.30.p.m. for instructions. 1 Regimental policeman & two prisoners will accompany this party.

6. One officer per Coy will reconnoitre the route to LE BUCQUIERE by daylight.

7. Meals will be served under Coy arrangements.

8. All work in progress will be handed over to the relieving Bn.

9. All sketches, aeroplane photos, trench stores, etc., will be handed over and receipts forwarded to Bn.H.Q. by 6.p.m. 24th.inst.

10. Completion of all reliefs will be reported to Bn.H.Q. Code word for this will be LIMIT.

11. Separate orders have been issued to the Transport Officer.

12. ACKNOWLEDGE.

E P L Carter

Issued at 11.a.m.
23rd.June.1917.

Lieut & Actg Adjt,
1/5th.Bn.Royal Warwickshire Regiment.

Copies 1 & 2. War Diary. Copy.7. T.O.& Q.M.
" 3 - 6. Companies. " 8. R.S.M.

Copy No 1.

OPERATION ORDERS NO.109.
by
Lieut.Colonel W.C.C.GELL,M.C.,
Commdg. 1/5th Bn. Royal Warwickshire Regiment.
30th June, 1917.

Ref:Map. 57C.1/40,000.

1. The 143 Inf:Bde will be relieved by the 8th Inf:Bde to-day,30th inst.
2. The 5th R.War.R., will be relieved by the 8th E.Yorks at 1 p.m., and, on relief will march to GOMIECOURT. Distance, 10 miles.
   Route - FREMICOURT-X roads H.30.a.55-track to H.17.c.13-FAVREUIL- - X roads H.15.c.36-junction of track H.14.d.42-GOMIECOURT.
3. Coys will march off in the order in which they are relieved, by platoons at 100 yards distance. WEST of FREMICOURT the Bn will close to Coys at 200 yards distance.
   The transport will march in rear of the Bn.
   Dress - Full marching order. Shrapnel helmets will be worn; oil sheets & caps, folded beneath the cross straps of the valise.
4. Lewis Guns will be packed by 12.30 p.m., under the supervision of the Lewis Gun Officer and, on completion of move will remain with the transport.
5. Officers' valises will be stacked at X roads I.30.b.26 by 10 a.m. They will be loaded on to a lorry.
6. Officers' mess boxes will be stacked outside Coy.H.Q., at 12.30 p.m.
7. Receipts will be taken for all stores, tents, etc., handed over. These will be forwarded to Bn.H.Q., by 6 p.m., today.
8. Completion of all reliefs to be reported to Bn.H.Q.
9. Separate orders have been issued to the Transport.
10. A C K N O W L E D G E.

E P 2 Carter

Issued at 9 a.m.,
30th June,1917.

Lieut. & Acting Adjutant.
1/5th Bn. Royal Warwickshire Regiment.

Copies 1 & 2. War Diary.
" 3 - 6. Companies.
Copy No.7. Q.M. & T.O.
" " 8. R.S.M.

S E C R E T. 1/6th ROYAL WARWICKSHIRE REGIMENT.

OPERATION ORDERS
BY
LT.COL.F.S.HANSON,M.C., COMMANDING.
20th JUNE 1917.

Appendix I

---

1. A raid will be carried out on the night of the 21st/22nd June by "A" & "B" Coys, 1/6th R. Warwicks R., supported by 2 Coys, 1/6th R. Warwicks. R.

2. OBJECTS.
To seize the Copse in D.15.c., and the Dug-outs in rear at D.15.c.28, to kill or capture the garrison and to hold the Copse until about 2.15 a.m.

3. BARRAGES.
The raiding parties will be assisted by Artillery, Stokes Mortars and Machine Gun Barrages as follows:-
(a) Artillery.
Creeping barrage from line D.21.b.08 - D.14.d.14 moving at rate of 100 yards per 2 minutes, up to Standing Barrage. Standing Barrage - D.15.d.60 - D.15.b.17-D.15.c.05
Howitzers will fire on following points and lift with the creeping barrage:-
S.W.edge of Copse - Centre of Copse - Small trench about D.15.c.65 and dugouts at D.15.c.28.
Heavies on Copse in D.14 Central-on sunken road in D.14.b-on HINDENBURG line-and sunken roads in D.15.b.
(b) Stokes Mortars.
1 Gun at about D.21.b.41, to fire on post at D.15.c.60.
1 Gun at about D.20.[illegible]55 to fire on sunken road at D.15.c.05.
(c) Machine Guns.
2 Guns in No.28 post to sweep road from D.15.d.60 to about D.16.b.67.
2 Guns at D.20.b.[illegible] to fire along line D.14.d.50 - D.15.a.74.
1 Gun at No.24 post to fire on D.14.b.50 - D.14.b.16.
1 Gun at No.24 post to fire on D.15.b.16.
Stokes Mortars and Machine Guns will open and cease fire when artillery does.

4. METHOD OF ATTACK.

(a) - Right Company (A) will [illegible] (4 Platoons) in extended order, on either side of [illegible] about D.[illegible].65 and advance with the barrage and seize the following objectives:-

1st Platoon - Dugout at D.15.c.67.
2nd " - S.E. [illegible] of Copse.
3rd " - will move in support to 1st Platoon [illegible] edge of Copse.
4th " - in support to 2nd Platoon will move to about D.15.c.21.

One Platoon (1/5th R.War.R.) will follow this Coy. in reserve to about D.21.a.[illegible].

(b) - Left Company (B) will first seize cross roads at D.21.a.2585 (artillery will be prepared to barrage this point if required) they will then form up in depth (as Right Company) and advance with barrage and seize following objectives:-

2 Platoons will advance - 1 on top and 1 at bottom of steep bank - and seize the S.W. edge of Copse, and the post on road about D.15.c.85.
1 Platoon in support will advance close in rear of first two platoons.
1 Platoon in reserve will move to quarry about D.15.c.61.

5. DISPOSITIONS OF 2 COYS. 1/5th R. WAR. R.

1 Coy will be in [illegible] cover at suitable places round about cross roads ready to move forward if required.
They will cover the return of the raiding party and will be the last to withdraw.
1 Platoon will be with Right Coy. as above.
2 Platoons will be escort to Stokes Gun at D.21.b.41.
1 Platoon will be escort to Stokes Gun at D.20.d.9550.

6. COMMUNICATIONS.

Signalling Officer will make the following arrangements:-

1 Telephone Station connected to Coy.H.Q. at D.27.a.85, to be established near cross roads D.21.a.2585.

2 extensions will be run from there, one to Left Coy., and one to Right Coy.

A system of code words will be formed later.

7. POSITION OF H.Q.

The O.C. and O.C. Left Group Artillery will be at Coy.H.Q., D.27.a.85.

Major Whitehouse will be in charge of the raiding parties and will be near cross roads, D.21.a.2585. He will give orders when the parties are to withdraw.

A F.O.O., will be with Major Whitehouse and will be in communication with Forward Battalion H.Q., by a separate telephone.

8. EQUIPMENT.

Details as to equipment will be issued later.

9. ZERO HOUR. Will be notified later.

10. TIME.

All watches will be synchronised at [illegible], [illegible] inst.

11. A C K N O W L E D G E.

(Signed) [illegible], 2/Lt. & A/Adjt.
1/5th R. War. R.

29 T.
(11 sheets)

Vol 29

CONFIDENTIAL.

W A R D I A R Y

of

1/5th. Bn. R O Y A L W A R W I C K S H I R E R E G T.

From 1st July To 31st July, 1917.

****

Instructions regarding War Diaries and Intelligence Summaries are contained in F. S. Regs., Part II. and the Staff Manual respectively. Title pages will be prepared in manuscript.

WAR DIARY
or
~~INTELLIGENCE SUMMARY~~
(Erase heading not required.)

Army Form C. 2118.

1/5 Bn The Royal Warwickshire Regt
July 1917

Hour, Date, Place		Summary of Events and Information	Remarks and references to Appendices
GOMIECOURT	2.7.17	The Battn carried on training and improvement of the camp	EB
		Leave MAJ A.S. ALABASTER M.C. rejoined from Senior Officers Course and 1 OR	
	3.7.17	The Brigade moved by March Route. The Battn moved to BERLES-AU-BOIS	O.O 180 EB
	4.7.17	Decrease 3 OR. MAJ A.S. ALABASTER attached to 1/7 R.War.R. (5.7.17) (CAPT. E.A.M BINDLOSS appointed second in command	EB
BERLES-AU-BOIS	6.7.17	Decrease 22 O.R. Increase Lt Col C RETALLACK.M.C. rejoined. A Divisional Exercise without troops was held	EB
	7.7.17	Decrease 6 O.R. A Brigade exercise was carried out	EB
	4-6.7.17	The Battn carried out training. Special attention being paid to Route marching.	EB
	8.7.17	Lt Col N.C.C. GELL M.C. attached to 1/7 R.War.R and to command	EB
	night 7/8-7.17	Reinforcement 206 OR from 43 Training reserve Bn	EB
	9.7.17	The Battn carried out training	EB
	10.7.17	The Battn carried out training. Decrease 2 O.R	EB
	11.7.17	The Batt carried out training	EB
	12.7.17	The Battn carried out training.	EB
		Increase 2nd Lt R.S.E. WALSHE joined from 5 Res Bn R.WAR.R.	EB
		Increase 36 O.R.	
		Decrease 2 O.R.	EB
	13.7.17 ~~14.7.17~~	The Battn carried out training	EB
	14.7.17	A Brigade exercise was carried out	EB
	16.7.17	The Battn carried out training	
		Decrease CAPT F.J. BREEDEN transferred to 2/5 R.War.R	EB
		Increase 4 O.R.	
	17.7.17	The Battn carried out training	EB
		The Battn played the 48th Div Supply Column in the semi final of the FANSHAWE Cup and won 3-2	
	18.7.17	The Battn carried out training.	EB
	19.7.17	The Brigade was inspected by the Brigade Commander and a Brigade Route march was carried out	EB
		Decrease 2. O.R.	
		The Battn played the 1/7 WORCESTERS Regt in the final of the Fanshawe Cup result 2-2	

Instructions regarding War Diaries and Intelligence Summaries are contained in F. S. Regs., Part II. and the Staff Manual respectively. Title pages will be prepared in manuscript.

WAR DIARY
or
~~INTELLIGENCE SUMMARY~~
(Erase heading not required.)

Army Form C. 2118.

1/5 Bn. The Royal Warwickshire Regt.
July 1917

Hour, Date, Place	Summary of Events and Information	Remarks and references to Appendices
BERLES-AU-BOIS 20.7.17	The Brigade moved by March Route. The Battalion moved to POMMERA	O.O111 EB
POMMERA 21/22-7-17	The Brigade moved by March Route and Rail. The Battn. supplied 1 Officer and 100 O.R. ~~who~~ proceeded by the 1st Train to PROVEN and acted as detraining party for the Brigade Group. The Bn. (less detraining party) proceeded by March Route to AUTHIEULE STATION and thence by rail to PROVEN and thence by March Route to St. JANSTER BIEZEN	O.O.112 EB Administrative O. in connection with O.O.112 EB Entraining State EB
21.7.17	Decrease 2 OR.	EB
St. JANSTER BIEZEN 23.7.17	The Battalion carried out training. A Canteen was started in conjunction with 1/6 Rwr. R.	EB
24.7.17	The Battalion carried out training.	EB
	2nd Lt. (Temp Capt.) H.S BLOOMER (Manchester Regt.) appointed acting MAJOR whilst employed as such from 18.5.17 – 5.7.17	EB
	Decrease. 2 O.R.	EB
25.7.17	The Battalion carried out training which was interfered with by the heavy rain	EB.
	Decreases 6 OR w/from 1/7/17 2 OR " " 21/7/17 2 OR " " 25/7/17	EB
26.7.17	The Battalion carried out training. A party of Officers visited the Model of Trenches.	EB
27.7.17	The Battalion carried out training. Extensions were fitted to Box respirators.	EB
28.7.17	The Battalion carried out a route march by Coys and Lewis Gun firing on the Range	EB
29.7.17	The Battalion lost the replayed final of the Fonshawe Cup to the 1/7 Worcester Regt. by 5 goals to 0	

Instructions regarding War Diaries and Intelligence Summaries are contained in F. S. Regs., Part II. and the Staff Manual respectively. Title pages will be prepared in manuscript.

WAR DIARY
or
~~INTELLIGENCE~~ SUMMARY
(Erase heading not required.)

Army Form C. 2118.

1/5 Bn The Royal Warwickshire Regt
July 1917

Hour, Date, Place	Summary of Events and Information	Remarks and references to Appendices
ST JANSTER BIEZEN 29.7.17	Church Parade was cancelled on account of the weather	E.B.
30.7.17	The Battalion carried out training in the morning	E.B.
Night of 30.31-7.17 BELGIUM Sheet 28NW 1/20000 WOODS in A30	The Brigade moved by March Route. The Route was altered by an after order issued verbally to O's C Coy's, H.Q. officers and T.O and was POPERINGHE – POPERINGHE-ELVERDINGHE Rd – CHEMIN MILITAIRE. The Battalion less Transport reached its position of readiness at ~~[illegible]~~ 2.20 AM on 31.7.17 and rested there	O.O.113 E.B.
	The total effective strength of the Regt on 31.7.17 was 38 officers 999 O.R 1 " 4 " RAMC 1 " Interpreter 39 officers 1004 O.R	E.B.

Charles Retallack Lt Col
Cmdg 1/5 R.War.R.
July 31st 1917

Copy No 1

O P E R A T I O N O R D E R S NO.110.
BY
Lieut.Col. W.C.C.GELL,M.C.,
Commdg. 1/5th Bn. Royal Warwickshire Regiment.
2nd July, 1917.

Ref: Sheet 11 LENS.1/100,000.

1. The 143rd Inf:Bde will move to-morrow, 3rd July.
2. The 5th R.War.R., will move to BERLES AU BOIS.
   Route - COURCELLES - AYETTE - DOUCHY - MONCHY.Distance 10 miles.
3. Coys will parade in their own lines ready to move off at 8.20 a.m., in the following order:- H.Q.-B-C-D-A Coys.
   Coys will march at 200 yards distance. Dress - Full marching order: oil sheets and service caps folded under the cross straps of the valise.
4. Coy Commanders will parade outside Bn.H.Q., at 8 a.m., and will proceed in advance of the Bn., to reconnoitre the new training area
5. Lewis GUns will be packed under the supervision of the Lewis Gun Officer and, on completion of move will remain with their coys.
6. O/C D Coy will detail 1 Officer, 1 N.C.O.,& 6 men to march in rear of the Bn, and collect stragglers.
7. Men who are sick from inoculation or other causes, and are likely to become stragglers will parade outside the Orderly Room at 7 a.m., under their COy.Orderly Corporals who will hand them over with a nominal roll to the Bn.Orderly Sergeant. This N.C.O., will march the party to their destination.
8. Officers' valises will be stacked outside D Coy H.Q., by 6.15 a.m. They will be loaded on to a lorry.
9. Mess boxes will be stacked outside D Coy H.Q., by 7.45 a.m.
10. Coy.Quartermaster-Sergeants and the Sergt.Drummer will report to 2/Lieut.C.L.GORDON outside the Orderly Room at 5.30 a.m.
    This party will report to the Town Major,BERLES AU BOIS at 9 a.m.
11. Dinners will be served on arrival.
12. Separate orders have been issued to the Transport Officer.
13. A C K N O W L E D G E.

E P L Carter

Issued at 10.15 p.m. Lieut.& A/Adjt.
2nd July,1917. 1/5th Bn.Royal Warwickshire Regiment.

Copies 1 & 2. War Diary. Copy No.7. T.O. & Q.M.
" 3 - 6. Companies. " 8. R.S.M.

1/5th ROYAL WARWICKSHIRE REGIMENT.

ENTRAINING STATE. 21-22nd July 1917.

Officers	Other ranks	Horses	Vehicles Four-Wheeled	Vehicles Two-Wheeled
27	873	61	16	4

[illegible signature]
2/Lt & Asst Adjt

for O/C 1/5th Royal Warwickshire Regiment.

21st July 1917.

Out of the above state the following will travel by No 1 train:

Officers	OR's	Horses
1	119	13

Copy No_____

OPERATION ORDERS, NO.111.

BY

Lieut.Col. C.RETALLACK,M.C.,
Commdg. 1/5th Bn. Royal Warwickshire Regiment.
19th July,1917.

Ref: Map.LENS II.

1. The 5th R.War.R., will move to POMMERA to-morrow,20th inst. Route - POMMIER-ST.AMAND-HENU-PAS. Distance, 10 miles.

2. 1st Line Transport and baggage wagon will accompany the Bn.

3. The Bn. will fall in on the main street, facing S.E., in the following order:-
   H.Q. - B - C - D - A - Transport.
   Head of the column at the X roads by H.Q.Mess, ready to move at 9.10 a.m.

4. An Advance Party of 1 N.C.O. per coy and 1 for Bn.H.Q., will rendezvous outside Bn.H.Q., at 8 a.m.
   This party will be provided with bicycles and will be under 2/Lieut.R.CRICHTON. The party will report on arrival at the Town Major's Office, POMMERA at 10 a.m.

5. Officers' valises will be stacked outside Medical Inspection Room by 8.15 a.m.
   Mess boxes will be stacked outside Coy.H.Q., by 8.30 a.m.

6. Lorry arrangements will be notified later.

7. Dinners will be cooked on the march and eaten on arrival.

8. The Bde Group will entrain at AUTHIEULE on the night, 21/22 July,'17.

9. ACKNOWLEDGE.

E P L Carter

Issued at 11.15 p.m.
19th July,1917.

Lieut.& A/Adjt.
1/5th Bn. The Royal Warwickshire Regiment.

Copies 1 & 2. War Diary.
" 3 - 6. Companies.
Copies 7. Q.M. & T.O.
" 8. R.S.M.

Copy No. 1

O P E R A T I O N   O R D E R S   NO.112.

B Y

Lieut.Col. C.RETALLACK,M.C.
Commdg. 1/5th Bn. Royal Warwickshire Regiment.
21st July,1917.

---

1. The 5th R.War.R., will move by road and rail to the XVIII Corps area on the night, 21/22 July,1917.

2. The Bn.(less detraining party of 1 officer & 100 O.Rs) will fall in on the road running S.E., from the A of POMMERA, with the head of the column on the DOULLENS-ARRAS road, ready to march off at 9.50 p.m., 21st inst., in the following order:-

   H.Q.
   C Coy.
   D Coy.
   A Coy.(less detraining party of one officer & 100 O.Rs)
   B Coy.-
   Transport.

   Route:- GRENAS.
   HALLOY.
   AMPLIER.
   AUTHIEULE.

   Distance:- 5 1/2 miles.

3. The Bn.(less detraining party) will entrain at AUTHIEULE station by No.4 train, and detrain at PROVEN.
   The train will depart at 2.48 a.m., on 22nd inst.

4. On arrival at PROVEN units will be met by guides, and will march to 5. Bde Group area, at ST.JANSTER-BIEZEN. Distance 3 1/4 miles.

5. "A" Coy will detail one officer and 100 O.Rs to act as detraining party for the whole Brigade group.
   This party will travel by No.I train and will report to the Staff Captain at AUTHIEULE station at 7.30 p.m., 21st inst.

6. The Bn. will entrain rationed up to and including the 23rd.
   Rations for consumption on the 24th will be issued in the new area.

7. Officers' valises will be stacked outside Coy.H.Q., by 8 p.m., 21st.
   Mess boxes will be stacked outside Coy.H.Q., by 8.30 p.m.

8. A C K N O W L E D G E.

S. J. Knape
2nd Lt
Asst Adjt.

Issued at 9.15 a.m.,
21st July,1917.

For Lieut. & Actg.Adjt.,
1/5th Bn.Royal Warwickshire Regiment.

Copies 1 & 2. War Diary.
" 3 - 6. Companies.
Copy 7. Q.M. & T.O.
" 8. R.S.M.

1/5th Bn. Royal Warwickshire Regiment.

ADMINISTRATIVE INSTRUCTIONS ISSUED IN CONJUNCTION WITH Bn.OPERATION O.NO.112.

Ref:Maps. LENS II.1/100,000.
HAZEBROUCK,5A.1/100,000.

1. Bn.H.Q. and each coy will detail 1 N.C.O. to travel by No.1 train on the 21st. They will report to the Staff Captain at a field just S of AUTHIEULE Station at 7.45 p.m., bringing rations up to 23rd inclusive.

2. No rations will be carried to AUTHIEULE by the men. Rations for the personnel of units entraining by Nos.1 & No.4 trains will be dumped at AUTHIEULE Station Yard at 6 p.m.,21st, and each coy will send their Q.M.Sergt., to take over these rations at 8 p.m., (A Coy at 6 p.m.)

3. All water carts to be entrained full and fires will be drawn in sufficient time to allow travelling kitchens to be entrained cold.

4. As the journey is likely to occupy anything from 12 to 20 hours, each coy officers' mess is advised to make arrangements for meals en route. It is suggested that one mess box per coy be taken in the carriage.

21st July,1917. (Signed) E.P.Q.CARTER.
Lieut. & Actg.Adjt.,
1/5th Bn. Royal Warwickshire Regiment.

Copies to all recipients of O.O.No.112.

2	A	64
5	B	175
5	C	175
6	D	174
2	T.O.	90
3	HQ	60

24

24 | 250/31
42

30
29

450

31

3 L

23 | 6
15
24

O P E R A T I O N O R D E R S

B Y

Lieut. Col. C.RETALLACH,M.C.

Commdg. 1/5th Royal Warwickshire Regiment.

29th July 1917.

Copy No. 1......

No 113.

REF:MAP. HAZEBROUK 5a 1/100000.
28 N.W. 1/20000.

1. The Fifth British and First French Armies will, on a date, and at an hour to be notified later, attack the enemy opposite their fronts.

2. The 143 Inf: Brigade will move to a position of readiness in Corps reserve, in camps A30 c & d, G6 a & b, on the night of 30-31st July.

3. The 5th Royal Warwickshire Regiment (less Transport) will move from present camp at 11.5 p.m. 30th July.
ROUTE. Switch road N of POPERINGHE — POPERINGHE - ELVERDINGHE road — CHEMIN MILITAIRE.
DISTANCE. 6 1/2 miles.

4. Coys. will parade in their own lines ready to move off as under:-

H.Q.	11.5 p.m.
A Coy.	11.7 "
B Coy.	11.10 "
C Coy.	11.13 "
D Coy.	11.16 "

A distance of 200yds. between Coys. will be observed.
Transport will move under the orders of the B.T.O.

5. One Officer per Coy. will rendevous mounted outside BN. Headqrs. at 9 a.m. to reconnoitre the route.

6. An advanced party of 1 N.C.O. per Coy. and 1 for Bn. Headqrs. will report to 2/Lieut. HOGAN outside Bn. Headqrs. at 2.30 p.m.
This party will report to the Staff Captain at A 30 d.19 at 5 p.m.

7. Lewis Guns will be packed under the supervision of 2/Lieut. GOODE, and unpacked on arrival of transport.

8. Officers valises will be stacked on the Transport lines by 8 p.m. Mess boxes opposite the Cookers by 10.30 p.m.

9. Tea will be given before moving.

10. ACKNOWLEDGE.

J. Carter

ISSUED at 9.30 p.m. 2/Lieut. & A/Adjt.,

29th July 1917. 1/5th Bn. Royal Warwickshire Regiment

Copies 1 & 2 War Diary Copy 7 Q.M. & T.O.
" 3 - 6 Companies " 8 R.S.M.

30.T.

(27 sheets)

143/48

CONFIDENTIAL

WAR DIARY

of

1/5th ROYAL WARWICKSHIRE REGIMENT.

From 1st August,

To 31st August, 1917.

WO 95/2756 [illegible]

Instructions regarding War Diaries and Intelligence Summaries are contained in F. S. Regs., Part II. and the Staff Manual respectively. Title pages will be prepared in manuscript.

WAR DIARY
or
INTELLIGENCE SUMMARY.
(Erase heading not required.)

Army Form C. 2118.

1/5 Bn. The Royal Warwickshire Regt.

August 1917

Place	Date	Hour	Summary of Events and Information	Remarks and references to Appendices
BELGIUM Sheet 28 N.W. 1/20000. Wood in A 30	1/8/17		The Batt. remained in its position. There was very heavy continuous rain	EB
	2/8/17		Rain continued. Strength decrease 2 OR	EB
	3/8/17		Coy Commanders attended a lecture by Corps Commander. A & B Coys were allotted the latter. The state of the ground and the rain greatly interfered with training	EB
	4/8/17		The Batt. carried out a route march by platoons	EB
	5/8/17		The Batt. carried out a route march by platoons and practised the Lewis guns on the range.	EB
			Strength decrease 2 O.R.	
			Strength decrease LIEUT A J. FARRINGTON posted to 1/6 Bn. R. War. R.	EB
	6/8/17		Bn. at Training. Strength decrease 2nd LIEUT R. HEGAN posted to R.F.C.	EB
	8/8/17		MAJOR BINDLOSS appointed Liaison Officer between 48th Div and Divn. on Right for remainder of the present operations.	EB
	7/8/17		Strength decrease 2nd LIEUT J. J. FARMER posted to 1/5 R SUSSEX R	EB
			Appointments. CAPT W. C RETALLACK M.C. to be acting LT COL whilst Commanding 21.7.17	EB
			CAPT E.A.M. BINDLOSS to be acting MAJOR whilst employed as MAJOR on H.Q. 20.7.17	EB
			CAPT H S BLOOMER 6th Bn. MAN R relinquishes the acting Rank of MAJOR on ceasing to be so employed 5.7.17	[illegible] Lt Col Cmdg 1/5 R.War R.

Army Form C. 2118.

Instructions regarding War Diaries and Intelligence Summaries are contained in F. S. Regs., Part II, and the Staff Manual respectively. Title pages will be prepared in manuscript.

WAR DIARY
or
~~INTELLIGENCE~~ SUMMARY.
(Erase heading not required.)

1/5 Bn The Royal Warwickshire Regt
August 1917

Place	Date	Hour	Summary of Events and Information	Remarks and references to Appendices
DAMBRE	17.8.17		Appointments CAPT W C C GELL to retain the acting rank of Lt Col whilst commanding a Battn 6.7.17	EB
			2nd LIEUT E.P.Q CARTER to be Adjutant vice CAPT J H CROSSKEY	EB
			Strength decrease 7 O.R Strength increase 1 O.R	EB
~~[illegible]~~	20/8/17		W C C Gell Lt Col Cmdg 1/5 R War R	

Instructions regarding War Diaries and Intelligence Summaries are contained in F. S. Regs., Part II. and the Staff Manual respectively. Title pages will be prepared in manuscript.

Army Form C. 2118.

WAR DIARY
or
INTELLIGENCE SUMMARY.
(Erase heading not required.)

1/5 Battn The Royal Warwickshire Regt

August 1917

Place	Date	Hour	Summary of Events and Information	Remarks and references to Appendices
Camp A 30 d 19 Ref Map BELGIUM-28 N.W. 1/20 000	August 7	2.30 pm	Battn (less B Echelon) moved to REIGERSBURG Camp - B Echelon to HOUTKERQUE	Appendix I. CR
REIGERSBURG CAMP	8th	7.15 pm	The Bn. relieved the BUCKS Bn in the line at ST JULIEN. An outpost line was taken up with posts 100 x by the River STEENBEEK. Southern boundary CHEDDER VILLA - BORDER HOUSE - Northern boundary ALBERTA - C12a 6525. On our right the 36 Division; on our left 4th GLOSTERS	Ref Map ST JULIEN 1/10000 O.O. No 114 CR
VANHEULE FM. ST JULIEN	10/11		Bn relieved by 7th R. WAR. R and proceeded to CANAL del L'YSER BANK. Casualties during period 8th - 11th, killed 17 OR's - WOUNDED - 2nd Lt F. COULSON and 38 OR's. wounded (at duty) 2 Lt J.B. FLORENCE and 6 OR's	CR
CANAL BANK	12th	8.30 pm	2 officers + 120 OR's working party at ST JULIEN - Casualties Wounded 3 OR's wounded (at duty) 3 OR's	CR O.O. 115 CR
" "	13	8.30 pm	Bn. Relieved 7th R. War. R in line	
VANHEULE FM.	16	1.45 am	Bn (less outpost coy) to DAMBRE CAMP in accordance with O.O. No 116	O.O. 116 - CR
		2 pm	Outpost coy to DAMBRE CAMP - Casualties 13th - 16th killed 6 - wounded 11. wounded at duty 1	CR
	17		wounded 2/Lt D. ECKERSLEY (143 Inf Bde T.O)	
DAMBRE	18	7 pm	Bn. less C + D Coys to relieve 7 R Warwk (less two coys) on Canal Bank - C + D coys to REIGERSBERG	CR
CANAL BANK	19.	2 am	B Coy (Capt. E. HOLT) to ST JULIEN to take part in a combined Infantry - Tank attack on HILLOCK Fm and gunpits C12 a 94 (ST JULIEN - 1/10.000)	

[illegible] Lt Col
Cmdg 1/5 R War R

A7092). Wt. W12839/M1293 750,000 1/17. D. D & L., Ltd. Forms/C2118/14.

Army Form C. 2118.

Instructions regarding War Diaries and Intelligence Summaries are contained in F. S. Regs., Part II. and the Staff Manual respectively. Title pages will be prepared in manuscript.

WAR DIARY

or

~~INTELLIGENCE SUMMARY.~~

(Erase heading not required.)

1/5 R.War.R.

August 1917

Place	Date	Hour	Summary of Events and Information	Remarks and references to Appendices
CANAL BANK	night 19/20		B Coy returned to CANAL BANK having successfully taken HILLOCK FM and the gun pit having been occupied by the 1/6 R WAR.R.	EB
			Casualties 16-19 Previously Wounded at duty now evacuated 2 O.R.	EB
			Wounded 7 O.R.	EB
			Killed 1 O.R.	EB
			MISSING 1 O.R Missing (believed killed) 2 O.R.	EB
			Appointments 2nd LIEUT E.HOLT., OX & BUCKS L.I. to be acting CAPT whilst commanding a Coy 28.7.17	EB
			LIEUT W.G LEES to be acting CAPT whilst commanding a Coy 31.7.17	
			2nd LIEUT (T. CAPT) J.H.CROSSKEY M.C. retains the acting rank of MAJOR whilst so employed 29.5.17	EB
			2nd Lt (T.CAPT) (acting MAJ) J H. CROSSKEY M.C. to be ~~acting~~ Lt COL whilst commanding 1/4 GLOUC R	
			21.6.17 – 1.7.17 when he reverts to acting MAJOR.	EB
			Strength decrease 4 O.R.	EB
CANAL BANK	21.8.17	10.30 P.M	The Bn (less B Coy) moved to positions of assembly preparatory for the attack	O.O.116 A Appendix II & III EB
Dugout C 18a 5.4			The Bn attacked in accordance with O.O.117. On the right after protracted fighting the gunpits at C12d 7.3	
			were captured; on the left the leading wave gained its objective without serious opposition. Owing to	O O.117
			the tanks being unable to get on the main objective was not attained. About 9 AM the enemy counter attacked	

D. D. & L., London, E.C. (A7883) Wt. W809/M1672 350,000 4/17 Sch. 52a Forms/C/2118/14

[illegible] Lt Col Cmdg 1/5 R.War R

Instructions regarding War Diaries and Intelligence Summaries are contained in F. S. Regs., Part II, and the Staff Manual respectively. Title pages will be prepared in manuscript.

WAR DIARY
or
~~INTELLIGENCE~~ SUMMARY. 1/5 R War. R.
August 1917
(Erase heading not required.)

Army Form C. 2118.

Place	Date	Hour	Summary of Events and Information	Remarks and references to Appendices
			strongly and drove us back to our original position. Lt Col RETALLACK seriously wounded 9 AM	EB.
	Night 22/23		C. Coy attacked and reoccupied gunpits C12 d 7 3 ~~[illegible]~~.	Appendix IV EB
	Night 23/24		Moves took place as in appendices V & VI	App. V & VI EB
Dugout C12 C0 2	24	3 AM	Enemy attacked the gun pits in force and with flamenwerfer and drove ^out^ back C Coy &c.	EB.
	Night 24/25		Operations as in appendices VII & VIII were prepared for. The attack on the gunpits was postponed owing to the state of the ground and the gunpits were eventually retaken on the 25th by B Coy 1/8 RWarR	Appendix VII & VIII EB
			Throughout these operations communication was very difficult and slow owing to the state of the ground and the severity of the enemy's fire and the closeness of his observation and the runners suffered many casualties	EB.
	Night 26/27		C Coy were sent up to support 1/8 RWarR. to C12 d 2 2 and after the commencement of the attack moved forward to C 12 d 7 3 and were subsequently used for Stretcher bearing	EB
	27th	3.15 PM	A.B & D Coys were sent as part of a Composite Bn back to POPERINGHE.	EB
	28th	3.15 PM	C Coy was sent as part of a composite Bn back to POPERINGHE.	EB
POPERINGHE	29th	2.50 PM	The Bn moved by march Route to TUNNELLING CAMP St. JAN TER BIEZEN	OO 118 EB
			MAJOR BINDLOSS rejoined from liaison duty	EB
			Lt COL W. C. C. GELL took over the command vice Lt Col RETALLACK wounded.	EB,

(Sgd) W C C Gell Lt Col
Cmdg 1/5 RWarR

Instructions regarding War Diaries and Intelligence Summaries are contained in F. S. Regs., Part II. and the Staff Manual respectively. Title pages will be prepared in manuscript.

WAR DIARY
or
~~INTELLIGENCE SUMMARY.~~ 1/5 R War R
(Erase heading not required.)

August 1917

Army Form C. 2118.

Place	Date	Hour	Summary of Events and Information	Remarks and references to Appendices
POPERINGHE	29		Casualties 19–28 2nd Lt R. CRIGHTON Killed in action 22.8.17	EB
			2nd Lt T. C. MAGNESS Missing believed killed 22.8.17	EB
			2nd Lt L.T. O'HANLON Wounded (at duty) 22.8.17	EB
			2nd Lt H.L. WOSTENHOLM Wounded (at duty) 24/8/17	EB
			2nd Lt S F. SNAPE Wounded 25.8.17	EB
			Strength Increase 2nd Lt R.O. PICKERING Embarked Southampton 17.7.17	EB
			2nd Lt F.G. HALL Embarked FOLKESTONE 31.7.17	EB
			2nd Lt W. SHADBOLT Embarked SOUTHAMPTON 11.8.17	EB
			2nd Lt G.A. PALMER Embarked SOUTHAMPTON 11.8.17.	EB
			Strength decrease 7 O.R.	EB
St JAN TER	30		Coy Inspection by Coy Commanders	EB
BIEZEN			Strength Increase 2nd Lt G.T. GAUNTLEET and 20 OR	EB
			Casualties 19–28 Killed 26 O.R.	EB
			Wounded 127 O.R. of whom 5 have since died.	EB
			Wounded (at duty) 5 OR	EB
			Strength decrease 1 OR.	EB

[illegible] Lt Col
Cmdg 1/5 R War R

D. D. & L., London, E.C.
(A7883) Wt W809/M1672 350,000 4/17 Sch. 52a Forms/C/2118/14

Army Form C. 2118.

Instructions regarding War Diaries and Intelligence Summaries are contained in F. S. Regs., Part II, and the Staff Manual respectively. Title pages will be prepared in manuscript.

WAR DIARY
or
~~INTELLIGENCE~~ SUMMARY. 1/5 R War R.
(*Erase heading not required.*)
August 1917

Place	Date	Hour	Summary of Events and Information	Remarks and references to Appendices
St JAN TER BIEZEN	31·8·17		The Bn Carried at Training. Coys were marched to POPERINGHE for the Baths	EB
			The total effective strength of the Bn on 31·8·17 was	
			34 officers 757 O.R.	
			1 " 5 " RAMC attached	
			1 " Interpreter.	
			35 officers 763 O.R.	
				[illegible] Lt Col Cmdg 1/5 R War R

D. D. & L., London, E.C.
(A7883) Wt W809/M1672 350,000 4/17 Sch 52a Forms/C2118/14

Appendix I

PROVISIONAL ORDERS FOR MOVE.
BY
Lieut. Colonel C.RETALLACK, M.C.
Commdg. 1/5th Bn.Royal Warwickshire Regiment.
6th August 1917.

---

1. Reference tomorrow's move to REIGERSBURG.

2. Bn. will move at 2.30 p.m.
<u>ROUTE.</u> CHEMIN MILITAIRE - Cross roads ~~xx~~I. 1 c.15 - REIGERSBURG.
Distance 4 miles.
<u>DRESS.</u> Full Marching Order.

3. B Echelon personnel to be left out of action will parade outside Bn. Headqrs. at 11 a.m.
These will <u>not</u> accompany the Bn. on the move.

4. Officers valises will be stacked just SOUTH of the Officers lines by 12.30 p.m.
Mens boxes outside Coy. H.Q's by 2 p.m.

5. Cooks, Lewis Gun limbers, Water Carts, Mess Cart, Medical Cart and Baggage Wagon for ~~xxxxxx~~ Officers valises will accompany the Bn.

6. Lewis Guns will be packed under the supervision of Lieut. C.E. CARRINGTON.

7. Further details will be notified tomorrow.

8. Bn. will move into the line on the night of the 8/9th.

2/Lieut. & A/Adjt,
6/8/17. 1/5th Bn. Royal Warwickshire Regiment.

OPERATION ORDERS
BY
Lieut. Colonel C.RETALLACK,M.C.
Commdg. 1/5th Bn. Royal Warwickshire Regiment.
8th Aug. 1917

Copy No...1...

No. 114.

Ref: Map 28 N.W. 1/20000.

1. The 5th R.War. R. will relieve the Bucks Bn. in the front line tonight, 8/9th Aug. 1917.

2. Coys. will parade ready to pass Bn. H.Q. as under; with 3 minutes between platoons:

B Coy.	~~7.15~~ p.m.	7.00 pm
A Coy.	~~7.30~~ p.m.	7.15 pm
C Coy.	~~7.45~~ pm.	8.15 "
H.Q. Coy.	~~8.0~~ p.m.	8.30 "
D Coy.	~~8.3~~ p.m.	8.33 "

ROUTE. REIGERSBURG - Cross Roads I.1 c. 15. - Road Junction ~~xxxxx~~ I.1 b. 35.- Road Junction I.1 b.09 - Bridge 2 a. - Trench Board track to C 21 d. 15.

DRESS. Fighting Order, with Box Respirators at the ALERT position.

3. Guides from the Bucks Bn. will be at junction of BUFFS ROAD and Trench Board track, C 21 d. 15 at 8.30 p.m.
Coys. will relieve corresponding Coys. of the Bucks Bn.

4. On arrival Coys. will be disposed as under:
B Coy. on the Right.
A Coy. on the Left.
C Coy. in Support.
D Coy. in Reserve.

5. Bn. H.Q. will be at C 28 b. 8340; Advanced Bn. H.Q. at VENHEULE FARM.

6. Mens packs and Officers valises will be stacked outside Bn. H.Q. by 6.30 p.m. Mess boxes outside Bn. H.Q. by 7 p.m.

7. Lewis Guns will be carried by the Teams.

8. Porridge will be issued before moving.

9. S.O.S. Signals, Very Lights and tools, etc. will be taken over from the Bucks Bn. and copies of receipts given forwarded to Bn. H.Q. as soon as possible.

10. ACKNOWLEDGE.

E.P.L. Carter
2/Lieut. & A/Adjt.,
1/5th Bn. Royal Warwickshire Regiment.

Issued at 3 p.m.
8th Aug. 1917.

Copies 1 & 2 War Diary
" 3 - 6 Coys.
Copies 7 T.O. & Q.M.S.
" 8 R.S.M.

OPERATION ORDERS BY Copy No.....

Lieut. Colonel C.RETALLACK, M.C.
Commdg. 1/5th Bn. Royal Warwickshire Regiment.
13th August 1917. No.115.

REF: MAP. 28 N.W. 1/20000.

1. The 5th R. War. R. will relieve the 7th R. War. R. in the front line tonight 13/14th August.

2. Coys. will parade ready to pass Bridge 2 a. as under, with 3 minutes between platoons:

C Coy.	8.30 p.m.
D Coy.	8.45 p.m.
A Coy.	9.0 p.m.
B Coy.	9.15 p.m.
H.Q.	9.30 p.m.

ROUTE. Trench Board Track toC.21 d. 15.
DRESS. Fighting Order, with Box Respirators at the ALERT position.

3. Guides from the 7th R. War. R. will be at C.21 d. 15. at 8.30 p.m.

4. On arrival, Coys. will be disposed as under:
D on the Right
C on the Left
A in Support
B in Reserve

5. Officers valises and mens' packs will be stacked under arrangements to be made by the R.S.M. by 7 p.m.
Mess boxes will be stacked in the same place half and hour before each Coy. moves off.

6. Lewis Guns will be carried by the Teams.

7. 1 Pack Mule per Coy. and 2 for H.Q. will be available. These will carry back empty petrol tins from the front line.

8. Porridge will be issued before moving.

9. S.O.S. Signals, Very Lights and tools, etc. will be taken over from the 7th R. War. R. and copies of receipts given forwarded to Bn. H.Q. as soon as possible.

10. ACKNOWLEDGE.

E P L Carter

Issued at 4 p.m.
13/8/17.

2/Lt. & A/Adjt.,
for O.C. 1/5th Bn. Royal Warwickshire Regt.

Copies to 1 & 2 War Diary.
" " 3 to 6 Coys.
Copy No 7 to Q.M. & T.O.
" " 8 " R.S.M.

To O.C. PLEASE. Appendix II

From H.S. BLOOMER Capt.

I have made the following arrangements with Major PRIOR.:–

1. Instead of 1 guide per platoon there will be guides as follows:– D Coy 2 – A Coy 2 – C Coy 2 for 11 & 10 platoons and 2 for 12 & 9 platoons – H.Q. 1 (9 in all) L. This has been done on the advice of Major PRIOR. He says he cannot find any more intelligent fellows. He also says that Coys should keep closed up in single file no interval between platoons or sections. A Coy platoons to come in following order – 1.4.3.2 as they deploy from the road.

Please instruct all ranks that when proceeding to assembly position immediately a very light goes up they must get down as owing to nature of ground appendix III

our : men stand out very much against skyline

2. Advance H.Q. under SHAPE please bring up one or two shovels.

3. Major PRIOR and I will be at assembly position

4. Men must be quiet.

5. D Coy form up behind hedge with swamp in front. They are slightly behind line of A Coy & should – immediately barrage starts – get through the swamp.

6. Guides will be at CHEDDAR VILLA at 12.15 prompt and Major PRIOR thinks that the leading Coy should pass Canal at 10.0 pm. He says 1130 pm will be too late. It is essential that first Coy should clear CHEDDAR at 12.15 am

21.8.17
6.0 pm

[illegible] Capt.

D Coy pass at 10.30

Operation Orders No 106

By Lt Col C. R[illegible] M.C.

Comdg 1/5 R. War. R.

Copy No 1

August 15th

Ref Maps

1/20.000. 28 NW

1/10.000. St JULIEN

1a. The Fifth Army is attacking the enemy on his front at dawn August 16th

b. The 48th Div. with the 145 Inf Bde is attacking the green line on the Right sector of the XVIII Corps front with the 11 Div on our left and the 36 Div on our right

c. The 143rd Bde will be in Divisional Reserve on the Right and the 144th Bde on the left

2 The 145 Bde will attack with the 5 Glosters on right - Bucks Bn in centre 4 Oxford & Bucks on left and 4 R Berks in Bde Reserve.

3.a. Two coys will be detailed - one by the 4 Glosters and one by the 5th R. War. R. will be left out to cover assembly of 145 Bde. These two outpost coys will be under the command of Capt H.S. BLOOMER who will be with the G.O.C. 145 Bde at Cheddar Villa.

They will remain in their present position when the attack commences and will not be withdrawn until the green line is captured.

They will then be withdrawn as and when ordered by O/C outposts (Capt. Bloomer)

b. The outpost coy of the 5 R.Warks will be employed as follows.

D coy – Two platoons under an officer

C coy – Two platoons under an officer.

In each case this will be the platoons East of the STEENBEEK and the platoons in close support on the West of the Steenbeek.

c. The officers of D & C detailed in para b will be at HQrs of D coy C18 a 0065 by 4 a.m and will remain there during operations.

d. Two runners from D and two from C will report to Capt Bloomer at Cheddar Villa at 3.30 a.m

4. a. The 5th Bn (less outpost coy) will move from present position in the line to DAMBRE camp B27 d and H3 b as soon as the leading troops of 145 Bde reach the Steenbeek. The 145 Bde will be in position of readiness by 3.45 a.m

b. The outpost coy will move to DAMBRE when relieved by 1/4 outposts.

5. Troops moving back will give way to all Eastward traffic, and will move in file by platoons at 100 yds distance ~~in file~~ East of Canal and by Coys at 200 yds distance West of Canal.

Route. Trench board track
Bridge 2A
Chemin Militaire
road junction H3d 23

6. In order to obtain the latest information of the enemy, the following patrols will be sent out as soon as possible after dusk tonight

Unit	Strength	Objective	Information Required
D Coy.	1 NCO + 6 ORs.	Border House –	If occupied or not
C.	1 NCO + 6 ORs.	Houses on St Julien – Poelcapelle Rd.	If occupied or not –

Reports as soon as possible to Vanheule Fm.

7. The Bn will be prepared to move from Dambre at short notice at zero + 2 hours

Copy 1 + 2 War Diary
3 – 6 – Coys

Issued by orderly at

2 Lt.
Adj 5 R Warwicks

To Recipients of OO No 116

Re/ para 3.b. The 2 officers detailed will report to Bn HQ's Kenkenle Pm as soon as possible tonight for detailed instructions

Re/ para 4.a. One officer from A and one from B will report to Bn. HQrs as soon as possible tonight for detailed instructions

Rations for outpost company will be delivered to HQrs D coy tonight

3 pack animals per Coy & 2 for Bn HQ will be available for carrying pack empties, petrol tins, mess kit etc

[signature]
2/Lt a/Adjt 1/5 R.Dub

15/8/17

31.T.
(6 sheets)

Vol 31

C O N F I D E N T I A L.

W A R D I A R Y.

of

1/5th ROYAL WARWICKSHIRE REGIMENT.

From 1st September,

To 30th September, 1917.

* * * * * *

Instructions regarding War Diaries and Intelligence Summaries are contained in F. S. Regs., Part II, and the Staff Manual respectively. Title pages will be prepared in manuscript.

WAR DIARY
or
~~INTELLIGENCE SUMMARY.~~
(Erase heading not required.)

September 1917

1/5 Bn The Royal Warwickshire Regt

Army Form C. 2118.

Place	Date	Hour	Summary of Events and Information	Remarks and references to Appendices
St JANTER	1st		Btn at training. Casualties not previously recorded Killed 1 OR Wounded 5 OR	EB
BIEZEN			Strength Increase 6 O.R. Strength decrease CAPT. O. W. SICHEL ordered Medical Board with a	EB
			sick leave in England.	
			No 200235 Pte J SORRELL No 200139 Pte E.W. BURROWS No 200455 Pte W. WEBSTER awarded	EB
			Military Medal by Corps Commander (XVIII Corps)	
	2nd		Church Parade. Casualties. Not previously recorded 1 OR Previously reported Wounded & Missing now reported dead 3 OR	EB
			Previously reported wounded now reported died of wounds 2 OR.	EB
			Strength Increase 7 OR Strength decrease 2 OR transferred to T.M.B.	EB
	3rd		Bn at Training and Firing on Range. Casualties. Previously reported Missing now reported gassed 1 O.R.	EB
			Previously reported sick now reported gassed 1 O.R. Previously reported Wounded now died of Wounds 5 OR	EB
			Strength Increase 3. OR	EB
			MAJ E.A.M. BINDLOSS assumed command of Bn during absence of Lt COL W. C. C. GELL on leave	EB
	4th		Bn at Training. Casualties Not previously reported. Missing 25 O.R.	EB
			Strength decrease 2 OR. Casualty Previously reported Wounded now reported Killed in action 1 OR	EB
	5th		Bn at Training. Strength Increase 1 OR Strength decrease 1 O.R.	EB
			No 200983 Sergt F. ORETON awarded bar to Military Medal by Corps Commander	EB
	6th		Bn at Training. Strength Increase 1. OR	

D. D. & L., London, E.C. (A7883) Wt W.... /M1672 350,000 4/17 Sch 52a Forms/C/2118/14

Instructions regarding War Diaries and Intelligence Summaries are contained in F. S. Regs., Part II, and the Staff Manual respectively. Title pages will be prepared in manuscript.

WAR DIARY or ~~INTELLIGENCE SUMMARY~~.

(Erase heading not required.)

1/5 R. War. R.
Sept 1917

Army Form C. 2118.

Place	Date	Hour	Summary of Events and Information	Remarks and references to Appendices
St. JAN TER BIEZEN	6th		Strength Increase 2nd Lt. H.A. SPENCER Joined Bn. 5.9.17	EB
			2nd Lt. F.H. WEBB Joined Bn. 5.9.17	EB
	7th		Bn. at Training. Inspection of Anti Gas appliances by Divl. Gas Officer.	EB
			Strength Increase 1 OR Strength decrease 2 O.R.	EB
	8th		The Brigade Paraded and was addressed by the G.O.C. Divn. The G.O.C. Divn. presented to the Football team of the Bn. medals and a cup to commemorate the fact that they had been the runners up in the FANSHAWE Cup in 1917	EB
			Strength decrease 6. OR.	EB
	9th		Church Parade. Not previously reported 1 O.R.	EB
			Strength decrease 1 OR.	EB
	10th		Bn. at Training.	EB
	11th		Bn. at Training Casualty Not previously reported 1 OR	EB
			Strength Increase 1 OR.	EB
	12th		Bn. at Training. Casualty 1. OR (previously reported missing now rejoined from Field Ambulance) Strength Increase	EB
			No. 242278 Pte. R. EGGINGTON No. 201797 Pte. J. RILEY & No. 203036 Pte. A. JOHNSON awarded Military Medal by Corps Commander	EB

D. D. & L., London, E.C. (A7883) Wt W809/M1672 350,000 4/17 Sch 52a Forms/C/2118/14

Instructions regarding War Diaries and Intelligence Summaries are contained in F. S. Regs., Part II, and the Staff Manual respectively. Title pages will be prepared in manuscript.

WAR DIARY ~~or~~ ~~INTELLIGENCE SUMMARY.~~

(Erase heading not required.)

1/5 R. War. R.

Sept 1917

Army Form C. 2118.

Place	Date	Hour	Summary of Events and Information	Remarks and references to Appendices
St JAN TER BIEZEN	13th		Bn at Training and at Baths. Strength Increase 2nd Lt S. G. MINCHER	EB
	*		" " 2nd Lt E. CURTIS	EB
	14th		Bn at training. strength decrease 2nd Lt (T. Capt)(A. Lt Col) J. H. CROSSKEY M.C Transferred to 1/4 GLOUCESTER Regt	EB
			Strength decrease Capt (A. MAJ) A. S. ALABASTER M.C. Transferred to 1/7 R. War R.	EB
			" " 6. O.R.	EB
	15th		Bn at training. Lt COL J. C. C. GELL returned from leave and resumed command of the Bn	EB
			Strength decrease 5 O.R.	EB
	16		Church Parade. Strength increase 2nd Lt H. J. PATTERSON and 2nd Lt G. H. WILSON	EB
	17		The Bn moved by March Route and rail to NORDAUSQUES	O.O.119 EB
NORDAUSQUES	18		Inspection of Coys by Coy Commanders. Strength increase 3. OR Strength decrease 1. OR.	EB
	19th		Bn practised holding a defensive position in conjunction with an attack practice by the 144 Bde	EB
	20th		Bn at training and firing on the Range. Strength increase 81 O.R.	EB EH.
	21st		Bn carried out Field firing. Strength Increase one O.R. Strength decrease 5 O.R. Casualties previously reported wounded, since died of wounds 2 O.R.	EB
	22nd		~~Church Parade~~. ~~Baths~~ Bn training. CAPT H. L. WOSTENHOLM granted ext. of leave to 25-9-17.	EH
	23rd		Church Parade. Baths.	EH.
	24th		Bn at training. 1 Coy. Field firing. Strength increase 19 OR.	EH.

D. D. & L., London, E.C. (A7889) Wt W2591/M1672 350,000 4/17 Sch 52a Forms/C/2118/14

Army Form C. 2118.

Instructions regarding War Diaries and Intelligence Summaries are contained in F. S. Regs., Part II, and the Staff Manual respectively. Title pages will be prepared in manuscript.

WAR DIARY
or
~~INTELLIGENCE SUMMARY.~~
(Erase heading not required.)

1/5 R War R.
Sept. 1917

Place	Date	Hour	Summary of Events and Information	Remarks and references to Appendices
NORDAUS-QUES	25th		Bn. training. (T.F. eff. medal (A.O. 1-5-17)	EH.
	26th		Bn. practice attack. CQMS TRIMNELL, SGT. LEACH, CPL. EVANS awarded. str. decrease 7 OR.	EH.
	27th		Coy. schemes against strong point.	EH.
	28th		Bn. carried out Bde. scheme. QM & HON. LT. E.V. JEAVONS to be HON. CAPTAIN. (London Gazette. 12-9-17)	EH. EH.
	29th		Inspection by C.O. 5% moved to HOUTKERQUE.	EH.
	30th		Bn. moved by route march & rail to DAMBRA CAMP.	O.O.120. EH.

E Holbart
for O.C. 1/5 R War R

OPERATION ORDERS BY Lieut. Col. C.RETALLACK, M.C. Commdg. 1/5th Bn. Royal Warwickshire Regiment. — Copy No........

21st Aug. 1917. — No 117.

Ref? Maps. 1/10000 PILKEM sheet
1/20000 Sheet 28 N.W.

1. PLAN.
The 143rd Inf: Bde: in conjunction with the 184 th Inf. Bde. on the right and the 144th Inf: Bde: on the left will capture on the 22nd inst. the WINNIPEG - SPRINGFIELD line from road junction D.7.c.35. - building C.12. b.47 (both exclusive).

2. BOUNDARIES.
Right. C.18 a.21. - C.18 b.08. - road junction D.7 c.35.(exclusive)
Left. HILLOCK Fme. - BUILDING C12 b.47. (both exclusive)
INTER BATTALION. C 12c9075 - Cemetery C 12 b.80 (inclusive to right Battalion)

3. ATTACK.
The attack will be carried out by tanks in conjunction with Infantry. Five tanks will co-operate with the 143rd Inf:Bde: moving up the ST.JULIEN - WINNIPEG road, and two tanks moving up the ST.JULIEN - TRIANGLE FARM road; clearing all the enemy's positions along the WINNIPEG - SPRINGFIELD line.

4. INFANTRY CO-OPERATION.
(a) The 5th R.War.R. (less B Coy.) will co-operate with tanks on the right. 7th R.War.R. (less 2 Coys.) on the left.
(b) The 5th R.War.R. will attack with 3 Coys. - A on right, D on left and C in support.
Boundry between Coys. will be the ST.JULIEN - WINNIPEG road (inclusive to D Coy.)
(c) At Zero hour the leading waves of 5th Bn. (Nos.1. 4; 15 &14) platoons and 7th Bn. will advance, mopping up any enemy posts to within 150 yds. of the WINNIPEG - SPRINGFIELD line.
The rear platoons (Nos. 3. 2. 13. & 16) will be prepared to move forward as soon as the tanks are reaching their objectives and to consolidate the WINNIPEG - SPRINGFIELD line as soon as the tanks have dealt with the enemy positions.
No 11 platoon will take up a position about C 12 d. 7535 and No 10 platoon about C 12 d. 3005 to protect the right flank until the 184th Inf:Bde: has made good that ground.
No 11 platoon will advance with the rear platoons, and No 10 with the leading platoons.
C Coy. (less 10 & 11 platoons) will be in Bn. Reserve at C 18 a.
Bn. Hqs. C 18 a.54.
Adv. Bn. Hqs. and Report Centre at JANET FARM.
~~(d) 143 M.G.C.~~
d. Troops of the 6th Bn. R.War.R. will continue to hold our present posts till orders are received from Bde. H.Q. that they may be withdrawn.

5. ARTILLERY.
At zero hour the artillery barrage will commence for 10 minutes on the line C. 12 d.60 - C.12 a.94. and then move in lifts of 100 yds, at the rate of 100 yds. in 8 minutes till it reaches the LANGEMARCK line where it will remain for 2 hours.
From zero a smoke barrage will be placed on WINNIPEG -SPRINGFIELD line and LANGEMARCK line; will lift off WINNIPEG-SPRINGFIELD line at zero plus 21 minutes, but will remain on the LANGEMARCK line till zero plus 3 hours.

6. Strong points will be made by 5th Bn. at WINNIPEG and by 7th Bn. at SPRINGFIELD.

7. ASSEMBLY.
The leading wave (1. 4. 15. 14.platoons) will assemble on a taped line from C12 d. 20 - C12 c.9075. The rear wave will assemble on a taped line 50 yds. in rear.
No11 platoon on right of No 3 platoon.
No 10 platoon behind No 11 platoon.

Copy No........1

OPERATION ORDERS
BY
Lieut. Col. C.RETALLACK, M.C.
Commdg. 1/6th Bn. Royal Warwickshire Regiment.
21st Aug. 1917.

No116./A

Ref: Map. 28 N.W. 1/20000.

1. The 6th R.War.R. (less B Coy.) will move to positions of assembly already detailed tonight 21/22nd Aug. 1917.

2. Coys. will parade in the following order, under the arrangement of O.C. Coys. in time for their leading platoons to pass - Bridge 2. at the times stated:

D Coy. ~~11~~ 10.30 p.m.	A Coy. ~~11.5~~ 10.35 p.m.	C Coy. ~~11.10~~ 10.40 p.m.
14 Platoon	~~4~~ 1 Platoon	11 Platoon
15 "	~~1~~ 4 "	10 "
16 "	3 "	12 "
13 "	2 "	9 "

DRESS. - Fighting Order.

3. Coys. will march by platoons at 100 yds. distance, and will be met by one guide per platoon, found by B Coy., at Bridge 2.
ROUTE. Bridge 2. via SOUTHERN TRACK (the Southern Track is marked by posts with square heads and goes by Bridge 2.) - PITTSBURG - 26 central - WILSON FARM - C 26. d.90 - Cross Roads Farm - BUFFS ROAD - CHEDDAR VILLA.
At CHEDDAR VILLA platoons will be met by guides from 6th Bn. who will lead them to positions of assembly by a track SOUTH of ST. JULIEN.

4. Lewis Guns will be carried on the man.

5. Officers valises and mens packs of Bn. H.Q. and A Coy. will be dumped under arrangements to be made by O.C. B Coy. by 8.30 p.m.. Mess boxes will be stacked on Bridge 2 by 10 p.m.
C and D Coys. will arrange direct with T.O.

6. All troops moving WEST will give way to troops moving EAST.

7. 6th R.War.R. (less outpost platoons) will withdraw as soon as Coys. reach the position of assembly.

8. ACKNOWLEDGE.

[signature] Carter

Issued at 6.15 p.m.

CAPT. & ADJT.

21/8/17.

for O.C. 1/6th Bn. Royal Warwickshire Regiment.

Copies 1 & 2 War Diary
" 3 to 6 Coys.
Copy No 7 Q.M. & T.O.
" " 8 R.S.M.

8. CONTACT.

The signal by tanks to infantry to rush and occupy the objective will be made with a signalling flag from the top of the tank.

A contact aeroplane will fly over the objective at zero plus one hour and zero plus 2 hours, at which hours leading infantry will light RED flares, whether called for or not.

At all other times, flares will only be lit when called for by the aeroplanes.

9. Zero hour will be at 4.45 a.m. - at which hour the leading waves will commence to advance up to the barrage.

10. ACKNOWLEDGE.

E A L Carter

Capt. & Adjt.,

Issued at 8 p.m.

1/5th Bn. Royal Warwickshire Regiment.

21/8/17.

Copies 1 & 2 War Diary
" 2 - 6 Coys.

Copy No 7 1/7th Bn. R.War.R
" " 8 T.O. & Q.M.

Ref. Para 4 INFANTRY COOPERATION.

(d) 143 M.G.Coy. add: will detail 6 guns to advance behind the Infantry and take up positions - 2 guns WINNIPEG - 2 guns CEMETERY - 2 guns SPRINGFIELD

Copy No......

OPERATION ORDERS
BY
Capt. H.S.BLOOMER
Commdg. 1/5th Bn. Royal Warwickshire Regiment.
29th August 1917.

No 118.

Reference Map. 1/100000 Hazebrouk 5 A.

1. The 143 Inf. Bde. will move to TUNNELLING CAMP, ST.JANSTER BEIZEN today, 29th August.

2. The 5th R.War.R. will parade as under:

H.Q. outside Bn. H.Q. facing WEST at 2.50 p.m.
B Coy. 200 yds. in rear of H.Q. at 2.50 p.m.
A and D Composite Coy. 200 yds. in rear of B Coy. at 2.50 p.m
C Coy. outside C Coy. H.Q. at 3 p.m.

DRESS. Full Marching Order. Steel helmets will be worn.

ROUTE. POPERINGHE - PROVEN road.
Distance about 3 1/2 miles.
A distance of 200 yds. between Coys. will be observed.

3. Officers valises will be stacked outside Coy. H.Q. by 2 p.m.
Mess boxes by 2.15 p.m.

4. Tea will be served on arrival.

5. ACKNOWLEDGE.

E P L Carter
Capt. & Adjt.,
for O.C. 1/5th Bn. Royal Warwickshire Regiment.

Issued at 12 noon.
29/8/17.

Copies 1 and 2 War Diary.
" 3 to 6 Coys.
Copy No 7 Q.M. & T.O.
" " 8 R.S.M.

[illegible] Coy

Appendix IV

1. The 5th R.War.R. will advance under a barrage at 9 pm tonight & will capture the following objectives
1st – Gn. Pt. C 12 d 73 & C 12 d 82
Final – [illegible] – SPRINGFIELD Rd from [illegible] Junction D 7 c 35 to Cemetery both inclusive.

2. C Coy will attack on the right & will capture Gun pit C 12 d 73, Junction D 7 c 35 & Cemetery D 7 c [illegible].
Two platoons of D Coy will attack on the left & will capture Gun pit C 12 d 82 & the [illegible].

3. The Coy Commanders
[illegible] – [illegible] will be under [illegible] C.C.

4. 'A' Coy will remain in the present position.
B Coy will [illegible] & form a defensive flank [illegible] – [illegible] about C 12 d 14.

5. SAA [illegible]
[illegible]
[illegible]

[signature]
2/9 Capt. Adjt. 1/5 R.War.R.
5 pm. for Capt [illegible] in command

To OC Coy

Appendix V

1/ Following moves & reliefs will ~~be taken~~ take place to-night 23–24 August

2/ C Coy will hold the front line & will then be disposed as under:–
a] Liaison Post with Rt Bn about C 12 d 92
Left Post of Rt Bn (2/4 Oxford & Bucks) is at D 7 c 0025
b] Post under 2/Lt COCHRANE in Gunpit C 12 d 73
c] Post in or EAST of JANET FARM
d] Liaison Post with Left Bn (7th Worcs) about C 12 d 58
These posts will be as strong as possible especially "b" in Gunpits

3/ B Coy will be disposed as under in Support:–
1 platoon in line of gunpits C 12 d 23
1 platoon in line of gunpits C 12 d 15
These two platoons are available for reinforcing the front line or for immediate counter attack if the front line is lost
2 platoons in their present positions at C 12 c 91
These two platoons will form a reserve at the disposal of Capt HOLT (Adv Bn HQ)

4/ A & D Coys on relief will move back from CHEDDAR VILLA where they will be met by 2/Lt SNAPE who will show them accommodation in the OG lines where they will remain & reorganize.

5/ Bn HQ will move to dugouts C 12 c 02
Adv Bn HQ at present Bn HQ at C 18 b 54

Appendix VII

6/ Regimental Aid Post will remain at C18a0065

7/ Completion of all moves & reliefs together with Map Reference of Coy HQ, to present Bn HQ at C18a54

8/ Rations & water for A & D Coys will be dumped at CHEDDAR VILLA & will be drawn as the Coy move back.

Rations & water for B & C Coys will be dumped where the tape from CHEDDAR VILLA to present Bn HQ crosses the STEENBEEK, & drawn by B Coy under the direction of Capt HOLT

9/ Every effort will be made to make up deficiencies in Lewis Guns, LG drums, ammunition etc from derelict tanks etc

23/8/17

E R L Carter
Capt & Adjt for OC 1/5 R War R

To Capt Holt
O.C. B Coy

Adjutant's Copy

appendix VII

1/ B Coy 5th R War R will occupy the Gunpits at C12a 73 at midnight 24–25 Augst.

2/ 2 platoons will be used for the assault with 1 platoon in close support.

3/ At dusk tonight ~~a patrol~~ it will be ascertained by a patrol detailed by Capt Holt whether the Gunpits are occupied by the enemy or not.

4 Before midnight the 4th platoon of B Coy will establish one post in or about JANET FARM & one post at C12d 42 in liaison with the front posts of B Coy 1/7th R Warwk.

5/ There will be no barrage but the artillery will shell SPRINGFIELD, the CEMETERY, WINNIPEG & SCHULER FARM.

6/ Before midnight one coy 8th R War R will move in night support & take over present dispositions of B Coy 5th R Warwk

7/ After the Gunpits have been occupied a patrol will obtain & touch with 61st Div at D/C 22

Appendix VIII

8/ As soon as the coy of 8th R Wark are in position C Coy 5th R Wark will withdraw to CANAL BANK. On his way out OC C Coy will report at CHEDDAR VILLA.

All arrangements for billeting & rationing C Coy 5th R Wark have been made.

9/ Two Vickers M.G's will take up positions in gunpits as soon as they have been occupied. Until the Gunpits are occupied these MG's will be at C 12 d 22

10/ If ~~[illegible]~~ the Gunpits have been occupied a protective barrage will be put down in front of them from 4.30am — 5am 25th inst.

11/ If the Gunpits are not occupied by the 5th R Wark the Coy of the 8th R Wark will attack with a barrage at 4.45 am 25th inst

12/ Rations for B Coy 5th R Wark will be issued before the operation & carried on the man.

24/8/17

E H L Carter

Capt & Adjt for OC 1/5 R Wark

7.10 pm

1/5 R Warwick R.

Vol 32

October 1917

32.T.

(89 sheets)

On His Majesty's Service.

Confidential

D.A.G.

3rd Echelon

164690/24

CONFIDENTIAL.

W A R   D I A R Y

of

1/5th ROYAL WARWICKSHIRE REGIMENT.

From 1st October,

To 31st October, 1917

Instructions regarding War Diaries and Intelligence Summaries are contained in F. S. Regs., Part II, and the Staff Manual respectively. Title pages will be prepared in manuscript.

WAR DIARY
or
~~INTELLIGENCE SUMMARY.~~
(Erase heading not required.)

1/5 Bn The Royal Warwickshire Regt Army Form C. 2118.

Oct. 1917

Place	Date	Hour	Summary of Events and Information	Remarks and references to Appendices
DAMBRE CAMP	1st		Forward positions reconnoitred	
	2nd		Casualties 1 – 2nd Lieut GORDON G.L. (Seaforth Highlanders attached)	
REIGERSBURG CAMP	2nd		Battalion moved to REIGERSBURG CAMP O.O. 121	O.O. 121
			Orders for attack on 4th issued O.O. 122	O.O. 122
" "	3rd		Bn moved into front line O.O. 123.	O.O. 123
FRONT LINE	4th		Bn attacked as per O.O. 123	
"	5-7th		Bn held new line. For account of attack & ensuing days see Appendices I. II. III	App I II III
"	4th-7th		Casualties – Killed ORs 55	
			Officers – CAPT TURNER R.S.; CAPT. A.C. BRATT; 2nd Lt C.W. WHITE	
			Wounded – ORs 177 (includes 9 since died of wounds)	
			Officers – 2nd Lt LADE J.H. (died of wounds 4th Oct)	
			2nd Lt W. SHADBOLT.	
			" A.G. FOSTER-SUTTON.	
			CAPT E. HOLT.	
			2nd Lt S.G. MINCHER.	
			" G.A. PALMER.	
			Missing – 7 ORs	

D. D. & L., London, E.C. (A7853) Wt W829/M1672 350,000 4/17 Sch 52a Forms/C/2118/14

Instructions regarding War Diaries and Intelligence Summaries are contained in F. S. Regs. Part II. and the Staff Manual respectively. Title pages will be prepared in manuscript.

WAR DIARY or ~~INTELLIGENCE SUMMARY~~.

(Erase heading not required.)

1/5th Bn The Royal Warwickshire Regt — Army Form C. 2118.

October 1917

Place	Date	Hour	Summary of Events and Information	Remarks and references to Appendices
IRISH FARM	7/8		Bn moved to IRISH FARM CAMP	lobb
SIEGE CAMP	8th		Bn moved in motor buses to SIEGE CAMP near ELVERDINGE	lobb
POPERINGE	9th		Bn moved to billets in POPERINGHE OO 124	OO124 lobb
"	9-13th		Bn remained in billets in POPERINGHE and spent the time cleaning up, making up deficiencies, with some drill	lobb
MAROEUIL	13th		Bn entrained at PESELHOEK and moved to MAROEUIL. Train departed at 11.30 am & arrived MAROEUIL 7.30 pm. The Bn detrained & marched to hutments at Mt. ST. ELOI	O.O.125 lobb
Mt St ELOY	13-16th		Bn carried out training. Front line in MERICOURT sector reconnoitred with a view of relieving the CANADIANS	lobb
MERICOURT SECTOR	16th		The Bn relieved the 24th CANADIAN Inf. Bn. in the front line MERICOURT OO125	O.O.126
			The Bn entrained on light railway and was taken to siding. From there they marched. Relief complete about 11.30	lobb
			The trenches were very fair. Long communication trenches trench boarded but not revetted. The front line was continuous, trench boarded in places but not revetted. Much work was done during the tour in working on the posts & support trenches	

D. D. & L., London, E.C. (A7831) Wt W5o9/M1672 350,000 4/17 Sch 52a Forms/C2118/14

Instructions regarding War Diaries and Intelligence Summaries are contained in F. S. Regs., Part II, and the Staff Manual respectively. Title pages will be prepared in manuscript.

WAR DIARY
or
INTELLIGENCE SUMMARY.
(Erase heading not required.)

Army Form C. 2118.

Place	Date	Hour	Summary of Events and Information	Remarks and references to Appendices
	Oct			
POPERINGHE	9th		Increase Officers - 2nd Lts NORWOOD JE - MARVIN FWH - THURSFIELD JT.	lobb
"			SUMNER JS - FILER GA - FROST RAM - TUCKER RF	
"	12th		Increase - 6 ORs from CCS	lobb
"			Officers - 2nd Lts HASELER JW. - PERKINS WC	
MT ST ELOY ~~[illegible]~~	14th		" 4 ORs from base	lobb
MT "	15th		" 1 OR CCS	lobb
MERICOURT Sects	18th		" Officers - 2nd Lt W.O. BUTLER.	lobb
			Decrease	
DAMBRE Camp	1st		ORS 7 to CCS	lobb
Front line	6th		Officers - Lt WG LEES Sick to England	lobb
"	7th		ORS - 1 to CCS	lobb
POPERINGHE	9th		" " - 8 " "	lobb
"	10th		Officers - 2nd Lt GURDON GL to England wounded	lobb
	12th		Officers - Capt LV SEAVONS / Lt L.T. O'HANLON } To England on duty.	lobb
"	13th		ORS 1 - to hospital	lobb
	26th		" 1 - to CCS	lobb
FRASER CAMP	27th		6 - " "	lobb

[signature] LIEUT.-COLONEL.
COMMANDING 1/5th Bn. ROYAL WARWICKSHIRE R. G!

D. D. & L., London, E.C. (A7883) Wt W829/M1672 350,000 4/17 Sch. 52a Forms/C/2118/14

Army Form C. 2118.

Instructions regarding War Diaries and Intelligence Summaries are contained in F. S. Regs., Part II, and the Staff Manual respectively. Title pages will be prepared in manuscript.

WAR DIARY
or
INTELLIGENCE SUMMARY.
(Erase heading not required.)

Place	Date	Hour	Summary of Events and Information	Remarks and references to Appendices
	October			
MERICOURT Sector			Casualties - Nil -	
"	20		The Corps boundary was changed ~~See Appendix~~ See Appendices IV	app IV. wbbG.
"	21st		The Bn was relieved by 1/8 R.War.R. & on relief moved to FRASER CAMP Mt St ELOI 00.126	wbbG. 00.126
FRASER CAMP	21-27		Bn carried out training	wbbG.
"	25/26		25/26th working party of 200 to work in front line. 5pm - 4.0 am.	wbbG.
MERICOURT Sector	27th		Bn relieved 1/8th R.War.R. in front line 0.0. 127	wbbG. 00.127
"			Work carried on in the posts & support reserve lines. Weather good.	
"			Casualties . ORs 2 ~~and [illegible]~~ killed.	
			8 wounded	
			Officers - Nil.	
"	Nov 1st		Bn relieved by 1/5th Bn The Glos: Regt	wbbG. 0.0.128
	Oct 2nd 4th		Increase & decrease in strength Increase - From Base 1 - from XVIII Corps. 1. Reinforcements ORs 133.	wbbG.
	9th		Increase - 7 from base 2 " CCS	wbbG.

Lt Col [illegible] Lt Col
Cmdg 1/5 R.War.R.

D. D. & L., London, E.C.
(A7859) Wt W3079/M1672 350,000 4/17 Sch 52a Forms/C/2118/14

War Diary

SECRET.

Copy No. 3.

143rd Inf. Bde. OPERATION ORDER NO. 169

Ref. maps
1/20,000 Sheet 28 N.W.
1/10,000 POELCAPPELLE

2nd October 1917.

1. Moves will take place to-day, 2nd Oct., in accordance with March Table on reverse.

2. On completion of the relief of the 4th Ox. and Bucks in CALIFORNIA DRIVE the 8th R.War.R. will be under the orders of the 145th Inf. Bde. but will only be used in the case of an enemy attack.

3. Distances of 400 yds. between Bns. and 200 yds. between Coys. will be maintained.

4. Units will report completion of move to Bde. Hdqrs.

5. ACKNOWLEDGE.

C.W. Deart.
Captain,
B.M. 143rd Inf. Bde.

Issued through Signals
at 2 p.m.

Copy No. 1 and 2 retained
3 to 10 Bde. Units.
11 145th Inf. Bde
12 and 13 48th Division.
14 and 15 War Diary.

UNIT	POSITION	STARTING POINT	PASSING S.P.	ROUTE	DESTINATION	REMARKS
6th R.War.R.	DAMBRE CAMP	X ROADs where BATH ROAD cuts VLAMERTINGHE-ELVERDINGHE Road.	5 p.m.	BATH ROAD	CANAL BANK	Guides at X roads C.25.d.31
7th R.War.R.	,,	,,	5-20 p.m.	,,	,,	,,
5th R.War.R.	,,	,,	5-45 p.m.	,,	REIGERSBERG CAMP	Take over camp vacated by the 8th R.War.R.
143 M.G.Coy.	,,	,,	6-5 p.m.	,,	,,	
143 T.M.Batt.	,,	,,	6-15 p.m.	,,	,,	
8th R.War.R.	REIGERSBERG CAMP			BATH ROAD -Bridge 2A -MOUSE TRAP Fm.	CALIFORNIA DRIVE	Time will be notified later.

OPERATION ORDERS
BY
Lieut. Col. W.C.C.GELL, M.C.
Commdg. 1/5th Bn. Royal Warwickshire Regiment.
2nd Oct. 1917.

Copy No. 1

No 121.

Ref. Map 28 N.W. 1/20000.

1. The 5th R.War.R. will move to REIGERSBURG (C) Camp today, 2nd October.

2. Coys. will parade in their ~~old~~ own lines ready to pass the entrance to Camp as under:-

H.Q.	4.30 p.m.
B Coy.	4.32 p.m.
C Coy.	4.34 p.m.
D Coy.	4.36 p.m.
A Coy. under orders of O.C."A"Coy.	

ROUTE. BATH ROAD. Distance 2 miles.
DRESS. Full Marching Order. Steel Helmets will be worn. Blankets rolled and fastened on the top of pack.

3. Lewis Guns will be packed under the supervision of Sgt. RILEY by 4 p.m.

4. Officers valises and Mess boxes will be stacked outside the ORDERLY ROOM by 4 p.m.

5. Teas will be served on arrival.

6. Transport will march in rear of D Coy.

7. ACKNOWLEDGE.

E F L Carter
Capt. & Adjt.,
1/5th Bn. Royal Warwickshire Regiment.

Issued at 2.45 p.m.
2/10/17.

Copies 1 & 2 War Diary.
" 3 to 6 Coys.
Copy No 7 Q.M. & T.O.
" No 8 R.S.M.

OPERATION ORDERS
BY
Lieut.Col.W.C.C.GELL, M.C.
Commdg, I/5th,Bn. Royal Warwickshire Regiment.
3rd, October 1917.

Copy No....1....

No. ~~I2I~~. ~~I22~~. 123

Ref:Map 28 N.W. I/20,000.
POELCAPPELLE I/IO,000.

I. With reference to O.O.I22, the 5th R.War.R. will move into the front line tonight 3/4th October.

2. Coys.will parade in their own lines ready to move as under:-

H.Q.	5.30 p.m.
B.Coy.	5.3I p.m.
A.Coy.	5.37 p.m.
D.Coy.	5.43 p.m.
C.Coy.	5.49 p.m.

ROUTE. BATH ROAD, Bridge 2, MOUSETRAP track.
DRESS. Fighting Order.

3. I guide per platoon & 2 for Bn. H.Q. will be at C I7 b 96 at 8 p.m. to lead Coys.to the forming up positions.

4. Lewis Guns will be carried by the teams.
One limber for A & B. & one for C & D, will be available for carrying L.G.drums (I6 per gun),Mess kit, Tools etc, & will be accompanied by I man per Coy. These limbers will reach VANHEULE FARM by 7 p.m. & will be offloaded there.
The limbers will then proceed to ST JULIEN to pick up salved petrol tins. T.O. will arrange for personnel to assist in this.

5. Officers valises & Messboxes will be stacked under arrangements to be made by the R.S.M. by 5.30 p.m.

6. ACKNOWLEDGE.

E R Carter
Capt. & Adjt.
I/5th Bn. Royal Warwickshire Regiment.

Issued at 3 p.m.
3/IO/I7.

Copies I & 2 War Diary.
" 3 to 6 Coys.
Copy No 7 Q.M. & T.O.
" No 8 R.S.M.

OPERATION ORDERS. Copy No.....9.

BY

Lieut.Col.W.C.C.GELL. M.C.

Commdg,I/5th,Bn.Royal Warwickshire Regiment.

3rd.October I917.— No. I[illegible].

Ref:Map. POELCAPPELLE I/IO.000.

I. On the morning of the 4th.October the I43 Inf:Bde will attack. 5th,R.War.R. on the right; 6th,R.War.R. in the centre; 7th,R.War.R, on the left; 8th,R.War.R. in reserve.

2. Ist,Auckland Bn. & 2nd,Wellington Bn. will be attacking on the right of the 5th,R.War.R.

3. Boundaries of 5th,R.War.R. are:-

Right Boundary. CLIFTON HOUSE (inclusive)
ALBATROSS FARM(inclusive) D.3 central.

Left Boundary; STROPPER STRAPPE FARM. (inclusive) D.2 central.(XXXXXXXXXX
(blockhouse inclusive) then the line of road & tramway to V.27 c.00.

4. The Bn. will form up on a line of posts & tape running from CLIFTON HOUSE to D.I d.48 as follows:-
A.Coy on the right. B.Coy on the left. C.Coy behind A.
D.Coy behind B.

5. Objectives will be as follows:-

A.Coy. I platoon will take VALE HOUSE.
I platoon will take WINZIG.
2 platoons will take ALBATROSS FARM.

B.Coy. I platoon will take dug-outs at D.I d.87.30 & trench D.2 c.I.4.
I platoon dug-outs D.2 c.45.45.
I platoon dug-outs D.2 d.I5.~~35~~. 65
I platoon concrete emplacement D.2 central & to assist I/6th,R.War.R. at STOKES FARM.

C.Coy. I platoon via ALBATROSS FARM for emplacements at D.2 d.70.55 & D.3 c.I8.
I platoon to assist in capture of KRONPRINZ from the N.E. 1 PLATOON FOR D2.d69
I platoon for D.2 d.89.

D.Coy. I platoon WELLINGTON FARM.
I platoon trench area D.2 b.5.3.
I platoon trench area D.2 b.[illegible].
I platoon in reserve at WELLINGTON FARM.

6. Ist N.Z. Bde are prepared to assist in the capture of VALE HOUSE, WINZIG & ALBATROSS FARM.

7. BARRAGE. The attack will be made under an artillery barrage. This barrage will come down I50 yds in front of the forming up positions at zero. It will lift every 50 yds.

For the Ist 200 yds, the barrage will move forward at the rate of 50 yds every [illegible] minutes. After the first 200 yds., & up to the dotted Red Line (Ist objective,)it will move forward at the rate of 50 yds every 3 minutes.

From the dotted Red Line (Ist objective)to the Red Line (Final Objective) the barrage will move forward at the rate of 50 yds every 4 minutes.

The following points will be boxed:-
WINCHESTER FARM, WELLINGTON, Concrete & Dug outs, in V.26 d.49 & BURNS HOUSE.

VACHER FARM will be in the "standing" barrage. The barrage will lift off VACHER FARM & form a box at about zero plus 5 hours.

The 6th,R.War.R. will then send forward and occupy it, if possible.

The Protective Barrage will lift after standing in front of the Dotted Red Line at Zero plus [illegible] hours IO minutes.

It will thicken for [illegible] minutes before lifting.

8. Companies will arrange to have a reserve.
Companies will form up in shell holes behind a taped line.
All troops to be in position by half an hour before dawn.

9. Companies will form strong points as follows:-
A.Coy. at ALBATROSS FARM.
C.Coy. at Houses at D.3 c.I.8.
D.Coy. at WELLINGTON FARM.

IO. Following liason posts will be astablished:-
A.Coy. with Ist Auckland Bn. at ALBATROSS FARM.
C.Coy. with 2nd Wellington Bn. at D.3 c.I.8.
B.Coy. with I/6th R.War.R. at STOKES FARM.
D.Coy. with I/6th R.War.R. at junction of trench with road D3.b86.

II. MACHINE GUNS. 2 sections will follow Coy's. assaulting the Dotted Red Line & take up positions when this has been captured:-
2 Guns about ALBATROSS FARM.
4 Guns about WINCHESTER FARM.
2 Guns about TWEED HOUSE.
I section will follow Coys. assaulting the Red Line & take up positions:-
2 Guns about WELLINGTON FARM.
2 Guns about BURNS HOUSE.
The remaining 4 Guns will be in reserve.

I2. I Trench Mortar will be in position behind I/8th R.War.R. to fire at any enemy strong points holding out.

I3. AEROPLANES. (A) Contact aeroplanes will fly over the objectives at:-
Zero plus I hour 30 minutes.
Zero plus 3 hours 30 minutes.
and when ordered by Corps H.Q.

Infantry will be ready to light RED flares (in line not in groups) at these hours, but will not do so unless called for by Klaxon Horn, or by dropping of WHITE lights.

(B) Counter-attack machine - An aeroplane will be up continuously from zero onwards, the mission of which will be to detect the approach of enemy counter-attacks.
When this patrol observes hostile parties of IOO or over moving to counter-attack it will drop a Smoke bomb over that portion of the front to which the enemy is moving.
The Smoke bomb will burst about IOO feet below the machine, into a white parachute flare, which descends slowly leaving a long trail of brown smoke about I foot broad behind it.

I4. Brigade Battle H.Q. - ARTILLERY HOUSE (C.I2 d.34)
Bde command post. - D.7 a. 37.
Bn. H.Q. - VICTORIA HOUSE. D.7 b.3I.
Forward Bn.H.Q. - probably either CLIFTON HOUSE or VALE HOUSE.
H.Q. I/6th R.War.R. - HUBNER FARM.

I5. Regimental Aid post will be at JANET FARM.

I6. ACKNOWLEDGE.

Issued at 8.0 a.m.
3/IO/I7.

(Sgd.) E. P. ? Capt & Adjt.
I/5th.Bn. Royal Warwickshire Regiment.

Copy No.I. retain.
" 2 to 5 Bn. Units.
" No.6. 6th,R.War.R.
" No.7. 8th,R.War.R.
" No.8. I43 M.G.Coy.
" No.9. File.

Appendix I

To All Companies.

1. C Coy will take over from 3rd Coy 1st Aucklands as soon as possible. Coy H.Q. about D 2 central. Line of posts from D2c12 to D2d29.

2. D Coy will take over from 15 Coy 1 Aucklands posts situated from D2d29 to D2a56. Coy H.Q. [illegible] front line posts.

3. A Coy will take over from 16 Coy 1 Auckland line of posts from D2a56 to D2c74 including two advanced posts at D2d55.80 & D3c14. Coy H.Q. [illegible] of posts.

4. B Coy will be support company on a line about ALBATROSS FARM to D2d04.

5. Reliefs will take place in daylight as far as possible but must be by small parties 4 or 5 men & will have two hours interval with [illegible] as the 1st Aucklands have been. Reconnaissance parties will be sent forward with a view to taking over.

6. 1/8 R. War. R. will be on the left of C Coy tonight & the 2nd Wellingtons will be on the right of D Coy tonight.

7. Companies will send the following [illegible] their present company strength, present dispositions stating their requirements in the way of ammunition, bombs, Lewis gun magazines & S.O.S. rockets.

8. Rations will be drawn from Bn H.Q. tonight after relief of 1st Aucklands has taken place.

9. Patrols with flanks and supporting units will be continuous throughout the night.

Reconnaissance patrols will ascertain location of present enemy posts.

10. Disposition maps after relief of 1st Auckland will be sent to BN HQ by 5.0 AM tomorrow. Detailed casualty reports will be sent in at 5.0 AM.

11. C Coy will establish visual communication with BN HQ.

5/10/17
2 PM
All companies
Repeated to [illegible] of Reserve

[illegible]

5/10/17

Capt [illegible] 1st [illegible]

Appendix II

I/5TH BN. ROYAL WARWICKSHIRE REGIMENT.

1917.

Map Ref: ~~POELCAPPELLE~~ I/10.000.

Mon. Ist Oct. C.O, 2nd in Command, & Signal Officer went up to reconnoitre from VICTORIA HOUSE (re-named "P" HOUSE) D 7 b 3I. 2nd in Command stayed up, Company Commanders & their 2nd in Commands joining him. The Objectives were observed as much as possible from O.P's and landmarks noted. At dusk these Officers went over theit forming up ground & put in marking posts. All returned before dawn except 2nd in

Tue. 2nd Oct. Commands of Coys who stayed in the front line trenches all day returning at dusk. I Officer & 2 N.C.O's per Coy went up at dusk, reconnoitred the forming up position under 2nd in command. Signal Officer & Intelligence Officer laid directing tapes from JANET FARM to "P" HOUSE & from JANET FARM to ARBRE.

Signal Officer (Lieut, C.L.GORDON. Wounded)

Wed, 3rd Oct. These Officers & N.C.O's stayed in the front line all day taking compass bearings etc.,

Forming up tapes laid out under 2nd in command (Capt.E.HOLT.) & Bn. in position by II.30 p.m. with only one casualty.

Thur. 4th Oct. The Bn. was formed up as follows:-

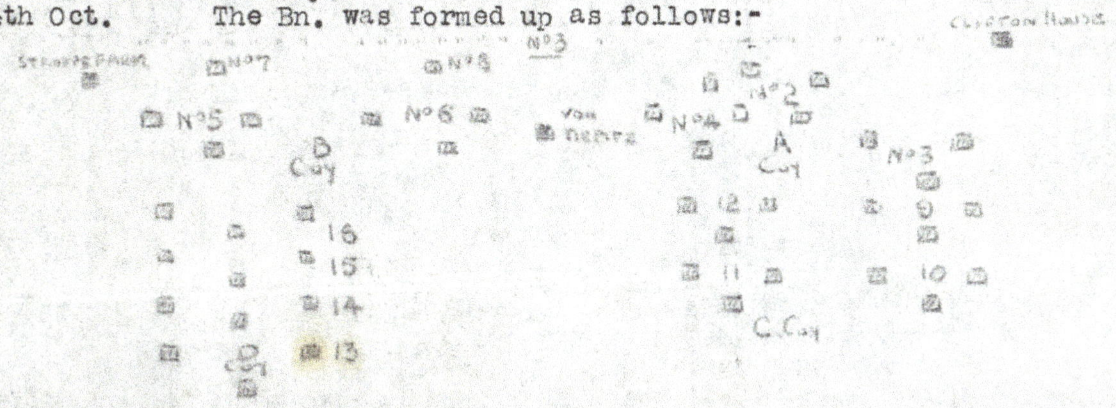

The ~~evening~~ enemy opened a heavy fire along our forming up line at twenty minutes before zero, & B.Coy suffered 7 casualties (O.R's) and I Officer before zero.

Right Company. (A.Coy.)

No.I platoon under 2/Lieut.W.SHADBOLT got to VALE HOUSE with only a few casualties & consolidated the flanks.

No.2 platoon passed through No.I, had some severe fighting around WINZIG took 20 prisoners & consolidated.

No.3 & 4 platoons came through Nos.I & 2 but the NEW ZEALANDERS (I. AUCKLAND BN.) lost direction & pushed our men over to the left.

NO.3 platoon under 2/Lieut.A.F.FOREMAN got on to the high ground about D.2 central & consolidated with the I/6th R.War.R. on the left & the NEW ZEALANDERS on the right, he had about IO men remaining.

No.4 platoon after casualties from M.G. fire on the left reached D.2 c 7.I & dug in.

About zero + 50 minutes heavy shelling of VALE HOUSE commenced almost wiping out No.I platoon, wounding the platoon Commander & killing or wounding all of the forward H.Q. which had just moved up there.

(Capt.E.HOLT. 2/Lieut.S.G.MINCHER. & 2/Lieut.W.SHADBOLT. wounded.)

B.Coy. (left front Company).

As soon as the leading platoons commenced moving forward heavy M.G. fire was opened from the front from about D.2 c I.4 D.2 c 5!5! in all about 5 (light pattern) M.G's & many snipers. These placed were eventually cleared up but the Coy. was only about 30 strong. Lieut.C.E.CARRINGTON with about IO men worked across to D.2 central & consolidated there. The remainder of the Coy consolidated in the positions they had taken .

C.Coy. (right support Coy.)

Moved up at zero + 20 minutes & some of the leading men became somewhat involved in the fighting round WINZIG.

The pressure from the NEW ZEALANDERS on the right pushed the Coy. over & 2/Lieut.F.W.HALE with No.9 platoon got to about D.2 central & consolidated just in rear of the NEW ZEALANDERS.

No.IO & II lost direction & I found them about 9.I5 a.m. about D.2 c 3.3. & sent them off in the direction of their objective. D.3 c 0.6 & D.3 c 2.8 but apparently they crossed the STROMBEEK about D.2 c I.6. & working to the left consolidated behind the NEW ZEALANDERS about D.2 b 2.I.

D.Coy. (left support Coy.)

Moved up at zero + 20 minutes & soon lost all its Officers & 3 platoon Sergeants from shell fire & snipers who still held out about D.2 c 5.3.

The remains of 2 platoons I found about D.2 d I4 where they dug in close to the 2 M.G's of A.Section(Lt.WHYLE) the other 2 platoons were in shell holes when I arrived up about 9.30 a.m. & I ordered C.S.M.SCOTT to dig in along the line of the STROOMBEEK about D.2 c 5.5.

About IOO prisoners (wounded & unwounded) were taken by the Bn.

During the day Lieut.C.E.CARRINGTON was ordered to withdraw & form a support Coy. about ALBATROSS FARM. Also in the afternoon the NEW ZEALANDERS moved to the right, thereby leaving about 30 men of the I/5th R.War.R. under 2/Lieut. F.W.HALE & 2/Lieut.A.F.FOREMAN between D.2 central & WELLINGTON FARM. This thinning out was very necessary as there were too many men in the area & it was being heavily shelled.

About 4.45 p.m. 3.Coys.of the I/5th Gloucesters advanced to advance our line but although Capt.E.P.Q.CARTER & 2/Lieut.G.T.GAUNTLET directed them on our front the high ground around D.2 central & the fact of having to cross the stream diagonally if they kept in the right direction attracted them towards D 2 central where they dug in.

5th Oct./17. Area round WINZIG -- VALE HOUSE and valley of STROOMBEEK heavily shelled. At dusk relieved the New Zealanders who had come into our area by 3 Coys. with 1 Coy. in support about D2 a1.4.

6th Oct/17. A Coy. 1/4th Oxfords relieved A.C. &D companies in the front line.

B & C went back to the line. CLIFTON HOUSE, STROPPE FARM. A & D to the line ALBATROSS FARM D 2 c 55.

A Coy. 1/4th Oxfords advanced their outpost line about 100 yds. and sent out a patrol which located an enemy M.G. about D.2 b 7.8. & was fired on by rifles from about D.3 a 0.5.

7th Oct/I7. Heavy enemy shelling about 4.I5 p.m. to 5.0 p.m. all along the valley of STROOMBEEK & about IOO yards to the N.E. of the stream also the area VALE HOUSE, WINZIG, & the high ground of the LANGEMARCK LINE.

The Bn. & A.Coy I/4th Oxfords was relieved about 2.0 a.m. 8th October by two Coys. of I/4th Royal Berks.

CASUALTIES.	Killed.	Missing.	Died of wounds.	Wounded at duty.	TOTAL.
Officers.	3	-	I	-	IO
O.Ranks.	55	9	6	7	254
TOTALS.	58	9	7	7	264

	Wounded
Officers.	6
O.Ranks.	I77
Total.	I83

LESSONS ON RECENT FIGHTING.

Supporting Coys. must not move up too close behind leading waves, otherwise they become engaged & disorganized.

Tape tracks should be supplemented by lamps at the destination with diffenent coloured lenses.

(Many times parties who did not know where Bde.H.Q, was were shown the flash of the visual lamp. Bde signals were asked to é dot dash for about 1/4 of an hour & the party found its way all right.)

The men seemed to be too thin for the ground to be covered especially if there are anything in the nature of block-houses or strong points suspected.

10th October 1917.

Lieut.Col.

Commdg. 1/5th Bn. Royal Warwickshire Regiment.

Appendix III

48th DIVISION - F.126

11.10.17.

1. I would like your report on the attack carried out by the Brigade, to be accompanied by copies of each Battalion Commander's report. I would like your report and the Battalion Commanders to include answers to the following questions.
The conditions under which the operations were carried out were so difficult that it is of great importance that these points should be brought out and the experience not be lost.

2. (1) Where did each Battalion assemble ?

(2) How did they get there ?

(3) What time were they in position ?

(4) Did any parties lose their way ?

(5) Was it possible to feed or rest after arrival ?

(6) Where was each Battalion Command Post ?

(7) Did Battalion C.Os move forward ?

(8) How was communication kept between Battalions and Companies ?

(9) Did Brigade move its Command Post forward at all, or Bde Commander or Staff go forward ?

(10) Did communication keep open between Brigade & Battalion ?

(11) Were the dogs used ? What were the means of communication ?

(12) Did the barrage come down well ?

(13) Were there any weak places ?

(14) Was it effective ?

(15) How soon was the situation clear enough for you to want to alter it ?

(16) What was furtherest point known to be reached by each Battalion ?

(17) Was that point maintained ?

(18) If not, why not ?

(19) Where were prisoners captured ?

(20) How were they escorted back ?

(21) Who selected the line to be held ?

(22) What consolidation was carried out ?

/ (23) ....

(23) What covering parties were placed out to cover consolidation and keep enemy under observation ?

(24) What Observation Posts were used ?

(25) What covering fire was usdd from front line ?

(26) What covering fire was used from back positions to keep enemy's fire down ?

(27) How did the rifles and machine guns keep in action ?

(28) What fifle shooting was done ?

(29) Were any rifle grenades used ?

(30) Were any T.Ms used, if so where from ?

(31) Were the machine guns used ?

(32) Was a ny enemy counter attack seen ?

(33) Were there any enemy seen to shoot at ?

(34) In what formation did Battalion fight ?

(35) Were there enough men ?

(36) Were all the wounded got in ?

(37) How far did each Battalion bury its own dead ?

(38) How many are missing ? — 10 MISSING

(39) Are a ny missing men known to be prisoners ?

3. I would like these reports to be sent in as early as possible.

(Sd) R. FANSHAWE,
Major-General,
Commanding 48th. Division.

I/5TH BN. ROYAL WARWICKSHIRE REGIMENT.

12th October 1917.

Reference 48th Divn. F.126. dated 11/10/17.

Question.

1. Along a line of tape from CLIFTON HOUSE to a point 150 yards N.E. of STROPPE FARM. The two support Coys. were formed up about 50 yards S.W. of their line.

2. From REIGERSBURG CAMP BRIDGE 2. MOUSE TRAP FARM track to the the BUFFS ROAD then via main ST JULIEN road through ST JULIEN, WINNIPEG Cross Roads, to "P" House (D.7 b 3 1)

3. (See narrative).

4. No.

5. Some men got a little sleep in the shell holes they formed up in. Only haversack ration available. Rum was issued about threequarters of an hour before Zero.

6. Rear."P" HOUSE. (D.7 b 3 1)
Forward. In trench D.7 b 7.7. this moved forward to VALE HOUSE after the leading Coy. had passed through, but all became casualties about 6.45 a.m.

7. Yes, commenced moving forward at 7.15 a.m. via STROPPE FARM, D.1 d 5.3.- D.1 d 9 4 - D. 2 c 1 4 - D.2 c 5 5, along the line of the 20 contour to ALBATROSS FARM, back via WINZIG and VALE HOUSE, arriving Bn.H.Q. 10.30 a.m. Observation became worse N.E. of CLIFTON HOUSE.

8. Runners.

9.

10. All the time by lamp messages could be sent both ways by visual.

11. Dogs were not used. Method of communication was by runners, towards evening of 4th October lamp station got going close to D.2 d 1.6. from forward Coy, & also visual both ways to HUBNER FARM.

12. Yes.

13. No. Barrage became a bit ragged just before it became protective beyond the first objective.

14. Yes.

15.

16. WELLINGTON FARM.

17. Yes.

18.

19. Chiefly round WINZIG the S.W. corner of square D.2 c & D.2 c central.

20. By anyone available.
Men were told off as escort before action butmany had become casualties.

2I. The forward positions around D.2 central & WELLINGTON FARM were selected by the Officers on the spot. I chose the positions along the line ALBATROSS FARM D.2 d 0 5 - D.2 c 5|5|

22. Small lengths of trench were dug linking up shell holes.

23. Covering parties were provided by the Lewis Guns in shell holes.

24. "P" HOUSE D.7 b 3 I & CLIFTON HOUSE.

25. Lewis Guns.

26.

27. Very well.

28. Small amount round D.2 c 5.5 and WELLINGTON FARM.

29. About IO on Machine Guns ~~parties~~ POSITIONS round the area D.2 c 5 3.

30.

3I.

32. No.

33. Yes, a few about N.E. corner of square D.2 b.

34. Line of skirmishers in pairs in front, remaining sections in Artillery formation until deployment became necessary.

35. No. not to deal with the final objective.

36. Yes, so far as could be found by the evening of 8th Octr.

37. There was only time to bury Officers.

38. 9.

39. One may be, it is uncertain whether he was killed or taken prisoner wounded.

I2/IO/I7.

Lieut. Col.
Commdg. I/5th Bn. Royal Warwickshire Regiment.

S E C R E T.

Copy No. 3 . . .

143rd Infantry Brigade OPERATION ORDER NO. 171

Ref. Map.
Sheet 28 1/40,000

8th October, 1917.

1. The Brigade will move to POPERINGHE to-morrow the 9th instant in accordance with March Table overleaf.

2. Transport will be brigaded and will move under the orders of B.T.O.

3. Distances of 200 yards between double Companies will be maintained.

4. Advance parties from all Units will meet the Staff Captain at Town Major's Office, the Square, POPERINGHE at 9 a.m.

5. Arrangements for lorries will be issued later.

6. ACKNOWLEDGE.

[signature]

Captain,

B.M. 143rd Inf. Bde.

Issued thro' Sigs. at
8.30 p.m.

Copy No 1 & 2 retained.
3 -10 Bde. Units.
11 &12 48th Division.
13 &14 War Diary.

MARCH TABLE TO ACCOMPANY O.O.171.

UNIT	POSITION	STARTING POINT	PASS S.P. AT	DESTINATION	REMARKS
143rd Bde. H.Q.	SIEGE CAMP	Cross roads CHEMIN MILITAIRE - POTTENHOEK- VLAMERTINGHE Road, H.3.d.23.	10 a.m.	POPERINGHE	
7th R.War.R.	-do-	-do-	10.5 a.m.	-do-	
6th R.War.R.	-do-	-do-	10.15	-do-	
5th R.War.R.	-do-	-do-	10.25 a.m.	-do-	
8th R.War.R.	-do-	-do-	10.35 a.m.	-do-	
143rd T. .Batt.	-do-	-do-	10.45 a.m.	-do-	
143rd M.G.Coy.	-do-	-do-	11 a.m.	-do-	
Bde. Transport	POTTEN FARM	-do-	11.10 a.m.	-do-	

Addendum to Operation Order No.171.

Lorries are allotted tomorrow as follows:-

Each Battalion	2.
M.G.Coy.	1.
Bde.H.Q. & T.M.B.	1.

Units will send guides for above to be at Brigade Headquarters at 9-15 a.m.

- - - - - - - - - - - - - - -

O P E R A T I O N   O R D E R S
BY
Lieut.Col. W.C.C.GELL. M.C.
Commdg. I/5th Bn. Royal Warwickshire Regiment.
12th October 1917.

Copy No....1....

No. 125

I. The 5th R.War.R. will entrain at PESELHOEK & will proceed by rail to Ist. Army Area tomorrow 13th inst.,
Detraining Station MAROEUIL.

2. Coys will parade in their own billetting area ready to pass the Coy.Officers Billet in the square as under:-

H.Q.	9.20 a.m.
B.Coy.	9.22 a.m.
C.Coy.	9.24 a.m.
D.Coy.	9.26 a.m.

A distance of 200 yards between Coys will be observed.
Route via PESELHOEK Road. Distance 11/2 miles.
Dress. Full Marching Order.

3. A detraining party of 100 O.R's from A.Coy under 2/Lt.F.H.WEBB will parade outside the Q.M.Stores at 9.5 a.m. & will report to the R.T.O. PESELHOEK at 9.45 a.m.
This party will proceed by the first train & will carry ration for the 13th & 14th.

4. Blankets rolled in tens & labelled will be stacked outside the Q.M.Stores by 6.30 a.m.
Officers valises will be stacked outside Q.M.Stores by 8.0 am.
One Mess box only per Coy " " " " " 8.0 am.
Remainder of Mess kit " " " " " 6.30. am.

5. Breakfast will be at 7.0 a.m.
Tea will be served at ~~XXXXXX~~ the Entraining Station.

6. ACKNOWLEDGE.

E P L Carter

Issued at 7.0 p.m.
12/10/17.

Capt. & Adjt.
I/5th Bn. Royal Warwickshire Regiment.

Copies 1 & 2 War Diary
" 3 to 6 Coys

Copy No. 7 Q.M. & T.O.
" 8 R.S.M.

OPERATION ORDERS.

Copy No. 2

BY

Lieut.Col.W.C.C.GELL. M.C.
Commdg, I/5th Bn. Royal Warwickshire Regiment.
8th October 1917.

No. 124.

GGGG

Ref:Map 28 N.W. 1/20,000.

I. The 143 Inf: Bde will move to POPERINGHE tomorrow, 9th inst.

2. The 5th R.War.R. will parade ready to move as under:-

H.Q.	9.55 a.m.
A.Coy.	9.57 a.m.
B.Coy.	9.57 a.m.
C.Coy.	9.59 a.m.
D.Coy.	9.59 a.m.

DRESS. Full Marching Order. Steel helmets will be worn. Transport will be brigaded & will march under the orders of the B.T.O.

3. Blankets, Officers valises & Mess boxes will be stacked under arrangements to be made by the R.S.M. by 9.25 a.m.

4. An advance party of Coy. Q.M.S's & Sgt PLESTER will report to 2/Lieut.A.F.FOREMAN outside Bn.H.Q's at 6.30 a.m. This party will report to the Staff Captain at the Town Majors Office in the Square POPERINGHE at 9.0 a.m.

5. Names of all men who are likely to become stragglers will be sent in to Orderly Room by 8.0 a.m. These men will parade outside the Orderly Room at 8.30 a.m. & will bemarched to their destination by the Bn. Orderly Sgt

6. Dinners will be served on arrival.

7. ACKNOWLEDGE.

Issued at II.0 p.m.

8/10/17.

E.A.L. Carter
Capt & Adjt.
I/5th Bn. Royal Warwickshire Regiment.

Copies I & 2 War Diary.
" 3 to 6 Coy's.

Copy No. 7 Q.M. & T.O.
" 8 R.S.M.

ENTRAINING TABLE issued with O.O.17[illegible].

Train Nos. from Station.	Serial No.	Unit	Date	Time of Departure.	Time of arrival at detraining sta.	Detraining Station.	Remarks.
2	4811	5th R.War.R.	13.10.17	11.20	Journey should take about 7 hours.		Trains will be composed as under:-
6	4810 4815 4816 4817	Bde. H.Q. Bde. Sig. Sec. 143 M.G.Coy. 143 T.M.Batt.	-do-	19.20		-do-	1 Coach (to hold 40) 30 covered wagons. 17 flats (each to take 4 vehicles) 2 brake vans.
10	4812	6th R.War.R.	14.10.17	3.30		-do-	
12	4813	7th R.War.R.	-do-	7.30		-do-	
14	4814	8th R.War.R.	-do-	11.20		-do-	

T A B L E 'B'.

To accompany 48th Division Order No. 225.

Date	Unit	Time parties report		To R.T.O. at
		entraining party	detraining party	
13th Oct.	143rd Inf. Bde.	8	9.45	PESELHOEK
13th Oct.	144th Inf. Bde.	6	7.50	HOPOUTRE
14th Oct.	5th R. Sussex R.	16	15.45	PESELHOEK
14th Oct.	145th Inf Bde.	6	7.50	HOPOUTRE

Entraining parties proceed by last train of their respective group.
Detraining parties " " first " " " " "

Table C

MOVE OF 48th DIVISION (Less Artillery)

From Fifth Army.

Entraining Stations.

A. HOPOUTRE.

B. PESELHOEK.

To First Army.

Detraining Stations.

A. WAVRANS.

B. DIEVAL.

Train Numbers. From Stations. A	B	Serial Numbers.	Date.	Marche.	Dept.	Time of Arrival at detraining Stations. A	B
1	2	3	4	5	6	7	8
1		4821	13.9	H.T.61	9.25		
	2	4811.	"	H.T.63	11.20		
3		4820. 25. 26. 27.	"	H.T.65	13.25		
	4	4801. 02. 03. 05.	"	H.T.67	15.30		
5		4877. 86.	"	H.T.69	17.45		
	6	4810. 15. 16. 17.	"	H.T.71	19.20		
7		4822.	"	H.T.73	21.45		
	8	4875. 76. 81.	"	H.T.51	23.30		
9		4823.	14/9	H.T.53	1.45		
	10	4812.	"	H.T.55	3.30		
11		4824.	"	H.T.57	5.45		
	12	4813.	"	H.T.59	7.30		
13		4831.	"	H.T.61	9.25		
	14	4814.	"	H.T.63	11.20		
15		4830. 35. 36. 37.	"	H.T.65	13.25		
	16	4804a. 88. 90.	"	H.T.67	15.30		
17		4878. 87.	"	H.T.69	17.45		
	18	4804.	"	H.T.71	19.20		
19		4832.		H.T.73	21.45		
	20	4882.	"	H.T.51	23.30		
21		4833.	15/9	H.T.53	1.45		
	22	4883.	"	H.T.55	3.30		
23		4834.	"	H.T.57	5.45		

H. Marriott

Captain, for

A.D.R.T.

Traffic Office,
HAZEBROUCK AREA.
10th October 1917.

143rd Inf. Bde. O.O.172

Copy No. 1 and 2 retained.
3 to 10 Bde. Units.
11 3rd S.M.Fd. Amb.
12 and 13 48th Division.
14 and 15 War Diary.

SECRET.

Addendum No. 1 to
143rd Inf. Bde. OPERATION ORDER NO.172
****

Bde. Hdqrs. will close at POPERINGHE at 5 p.m. on 13th inst. and will open in the new area at a place and time to be notified later.

L Crockford

Captain,

a/B.M. 143rd Inf. Bde.

10-30 am.
12-10-17.

Copies to recipients of O.O.172

S E C R E T.

Copy No. 3

143rd Infantry Brigade OPERATION ORDER NO.172.

Map Ref.
HAZEBROUCK 5A, 1/100,000
LENS 11. ,,

12th October, 1917

1. The Brigade will proceed by rail to First Army Area on the 13th/14th October, in accordance with the attached Table.

2. The entraining station will be PESELHOEK. One Officer from each Unit of the Bde. will meet the Staff Captain there at 3 p.m. on the 12th inst. to reconnoitre approaches etc.

3. Transport of all Bns. will arrive at entraining station 3 hours, and the Infantry personnel 1½ hours, before the train is due to depart. Other Units will arrive complete 3 hours before the time of departure of the train.

4. Supply and baggage Wagons will accompany the Units in every case.

5. The entrainment of all Units must be completed ½ hour before departure of the train.

6. Units must provide their own breast ropes.

7. Rations for 13th and 14th October will be issued to Units on 12th inst., and Units will entrain with the unexpended portion.
Rations for 15th inst., will be carried on the Supply Wagons.
Rations for 16th inst., will be issued in the new area.

8. Lorries will be provided by 48th Div. Supply Column for conveying blankets and stores to the entraining station as follows:-

Bde. H.Q 1
Each Bn. 1

These will report to Bde. H.Q. 5 hours before the departure of the train, at which hour Bns. will have a guide with written instructions as to where he is to guide the lorry.

9. The usual distances when moving to the entraining station, will be observed in this area.
In First Army Area a distance of 500 yds. will be maintained in rear of each Bn.

10. The following officers will be detailed to assist R.T.Os.-

Captain W.N.BUSHILL, 7th R.War.R. at Entraining Station
Captain J.BOWATER, 6th R.War.R. at Detraining Station.

11. An entraining party of 1 Officer and 100 men will be detailed by 8th R.War.R. to report to R.T.O. at the entraining station at 8 a.m. on 13th inst. These will proceed by the last train.
A detraining party of 1 officer and 100 men will be detailed by 5th R.War.R. to report to R.T.O. entraining station at 9.45 a.m. on 13th inst. This party will proceed by the first train.
Both these parties should carry rations for 13th and 14th inst.

12. Each Unit will hand to R.T.O. at entraining station 3 hours before the train is due to depart, an entraining state showing numbers of Officers, O.Rs, animals and vehicles by axles, to proceed.
A copy of this will be sent to Bde. H.Q. by 9 p.m. 12th inst.

13. ACKNOWLEDGE.

L. C. Brockford
Captain,
a/B.M.143rd Inf.Bde.

Issued at 10.30am

5th Bn.
6th Bn.
7th Bn.
8th Bn.
M.G.Coy.
T.M.Batt.

Addendum issued with O.O. 173

The following arrangements, with the 5th Can. Inf. Bde., have been made for reconnoitring the new line and for providing advanced parties :-

1. At 11 a.m. on 15th inst. C.O.s, Adjutants and Seconds-in-Command of the 3 forward Bns. (5th, 6th and 7th) and O.C. 143 T.M.Batt. will meet guides at 5th Can. Inf. Bde. Hdqrs. who will guide them to their respective Bns.

   (Route to 5th Can. Inf. Bde. HDqrs. - ST ELOY- NEUVILLE ST VAAST- TILLEULS CORNER- turn North up LENS Road- turn right where traffic man will show- to THELUS CAVES.)

2. One Coy. Officer per Coy. and 1 N.C.O. per platoon from each of the 3 forward Bns. will report to 5th Can. Inf. Bde. Hdqrs. (see route above in 1.) at 3 p.m. on 15th inst. These will remain with the Bns., to be relieved, during night 15th/16th and will rejoin their own Bns. in the ~~relief~~ line on relief.
   Application has been made for a train to convey the party (time and place of starting and arrival will be notified as soon as possible).

3. The C.O., Second-in-Command and Adjutant of the Reserve Bn. (8th) will be at Reserve Bn. Hdqrs. NEUVILLE ST VAAST on afternoon of the 15th inst. to reconnoitre positions and routes up to the line.

Captain,

14-10-17.

a/B.M. 143rd Inf. Bde.

'Copy to 5th Can. Inf. Bde.'

S E C R E T.

Copy No. . . . 3

143rd Infantry Brigade OPERATION ORDER NO.173.

Ref maps.
LENS 11 1/100,000.
36 C 1/40,000.

14th Oct.1917

1. The 143rd Inf. Bde. will relieve the 5th Canadian Inf. Bde. on the night of 16/17th October, in the Right Sector of the Divisional front.

2. (a) Moves and reliefs will take place as per attached table.
(b) Details of reliefs as to guides etc., will be arranged direct between Unit commanders concerned.
(c) The 143rd M.G.Coy. will relieve the 4th Can. M.G.Coy. in the line on the night 15/16th Oct. under arrangements to be made direct between commanders concerned.

3. (a) No movement by day will take place East of the VIMY RIDGE, except by MERSEY and HUMBER Trenches.
(b) West of the VIMY RIDGE, Units will move by Coys: 500 yds. interval to be maintained between Coys.

4. Instructions for advance and reconnoitring parties are issued on a separate Memo herewith.

5. G.O.C. 143rd Inf. Bde. will take over command of the line on complet ion of relief, at which time Bde. H.Q. will open at THELUS CAVE (A.6.c.84. Ref. Sheet 36C 1/40,000).

6. Completion of reliefs will be reported in Code to Bde. H.Q.

7. ACKNOWLEDGE.

L. C. Croitford.
Captain,
a/B.M.143rd Inf. Bde.

Issued at

Copy No. 1 & 2 retained
3 - 10 Bde. Units.
11 5th Can. Inf. Bde.
12 Flank Bde.
13 - do -
14 & 15 48th Division.
16 & 17 War Diary.

Table of Reliefs and Moves. Issued with O.O. 173

SERIAL NO.	DATE	UNIT	FROM	TO	RELIEVING UNIT OF 5th Can. Inf. Bde.	REMARKS.
1.	Night 15th/16th Oct.	143 M.G.Coy.	ST ELOY	Line.	4 Can. M.G.Coy.	12 guns will be in the line and the remaining 4 at Coy. H.Q..
2.	Night 16th/17th Oct.	5th R.War.R.	BOIS DES ALLEUX	Right Sector of Line.	24th Can. R.	
3.	,,	6th R.War.R.	,,	Line. (In support)	25th Can. R.	
4.	,,	7th R.War.R.	,,	Left Sector of Line.	26th Can. R.	
5.	,,	8th R.War.R.	"	Reserve. NEUVILLE ST VAAST.	22nd Can. R.	This relief may take place on day of 16th. Time to be arranged between C.O.s concerned.
6.	,,	143 T.M.Batt.	ST ELOY.	Line.	Can. T.M.Batt.	

MOVE OF 48th DIVISION (Less Artillery).

TABLE "D".

U N I T .	Serial Nos.	Description.
DIVISIONAL UNITS.	4801	Divisional Headquarters.
	4802	H.Q., Divisional R.A.
	4803	H.Q., Divisional R.E.
	4804	1/5th Royal Sussex Regt (Pioneers) less 4804a.
	4804a	1 Company, cooker and teams of 1/5th Royal Sussex Regt.
	4805	H.Q., Divisional Signals.
	4806	
143rd INFANTRY BRIGADE.	4810	Brigade Headquarters.
	4811	1/5th Royal Warwick Regt.
	4812	1/6th " " "
	4813	1/7th " " "
	4814	1/8th " " "
	4815	Brigade Signal Section.
	4816	Brigade Machine Gun Company.
	4817	Brigade Trench Mortar Battery (Light)
144th INFANTRY BRIGADE.	4820	Brigade Headquarters.
	4821	1/4th Gloucester Regt.
	4822	1/6th " "
	4823	1/7th Worcester Regt.
	4824	1/8th " "
	4825	Brigade Signal Section.
	4826	Brigade Machine Gun Company.
	4827	Brigade Trench Mortar Battery (Light)
145th INFANTRY BRIGADE.	4830	Brigade Headquarters.
	4831	1/5th Gloucester Regt.
	4832	1/4th Oxford & Bucks Light Infantry.
	4833	1/1st Buckingham Battalion.
	4834	1/4th Royal Berkshire Regt.
	4835	Brigade Signal Section.
	4836	Brigade Machine Gun Company.
	4837	Brigade Trench Mortar Battery (Light).
DIVISIONAL TRAIN.	4875	H.Q., Divl. Train.
	4876	No. 2 Company., A.S.C.
	4877	No. 3 Company., A.S.C.
	4878	No. 4 Company., A.S.C.
DIVISIONAL ENGINEERS.	4881	474th (South Midland) Field Coy. R.E.
	4882	475th (" ") " " "
	4883	477th (" ") " " "
MEDICAL UNITS.	4886	1/1st South Midland Field Ambulance.
	4887	1/2nd " " " "
	4888	1/3rd " " " "
VETERINARY UNITS.	4890	1/1st South Midland Mobile Vety. Section.

OPERATION ORDERS. Copy No. 1.....
BY
Lieut.Col. W.C.C.GELL. M.C.
Commdg. I/5th Bn. Royal Warwickshire Regiment. 126
16th October 1917. No. ~~124~~.

I. The 5th R.War.R. will relieve the 24th Can.Inf:Bn. in the line today 16th inst.,

2. Coys will march in the following order:-
H.Q.- D - C - B - A.
DRESS Old Fighting Order, Haversack on the back, greatcoat rolled round the haversack.
Probable time of move 1.30 p.m. Exact time will be notified later.

3. 2 Guides per platoon & 2 for Bn.H.Q. will be met at the entrance to HERSEY TRENCH near Bde.H.Q. at THELUS CAVES.

4. On relief Coys will be disposed as under:-
B.on the right.
C.in the centre.
D.on the left.
A.in support.
Bn.H.Q. & R.A.P. will be at T.22 d 9 3 junction of HUDSON & NEW BRUNSWICK.

5. Officers valises & Mess boxes will be stacked outside the Q.M.Stores by 12.30 p.m.
Mess kit which is to be taken into the line will be stacked outside the Q.M.Stores on a separate dump by 1.0 p.m.

6. Dinners will be served at 12 noon. Tea will be served on arrival at TILLEUL CROSS ROADS.

7. Completion of all reliefs will be reported to Bn.H.Q. in Code.
Duplicate lists of all Trench Stores taken over will be sent to Bn.H.Q. by 12 noon 17th inst.,

8. ACKNOWLEDGE.

E P L Carter

16/10/17. Capt. & Adjt.
I/5th Bn. Royal Warwickshire Regiment.

Copies No.1 & 2 War Diary. Copy No.7 R.S.M.
" 3 to 6 Coys. " 8 Q.M. & T.O.

SECRET.

Copy No . . 3 . .

143rd Infantry Brigade OPERATION ORDER No.174.

Ref Map.
MERICOURT Rd. 1/10,000.

19th October, 1917.

1. The boundary between the Vth and XIIIth Corps will be changed to-morrow the 20th inst., in accordance with attached plan (issued to 5th and 6th R.War.R).

2. The platoon of the 6th R.War.R. in MONTREAL Trench will not be relieved but will rejoin the 6th R.War.R. as soon as possible after dark.

3. The Coy. of the 6th R.War.R. in NEW BRUNSWICK Trench will be relieved by 12th Yorksand Lancs. R. at 4 p.m.
The Coy. so relieved will move to a reserve position in the Railway Bank.
An Officer of the 6th R.War.R. will meet the Staff Captain at the Railway Bridge, T.26.a.39 at 10 a.m. to arrange accommodation.

4. The Bn. H.Q's at BEEHIVE and ABERGELE and M.G.Coy. H.Q. at BUSHY will not be moved but will be retained.

5. The Bde. can use C.P.R. and HUDSON communication trenches and NEW BRUNSWICK as far as is necessary.

6. 143 M.G.Coy. will hand over all gun positions S. of the new boundary and place the guns in positions as arranged with C.O. on relief.

7. Completion of reliefs will be wired to Bde. by the code word 'DRAKE'.

8. ACKNOWLEDGE.

Captain,
a/B.M. 143rd Inf. Bde.

Issued thro' Sigs. at

Copy No.1 & 2 retained.
3 - 8 Bde. Units.
9 Right Flank Bde.
10 48th Division.
11 War Diary.
12 - do -

SECRET.

OPERATION ORDERS. Copy No. 1

BY

Lieut.Col. W.C.C.GELL. M.C.

Commdg. I/5th Bn. Royal Warwickshire Regiment.

21st October 1917. No. 126/1

Map Ref: Trench Map. MERICOURT ROAD. I/10,000
MAROEUIL. I/20,000.

....

I. I/5 R.War.R. will be relieved by I/8th R.War.R. in the right Bn. area, Mericourt sector on 22nd inst.,

2. I/5th R.War.R. will be relieved as follows:-
B.Coy by 2 platoons of A.Coy I/8th R.War.R.-
I.platoon for posts in bays 5 & 18 & I platoon in QUEBEC trench S.W. of 12th Av.

C.Coy. by 2 platoons & Coy.H.Q. of A.Coy I/8th R.War.R.
I. platoon 30 to 35 bays & I platoon in bays 44 & 45 the last platoon will also provide post in 54 bay.

D.Coy. will be relieved in 54 post by I section of A.Coy. I/8th R.War.R. & on QUEBEC by I platoon of B.Coy. I/8th R.War.R. which will be placed around junction of TORQUAY & QUEBEC.
A.Coy. will be relieved by B.Coy. I/8th R.War.R.

3. Guides will report as follows at Bn.H.Q. at 12 noon 22nd:-
A.Coy. I Officer & I guide per platoon.
B.Coy. 2 guides I.for No.5 & 18 bay. I.for QUEBEC 12 Av.
C.Coy. 3 guides I.for bay 30-35. I.for bays 40-45,
I.for Coy.H.Q.
D.Coy. I/guide for area junction of TORQUAY & QUEBEC.
The Officer will be in charge of these guides & meet A.Coy. & B.Coy. I/8th R.War.R. at head of Mersey C.T. at I.30 p.m.

Right front Coy.(A.Coy.I/8th R.War.R).
The order will be No.5 bay platoon. No.44 bay platoon. No. 30 bay platoon, junction QUEBEC & 12 Av. platoon, junction TORQUAY & QUEBEC platoon.
Right Reserve Coy.(B.Coy.I/8th R.War.R).
Tunnel platoon, left platoon, centre platoon, right platoon.

4. O.C. C & A Coys will hand over one trench map each to the relieving units.

5. All periscopes, wire cutters,&very pistols will be brought out.

6. All petrol tins, dixies & Lewis gun drums (not Lewis Guns) will be taken to A.Coy dump in NEW BRUNSWICK trench.

O.C. A.Coy. will detail I. Officer, I.N.C.O. & 4 men to load these into Bn. transport at dusk. Each Coy. will detail I.N.C.O. to supervise the loading & unloading of his Coy. L.G.drums.

7. Duplicate lists of trench stores handed over will be forwarded to Bn.H.Q. by 6 p.m. 23rd inst.,
O.C. A.Coy. I/8th R.War.R. will take over the entire trench stores of B.C & D.Coys.I/5th R.War.R.

8. Location of rest billets & details of march will be notified later.

9. ACKNOWLEDGE.

E P L Carter
Capt. & Adjt.
I/5th Bn. Royal Warwickshire Regt.

21/10/17.
issued at 5.0 p.m.

Copies No.I & 2 War Diary.
" 3 to 6 Coys.
Copy No.7 8th R.War.R
" 8 Q.M. & T.O.

S E C R E T. Copy No. 3

143rd Infantry Brigade OPERATION ORDER NO.175

Ref. Maps.
MERICOURT RD. 1/10,000
LENS 11 1/100,000. 21st October, 1917

1. The 8th R.War.R will relieve the 5th and 7th R.War.R. in the Brigade Sector to-morrow 22nd inst., and thenceforward the line will be held in accordance with memo issued herewith - G.O.158.

2. All arrangements for relief to be made direct between C.O's of the Units concerned.

3. The Coys. of 8th R.War.R. relieving 7th R.War.R. will move by MERSEY C.T. (to the VIMY Rd.) - VIMY Rd. - GRAND TRUNK and TOAST.
The 7th R.War.R. will return by the same route.

The Coys of the 8th R.War.R. relieving 5th R.War.R. will move by MERSEY - C.P.R. - HUDSON - NEW BRUNSWICK - TOPER.
The 5th R.War.R. will move out by the same route.

Troops returning by VIMY Rd. and MERSEY will not on any account be held up at the junction of VIMY Rd. and MERSEY, troops returning by C.P.R. will give way in all cases.

4. Troops moving to and from the line will proceed by half platoons at 250 yds. distance East of the LENS-ARRAS Rd.

5. On relief 7th R.War.R. will proceed to NEUVILLE ST VAAST Camp and the 5th R.War.R. will proceed to camp in BOIS DES ALLEUX.

6. The 7th R.War.R. will send an Officer to report to H.Q. 8th R.War.R. at 11 a.m. to-morrow, 22nd inst., to take over the accommodation.

7. The 5th R.War.R. will send an Officer and billeting party to meet the Staff Capt. at the Town Major's office MONT ST ELOY at 12 noon to-morrow, 22nd inst.

8. Trains will be at ZIVVY to convey 5th R.War.R. to FRASER's Camp at 5 p.m. to-morrow.

9. Completion of relief will be wired to Bde. Hdqrs. by the code word 'DUCK'

10. ACKNOWLEDGE.

L. Blackford
Captain,
a/B.M. 143rd Inf. Bde.

Issued through Signals
at

Copy No. 1 and 2 retained
3 to 10 Bde. Units.
11 144th Inf. Bde,
12 94th Inf. Bde.
13 and 14 48th Division,
15 and 16 War Diary.

S E C R E T.

Copy No 3

143rd Infantry Brigade OPERATION ORDER No.176.

Ref. Maps.
MERICOURT 1/10,000
MAROEUIL 1/20,000

25th October, 1917.

1. Battalions will carry out movements and reliefs on the 27th inst., according to attached table.

2. All arrangements for the relief will be made direct between C.O's of Units concerned.

3. Troops moving East of the VIMY RIDGE will maintain distances of 100 yds. between platoons.

4. The Brigade is being relieved in the line on the 1st November.

5. All receipts taken for trench stores will be sent to Bde. H.Q. within 24 hours of relief.

6. Completion of relief will be wired to Bde. H.Q. by code word 'AMENA'.

7. ACKNOWLEDGE.

C.W. Beart
Captain,
B.M. 143rd Inf. Bde.

Issued at 5 p.m.

Copy Nos 1 & 2 retained.
3 - 10 Bde. Units.
11 94th Inf. Bde.
12 144th Inf. Bde.
13 48th Division 'G'.
14 -do- 'Q'.
15 & 16 War Diary.

RELIEF TABLE issued with 143rd Inf. Bde. O.O.178.

DATE	UNIT	FROM	TO	RELIEVING	ROUTE	REMARKS
Oct.,27th	5th R.War.R.	MONT ST ELOY	FRONT SYSTEM.	8th R.War.R.	MERSEY - GRAND TRUNK - TOAST & MERSEY - C.P.R. - HUDSON - BRUNSWICK.	Entrain FRASER Camp 10 a.m. Detrain BONSUMMIT (A.5.b.58).
-do-	8th R.War.R.	FRONT SYSTEM.	RESERVE SYSTEM.	6th R.War.R.	TOAST - GRAND TRUNK.	
-do-	6th R.War.R.	RESERVE SYSTEM.	CUBIT CAMP A.9.central		GRAND TRUNK - MERSEY Train ZIVY Dump.	Entrain at 6 p.m. BON SUMMIT (A.5.b.58)

Copy No. 1........

O P E R A T I O N   O R D E R S.
BY
Lieut.Col. W.C.C.GELL. M.C.
Commdg. I/5th Bn. Royal Warwickshire Regiment.
26th October 1917.

No. I27.

I. The 5th R.War.R. will relieve the 8th R.War.R. in the front line tomorrow 27th.

2. The Bn. will entrain at FRASER CAMP & will detrain at BONSUMMIT.

3. Coys. will parade ready to pass the entrance to camp as under:-

C.	9.45 a.m.
D.	9.47 a.m.
H.Q.	9.49 a.m.
A.	9.50 a.m.
B,	9.52 a.m.

DRESS. Old Fighting Order, Overcoat rolled round the the haversack. Puttees & Soft Caps will be left in the pack. Sandbags will be worn in place of puttees.

4. Lewis Guns & 20 Drums per gun will be carried by the teams.

5. Officers valises & mess boxes will be stacked under arrangements to be made by the R.S.M. by 9.I5 a.m. Mens packs, & blankets (rolled in tens) will be stacked near the railway siding by 9.I5 a.m.

6. Copies of receipts given for trench stores will be forwarded to Bn.H.Q. by I2 noon 28th.

7. Completion of all reliefs will be wired to Bn.H.Q. by the Code Word WILLS.

8. A C K N O W L E D G E.

Copies No I & 2 War Diary. Copy No. 7 R.S.M.
" " 3 to 6 Coys. " 8 Q.M. & T.O.

E P L Carter

Capt, & Adjt.
I/5th Bn. Royal Warwickshire Regiment.

26/I0/I7.
issued at 4 o'clock.

OPERATION ORDERS. Copy No. 2

BY

Lieut.Col. W.C.C.GELL. M.C.
Commdg. I/5th Bn. Royal Warwickshire Regiment.
31st October 1917.

No. 128.

Ref:Map. ROUVEROY I/10,000.
VIMY I/10,000.
MAROEUIL I/10,000.

1. The 5th R.War.R. willbe relieved by the 5th Glos'ters tomorrow 1st November & on relief will move to CUBITT CAMP at NEUVILLE ST VAAST.

ROUTES C & D NEW BRUNSWICK - CPR - HUDSON - MERSEY - THELUS VILLAGE (not via BONSUMMIT) - NEUVILLE ST VAAST.

A & B GRAND TRUNK - MERSEY - THELUS VILLAGE (not via BONSUMMIT) - NEUVILLE ST VAAST.

2. Distances of 100 yards between platoons will be kept E of the VIMY RIDGE & 500 yards between Coys. W of the VIMY RIDGE.

If observation is good movement across the ridge will be by parties of 6 men at distances of 100 yards.

3. 1 guide per platoon & 1 for Bn.H.Q. will report to 2/Lieut.NORWOOD at Bn.H.Q. at 10.30 a.m.

4. Receipts taken for trench stores will be forwarded to Bn.H.Q. by 12 noon 2nd November.

5. Lewis Guns will be carried by the teams.

6. 1 limber for A & B Coys. & 1 for C & D Coys. will be at the old ration dumps as soon as possible after dusk. These will be used for L.G. drums, Mess kit, Petrol tins, Dixies & Salvage.

1 limber will be at Bn.H.Q. for Mess kit, Orderly Room, Signals & Dixies etc.,

X. A guard must be left on the above stores to assist in the loading.

7. All periscopes, Wire cutters, Very pistols & Grenade cups will be brought out.

8. Completion of all reliefs will bw wired to Bn.H.Q. by the Code Word CLOSED.

9. ACKNOWLEDGE.

E R J Carter

Issued at 4 p.M,
31/10/17.

Capt. & Adjt.
I/5th Bn. Royal Warwickshire Regiment.

Copies No 1 & 2 War Diary.
" " 3 to 6 Coys.

Copy No.7 R.S.M.
" 8 Q.M. & T.O.
" 9 I/5th Glos'ters.

www.ingramcontent.com/pod-product-compliance
Lightning Source LLC
Chambersburg PA
CBHW080854010526
44117CB00014B/2250
* 9 7 8 1 4 7 4 5 2 6 8 1 4 *